SAMUEL TAYLOR COLERIDGE

Selected Letters

Samuel Taylor Coleridge, by James Northcote (1802); the portrait was commissioned by Sir George Beaumont of Coleorton. *The Master and Fellows of Jesus College, Cambridge.*

SAMUEL TAYLOR COLERIDGE

Selected Letters

Edited by

H. J. JACKSON

CLARENDON PRESS · OXFORD

1987

Oxford University Press, Walton Street,Oxford OX2 6DP

New York Toronto
Delhi Bombay Calcutta Madras Karachi
Petaling Jaya Singapore Hong Kong Tokyo
Nairobi Dar es Salaam Cape Town
Melbourne Auckland

and associated companies in
Beirut Berlin Ibadan Nicosia

Oxford is a trade mark of Oxford University Press

Published in the United States
by Oxford University Press, New York

British Library Cataloguing in Publication Data
Coleridge, Samuel Taylor
Selected letters.
1. Poets, English—19th century—
Biography
I. Title   II. Jackson, H. J.
821'.7   PR4483
ISBN 0-19-818540-5

Library of Congress Cataloging in Publication Data
Coleridge, Samuel Taylor, 1772-1834.
Selected letters.
Bibliography: p.
Includes index.
1. Coleridge, Samuel Taylor, 1772-1834—Correspondence.
2. Authors, English—19th century—Correspondence.
I. Jackson, H. J. II. Title.
PR4483.A4 1987   821'.7   86-18150
ISBN 0-19-818540-5

Set by Hope Services, Abingdon
Printed in Great Britain by
Butler and Tanner Ltd, Frome, Somerset

CONTENTS

INTRODUCTION

THE introduction of the postage stamp in England in 1840, six years after Coleridge's death, significantly altered the situation of correspondents. Until then, recipients paid postage; the writers themselves were responsible for making letters worth paying for. As objects paid for, letters had a special status: they were shared with family and friends; in most households, they were preserved and periodically re-read; and on the death of the letter-writer, they were customarily returned to the family as part of the estate. Besides these postal arrangements, other historical circumstances contributed to making Coleridge's period a golden age of letter-writing. To this one means of communication, people entrusted their pressing commercial, intellectual, and emotional concerns. Everyone who wrote also received letters and had learnt how to tell the good from the bad. Their standards were established both by general practice and by the art cultivated in the enormously popular eighteenth-century mode of the epistolary novel. Even sophisticated modern readers familiar with Richardson's *Pamela* and *Clarissa* and Smollett's *Humphry Clinker*, who may know that the first version of Austen's *Sense and Sensibility* was written as a series of letters, can hardly conceive of the amount of real or fictional correspondence that passed under the eyes of a reader of the late eighteenth or early nineteenth century.

It is fairly common now to hear readers admiring the bluntness of Blake's letters or the raciness of Byron's by saying how modern they seem. The main reason for this judgement appears to be that although circumstances have changed, we have inherited the standards of the age of Blake and Byron; in fact, the conventions of the familiar letter have for centuries been comparatively stable. Those conventions, which I shall outline here, might have been tailor-made for Coleridge. His earliest letters reveal an awareness, formed or at least fostered by classical studies at school, of traditional guidelines for letter-writing. As his experience as a correspondent increased, so did his command of the medium. In a marginal note to one of Donne's published letters, he wrote appreciatively, 'A noble Letter in the _next_ to best Style of Correspondence, in which Friends communicate to each other the accidents of their meditations, and baffle absence by writing what, if present, they would have talked.' Coleridge was describing the kind of familiar letter in which he himself excelled; I do not know what sort of communication he considered superior to it.

Coleridge's comment on Donne introduces perhaps the most conspicuous of the conventions of the familiar letter, that of spontaneity. As a young woman, Fanny Burney was given the standard advice that 'there is no fault in epistolary correspondence, like stiffness, & study—Dash away, whatever comes uppermost'. 'My pen writes to others, but it _talks_ to you,' is the way Coleridge puts it in the first letter in this collection. A letter is _sermo absentis ad absentem_, the _talk_ of one who is absent to his absent friend. Even as a schoolboy, Coleridge had the reputation of being an enthralling talker, and in his maturity the most grudging of his contemporaries acknowledged his exceptional powers of speech. Although we cannot hear him, we feel closest to his famous talk in the apparent spontaneity of the letters. What one shrewd observer after another said about his conversation will also be found to be true of his correspondence, that is, that the impression of desultoriness, of dazzling variety and abrupt changes of topic, is superficially pleasing, but that there are generally concealed connections and an underlying harmony in what Coleridge has to say.

A related convention, that of informality, decrees that familiar letters should show off the writer's intellectual agility by representing the free play of the mind; one avoids rigorously logical connections in favour of rapid and un-announced transitions from one subject to the next, just as one may avoid formal sentence structure and take liberties with punctuation. Some of Coleridge's letters seem to push the principle of freedom of form to its limits, so sweeping readers off their feet with abrupt changes of topic and tone that the letters approach incoherence, but even in those extreme cases, if they are read attentively and without hostility, connections will appear. Such letters have the vivacity of _Tristram Shandy_ and, like that supposedly shapeless book, an energy that arises from integrity of purpose. (This may be the place to observe also that the Shandean humour and playfulness of the letters often surprise readers familiar only with Coleridge's influential poems and critical work.)

A third feature of the familiar letter is what might be called the intimacy convention. The familiar letter is generally a private communication and a tribute to friendship: it should evoke qualities both of the absent friend and of the friendship itself. It thrives on candour and minuteness, expressing a sympathetic concern in the interests and anxieties of the correspondent, and taking a reciprocal concern for granted. So Coleridge unaffectedly gives accounts of his health, of distresses and successes, and urges his correspondents to write with similar frankness to him. He does not shy away from serious subjects, or from silliness either. In a letter of 1819 (not in this volume), he said he would rather see his friend than write to him, but 'On the other hand, Letters are more permanent, and an epistolary correspondence perhaps more endearing—like all marks of remembrance in absence.' Like the others, the intimacy convention was comfortable to Coleridge, who was a demanding but at the same time an extraordinarily generous friend. A craving for intimacy is evident in the history of his personal relations, and if the story of his life had to be reduced to a single theme it might be told as a quest for the perfect friend. He hopefully bound himself to a succession of candidates—Southey, Poole, Wordsworth, Sara Hutchinson, Gillman, Green—only to be disappointed by them in one way or another. Many letters or parts of letters involve remarkably direct and delicate probing of himself and of his relationship with the correspondent, notably the dignified letters of reproach to Southey (pp. 13–25) and Wordsworth (pp. 167–72), and a less creditable one to his wife (pp. 117–21), in honest attempts to air or ease or end difficulties.

Sometimes Coleridge seems to have had unreasonable expectations of his audience: the 'best friend' whom he addressed in letters was always to some extent 'another Self' (p. 90), an idealized version of himself. On the other hand, it is impossible to read many of these letters without realizing the extent to which Coleridge made allowance for the character of his correspondent, and adapted his words to suit a particular reader and a particular occasion. This tendency is one we recognize in ourselves if we write different sorts of letters to our grandmothers and our drinking companions, but Coleridge reveals an unusually high degree of chameleon-like changing of colour according to circumstances. When he writes to his censorious brother George (a schoolmaster) or to James Gooden (a classical scholar), his letters become heavily freighted with Latin quotations and rather creaking classical jokes; the language of his letters to Benjamin Flower, an active Unitarian, seems rather sanctimoniously biblical; his letters to Gillman are full of puns; and so on. The occasion of the letter needs to be kept in mind, as a context that often qualifies what is actually said. When Coleridge disparages his own literary talent to Godwin (p. 93) with the memorable and moving remark, 'If I die, and the Booksellers will give you anything for my Life, be sure to say—"Wordsworth descended on him, like the Γνῶθι σεαυτόν from Heaven; by shewing him what Poetry was, he made him know, that he himself was no Poet"', it is important to realize that Godwin had asked Coleridge to make critical comments on the draft of a tragedy; that Godwin was sensitive to criticism; and that Coleridge, anticipating trouble, wanted to provide Godwin with the means for dismissing his remarks without losing his friendship. This is not to say that his letters are deliberately calculated— let alone hypocritical—compositions, rather that Coleridge possessed and valued and cultivated the power of sympathetic identification, that he wanted very much to please his correspondents, and that he was therefore inclined, probably unconsciously, to exaggerate congenial qualities in himself as he wrote. Samuel Johnson's sombre remark about Pope's letters is apposite: 'There is, indeed, no transaction which offers stronger temptations to fallacy and sophistication than epistolary intercourse.' His is a warning one must bear in mind in approaching any correspondence, along with the awareness that spontaneity, informality, and intimacy are requirements of the art and not necessarily evidence of absolute veracity.

The Chronology below indicates major events in Coleridge's life, but as a guide through the letters a sketch of the significant phases in his career may be a useful supplement to it. I should take the first phase, the period of promise, to end with the collapse of Pantisocracy at the end of 1795; the second, with the quarrel with Wordsworth in 1810; the third, with Coleridge's moving into the Gillman household in 1816; and the fourth, with his death. Although they are obviously disproportionate, each has a fairly coherent character. Coleridge was something of a prodigy as a child, and the promise of the early years became one of the burdens of his maturity: much was expected of him, and circumstances internal and external denied him any conventional kind of success. His self-introduction to Thelwall (pp. 31–2) provides a sharp impression of him as a youth, when his fervent political and religious convictions were given an outlet by the turbulent conditions of the time, the period of the French Revolution. As a young man, he rashly sacrificed his prospects for worldly success and personal happiness, for he left Cambridge without a degree in order to join Southey and others in the Pantisocracy scheme, and he married the sister of Southey's fiancée. There followed a period of increasing financial instability, domestic friction, and ill health, in which Coleridge tried one way after another of earning money for his family—hence the years of study in Germany, of journalism in London, and of public office in Malta. The Wedgwood annuity, however, gave him a measure of security, and the company of William and Dorothy Wordsworth and their expanding household gave him periods of great happiness. After the quarrel with Wordsworth, Coleridge entered the darkest phase of his career. He lived mostly with John Morgan, a friend who was himself in difficult circumstances, who indeed temporarily fled the country to escape his creditors, leaving Coleridge in charge of his wife and sister-in-law. Coleridge led a nomadic life, giving lectures in London and Bristol, and changing his lodgings at least twenty times in six years. He struggled against opium addiction and suicidal depression. In April 1816, still attempting a cure, he took up residence with James Gillman, a surgeon, in Highgate, and lived the rest of his life in comparative serenity, writing and acting as a spiritual advisor and what we might now call a literary consultant to the many visitors who sought him out. His own rather bitter account of his career from the perspective of Highgate appears on pp. 212–14.

The letters in this volume, representing only a tenth of Coleridge's published correspondence, come from every period of his life but are not intended to provide a complete biographical or autobiographical portrait; nor do they include the formal letters that are virtually essays in epistolary form. They have been chosen to do several things at once: to display his achievement as a writer in the minor genre of the familiar letter; to reveal his complex personality in evolution; and to record his astute judgement, especially in literary matters. All the letters are printed unabridged, following the text established by Earl Leslie Griggs in his edition of the *Collected Letters* in six volumes (1956–71), with only typographical errors silently corrected. I am grateful to the Oxford University Press for permission to use the text of this standard edition. I have made no attempt to modernize the text, having found by experiment upon students that after a page or two the irregularities of Coleridge's practice cease to be distracting, and that his pre-Victorian freedom from the bugbear of consistency in matters of capitalization, spelling, and punctuation comes to be thought of as refreshing. As a rule, what appear to be eccentricities—the slant line marking a pause and the apostrophe in the possessive 'it's', for example—are not idiosyncracies but accepted and common usage of the period. In view of the spontaneity convention, it is essential to retain the peculiarities of the original letters, especially their use of italics, small capitals (single and double underlining respectively, in the manuscripts), and capitals to indicate degrees of emphasis. Where these characteristic features do *not* appear, as in pp. 86–7, it is because the manuscript has been lost, and the letter printed from a 'corrected' published text. The layout of the farewell or 'valediction' at the end of a letter has been standardized, with a vertical rule to indicate a change of line in the original. Square brackets always indicate editorial insertions, and points of ellipsis within square brackets ([. . .]) indicate an illegible word or words. For ease of reading, however, I have removed the square brackets with which Professor Griggs scrupulously surrounded his reconstruction of words or passages deleted by Coleridge's correspondents or editors after the letters had left his hands.

Terms and phrases in foreign languages are translated on

the spot except in cases where Coleridge's text itself contains a translation. I am indebted to my colleague John Grant, of the Classics Department of the University of Toronto, for more than a helping hand with passages in Latin and Greek, and to Andrew Patenall of the Division of Humanities at Scarborough College in the University of Toronto, for locating an intractable allusion to Shakespeare. The degree sign ° indicates that there is a note at the end of the book. In annotating the letters, I have tried to cover basic needs by identifying persons and sources of quotations, and occasionally explaining the context of a remark, but readers who want help with Coleridge's vocabulary should supplement the notes by using a comprehensive English dictionary. Where something is not annotated that looks as though it ought to be, the Index may supply an earlier, annotated instance, or at least a useful cross-reference.

LIST OF LETTERS

Correspondent

Correspondent

CHRONOLOGY

1772   Birth of Samuel Taylor Coleridge at Ottery St Mary, Devon, 21 October.

1781   Death of father.

1782   Sent to Christ's Hospital School; Charles Lamb a schoolmate, James Boyer a memorable master.

1789   Fall of the Bastille 14 July, beginning of the French Revolution.

1791   Enters Jesus College, Cambridge, with scholarships.

1793   Execution of the King (January) and Queen (October) of France. Declaration of war between France and England (February). Reign of Terror begins in March, ending July 1794 with execution of Robespierre. Coleridge publishes his first poem but, fearing disgrace for debts, enlists in a company of dragoons (as Silas Tomkyn Comberbache) in December.

1794   Returns to Cambridge in April. In June, on a walking tour, meets Robert Southey at Oxford, and plans with him to establish a Utopian community ('pantisocracy') in America; becomes engaged to Sara Fricker, the sister of Southey's fiancée; leaves Cambridge in December, without a degree.

1795   Lectures with Southey at Bristol (January to June), but pantisocracy is abandoned. Meets Wordsworth (September?). Marries Sara Fricker 4 October.

1796   Publishes a political newspaper, *The Watchman*, in ten numbers (March to May). Publishes *Poems on Various Subjects*. Birth of Hartley Coleridge 19 September. Moves with family to Nether Stowey, near Thomas Poole (December).

1797   William and Dorothy Wordsworth rent Alfoxden House, not far from Stowey (July); *The Rime of the Ancient Mariner* begun (November).

1798   Accepts an annuity of £150 from Thomas and Josiah Wedgwood (reduced to £75 in November 1812). Birth of Berkeley Coleridge 14 May. *Lyrical Ballads* published

anonymously (September). Coleridge and the Wordsworths set out for Germany.

1799   Wordsworths at Ratzeburg, Coleridge at Göttingen and
travelling. Death of Berkeley Coleridge 10 February.
Return to England in July. On a walking tour with
Wordsworth, Coleridge meets Sara Hutchinson, whom
he is to love hopelessly for many years. In London as a
regular contributor to the *Morning Post* December 1799
to April 1800.

1800   Birth of Derwent Coleridge 14 September.

1801   *Lyrical Ballads* (1800) published January, with Preface.
Coleridge an occasional contributor to the *Morning Post*
September 1801 to August 1803.

1802   Napoleon made life consul (May); French invasion of
Switzerland (October). Wordsworth marries Mary
Hutchinson (October). Founding of the *Edinburgh
Review* (October). Birth of Sara Coleridge 23 December.

1804   Napoleon made emperor (May). Spain declares war on
Britain (December). Coleridge leaves England in April
to live in Malta and Italy, acting for part of the time as
Public Secretary in Malta; on return (August 1806) resolved to separate from his wife.

1808   Lectures on poetry at the Royal Institution; fitful contributor to the *Courier* (until 1818).

1809–10   Dictates *The Friend*, in 28 numbers, to Sara Hutchinson
during a prolonged domestication with the Wordsworths
at Allan Bank, Grasmere. Serious break with Wordsworth (October 1810); partial reconciliation May 1812.
Goes to live with John Morgan and his wife and sister-
in-law, at first in London.

1811–12   Three series of lectures on literature. Contributions to
Southey's miscellaneous *Omniana*.

1813   Coleridge's tragedy, *Remorse*, has a successful run at
Drury Lane. Lectures at Bristol October to November.

1814   Lectures at Bristol (April). Wordsworth's *Excursion*
published.

1815   Waterloo (18 June); restoration of Louis XVIII.
Wordsworth's *Poems* (1815) and *The White Doe of Rylstone*.
Biographia Literaria dictated to John Morgan at Calne,
Wiltshire.

1816 Accepted as patient and housemate by James Gillman, surgeon, at Highgate. *Christabel, Kubla Khan, The Pains of Sleep* published in May; *The Statesman's Manual* in December. Composes 'Theory of Life' (pub. 1848).

1817 Publication of *A Lay Sermon, Biographia Literaria, Sibylline Leaves,* and a play, *Zapolya.*

1818–19 Lectures on poetry and drama (January to March 1818) and alternately on literature and on the history of philosophy (December 1818 to March 1819). Bankruptcy of Coleridge's publisher, Rest Fenner.

1825 Address to the Royal Society of Literature 'On the Prometheus of Aeschylus'. *Aids to Reflection* published.

1828 Rhine tour with William Wordsworth and his daughter Dora. Publication of Coleridge's *Poetical Works* (3 vols.).

1829 Second edition of *Poetical Works.* Publication of *On the Constitution of the Church and State* (December).

1834 *Poetical Works* (3rd edn.). Death of Coleridge, 25 July.

BIOGRAPHICAL REGISTER OF CORRESPONDENTS AND PERSONS FREQUENTLY CITED

ALLSOP, THOMAS (1795–1880). A businessman and speculator in London, Allsop introduced himself to Coleridge after attending one of the 1818 lectures, and soon became an intimate of the household.

ALLSTON, WASHINGTON (1779–1843). An American artist whom Coleridge met in Rome in 1805. While Allston was in England in 1812–14, Coleridge nursed him through an illness, and wrote a series of 'Essays on Genial Criticism' on the occasion of a Bristol exhibition of Allston's work; Allston at the same time painted a fine portrait of Coleridge, now in the National Portrait Gallery.

BEAUMONT, Sir GEORGE (1753–1827). Connoisseur, patron of the arts, and himself an accomplished landscape painter, Sir George met Coleridge in 1803 and through him made the acquaintance of Wordsworth.

BOOSEY, THOMAS (1767–1840). London bookseller, member of an important family in the trade. His Broad St. shop appears to have specialized in foreign titles, and may have combined (as many bookshops did) the functions of shop and private circulating library.

BOWLES, Revd WILLIAM LISLE (1762–1850). Popular writer of reflective and topographical poetry. The 1789 collection of his *Sonnets* made so lasting an impression on Coleridge that he paid tribute to it in the first chapter of *Biographia Literaria* (1817). Coleridge was briefly (1814–15) a neighbour of Bowles's.

BRABANT, R. H. (1781–1866). A surgeon at Devizes in Wiltshire, on friendly terms with Coleridge while he lived in the neighbourhood (at Calne) in 1815.

BURNETT, GEORGE (1776?–1811). A college-mate of Southey's who joined Coleridge and Southey in Bristol and was to have been one of the founders of Pantisocracy; he is said to have been an unsuccessful suitor to Martha Fricker (see Coleridge, Sara). He died a pauper in a workhouse.

CARY, Revd HENRY FRANCIS (1772–1844). Attributed the public success of his translation of Dante to Coleridge, who had praised it in his lectures after encountering Cary on holiday in 1817. Coleridge's publishers, Taylor and Hessey, brought out the second edition of the translation, and took Cary on as a contributor to their *London Magazine*. Cary gave Coleridge some literary assistance, especially after becoming an assistant keeper at the British Museum in 1826.

COLERIDGE, DERWENT (1800–83). Coleridge's younger son. Attended St John's College, Cambridge, where he caused his parents some anxiety by declaring atheistical convictions and neglecting his studies; but eventually took orders (becoming 'my right reverend boy'), became the first principal of St Mark's College, Chelsea, and edited several of Coleridge's works after his death.

COLERIDGE, Revd GEORGE (1764–1828). Coleridge's older brother, a second father to him after their own father died; a teacher, who at one time considered taking S.T.C. as a partner in a school; but apparently a man of rigorous social, political, and religious orthodoxy, who was therefore continually disappointed by his youngest brother.

COLERIDGE, HARTLEY (1796–1849), Coleridge's eldest and initially most promising child; took his degree at Merton College, Oxford, but was removed from a fellowship at Oriel on charges of drunkenness; settled in the Lake District as a schoolmaster and occasional writer of poems, essays, and biographical sketches.

COLERIDGE, Sir JOHN TAYLOR (1790–1876). Coleridge's nephew. Brilliant student, lawyer, and man of letters, editor of the *Quarterly Review* temporarily in 1824, he chose a legal career and became an eminent judge.

COLERIDGE, SARA, née FRICKER (1770–1845). One of five sisters caught up in the Pantisocratic scheme of 1794–95; engaged to Coleridge in Bristol in August 1794, married October 1795. After the final breakdown of the marriage, Mrs Coleridge and the Coleridge children continued to live at Greta Hall in Keswick, sharing the house with the Southeys, her sister and brother-in-law.

COTTLE, JOSEPH (1770–1853). As a young Bristol bookseller and fellow poet, Cottle provided money and encouragement to Coleridge and Southey, and was the original publisher of *Lyrical Ballads* (1798).

DAVY, Sir HUMPHRY (1778–1829). Although he was to become the foremost chemist of his day in England, Davy was only an assistant to Thomas Beddoes at the Pneumatic Institution near Bristol when he was introduced to Coleridge and Southey in 1799. Coleridge encouraged his interest in poetry, and he perhaps formed Coleridge's in chemistry. Davy's increasing success (and 1812 knighthood, and marriage to an heiress) gradually forced them apart.

DAWES, Revd JOHN (d. 1845). Kindly schoolmaster to Coleridge's two sons, Dawes offered Hartley a teaching position at his small school in Ambleside when he was forced to leave Oxford.

DE QUINCEY, THOMAS (1785–1859). An admirer of the *Lyrical Ballads*, De Quincey sought Coleridge out in 1807 and became for a time a trusted friend. Later, having turned to miscellaneous essay-writing, he was widely known as 'the English Opium-Eater', after the title of his 1822 *Confessions*.

EVANS family. Mrs Charlotte Evans, a widow, living in London. Her son Tom was a schoolfellow of Coleridge's at Christ's Hospital, and Coleridge fell in love with Mary, one of her three daughters.

FLOWER, BENJAMIN (1775–1829). Coleridge met Flower at Cambridge, where he was an active Unitarian and editor of the *Cambridge Intelligencer*, remarkable among provincial newspapers for its steady opposition to the war with France. Coleridge's first published verses appeared in Flower's paper.

FRERE, JOHN HOOKHAM (1769–1846). Diplomat, poet, translator of Aristophanes, an encouraging and useful friend to Coleridge from about 1816. Coleridge referred to him habitually as a model of good taste.

FRICKER. See Coleridge, Sara.

GILLMAN, ANNE, née HARDING (*c.*1799–1860). Wife of James Gillman and mistress of the Highgate household in which Coleridge spent the last 18 years of his life; treated Coleridge with sisterly affection, and with the two Gillman children accompanied him on several autumn holidays at the seaside.

GILLMAN, JAMES (1782–1839). Surgeon at Highgate, with a busy local practice; author of a treatise on hydrophobia before Coleridge knew him, and of the first volume of a biography of Coleridge after the death of his housemate. Coleridge described him to a new neighbour once as 'an agreeable man, an honest man, and a man of sound common sense'.

GILLMAN, JAMES, Jr. (1808–77). Elder son of Anne and James Gillman, tutored in classics occasionally by Coleridge; attended St John's College, Oxford; took orders and eventually became the Vicar of Holy Trinity Church, Lambeth, Chairman of the Prudential Insurance Co., and father of seven children.

GODWIN, WILLIAM (1756–1836). Philosopher, author of the widely influential *Enquiry concerning Political Justice* (1793); also novelist, bookseller, and hack writer constantly in quest of money-making projects. Husband of Mary Wollstonecraft (1759–97) and father of Mary Shelley (1797–1851).

GOODEN, JAMES. Little is known of Gooden: he appears to have been contemporary with Coleridge (but was still alive in 1849); he was a scholar and an admirer of Wordsworth's.

GREEN, JOSEPH HENRY (1791–1863). Though Green was destined for a surgeon's career when he met Coleridge in 1817, he was also a student of German philosophy, and he and Coleridge began to work together one day a week—an arrangement that lasted the rest of Coleridge's life. Green became in time President of the Royal College of Surgeons and one of Coleridge's literary executors.

HAZLITT, WILLIAM (1778–1830). On good terms with Wordsworth as well as Coleridge from the time he heard the latter preach in 1798 (an experience recorded in 'My First Acquaintance with the Poets'), Hazlitt forfeited their friendship after an embarrassing incident in the Lakes in 1803. He turned to journalism and became a distinguished essayist and lecturer. His reviews of Coleridge are among the most colourful adverse reviews ever written.

HUTCHINSON, SARA (1775–1835). Wordsworth's sister-in-law, whom Coleridge met in 1799 and loved for many years. To her he dictated his periodical *The Friend* during a long period of residence in the Wordsworths' house. The quarrel with Wordsworth effectively separated him from her: they did not correspond, and only rarely encountered one another again.

KENNARD, ADAM STEINMETZ (b. 1833). One of Coleridge's godsons, named for a mutual friend of his father's and godfather's who had died in 1832.

LAMB, CHARLES (1775–1834). Schoolfellow and lifelong friend to Coleridge. Clerk in the East India House until 1825; author of the much-loved *Essays of Elia* (1823), written for the *London Magazine* to which he was a regular contributor.

LAMB, MARY (1764–1847). Sister of Charles Lamb. In 1796, in a fit of insanity, she killed her mother with a kitchen knife. Apart from occasional periods spent in private madhouses, she lived with her brother, collaborating with him in two works for children, *Tales from Shakespeare* and *Mrs. Leicester's School*.

MORGAN, JOHN JAMES (c. 1775–1820). Originally a Bristol acquaintance of Southey's—he had a legal practice there about 1800—Morgan married and moved to London, and offered Coleridge a home with his family at the time of the quarrel with Wordsworth. With a few intervals, Coleridge lived with the Morgans from 1810 to 1816, weathering with them several changes of address and Morgan's personal bankruptcy.

POOLE, THOMAS (1765–1837). A prosperous tanner in Nether Stowey, Somerset, so well known for liberal social views that Southey tried to enlist him in the Pantisocracy scheme in 1794. Coleridge moved to Stowey at the end of 1796 chiefly to be near Poole, who combined with an interest in ideas practical talents that were especially helpful to Coleridge and his young family.

ROBINSON, HENRY CRABB (1775–1867). Lawyer, diarist, Germanist acquainted with Goethe and Schiller, and admirer of Wordsworth. Robinson was introduced to Coleridge in 1810, and gave him access to his German library; in 1812, he was instrumental in patching up the quarrel between Coleridge and Wordsworth.

ROSE, HUGH J. (1795–1838). A student at Cambridge in 1816 when he wrote to express his admiration for *The Friend* and entered into correspondence with Coleridge, Rose was ordained in 1818 and later became known as a Greek scholar and High-Church theologian.

SCOTT, WALTER (1771–1832). Trained in the law, Scott was successively the most popular poet and the most popular writer of fiction of his generation. The poem with which his career began, *The Lay of the Last Minstrel* (1805), was influenced by Coleridge's then unpublished *Christabel*. Scott was generous with compliments to Coleridge's poetry in later years, and although Coleridge did not think highly of Scott's verse, he enjoyed the novels, which he said had been his comforters 'in many a sleepless night when I should but for them have been comfortless'.

SOTHEBY, WILLIAM (1757–1833). A minor poet with independent means, Sotheby shared many of Coleridge's interests: he was a good classical scholar, and he taught himself German in order to translate Wieland's *Oberon* in 1798. Coleridge acted informally as a critic of several of Sotheby's plays, poems, and translations before publication.

SOUTHEY, ROBERT (1774–1843). For a year after their first meeting as students in 1794, Coleridge and Southey worked to realize their dream of establishing a classless society ('Pantisocracy') in America. The project failed, leaving Coleridge engaged to Sara Fricker, the sister of Southey's fiancée, and there followed a few years of alienation between the two poets. In 1801, however, Southey and his wife joined the Coleridges at Greta Hall, and after Coleridge separated from his wife, she and their children stayed on with the Southey household. Southey was a prolific reviewer, editor, biographer, and poet, best known in his time for such exotic epics as

Thalaba (1801) and *The Curse of Kehama* (1810); he was appointed Poet Laureate in 1813.

STERLING, JOHN (1806–44). Introduced to Coleridge about 1828, Sterling became an enthusiastic disciple and intended, after Coleridge's death, to edit his works. Carlyle's famous *Life of John Sterling* (1851) gives an unsympathetic account of Coleridge's influence.

STUART, DANIEL (1766–1846). In 1797, following an introduction to Stuart, who at the time owned two newspapers, Coleridge began occasionally to write poems and 'leaders' first for the *Morning Post* and then (1804–18) for the *Courier*. For a few months in 1799–1800 he attempted to work full-time as a journalist for Stuart; in 1808, when he was lecturing in London, he occupied rooms above the *Courier* office. Although their professional connection ended shortly after Coleridge went to Highgate, Stuart and Coleridge remained friends.

THELWALL, JOHN (1764–1834). Political radical, lecturer, and poet, one of the popular heroes of the time when he and Coleridge began to correspond in 1796, Thelwall having been tried for treason and acquitted in 1794 along with Thomas Hardy (founder of the subversive London Corresponding Society) and John Horne Tooke. In 1798, when it became dangerous for Thelwall to stay in London, Coleridge and Wordsworth tried unsuccessfully to find him accommodation near them in Somerset. It was felt that the neighbourhood would not bear another trouble-maker, and Thelwall went and lived peacefully in Wales instead.

TOBIN, JAMES WEBBE (1767–1814). Part of Coleridge's Bristol circle, a friend of Davy's and of Wordsworth's. Tobin's failing eyesight prevented him from taking any regular professional employment, but he published some verse and encouraged other writers. He left England in 1809 to supervise his father's plantation in the West Indies and to work, though blind, for the abolition of slavery.

TULK, CHARLES AUGUSTUS (1786–1839). Although he was not himself a member of the Swedenborgian New Church, Tulk was a serious student of Swedenborg's works and one of the founders (in 1810) of the Swedenborg Society, established to ensure the publication of Swedenborg's writings. He met Coleridge during a holiday at Littlehampton in 1817. He later served as MP from 1820 to 1826, and from 1835 to 1837.

WADE, JOSIAH (*fl.* 1794–1814). Bristol businessman, a witness at Coleridge's wedding, and a loyal friend through the failure of the *Watchman* and the worst crisis of Coleridge's opium addiction.

WEDGWOOD, THOMAS (1771–1805). Younger son of the founder of the pottery; scientific speculator and 'the first photographer'; patron of promising young men. In Jan. 1798, with his brother Josiah, he offered Coleridge an annual income of £150 with no conditions attached, to allow him to study and write independently rather than become a clergyman.

WORDSWORTH, DOROTHY (1771–1855). Devoted sister of William Wordsworth. Her well-known *Journals* and letters vividly record the character of their life together, including periods (1797–8, 1800–3, 1808–10) in which Coleridge was a housemate or near neighbour.

WORDSWORTH, WILLIAM (1770–1850). Met Coleridge in Sept. 1795, became his closest friend 1797–1810. They were collaborators in the controversial *Lyrical Ballads* (1798), and for at least a decade continued to influence one another's work. Even after the serious rupture of 1810 (patched up in 1812), Coleridge exerted himself, notably in *Biographia Literaria* (1817), to educate readers to appreciate Wordsworth's poetry. For years before its publication in 1850, Wordsworth's *Prelude* was known in the family simply as 'the poem to Coleridge'.

To Mrs Evans

Feb: 5th [1793]

My dear Mrs Evans

   This is the third day of my resurrection from the Couch, or rather, the Sofa of Sickness. About a fortnight ago a quantity of matter took it into it's head to form in my left gum, and was attended with such violent pain, inflammation, and swelling, that it threw me into a fever—however—God be praised—my gum has at last been opened, a villainous tooth extracted, and all is well. I am still very weak—as well I may, since for 7 days together I was incapable of swallowing anything but Spoon meat—so that in point of Spirits I am but the Dregs of my former self—a decaying flame agonizing in the Snuff of a tallow Candle—a kind of hobgoblin, clouted and bagged up in the most contemptible Shreds, Rags, and yellow Relics of threadbare Mortality. The event of our examination was such, as surpassed my expectations, and perfectly accorded with my wishes. After a very severe trial of 6 days' continuance the Number of the Competitors was reduced from 17 to 4—and after a further process of ordeal we, the Survivors, were declared equal—each to the other—and the Scholarship according to the will of it's founder awarded to the Youngest of us—who was found to be a Mr Butler of St John's College.—I am just two months older than he is—& tho' I would doubtless have rather had it myself, I am yet not at all sorry at his success—for he is sensible, and unassuming—and besides—from his circumstances such an accession to his annual income must have been very acceptable to him. So much for myself.—

   I am greatly rejoiced at your Brother's recovery—in proportion indeed to the anxiety and fears, I felt, on your account during his illness.—I recollected, my most dear Mrs Evans, that you are frequently troubled with a strange forgetfulness of yourself, and too too apt to go far beyond your strength, if by any means you may alleviate the Sufferings of others—ah! how different from the majority of those, whom we courteously dignify with the Name of human:—a vile herd, who sit still in the severest distresses of their *Friends*, and cry out, There is a Lion in the way!—animals, who walk with leaden sandals in the paths of Charity, yet to gratify their own inclinations will run a mile in a breath. Oh!—I do know a set of little, dirty, pimping, petyfogging, ambi-dextrous fellows, who would set your house on fire, tho' it were but to roast an egg for themselves! Yet surely—considering it even in a selfish view, the pleasures that arise from whispering peace to those who are in trouble, and healing the broken in heart are far superior to all, the unfeeling can enjoy.

—I need not say how concerned I am for my poor Anne, whose frame is a system of such sweet tones and modulations, that I am perfectly enraged with any Sickness, that untunes so harmoniously attuned an instrument. I hope, that my Condolances will come too late, and should rather have been exchanged for Congratulations. I have enclosed a little work of that great and good man, Archdeacon Paley—it is entitled motives of Contentment—addressed to the poorer part of our fellow Men—the 12th page I particularly admire—& the 20th.° The Reasoning has been of some Service to *me*—who am of the Race of the Grumbletonians.—My dear friend, Allen,° has a resource against most misfortunes in the natural gaiety of his temper—whereas my hypochondriac gloomy Spirit *amid blessings* too frequently warbles out the hoarse gruntings of discontent—!—Nor have all the lectures, that Divines and Philosophers have given us for these 3000 years past, on the vanity of Riches, and the Cares of greatness, &c—prevented me from sincerely regretting, that Nature had not put it into the head of some *Rich* Man to beget *me* for his *first born*—whereas now I am likely to get bread, just when I shall have no teeth left to chew it.—Cheer up, my little one! (thus I answers I) *better late than never.* Hath Literature been thy choice—and hast thou food and raiment—? Be thankful, be *amazed* at thy good fortune! Art thou dissatisfied and desirous of other things? Go, and make twelve votes at an election: it shall do thee more service, and procure thee greater preferment, than to have made twelve commentaries on the twelve Prophets.—

My dear Mrs Evans! excuse the wanderings of my castle building Imagination—I have not a thought, which I conceal

from you—I *write* to others, but my Pen talks to you.—Convey
my softest Affections to Betty, and believe me,

> Your grateful & affectionate Boy
> S T Coleridge.

To George Coleridge

—Sunday night. Feb. [23,] 1794

My Brother would have heard from me long ere this, had I
not been unwell—unwell indeed—I verily thought, that I was
hastening to that quiet Bourne, Where grief is hush'd—And
when my recovered Strength would have enabled me to have
written to you, so utterly dejected were my Spirits, that my
letter would have displayed such a hopelessness of all future
Comfort, as would have approached to Ingratitude—

Pardon me, my more than brother—! if it be the sickly
jealousy of a mind sore with 'self-contracted miseries'—but
was your last letter written in the same tone of tenderness with
your former! Ah me! what awaits me from within and without,
after the first tumult of Pity shall have subsided—Well were it,
if the consciousness of having merited it could arm my Heart
for the patient endurance of it—.

Sweet in the sight of God and celestial Spirits are the tears
of Penitence—the pearls of heaven—the Wine of Angels!—
Such has been the Language of Divines—but Divines have
exaggerated.—Repentance may bestow that tranquillity, which
will enable man to pursue a course of undeviating harmless-
ness, but it can not restore to the mind that inward sense of
Dignity, which is the parent of every kindling Energy!—I am
not, what I was:—*Disgust*—I *feel*, as if it had—jaundiced all
my Faculties.

I laugh almost like an insane person when I cast my eye
backward on the prospect of my past two years—What a
gloomy *Huddle* of eccentric Actions, and dim-discovered
motives! To real Happiness I bade adieu from the moment, I
received my first Tutor's Bill—since that time since that
period my Mind has been irradiated by Bursts only of
Sunshine—at all other times gloomy with clouds, or turbulent

with tempests. Instead of manfully disclosing the disease, I concealed it with a shameful Cowardice of sensibility, till it cankered my very Heart.—I became a proverb to the University for Idleness—the time, which I should have bestowed on the academic studies, I employed in dreaming out wild Schemes of impossible extrication. It had been better for me, if my Imagination had been less vivid—I could not with such facility have shoved aside Reflection! How many and how many hours have I stolen from the bitterness of Truth in these soul-enervating Reveries—in building magnificent Edifices of Happiness on some fleeting Shadow of Reality! My Affairs became more and more involved—I fled to Debauchery—fled from silent and solitary Anguish to all the uproar of senseless Mirth! Having, or imagining that I had, no *stock* of Happiness, to which I could look forwards, I seized the empty gratifications of the moment, and snatched at the Foam, as the Wave passed by me.——I feel a painful blush on my cheek, while I write it—but even for the Un. Scholarship, for which I affected to have read so severely, I did not read three days uninterruptedly—for the whole six weeks, that preceded the examination, I was almost constantly intoxicated! My Brother, you shudder as you read——

When the state of my affairs became known to you, and by your exertions, and my Brothers' generous Confidence a fair Road seemed open to extrication—Almighty God! What a sequel!——

I loitered away more money on the road, and in town than it was possible for me to justify to my Conscience—and when I returned to Cambridge a multitude of petty Embarrassments buzzed round me, like a Nest of Hornets—Embarrassments, which in my wild carelessness I had forgotten, and many of which I had contracted almost without knowing it—So small a sum remained, that I could not mock my Tutor with it—My Agitations were delirium—I formed a Party, dashed to London at eleven o'clock at night, and for three days lived in all the tempest of Pleasure—resolved on my return—but I will not shock your religious feelings°—I again returned to Cambridge—staid a week—such a week! Where Vice has not annihilated Sensibility, there is little need of a Hell! On Sunday night I packed up a few things,—went off in the mail—staid about a week in a strange way, still looking forwards with a kind of recklessness to the dernier [last] resort of misery—An accident of a very singular kind prevented me—and led me to adopt my present situation—where what I have suffered—but enough—may he, who in mercy dispenseth Anguish, be gracious to me!

> Ulcera possessis alte suffusa medullis
> Non leviore manu, ferro sanantur et igni,
> Ne coeat frustra mox eruptura cicatrix—
> Ad vivum penetrant flammae, quò funditus humor
> Defluat, et vacuis corrupto sanguine venis
> Exundet fons ille mali. Claud.°——

[Ulcers deep in the marrow of the bone are cured, not by light touch of hand, but by steel and fire. In this way the scar will not heal in vain, only to burst open again. Flames penetrate to the quick. The humour drains away completely and the source of harm flows away when the veins are emptied of corrupted blood.]

I received a letter from Tiverton° on Thursday full of wisdom, and tenderness, and consolation—I answered it immediately—Let me have the comfort of hearing from you—I will write again to morrow night—

S.T.C.—

To Robert Southey

July 6th—[1794.] Sunday Morn. Gloucester
S.T. Coleridge to R. Southey—Health & Republicanism!

When you write, direct to me to be left at the Post Office, Wrexham, Denbighshire N. Wales. I mention this circumstance *now*, lest carried away by a flood of confluent ideas I should forget it.—You are averse to Gratitudinarian Flourishes—else would I talk about hospitality, attentions &c &c—however as I must not thank you, I will thank my Stars. Verily, Southey—I like not Oxford nor the inhabitants of it—I would say, thou art a Nightingale among Owls—but thou art so songless and heavy towards night, that I will rather liken thee to the Matin Lark—thy *Nest* is in a blighted Cornfield, where

the sleepy Poppy nods it's red-cowled head, and the weak-
eyed Mole plies his dark work—but thy soaring is even unto
heaven.—Or let me add (for my Appetite for Similies is truly
canine° at this moment) that as the Italian Nobles their new-
fashioned Doors, so thou dost make the adamantine Gate of
Democracy turn on it's golden Hinges to most sweet Music.

Our Journeying has been intolerably fatiguing from the
heat and whiteness of the Roads—and the un*hedged* country
presents nothing but *stone*-fences dreary to the Eye and
scorching to the touch—But we shall soon be in Wales.

Gloucester is a nothing-to-be-said-about Town—the Women
have almost all of them sharp Noses. As we walked last night
on the Severn Banks, a most lovely Girl glided along in a
Boat—there were at least 30 naked men bathing—she seemed
mighty unconcerned—and they addressing her with not the
most courtly gallantry, she snatched the Task of Repartee
from her Brother who was in the Boat with her, and abused
them with great perseverance & elocution. I stared—for she
was elegantly dressed—and not a Prostitute. Doubtless, the
citadel of her chastity is so impregnably strong, that it needs
not the ornamental Out-works of Modesty.

It is *wrong*, Southey! for a little Girl with a half-famished
sickly Baby in her arms to put her head in at the window of an
Inn—'Pray give me a bit of Bread and Meat'! from a Party
dining on Lamb, Green Pease, & Sallad—Why?? Because it is
impertinent & *obtrusive*!—I am a Gentleman!—and wherefore
should the clamorous Voice of Woe *intrude* upon mine Ear!?

My companion is a Man of cultivated, tho' not vigorous,
understanding—his feelings are all on the side of humanity——
yet such are the unfeeling Remarks, which the lingering
Remains of Aristocracy occasionally prompt. When the pure
System of Pantocracy° shall have aspheterized the Bounties of
Nature, these things will not be so—! I trust, you admire the
word 'aspheterized' from α non, σφέτερος proprius!° We
really *wanted* such a word—instead of travelling along the
circuitous, dusty, beaten high-Road of Diction you thus cut
across the soft, green pathless Field of Novelty!—Similies
forever! Hurra! I have bought a little Blank Book, and
portable Ink horn—as I journey onward, I ever and anon
pluck the wild Flowers of Poesy—'inhale their odours

awhile'°—then throw them away and think no more of
them—I will not do so!—Two lines of mine—

> And o'er the Sky's unclouded blue
> The sultry Heat suffus'd a *brassy* hue.°

—The Cockatrice is a foul Dragon with a *crown* on it's head.
The Eastern Nations believe it to be hatched by a Viper on a
Cock's Egg. Southey.—Dost thou not see Wisdom in her *Coan*
Vest of Allegory?° The Cockatrice is emblematic of Monarchy
—a *monster* generated by *Ingratitude* on *Absurdity*. When
Serpents *sting*, the only Remedy is—to *kill* the *Serpent*, and
besmear the *Wound* with the *Fat*. Would you desire better
Sympathy?—

Description of Heat from a Poem I am manufacturing—the
Title 'Perspiration, a Travelling Eclogue[']—

> The Dust flies smothering, as on clatt'ring Wheels
> Loath'd Aristocracy careers along.
> The distant Track quick vibrates to the Eye,
> And white and dazzling undulates with heat.
> Where scorching to th' unwary Traveller's touch
> The stone-fence flings it's narrow Slip of Shade,
> Or where the worn sides of the chalky Road
> Yield their scant excavations (sultry Grots!)
> Emblem of languid Patience, we behold
> The fleecy Files faint-ruminating lie.—

Farewell, sturdy Republican! Write me concerning Burnet
& thyself and concerning &c &c—My next shall be a more
sober & chastised Epistle—but you see I was in the humour
for metaphors—and to tell thee the Truth, I have so often
serious reasons to quarrel with my Inclination, that I do not
chuse to contradict it for Trifles.—To Lovell, Fraternity &
civic Remembrances. Hucks' Compliments!°

S.T. Coleridge

To Robert Southey

Sept—18th—[1794] 10 0 clock Thursday Morning

Well, my dear Southey! I am at last arrived at Jesus [College]. My God! how tumultuous are the movements of my Heart—Since I quitted this room what and how important Events have been evolved! America! Southey! Miss Fricker!— Yes—Southey—you are right—Even Love is the creature of strong Motive—I certainly love her. I think of her incessantly & with unspeakable tenderness—with that inward melting away of Soul that symptomatizes it.

Pantisocracy—O I shall have such a scheme of it! My head, my heart are all alive—I have drawn up my arguments in battle array—they shall have the *Tactician* Excellence of the Mathematician with the Enthusiasm of the Poet—The Head shall be the Mass—the Heart the fiery Spirit, that fills, informs, and agitates the whole—Harwood!—Pish! I say nothing of him——

SHAD GOES WITH US. HE IS MY BROTHER!°

I am longing to be with you—Make Edith my Sister—Surely, Southey! we shall be frendotatoi meta frendous. Most friendly where all are friends. She must therefore be more emphatically my Sister.

Brookes & Berdmore, as I suspected, have spread my Opinions in mangled forms at Cambridge—Caldwell the most excellent, the most pantisocratic of Aristocrats, has been laughing at me—Up I arose terrible in Reasoning—he fled from me—because 'he could not answer for his own Sanity sitting so near a madman of Genius!' He told me, that the Strength of my Imagination had intoxicated my Reason—and that the acuteness of my Reason had given a directing Influence to my Imagination.—Four months ago the Remark would not have been more elegant than Just—. Now it is Nothing.—

I like your Sonnets exceedingly—the best of any I have yet seen.—tho' to the eye Fair is the extended Vale—should be To the Eye Tho' fair the extended Vale—I by no means disapprove of Discord introduced to produce *effect*—nor is my Ear so fastidious as to be angry with it where it could not have

been avoided without weakening the Sense—But Discord for
Discord's sake is rather too licentious.—

'Wild wind' has no other but alliterative beauty—it applies
to a storm, not to the Autumnal Breeze that makes the trees
rustle mournfully—Alter it to

> That rustle to the sad wind moaning by.

''Twas a long way & tedious'—& the three last lines are
marked Beauties—unlaboured Strains poured soothingly
along from the feeling Simplicity of Heart.—The next Sonnet
is altogether exquisite—the circumstance common yet new to
Poetry—the moral accurate & full of Soul. '*I never saw*['] &c is
most exquisite——I am almost ashamed to write the following
—it is so inferior—Ashamed! No—Southey—God knows my
heart—I am *delighted* to feel you superior to me in Genius as in
Virtue.

> No more my Visionary Soul shall dwell
> On Joys, that were! No more endure to weigh
> The Shame and Anguish of the evil Day,
> Wisely forgetful! O'er the Ocean swell
> Sublime of Hope I seek the cottag'd Dell,
> Where Virtue calm with careless step may stray,
> And dancing to the moonlight Roundelay
> The Wizard Passions weave an holy Spell.
> Eyes that have ach'd with Sorrow! ye shall weep
> Tears of doubt-mingled Joy, like their's who start
> From Precipices of distemper'd Sleep,
> On which the fierce-eyed Fiends their Revels k[eep,]
> And see the rising Sun, & feel it dart
> New Rays of Pleasance trembling to the Heart.°

I have heard from Allen—and write the *third* Letter to him.
Your's is the *second*.—Perhaps you would like two Sonnets I
have written to my Sally.——

When I have received an answer from Allen, I will tell you
the contents of his first Letter.—

My Comp— to Heath——

I will write you a huge big Letter next week—at present I
have to transact the Tragedy Business, to wait on the Master,
to write to Mrs Southey, Lovell, &c &c—

God love you— &
S.T. Coleridge

To Robert Southey

[Although Coleridge had left Bristol in August engaged to marry Sara Fricker, and returned to Cambridge chiefly to oversee the publication of his and Southey's collaborative *Fall of Robespierre*, he neither wrote nor returned to Bristol as expected. He had heard that Mary Evans was engaged to someone else, and the rumour revived his feelings for her. This letter responds to a reproachful one from Southey; in the end, Southey traced Coleridge to London and brought him back to Bristol.]

[29 Dec. 1794]

I am calm, dear Southey! as an Autumnal Day, when the Sky is covered with grey moveless Clouds. To *love her*° Habit has made unalterable: I had placed her in the sanctuary of my Heart, nor can she be torn from thence but with the Strings that grapple it to Life. This Passion however, divested as it now is of all Shadow of Hope, seems to lose it's disquieting Power. Far distant, and never more to behold or hear of her, I shall sojourn in the Vale of Men sad and in loneliness, yet not unhappy. He cannot be long wretched who dares be actively virtuous. I am well assured, that she loves me as a favorite Brother. When she was present, she was to me only as a very dear Sister: it was in absence, that I felt those gnawings of Suspense, and that Dreaminess of Mind, which evidence an affection more restless, yet scarcely less pure, than the fraternal. The Struggle has been well nigh too much for me—but, praised be the All-merciful! the feebleness of exhausted Feelings has produced a Calm, and my Heart stagnates into Peace.

Southey! my ideal Standard of female Excellence rises not above that Woman. But all Things work together for Good.° Had I been united to her, the Excess of my Affection would have effeminated my Intellect. I should have fed on her Looks as she entered into the Room—I should have gazed on her Footsteps when she went out from me.

To lose her!—I can rise above that selfish Pang. But to marry another—O Southey! bear with my weakness. Love makes all things pure and heavenly like itself:—but to marry a woman whom I do *not* love—to degrade her, whom I call my Wife, by making her the Instrument of low Desire—and on the removal of a desultory Appetite, to be perhaps not displeased with her Absence!—Enough!—These Refinements are the wildering Fires, that lead me into Vice.

Mark you, Southey!—*I will do my Duty.*

I have this moment received your Letter. My Friend—you want but one Quality of Mind to be a—perfect character—. Your Sensibilities are tempestuous—you feel *Indignation* at Weakness—Now Indignation is the handsome Brother of Anger & Hatred—His looks are 'lovely in Terror'—yet still remember, *who* are his *Relations.* I would ardently, that you were a Necessitarian—and (believing in an all-loving Omnipotence) an Optimist.° That puny Imp of Darkness yclept Scepticism—how could it dare to approach the hallowed Fires, that burn so brightly on the Altar of your Heart?

Think you, I wish to stay in Town? I am all eagerness to leave it—and am resolved, whatever be the consequence, to be at Bath by Saturday—I thought of walking down.

I have written to Bristol—and said, I could not assign a particular Time for my leaving Town—I spoke indefinitely that I might not disappoint.

I am not, I presume, to attribute some verses addressed to S. T. C. in the M. Chronicle to you—. To whom?——

My dear Allen!—wherein has he offended? He did never promise to form one of our Party—But of all this when we meet.

Would a Pistol preserve Integrity?—To concentrate Guilt —no very philosophical mode of preventing it.——

I will write of indifferent Subjects.—

Your Sonnet 'Hold your Mad hands![']—is a noble Burst of Poetry—/ But my Mind is weakened—and I turn with selfishness of Thought to those milder Songs, that develope my lonely Feelings. Sonnets are scarcely fit for the hard Gaze of the Public—Manly yet gentle Egotism is perhaps the only conversation which pleases from these melancholy Children of the Muse.—I read with heart and *taste* equally delighted your Prefatory Sonnet / I transcribe not so much to give you my corrections as for the pleasure it gives me.

> With wayworn Feet a Pilgrim woe-begone
> Life's upland Steep I journeyed many a day,

And hymning many a sad yet soothing Lay
Beguil'd my wand'ring with the Charms of Song.
Lonely my Heart and rugged was my Way—
Yet often pluck'd I as I past along
The wild and simple Flowers of Poesy:
And as beseem'd the wayward Fancy's child
Entwin'd each random weed that pleas'd mine Eye.
Accept the wreath, Beloved! it is wild
And rudely-garlanded—yet scorn not thou
The humble Offering, where the sad Rue weaves
With gayer Flowers it's intermingled Leaves—
And I have twin'd the Myrtle for thy Brow!

It is a lovely Sonnet—Lamb likes it with tears in his Eyes.—His Sister has lately been very unwell—confined to her Bed dangerously—She is all his Comfort—he her's. They dote on each other. Her mind is elegantly stored—her Heart feeling—Her illness preyed a good deal on his Spirits—though he bore it with an apparent equanimity, as beseemed him who like me is a Unitarian Christian and an Advocate for the Automatism of Man.—

I was writing a poem which when finished you shall see—and wished him to describe the Character & Doctrines of Jesus Christ for me—but his low Spirits prevented him—The Poem is in blank Verse on the Nativity°——

I sent him these careless Lines which flowed from my Pen extemporaneously——

To C. Lamb.

Thus far my sterile Brain hath fram'd the Song
Elaborate & swelling—but the Heart
Not owns it. From thy spirit-breathing powers
I ask not now, my Friend! the aiding Verse
Tedious to thee, and from thy anxious thought
Of dissonant Mood. In Fancy, well I know,
Thou creepest round a dear-lov'd Sister's Bed
With noiseless step, and watchest the faint Look
Soothing each Pang with fond Solicitudes
And tenderest Tones medicinal of Love.
I too a Sister *had*—an only Sister—
She loved me dearly—and I doted on her—

On her soft Bosom I repos'd my Cares
And gain'd for every wound an healing Tear.
To her I pour'd forth all my puny Sorrows,
(As a sick Patient in his Nurse's arms)
And of the Heart those hidden Maladies
That shrink asham'd from even Friendship's Eye.
O! I have woke at midnight, and have wept
Because she was not!—Cheerily, dear Charles!
Thou thy best Friend shalt cherish many a year—
Such high presages feel I of warm Hope!
For not uninterested the dear Maid
I've view'd, her Soul affectionate yet wise,
Her polish'd Wit as mild as lambent Glories
That play around an holy Infant's head.
He knows (the Spirit who in secret sees,
Of whose omniscient & all-spreading Love
Aught to implore were Impotence of Mind)
That my mute Thoughts are sad before his Throne,
Prepar'd, when he his healing Ray vouchsafes,
To pour forth Thanksgiving with lifted heart
And praise him gracious with a Brother's Joy!

Wynne° is indeed a noble Fellow—more when we meet—
                              Your's
                                      S. T. Coleridge

To Robert Southey

[Responding point by point to accusations made by Southey, this long letter gives Coleridge's view of the decline and collapse of Pantisocracy. Originally planned as an emigration involving twelve couples, the scheme had suffered various setbacks and adjustments, and had been scaled down to a joint-stock farming venture in Wales before Southey himself withdrew. Southey's relations had intervened, urging him to enter the Church or to study law. Southey's friend Wynn had offered him an annuity of £160 provided he study law. Since the annuity could not be paid until Oct. 1796, one of Southey's uncles proposed that Southey and his wife should occupy the remaining months by accompanying him to Portugal.]

                      Friday Morning November [13], 1795
Southey! I *have* 'lost Friends'—Friends who still cherish for

me Sentiments of high Esteem and unextinguished Tenderness. For the Sum Total of my Misbehaviour; the Alpha and Omega of their Accusations, is Epistolary Neglect. I never spake of them without affection, I never think of them without Reverence. Not 'to this Catalogue', Southey! have I 'added *your* name'. You are *lost* to *me*, because you are lost to Virtue.

As this will probably be the last time I shall have occasion to address you, I will glance thro' the History of our connection, and regularly retrace your Conduct and my own. In the month of June, 1794, I first became acquainted with your person and character. Before I quitted Oxford, we had struck out the leading features of a Pantisocracy: while on my Journey thro' Wales, you invited me to Bristol with the full hopes of realizing it—: during my abode at Bristol, the Plan was matured: and I returned to Cambridge hot in the anticipation of that happy Season, when we should remove the *selfish* Principle from ourselves, and prevent it in our children, by an *Abolition* of Property: or in whatever respects this might be impracticable, by such similarity of Property, as would amount to a *moral Sameness*, and answer all the purposes of *Abolition*. Nor were you less zealous: and thought, and expressed your opinion, that if any man embraced our System, he must comparatively disregard 'his father and mother and wife and children and brethren and sisters, yea, and his own Life also': or he could 'not be our disciple'.° In one of your Letters alluding to your Mother's low Spirits and situation—you tell me, that I 'cannot suppose any *individual* feelings will have an undue weight with you[']—and in the same letter you observe (alas! your recent conduct has made it a prophecy!) 'God forbid! that the *Ebullience* of *Schematism* should be over. It is the Promethean Fire that animates my soul—and when *that* is gone, all *will be Darkness*!'——'I have DEVOTED myself!'——

Previously to my departure from Jesus College, and during my melancholy detention in London, what convulsive Struggles of Feeling I underwent, and what sacrifices I made, you know. The liberal Proposal from my Family affected me no farther than as it pained me to wound a revered Brother by the positive and immediate Refusal, which Duty compelled me to return. But there was a—I need not be particular—You

remember what a Fetter I burst, and that it snapt, as if it had
been a Sinew of my Heart. However I returned to Bristol, and
my addresses to Sara, which I at first payed from Principle not
Feeling, from Feeling & from Principle I renewed: and I met a
reward more than proportionate to the greatness of the Effort.
I love and I am beloved, and I am happy!——

Your Letter to Lovell, (two or three days after my arrival at
Bristol) in answer to some objections of mine to the Welsh
Scheme, was the first Thing that alarmed me. Instead of—'It
is our duty' 'such and such are the reasons'—it was 'I and I'
and 'will and will'—sentences of gloomy and self-centering
Resolve. I wrote you a friendly Reproof, and in my own mind
attributed this unwonted Stile to your earnest desires of
realizing our Plan, and the angry Pain which you felt when
any appeared to oppose or defer it's execution. However, I
came over to your opinion, of the utility and in course the duty
of rehearsing our Scheme in Wales—and so rejected the Offer
of being established in the Earl of Buchan's Family. To this
period of our connection I call your more particular attention
and remembrance, as I shall revert to it at the close of my
Letter.

We commenced lecturing. Shortly after, you began to
recede in your conversation from those broad Principles, in
which Pantisocracy originated. I opposed you with vehemence:
for I well knew that no Notion on morality or it's motives
could be without consequences. And once (it was just before
we went in to Bed) you confessed to me that you had acted
wrong. But you relapsed: your manners became cold and
gloomy: and pleaded with increased pertinacity for the
Wisdom of making Self an undiverging Center. At Mr
Jardine's your language was *strong indeed*—recollect it—You
had left the Table and we were standing at the Window. Then
darted into my mind the Dread, that you were meditating a
Separation. At *Chepstow* your Conduct renewed my Suspicion:
and I was greatly agitated even to many Tears. But in
Percefield Walks you assured me that my Suspicions were
altogether unfounded, that our differences were merely
speculative, and that you would certainly go into Wales. I was
glad and satisfied. For my Heart was never bent from you but
by violent strength—and heaven knows, how it leapt back to

esteem and love you. But alas! a short time passed, ere your departure from our first principles became too flagrant. Remember when we went to Ashton on the Strawberry Party. Your conversation with George Burnet on the day following he detailed to me. It scorched my throat. Your private resources were to remain your individual property, and every thing to be separate except on five or six acres. In short, we were to commence Partners in a petty Farming Trade. This was the Mouse of which the Mountain Pantisocracy was at last safely delivered! I received the account with Indignation & Loathings of unutterable Contempt. Such opinions were indeed unassailable—the Javelin of Argument and the arrows of Ridicule would have been equally misapplied—a Straw would have wounded them mortally. I did not condescend to waste my Intellect upon them; but in the most express terms I declared to George Burnet my opinion (and, Southey! next to my own Existence there is scarce any Fact of which at this moment I entertain less doubt) to Burnet I declared it to be my opinion, '*That you had long laid a Plot* of Separation, and were now developing it—by proposing such a vile mutilation of our Scheme, as you must have been conscious, I should reject decisively & with scorn.['] George Burnet was your most affectionate Friend: I knew his unbounded veneration for you, his personal attachment. I knew likewise his gentle Dislike of *me*. Yet him I bade be the Judge. I bade him choose his associate. I would adopt the full System or depart. George, I presume, detailed of this my conversation what part he chose: from him however I received your sentiments—viz—that you would go into Wales on what plan I liked.—Thus your System of Prudentials and your Apostacy were not sudden: these constant Nibblings had sloped your descent from Virtue.

You received your Uncle's Letter. I said—What Answer have you returned. [(]For to think with almost superstitious Veneration of you had been such a deep-rooted Habit of my Soul, that even then I did not dream, you could hesitate concerning so infamous a Proposal.) 'None.' (you replied) 'Nor do I know what Answer I shall return.' You went to Bed. George sat half-petrified—gaping at the pigmy Virtue of his supposed Giant. I performed the Office of still-struggling

Friendship by writing you my free Sentiments concerning the
enormous Guilt of that which your Uncle's doughty Sophistry
recommended.

On the next morning I walked with you towards Bath—
again I insisted on it's criminality. You told me, that you had
'little notion of Guilt', and that 'you had a pretty Sort of
lullaby Faith of your own'. Finding you invulnerable in
conscience, for the sake of mankind I did not however quit the
Field; but prest you on the difficulties of your System. Your
Uncle's Intimacy with the Bishop, and the Hush, in which
you would lie for the two years previous to your Ordination,
were the arguments (variously urged in a long and desultory
Conversation) by which you solved those difficulties.—'But
your Joan of Arc—the sentiments in it are of the boldest
Order.° What if the Suspicions of the Bishop be raised, and he
particularly questions you concerning your opinions of the
Trinity, and the Redemption?' O (you replied) I am pretty
well up to their Jargon and shall answer them accordingly. In
fine, you left me fully persuaded, that you would enter into
holy Orders. And after a week's Interval or more you desired
George Burnet to act independently of you, & *gave him an
invitation to Oxford.*—Of course, we both concluded that the
matter was now absolutely determined. Southey! I am not
besotted, that I should not know nor hypocrite enough not to
tell you, that you were diverted from being a Priest—only by
the weight of Infamy which you perceived coming towards
you, like a Rush of Waters!

Thus with good Reason I considered [you] as one who had
fallen back into the Ranks; as a man admirable for his abilities
only, strict indeed in the lesser Honesties, but like the majority
of men unable to resist a strong Temptation—FRIEND is a very
sacred appellation—You were become an Acquaintance, yet
one for whom I felt no common tenderness. I could not forget
what you had been. Your Sun was set: your Sky was clouded:
but those Clouds and that Sky were yet tinged with the recent
Sun. As I considered you, so I treated you. I studiously
avoided all particular Subjects, I acquainted you with nothing
relative to myself—literary Topics engrossed our Conversation.
You were too quicksighted not to perceive it. I received a
letter from you. 'You have withdrawn your confidence from

me, Coleridge! Preserving still the face of friendship when we meet, you yet avoid me and carry on your plans in secrecy'! If by 'the face of Friendship' you meant that kindliness which I shew to all because I feel it for all, your statement was perfectly accurate. If you meant more, you contradict yourself, for you evidently perceived from my manners, that you were 'a weight upon' me 'in company, an intruder unwish'd and unwelcome.['] I pained you by 'cold Civility, the shadow which Friendship leaves behind him.[']—Since that Letter I altered my conduct no otherways than by avoiding you more—. I still generaliz'd, and spoke not of myself excepting my proposed literary works. In short, I spoke to you as I should have done to any other man of Genius who had happened to be my *acquaintance*—Without the farce & tumult of a Rupture I wish you to sink into that Class.—'Face to face you never changed your manners to me'—And yet I pained you by 'cold civility[']—Egregious contradiction—— Doubtless, I always treated you with urbanity and meant so to do—but I *locked up* my heart from you, and you perceived it and I intended you to perceive it. 'I planned works in conjunction with you'—Most certainly—the *magazine*, which long before this you had planned equally with me, and if it had been carried into execution, would of course have retained your third Share of the Profits.—What had you done that should make you an unfit literary associate to me?— Nothing.—My opinion of you as a *man* was altered—not as a Writer. Our Muses had not quarrelled. I should have read your Poetry with equal Delight and corrected it with equal Zeal, if correction it needed.—I received you on my return from Shurton with 'My usual Shake of the Hand.' You gave me your hand—and dreadful must have been my feelings, if I had refused to take it. Indeed, so long had I known you, so highly venerated, so dearly loved you, that my Hand would have taken your's *mechanically*.—But is shaking the Hand a mark of Friendship?—Heaven forbid! I should then be a Hypocrite many days in the week—It is assuredly the *pledge of Acquaintance, and nothing more*. But after this did I not with most scrupulous care avoid you?—You know, I did.

In your former Letter you say that I made use of these words to you—[']You will be retrograde that you may spring

the farther forward'—You have misquoted, Southey!—You
had talked of rejoining Pantisocracy in about 14 years—I
exploded the probability—but as I saw you determined to
leave it, hoped and wished it might be so—*hoped* that you
might run backwards only to leap the farther forward.—Not
to mention, that during that *conversation,* I had taken the
weight and pressing Urgency of your motives as truths
granted—but when on examination I found them a shew &
mockery of unreal things, doubtless my opinion of you must
have become far less respectful.—You quoted likewise the last
sentence of my Letter to you, as a proof that I approved of
your design—you *knew* that sentence to imply no more than
the pious confidence of Optimism—However wickedly you
might act, God would make it ULTIMATELY the best—. You
knew, this was the meaning of it. I could find twenty Parallel
passages in the Lectures—indeed such expressions applied to
bad actions had become a habit of my Conversation—you had
named, not unwittily, Dr Pangloss.° And Heaven forbid, that
I should not now have faith, that however foul your Stream
may run here, yet that it will filtrate & become pure in it's
subterraneous Passage to the Ocean of Universal Redemption.

Thus far had I written when the necessities of literary
Occupation crowded upon me—and I met you in Red Cliff,
and unsaluted and unsaluting pass'd by the man to whom for
almost a year I had told my last thoughts when I closed my
eyes, and the first when I awoke! But 'Ere this I have felt
Sorrow![']°——I shall proceed to answer your Letters—and
first excriminate myself, and then examine your conduct. You
charge me with having industriously trumpeted your Uncle's
Letter. When I mentioned my intended journey to Clevedon
with Burnet, and was asked by my immediate friends why *you*
were not with us, should I have been silent and implied
something mysterious, or have told an open untruth and made
myself your accomplice? I could do neither. I answered that
you were quite undetermined: but had some thoughts of
returning to Oxford. To Danvers indeed and to Cottle I spoke
more particularly—for I knew their prudence, and their love
for you—: and my Heart was very full. But to Mrs Morgan I
did not mention it. She met me in the streets, and said—So!
Southey is going into the Church—'tis all concluded—'tis in

vain to deny it!—I answered —you are mistaken—you must contradict. Southey has received a splendid offer—but he has not determined—This, I have some faint recollection, was my answer—but of this particular conversation my recollection is very faint. By what means she received the Intelligence, I know not—probably from Mrs Richardson, who might have been told it by Mr Wade. A considerable Time after, the Subject was renewed at Mrs Morgan's, Burnet and my Sara being present. Mrs M. told me, that you had asserted to her, that with regard to the Church you had but barely hesitated, that you might consider your Uncle's Arguments—that you had not given up one Principle—and that *I* was more your Friend, than ever.——I own, I was roused to an agony of Passion; nor was George Burnet undisturbed. Whatever I said that afternoon (and since that Time I have but repeated what I then said, in gentler Language) George Burnet did give his *decided Amen* to. And I said, Southey!—that you had given up every Principle—that confessedly you were going into the Law, more opposite to your avowed principles, if possible, than even the Church—and that I had in my pocket a letter, in which you charged me with having withdrawn my friendship; and as to your barely hesitating about your Uncle's Proposal, I was obliged in my own defence to relate all that past between us, all on which I had founded a conviction so directly opposite.

I have, you say, distorted your conversation by 'gross misrepresentation and wicked and calumnious falsehoods. It has been told me by Mrs Morgan, that I said, I have seen my Error! I have been drunk with principle!'——Just over the Bridge, at the bottom of High Street, returning one night from Red Cliff Hill, in answer to my pressing contrast of your then opinions of the selfish kind with what you had formerly professed, you said—I was intoxicated with the novelty of a System! That you said, 'I have seen my error', I never asserted. It is doubtless implied in the sentence which you did say—but I never charged it to you as your expression. As to your reserving Bank Bills &c to yourself, the Charge would have been so palpable a Lie, that I must have been madman as well as villain to have been guilty of it—if I had, George Burnet & Sara would have contradicted it. I said, that your

conduct in little things had appeared to me tinged with
selfishness, and George Burnet attributed, and still does
attribute your defection to your unwillingness to share your
expected Annuity with us. As to the long Catalogue of other
Lies, they not being particularized, I of course can say nothing
about them—Tales may have been fetched & carried with
embellishments calculated to improve them in every thing but
the Truth. I spoke 'the plain & simple Truth' alone.

And now for your Conduct & Motives. My Hand trembles
when I think what a series of falsehood & duplicity I am about
to bring before the Conscience of a Man, who has dared to
write me, that 'his Conduct has been uniformly open.[']

I must revert to your first Letter, and here you say—

'The Plan you are going upon is not of sufficient Importance
to justify me to myself in abandoning a family, who have none
to support them but me.' The Plan, *you* are going upon! What
Plan was *I* meditating save to retire into the Country with
George Burnet & yourself, and taking by degrees a small farm
there be *learning* to get my own bread by my bodily
Labor—and there to have all things in common—thus
disciplining my body & mind for the successful Practice of the
same thing in America with more numerous Associates—?
And even if this should never be the Case, ourselves & our
children would form a society sufficiently large. And was not
this your own Plan? The Plan, for the realizing of which you
invited me to Bristol—the plan, for which I abandoned my
friends, and every prospect & every certainty, and the Woman
whom I loved to an excess which you in your warmest dream
of fancy could never shadow out?—When I returned from
London, when you deemed Pantisocracy a DUTY—a duty
unaltered by numbers—when you said, that if others left it,
you and George Burnet and your Brother would stand firm to
the post of Virtue—what then were our circumstances? Saving
Lovell, our number was the same—yourself & Burnet &
I—Our *Prospects* were only an uncertain Hope of getting 30
Shillings a week between us by writing for some London
Paper—for the remainder we were to rely on our agricultural
Exertions—And as to your family you stood precisely in the
same situation as you now stand. You meant to take your
Mother with you and your Brother—And where indeed would

have been the Difficulty? She would have earned her maintenance by her management & savings—considering the matter even in this cold-hearted Way. But when you broke from us, our Prospects were brightening—by the magazine or by Poetry we might and should have got 10 guineas a month.—

But if you are acting right, I should be acting right in imitating you—What then would George Burnet do—He, 'whom you seduc'd

> With other promises & other vaunts
> Than to repent, boasting *you* could subdue
> Temptation!'°——

He cannot go into the Church—for you did 'give him Principles'! And I wish that you had indeed 'learnt from him, how infinitely more to be valued is Integrity of Heart than effulgence of Intellect'. Nor can he go into the Law—for the same Principles declare against it—and he is not calculated for it. And his Father will not support any expence of consequence relative to his further education—for Law or Physic he could not take his degrees in or be called to, without a sinking of many hundred pounds.—What, Southey! was George Burnet to do??——

Thus even if you had persisted in your design of taking Orders, your motives would have been weak & shadowy and vile: but when you changed your ground for the Law, they were annihilated. No man dreams of getting Bread in the Law till six or eight years after his first entrance at the Temple. And how very few even then?—Before this Time your Brothers would have been put out—and the money which you must of necessity have sunk in a wicked Profession would have given your Brother an education, and provided a premium fit for the first Compting House in the world.

But I hear, that you have again changed your Ground. You do not now mean to study the Law—but to maintain yourself by your writings and on your promis'd Annuity, which, you told Mrs Morgan, would be more than 100£ a year. Could you not have done the same with *us*? I neither have or could deign to have an hundred a year—Yet by my own exertions I will struggle hard to maintain myself, and my Wife, and my Wife's

Mother, and my associate. Or what if you dedicated this
hundred a year to your family? Would you not be precisely as
I am? Is not George Burnet accurate, when he undoubtingly
ascribes your conduct to an unparticipating Propensity—to a
total want of the boasted *flocci-nauci-nihili-pilificating* Sense?° O
Selfish, money-loving Man! what Principle have you not given
up?—Tho' Death had been the consequence, I would have
spit in that man's Face & called him Liar, who should have
spoken that last Sentence concerning *you*, 9 months ago. For
blindly did I esteem you. O God! that *such a mind* should fall in
love with that low, dirty, gutter-grubbing Trull, WORLDLY
PRUDENCE!!

  Curse on all *Pride*! 'Tis a Harlot that buckrams herself up
in Virtue only that she may fetch a higher Price—'Tis a
Rock, where Virtue may be planted but cannot strike
Root.

  Last of all, perceiving that your Motives vanished at the
first ray of examination, and that those accounts of your
Mother & Family, which had—drawn easy tears down
wrinkled Cheeks—had no effect on keener minds, your last
resource has been—to calumniate me—If there be in nature a
Situation perilous to Honesty, it is this—when a man has not
heart to *be*, yet lusts to *seem*, virtuous. My INDOLENCE you
assigned to Lovell as the Reason for your quitting Pantisocracy.
Supposing it true, it might indeed be a Reason for rejecting
me from the System? But how does this affect Pantisocracy,
that you should reject *it*? And what has Burnet done,
that He should not be a worthy Associate! He who leaned
on you with all his head and his heart? He who gave his
all for Pantisocracy & expected that Pantisocracy would be at
least Bread & Cheese to Him?——But neither is the charge a
true one. My own lectures I wrote for myself—eleven in
number—excepting a very few pages, which most reluctantly
you eked out for me—And such Pages! I would not have
suffered them to have stood in a Lecture of your's. To your
Lectures I dedicated my whole mind & heart—and wrote one
half in *Quantity*—; but in Quality, you must be conscious, that
all the *Tug* of Brain was mine: and that your Share was little
more than Transcription. I wrote with vast exertion of all my
Intellect the parts in the Joan of Arc, and I corrected that and

other Poems with greater interest, than I should have felt for my own. Then my own Poems—and the recomposing of my Lectures—besides a Sermon—and the correction of some Poems for a friend—I could have written them in half the Time and with less expence of Thought.—I write not these things boastfully—but to excriminate myself. The Truth is—You sate down and wrote—I used to saunter about and think what I should write. And we ought to appreciate our comparative Industry by the quantum of mental exertion, not the particular mode of it: By the number of Thoughts collected, not by the number of Lines, thro' which these Thoughts are diffused.

But I will suppose myself guilty of the Charge. How would an honest Man have reasoned in your Case, and how acted? Thus. 'Here is a Man who has abandoned all for what I believe to be Virtue—But he professed himself an imperfect Being when he offered himself an associate to me. He confessed that all his valuable Qualities were "sloth-jaundiced["]°—and in his Letters is a bitter self-accuser. This man did not deceive me—I accepted of him in the hopes of curing him—but I half despair of it. How shall I act? I will tell him fully & firmly, that much as I love Him, I love Pantisocracy more: and if in a certain time I do not see this disqualifying propensity subdued, I must and will reject him.' Such would have been an honest man's reasonings—Such his conduct. Did You act so? Did you ever mention to me 'face to face' my indolence as a motive for your recent Conduct? Did you even mention it in Percefield Walks? And some time after, that night when you scattered some most heart-chilling sentiments, and in great agitation I did ask you *solemnly*, whether you disapproved of any thing in *my* Conduct. And you answered—Nothing. I like you better now than at the commencement of our Friendship!—An Answer which so startled Sara, that she affronted you into angry Silence by exclaiming, What a Story!—George Burnet, I believe, was present. This happened after all our Lectures—after every one of those Proofs of Indolence on which you must found your Charge—A charge which with what Indignation did you receive when brought against me by Lovell! Yet *then* there was some Shew for it—I *had* been criminally indolent! But since then I have exerted

myself more than I could have supposed myself capable.
Enough.

I heard for the first Time on Thursday that you were to set
off for Lisbon on Saturday Morning. It gave me great Pain on
many accounts—but principally, that those moments which
should be sacred to your Affections, may be disturbed by this
long Letter.

Southey! as far as Happiness will be conducive to your
Virtue, which alone is final Happiness, may you possess it!
You have left a large Void in my Heart—I know no man big
enough to fill it. Others I may love equally & esteem equally:
and some perhaps I may admire as much. But never do I
expect to meet another man, who will make me unite
attachment for his person with reverence for his heart and
admiration of his Genius! I did not only venerate you for your
own Virtues, I prized you as the Sheet Anchor of mine! And
even [as] a Poet, my Vanity knew no keener gratification than
your Praise—But these Things are past by, like as when an
hungry man dreams, and lo! he feasteth—but he awakes, and
his Soul is empty!——

May God Almighty bless & preserve you! And may you live
to know, and feel, and acknowlege that unless we accustom
ourselves to meditate adoringly on him, the Source of all
Virtue, no Virtue can be permanent.

Be assured that G. Burnet still loves you better than he can
love any other man—and Sara would have you accept her
Love & Blessing, accept it, as the future Husband of her best-
loved Sister!

Farewell!
S. T. Coleridge.

To Josiah Wade

Nottingham, Wednesday morning, January 27, 1796

My dear Friend,—You will perceive by this letter that I
have changed my route.° From Birmingham, which I quitted
on Friday last (four o'clock in the morning), I proceeded to
Derby, stayed there till Monday morning, and am now at

Nottingham. From Nottingham I go to Sheffield; from Sheffield to Manchester; from Manchester to Liverpool; from Liverpool to London; from London to Bristol. Ah, what a weary way! My poor crazy ark has been tossed to and fro on an ocean of business, and I long for the Mount Ararat on which it is to rest. At Birmingham I was extremely unwell; a violent cold in my head and limbs confined me for two days. Business succeeded very well there; about an hundred subscribers, I think. At Derby tolerably well. Mr. Strutt (the successor to Sir Richard Arkwright°) tells me I may count on forty or fifty in Derby and round about.

Derby is full of curiosities, the cotton, the silk mills, Wright, the painter, and Dr. Darwin, the everything, except the Christian!° Dr. Darwin possesses, perhaps, a greater range of knowledge than any other man in Europe, and is the most inventive of philosophical men. He thinks in a *new* train on all subjects except religion. He bantered me on the subject of religion. I heard all his arguments, and told him that it was infinitely consoling to me, to find that the arguments which so great a man adduced against the existence of a God and the evidences of revealed religion were such as had startled me at fifteen, but had become the objects of my smile at twenty. Not one new objection—not even an ingenious one. He boasted that he had never read one book in defence of *such stuff*, but he had read all the works of infidels! What should you think, Mr. Wade, of a man, who, having abused and ridiculed you, should openly declare that he had heard all that your *enemies* had to say against you, but had scorned to enquire the truth from any of your own friends? Would you think him an honest man? I am sure you would not. Yet of such are all the infidels with whom I have met. They talk of a subject infinitely important, yet are proud to confess themselves profoundly ignorant of it. Dr. Darwin would have been ashamed to have rejected Hutton's theory of the earth° without having minutely examined it; yet what is it to us *how* the earth was made, a thing impossible to be known, and useless if known? This system the doctor did not reject without having severely studied it; but *all at once he makes up his mind* on such important subjects, as whether we be the outcasts of a blind idiot called Nature, or the children of an all-wise and infinitely good God;

whether we spend a few miserable years on this earth, and
then sink into a clod of the valley, or only endure the anxieties
of mortal life in order to fit us for the enjoyment of immortal
happiness. These subjects are unworthy a philosopher's
investigation. He deems that there is a certain *self-evidence* in
infidelity, and becomes an atheist by intuition. Well did St.
Paul say: 'Ye have an evil *heart* of unbelief.'° I had an
introductory letter from Mr. Strutt to a Mr. Fellowes of
Nottingham. On Monday evening when I arrived I found
there was a public dinner in honour of Mr. Fox's birthday,
and that Mr. Fellowes was present. It was a piece of famous
good luck, and I seized it, waited on Mr. Fellowes, and was
introduced to the company. On the right hand of the president
whom should I see but an old College acquaintance? He
hallooed out: *'Coleridge, by God!'* Mr. Wright, the president of
the day, was his relation—a man of immense fortune. I dined
at his house yesterday, and underwent the intolerable slavery
of a dinner of three courses. We sat down at four o'clock, and
it was six before the cloth was removed.

What lovely children Mr. Barr at Worcester has! After
church, in the evening, they sat round and sang hymns so
sweetly that they overwhelmed me. It was with great difficulty
I abstained from weeping aloud—and the infant in Mrs.
Barr's arms leaned forwards, and stretched his little arms, and
stared and smiled. It seemed a picture of Heaven, where the
different orders of the blessed join different voices in one
melodious allelujah; and the baby looked like a young spirit
just that moment arrived in Heaven, startling at the seraphic
songs, and seized at once with wonder and rapture.

My kindest remembrances to Mrs. Wade, and believe me,
with gratitude and unfeigned friendship, your

S. T. Coleridge.

To Charles Lamb

[Lamb had sent an account of the murder of his mother by his sister, and asked Coleridge to reply with 'as religious a letter as possible'. Coleridge mentions the incident again below, p. 35.]

[28 September 1796]

Your letter, my friend, struck me with a mighty horror. It rushed upon me and stupefied my feelings. You bid me write you a religious letter. I am not a man who would attempt to insult the greatness of your anguish by any other consolation. Heaven knows that in the easiest fortunes there is much dissatisfaction and weariness of spirit; much that calls for the exercise of patience and resignation; but in storms like these, that shake the dwelling and make the heart tremble, there is no middle way between despair and the yielding up of the whole spirit unto the guidance of faith. And surely it is a matter of joy that your faith in Jesus has been preserved; the Comforter that should relieve you is not far from you. But as you are a Christian, in the name of that Saviour, who was filled with bitterness and made drunken with wormwood, I conjure you to have recourse in frequent prayer to 'his God and your God;'° the God of mercies, and father of all comfort. Your poor father is, I hope, almost senseless of the calamity; the unconscious instrument of Divine Providence knows it not, and your mother is in heaven. It is sweet to be roused from a frightful dream by the song of birds and the gladsome rays of the morning. Ah, how infinitely more sweet to be awakened from the blackness and amazement of a sudden horror by the glories of God manifest and the hallelujahs of angels.

As to what regards yourself, I approve altogether of your abandoning what you justly call vanities. I look upon you as a man called by sorrow and anguish and a strange desolation of hopes into quietness, and a soul set apart and made peculiar to God! We cannot arrive at any portion of heavenly bliss without in some measure imitating Christ; and they arrive at the largest inheritance who imitate the most difficult parts of

his character, and, bowed down and crushed underfoot, cry in
fulness of faith, 'Father, thy will be done.'°

I wish above measure to have you for a little while here; no
visitants shall blow on the nakedness of your feelings; you
shall be quiet, and your spirit may be healed. I see no possible
objection, unless your father's helplessness prevent you, and
unless you are necessary to him. If this be not the case, I
charge you write me that you will come.

I charge you, my dearest friend, not to dare to encourage
gloom or despair. You are a temporary sharer in human
miseries that you may be an eternal partaker of the Divine
nature. I charge you, if by any means it be possible, come to
me.

I remain your affectionate
S. T. Coleridge

To John Thelwall

Saturday Nov. 19th [1796]
Oxford Street, Bristol

My dear Thelwall

Ah me! literary *Adventure* is but bread and cheese *by chance!* I
keenly sympathize with you—sympathy, the only poor consolation I can offer you. Can no plan be suggested? I mention
one not as myself approving it; but because it was mentioned
to me—Briefly thus—If the Lovers of Freedom° in the
principal towns would join together by eights or tens, to send
for what *books* they want directly to you, & if you could place
yourself in such a line that you might have books from the
different Publishers at Booksellers' price.—Suppose now, that
12 or 14 people should agree together that a little order book
should be kept in the *Shop* of one of them—& when any one of
these wanted a book, to write it down. And as soon as enough
were ordered, to make it worth the carriage, to write up to you
for them?——I repeat, that I mention the plan merely
because it was mentioned to me. Shame fall on the friends of
Freedom if they will do nothing better! If they will do nothing
better, they will not do even this!—And the plan would

disgust the Country Booksellers, who ought not to be
alienated.

Have you any connection with the Corresponding Society
Magazine°—I have not seen it yet—Robert Southey is one of
it's benefactors—Of course, you have read the Joan of Arc.
Homer is the Poet for the Warrior—Milton for the Religionist
—Tasso for Women—Robert Southey for the Patriot. The
first & fourth books of the Joan of Arc are to me more
interesting than the same number of Lines in any poem
whatsoever.—But you, & I, my dear Thelwall! hold different
creeds in poetry as well as religion. N'importe [it doesn't
matter].—By the bye, of your works I have now all, except
your essay on animal vitality which I never had, & your *poems*
which I bought on their first publication, & lost them.° From
those poems I should have supposed our poetical *tastes* more
nearly alike, than I find, they are.—The poem on the Sols
flashes Genius thro' Strophe I. Antistrophe I. & Epode
I.—the rest I do not perhaps understand——only I *love* these
two lines—

> Yet sure the Verse that shews the friendly mind
> To Friendship's ear not harshly flows.—

Your larger *Narrative* affected me greatly. It is admirably
written—& displays strong Sense animated by Feeling, &
illumined by Imagination—& neither in the thoughts or
rhythm does it encroach on poetry.——

There have been two poems of mine in the New Monthly
magazine—with my name—indeed, I make it a scruple of
conscience never to publish any thing, however trifling,
without it. Did you like them? The first was written at the
desire of a beautiful little Aristocrat—Consider it therefore, as
a Lady's Poem. Bowles (the bard of my idolatry) has written a
poem lately without plan or meaning—but the component
parts are divine. It is entitled—Hope, an allegorical Sketch. I
will copy two of the Stanzas, which must be peculiarly
interesting to you, virtuous High-Treasonist, & your friends,
the other Acquitted Felons!—

> But see as one awaked from deadly Trance
> With hollow and dim eyes and stony stare

CAPTIVITY with faltering step advance!
Dripping & knotted was her coal-black Hair,
For she had long been hid, as in the Grave:
No sounds the silence of her prison broke,
Nor one Companion had she in her Cave
Save TERROR's dismal Shape, that no word broke,*
But to a stony Coffin on the Floor
With lean and hideous finger pointed evermore.

The lark's shrill song, the early Village Chime,
The upland echo of the winding Horn,
The far-heard Clock that spoke the passing time,
Had never pierc'd her Solitude forlorn:
At length releas'd from the deep Dungeon's gloom
She feels the fragrance of the vernal Gale,
She sees more sweet the living Landscape bloom
And whilst she listens to Hope's tender tale,
She thinks, her long-lost Friends shall bless her sight,
And almost faints with Joy amidst the broad Day-light!

The last line is indeed exquisite.—

Your portrait of yourself interested me—As to me, my face, unless when animated by immediate eloquence, expresses great Sloth, & great, indeed almost ideotic, good nature. 'Tis a mere carcase of a face: fat, flabby, & expressive chiefly of inexpression.—Yet, I am told, that my eyes, eyebrows, & forehead are physiognomically good—; but of this the Deponent knoweth not. As to my shape, 'tis a good shape enough, if measured—but my gait is awkward, & the walk, & the *Whole man* indicates *indolence capable of energies.*—I am, & ever have been, a great reader—& have read almost every thing—a library-cormorant—I am *deep* in all out of the way books, whether of the monkish times, or of the puritanical aera—I have read & digested most of the Historical Writers—; but I do not *like* History. Metaphysics, & Poetry, & 'Facts of mind'—(i.e. Accounts of all the strange phantasms that ever possessed your philosophy-dreamers from Tauth [Thoth], the Egyptian to Taylor, the English Pagan,°) are my darling Studies.—In short, I seldom read except to amuse myself— & I am almost always reading.——Of useful knowlege, I am

*for broke read spoke, as in Bowles.

a so-so chemist, & I love chemistry——all else is *blank*,—but I *will* be (please God) an Horticulturist & a Farmer. I compose very little—& I absolutely hate composition. Such is my dislike, that even a sense of Duty is sometimes too weak to overpower it.

I cannot breathe thro' my nose—so my mouth, with sensual thick lips, is almost always open. In conversation I am impassioned, and oppose what I deem [error] with an eagerness, which is often mistaken for personal asperity—— but I am ever so swallowed up in the *thing*, that I perfectly forget my *opponent*. Such am I. I am just about to read Dupuis' 12 octavos,° which I have got from London. I shall read only one Octavo a week—for I cannot *speak* French at all, & I read it slowly.——

My Wife is well & desires to be remembered to you & your Stella, & little ones. N.B. Stella (among the Romans) was a Man's name. All the *Classics* are against you; but our Swift, I suppose, is authority for this unsexing.°—

My little David Hartley Coleridge is marvellously well, & grows fast.—I was at Birmingham when he was born—I returned immediately on receiving the unexpected news (for my Sara had strangely miscalculated) & in the Coach wrote the following Sonnet. It alludes in it's first lines to a *Feeling* which if you never have had yourself, I cannot explain to you.

> Oft of some *Unknown Past* such fancies roll
> Swift o'er my brain, as make the Present seem,
> For a brief moment, like a most strange Dream
> When, not unconscious that [s]he dreamt, the Soul
> Questions herself in sleep: and Some have said
> We liv'd ere yet this *fleshly* robe we wore.*
> O my sweet Baby! when I reach my Door
> If heavy Looks should tell me, thou wert dead,
> (As sometimes, thro' excess of Hope, I fear)
> I think, that I should *struggle* to believe
> Thou wert a Spirit to this nether Sphere
> Sentenc'd for some more venial crime to grieve;
> Didst scream, then spring to meet heaven's quick reprieve
> While we wept idly o'er thy little Bier!

*Alluding to Plato's doc[trine] of Pre-existence

My feeling is more perspicuously, tho' less poetically, expressed thus—take which you like.

> Oft o'er my brain mysterious Fancies roll
> That make the Present seem (the while they last)
> A dreamy Semblance of some Unknown Past
> Mix'd with such feelings, as distress the [Soul]
> Half-reas'ning in her sleep: &c

Which do you like the best?—

Sonnet II

To a Friend who asked me *how* I felt when the Nurse first presented the Child to me.

> Charles! my slow heart was only *sad*, when first
> I scann'd that face of feeble Infancy:
> For dimly on my thoughtful spirit burst
> All I had been, and all my babe might be!
> But when I watch'd it on it's Mother's arm
> And hanging at her bosom (She the while
> Bent o'er it's features with a tearful smile)
> Then I was *thrill'd*, & *melted*, and most warm
> Imprest a Father's Kiss—and all beguil'd
> Of dark Remembrance and presageful Fear
> I seem'd to see an Angel's form appear——
> 'Twas even thine, beloved Woman mild!
> So for the Mother's sake the Child was dear,
> And dearer was [the] Mother for the Child!——

Write on the receipt of this—& believe me, as ever, with affectionate esteem | Your sincere Friend
S. T. Coleridge

P.S. I have inclosed a five guinea note——The five Shillings over please to [la]y out for me thus—In White's (of Fleet Street or the Strand, I forget which—O! the Strand, [I] believe—but I don't know which) well, in White's Catalogue are the following Books

4674 Iamblichus, Proclus, Porphyrius &c, One shilling & sixpence, One little volume—
4686 Juliani Opera, three shillings——

Which two books you will be so kind as to purchase for me & send down with the 25 pamp[h]lets. But if they should unfortunately be sold, in the same Catalogue are

		s	d
2109	Juliani Imp. Opera—	12	6
676	Iamblichus de Mysteriis	10	6
2681	Sidonius Apollinaris	6	0

& in the Catalogue of Robson, the Bookseller in New Bond Street,

	s	d	
Plotini Opera, a Ficino,—£1	1	0	——making all together

£2 10 0——°

If you can get the two former little books, costing only four & sixpence, I will [r]est content with them—if they are gone, be so kind as to purchase for me [t]he others, I mentioned to you, amounting to two pound, ten shillings—and, as in the course of next week I shall send a small parcel of books & manuscripts to my very dear Charles Lamb of the India House, I shall be [en]abled to convey the money to you in a letter, which he will leave at your house.——I make no apology for this commission—because I feel (to use a vulgar phrase) that I would do as much for you.

P.S. Can you buy them time enough to send down with your pamphlets? If not, make a parcel per se.

I hope, your hurts from the fall are not serious—You have given a *proof* now that you are no '*Ippokrite*——but I forgot, that you are not a Greekist, & perchance, you hate puns—but in Greek krités signifies a judge, & hippos an Horse—Hippo-crite, therefore, may mean a *Judge of Horses*—My dear fellow! I laugh more, & talk more nonsense in a week, than [mo]st other people do in a year—& I *let* puns [in]offensively [in the presenc]e of grave men, who smile, like verjuice putred.

Farewell!

(I have inclosed the five pound—write when you have received it.)

To Benjamin Flower

Sunday Night. [11 December 1796]

My much esteemed Friend

I truly sympathize with you in your severe Loss, and pray to God that he may give you a sanctified use of your Affliction. The death of a young person of high hopes and opening faculties impresses me less gloomily, than the Departure of the Old. To my more natural Reason, the former *appears* like a *transition*; there seems an *incompleteness* in the life of such a person, contrary to the general order of nature; and it makes the heart say, 'this is not all.' But when an old man sinks into the grave, we have seen the bud, the blossom, and the fruit; and the unassisted mind droops in melancholy, as if *the Whole* had come and gone.—But God hath been merciful to us, and strengthened our eyes thro' faith, and Hope may cast her anchor in a certain bottom, and the young and old may rejoice before God and the Lamb, weeping as tho' they wept not, and crying in the Spirit of faith, Art thou not from everlasting, O Lord God my Holy One? We shall not die!——I have known affliction, yea, my friend! I have been myself sorely afflicted, and have rolled my dreary eye from earth to Heaven, and found no comfort, till it pleased the Unimaginable High & Lofty One to make my Heart more tender in regard of religious feelings. My philosophical refinements, & metaphysical Theories lay by me in the hour of anguish, as toys by the bedside of a Child deadly-sick. May God continue his visitations to my soul, bowing it down, till the pride & Laodicean self-confidence of human Reason be utterly done away; and I cry with deeper & yet deeper feelings, O my Soul! thou art wretched, and miserable, & poor, and blind, and naked!——The young Lady, who in a fit of frenzy killed her own mother, was the Sister of my dearest Friend, and herself dear to me as an only Sister.° She is recovered, and is acquainted with what she has done, and is very calm. She was a truly pious young woman; and her Brother, whose soul is almost wrapped up in her, hath had his heart purified by this horror of desolation, and prostrates his Spirit at the throne of God in believing Silence. The Terrors of the Almighty are the whirlwind, the earthquake, and the Fire that precede the still small voice of his Love. The pestilence of our lusts must be scattered, the strong-layed Foundations of our Pride blown up, & the stubble & chaff of our Vanities burnt, ere we can give ear to the inspeaking Voice of Mercy, 'Why *will* ye die?'°——

My answer to Godwin° will be a six shilling Octavo; and is designed to shew not only the absurdities and wickedness of *his* System, but to detect what appear to me the defects of all the systems of morality before & since Christ, & to shew that wherein they have been right, they have exactly coincided with the Gospel, and that each has erred exactly where & in proportion as, he has deviated from that perfect canon. My last Chapter will attack the credulity, superstition, calumnies, and hypocrisy of the present race of Infidels. Many things have fallen out to retard the work; but I hope, that it will appear shortly after Christmas, at the farthest. I have endeavoured to make it a cheap book; and it will contain as much matter as is usually sold for eight shillings. I perceive, that in the New Monthly Magazine the Infidels have it all hollow. How our ancestors would have lifted up their hands at th[at] modest proposal for making experiments in favor of Idolatry!°

Before the 24th of this month I will send you my *poetic endeavor*—it shall be as good as I can make it. The following Lines are at your service, if you approve of them.

LINES to a Young Man of Fortune who abandoned himself to an indolent and causeless Melancholy.

Hence that fantastic Wantonness of Woe,
O Youth to partial Fortune vainly dea[r!]
To plunder'd WANT's half-shelter'd Hovel go,
Go, and some hunger-bitten Infant hear
Moan haply in a dying Mother's Ear;
Or when the cold and dismal fog-damps brood
O'er the rank Church-yard with sear elm-leaves strew'd
Pace round some WIDOW's grave, whose dearer Part
Was slaughter'd where o'er his uncoffin'd limbs
The flocking Flesh-birds scream'd! Then, while thy Heart
Groans, and thine eyes a fiercer Sorrow dims,

Know (and the Truth shall kindle thy young Mind)
What Nature makes thee mourn, she bids thee heal:
O abject! if to sickly Dreams resign'd
All effortless thou leave Earth's common weal
A prey to the thron'd Murderers of Mankind!
Bristol, Dec. 11th, ~~1796~~

S. T. COLERIDGE.

Do you keep a Shop in Cambridge?——I seldom see *any*
paper. Indeed, I am out of heart with the French. In one of the
numbers of my Watchman I wrote 'a remonstrance to the
French Legislators': it contain'd *my* politics, & the splendid
Victories of the French since that time have produced no
alterations in them. I am tired of reading butcheries and
altho' I should be unworthy the name of Man, if I did not feel
my Head & Heart awefully interested in the final Event, yet, I
confess, my Curiosity is worn out with regard to the
particulars of the Process.—The paper, which contained an
account of the departure of your friend, had in it a Sonnet
written during a Thunder-storm.° In thought & diction it was
sublime & fearfully impressive. I do not remember to have
ever read so fine a *Sonnet*—Surely, I thought, this burst from
no common feelings agitated by no common sorrow!—Was it
your's?—

A young man of fortune, (his name, Gurney°) wrote &
published a book of horrible Blasphemies, asserting that our
blessed Lord deserved his fate more than any malefactor ever
did Tyburn (I pray heaven, I may incur no Guilt by
transcribing it!)—& after a fulsome panegyric adds that the
name of *Godwin* will soon supersede that of Christ.—Godwin
wrote a letter to this Man, thanking him for his *admirable* work,
& soliciting the honor of his personal friendship!!!—

With affectionate Esteem | Your's sincerely
S. T. Coleridge

At the close of this week I go with my Wife & Baby to Stowey,
near Bridgewater, Somersetshire: where you will for the future
direct to me. Whenever there is any thing particular, I shall be
thankful for your Paper.

S. T. C.

To John Thelwall

[This letter answers point by point a letter in which Thelwall had challenged Coleridge's poetry and poetic theory, and gone on to attack the Christian religion.]

December 17th. Saturday Night. [1796]

My dear Thelwall

I should have written you long ere this, had not the settlement of my affairs previous to my leaving Bristol, and the organization of my *new plan* occupied me with bulky anxieties that almost excluded every thing but Self from my thoughts. And, besides, my Health has been very bad, and remains so—A nervous Affection from my right temple to the extremity of my right shoulder almost distracted me, & made the frequent use of Laudanum absolutely necessary. And since I have subdued this, a Rheumatic Complaint in the back of my Head & Shoulders, accompanied with sore throat, and depression of the animal Spirits, has convinced me that a man may change bad Lodgers without bettering himself. I write these things not so much to apologize for my silence, or for the pleasure of complaining, as that you may know the reason why I have not given you 'a strict account' how I have disposed of your Books. This I will shortly do, with all the Veracity, which, that solemn Incantation *'upon your honor'* must necessarily have conjur'd up.—

Your second & third part promise great things°—I have counted the subjects, and by a nice calculation find that eighteen Scotch Doctors would write fifty four Quarto Volumes; each chusing his Thesis out of your Syllabus. May you do good by them; and moreover enable yourself to do more good—I *should* say—to continue to do good. *My farm* will be a garden of one acre & an half; in which I mean to raise vegetables & corn enough for myself & Wife, and feed a couple of snouted & grunting Cousins from the refuse. My evenings I shall devote to Literature; and by Reviews, the Magazine, and other shilling-scavenger Employments shall probably gain 40£ a year—which Economy & Self-Denial, Gold-beaters, shall hammer till it cover my annual Expences.

Now in favor of this scheme I shall say nothing: for the more vehement my ratiocinations were previous to the experiment, the more ridiculous my failure would appear; and if the Scheme deserve the said ratiocination, I shall *live down* all your objections. I doubt not, that the time will come when all our Utilities will be directed in one simple path. That Time however is not come; and imperious circumstances point out to each one his particular Road. Much good may be done in all. I am not *fit* for *public* Life; yet the Light shall stream to a far distance from the taper in my cottage window. Meantime, do *you* uplift the *torch* dreadlessly, and shew to mankind the face of that Idol, which they have worshipped in Darkness!

And now, my dear fellow! for a little sparring about Poetry. My first *Sonnet is obscure;*° but you ought to distinguish between obscurity residing in the uncommonness of the thought, and that which proceeds from thoughts unconnected & language not adapted to the expression of them. When you *do* find out the meaning of my poetry, can you (in general, I mean) alter the language so as to make it more perspicuous—the thought remaining the same?—By 'dreamy semblance' I *did* mean semblance of some unknown Past, like to a dream—and not 'a semblance *presented* in a dream.'—I meant to express, that oftimes, for a second or two, it flashed upon my mind, that the then company, conversation, & every thing, had occurred before, with all the precise circumstances; so as to make Reality appear a Semblance, and the Present like a dream in Sleep. Now this thought is obscure; because few people have experienced the same feeling. Yet several have—& they were proportionably delighted with the lines as expressing some strange sensations, which they themselves had never ventured to communicate, much less had ever seen developed in poetry. (—The lines I have since altered to—

> Oft o'er my Brain does that strange Rapture roll
> Which makes the Present (while it's brief fits last)
> Seem a mere Semblance of some Unknown Past,
> Mix'd with such feelings, as distress the Soul
> When dreaming that she dreams.)

Next as to 'mystical'—Now that the thinking part of Man, i.e. the Soul, existed previously to it's appearance in it's present

body, may be very wild philosophy; but it is very intelligible poetry, inasmuch as Soul is an orthodox word in all our poets; they meaning by 'Soul' a being inhabiting our body, & playing upon it, like a Musician inclosed in an Organ whose keys were placed inwards.—Now this opinion I do not hold—not that I am a Materialist; but because I am a Berkleian°——Yet as you who are not a Christian wished you were, that we might meet in Heaven, so I, who do not believe in this descending, & incarcerated Soul, yet said, if my Baby had died before I had seen him, I should have *struggled* to believe it.——Bless me! a commentary of 35 lines in defence of a Sonnet!—And I do not like the Sonnet much myself——. In some (indeed in many of my poems,) there is a garishness & swell of diction, which I hope, that my poems in future, if I write any, will be clear of—; but seldom, I think, any *conceits*.—In the second Edition now printing I have swept the book with the expurgation Besom to a fine tune—having omitted nearly one third.—As to Bowles, I affirm, that the manner of his accentuation in the words 'broad daylight[']
(three long Syllables) is a beauty, as it admirably expresses the Captive's *dwelling* on the sight of Noon—with rapture & a kind of Wonder.

> The common Sun, the Air, the Skies,
> To Him are opening Paradise.
>   Gray.°

But supposing my defence not tenable, yet how a blunder in metre stamps a man, Italian or Della Cruscan,° I cannot perceive.——As to my own poetry I do confess that it frequently both in thought & language deviates from 'nature & simplicity.' But that Bowles, the most tender, and, with the exception of Burns, the only *always-natural* poet in our Language, that *he* should not escape the charge of Della Cruscanism / this cuts the skin & *surface* of my Heart.——
'Poetry to have it's highest relish must be *impassioned*!' true! but first, Poetry ought not always to have it's *highest* relish, & secondly, judging of the cause from it's effect, Poetry, though treating on lofty & abstract truths, ought to be deemed *impassioned* by him, who reads it with impassioned feelings.—
Now Collins' Ode on the poetical character—that part of it, I

should say, beginning with—'The Band (as faery Legends say) Was wove on that creating Day,' has inspired & whirled *me* along with greater agitations of enthusiasm than any the most *impassioned* Scene in Schiller or Shakspeare——using 'impassioned' in it's confined sense for writings in which the human passions of Pity, Fear, Anger, Revenge, Jealousy, or Love are brought into view with their workings.——Yet I consider the latter poetry as more valuable, because it gives *more general* pleasure—& I judge of all things by their Utility.——I feel strongly, and I think strongly; but I seldom feel without thinking, or think without feeling. Hence tho' my poetry has in general a *hue* of tenderness, or Passion over it, yet it seldom exhibits unmixed & simple tenderness or Passion. My philosophical opinions are blended with, or deduced from, my feelings: & this, I think, peculiarizes my style of Writing. And like every thing else, it is sometimes a beauty, and sometimes a fault. But do not let us introduce an act of Uniformity° against Poets—I have room enough in *my* brain to admire, aye & almost equally, the *head* and fancy of Akenside, and the *heart* and fancy of Bowles, the solemn Lordliness of Milton, & the divine Chit chat of Cowper: and whatever a man's excellence is, that will be likewise his fault.

There were some verses of your's in the last monthly Magazine,—with which I was much pleased. Calm good sense combined with *feeling*, & conveyed in harmonious verse, & a chaste & pleasing Imagery.—I wish much, very much to see your other poem. As to your Poems which you informed me in the accompanying letter that you had sent in the same parcel with the pamphlets,—whether or no your Verses had more than their *proper number of Feet*, I cannot say; but certain it is, that somehow or other they *marched off*. No 'Poems by John Thelwall' could I find.—

When I charged you with anti-religious Bigotry, I did not allude to your Pamphlet; but to passages in your Letters to me, & to a circumstance which Southey, I *think*, once mentioned—that you had asserted, that the *name* of God ought never to be introduced in poetry: which, to be sure, was carrying hatred to your Creator very far indeed!

My dear Thelwall! 'It is the principal felicity of Life, & the chief Glory of Manhood to speak out fully on all subjects.' I will avail myself of it—I will express *all* my feelings; but will previously take care to make my feelings benevolent. Contempt is Hatred without fear—Anger Hatred accompanied with apprehension. But because Hatred is always evil, Contempt must be always evil—& a good man ought to speak *contemptuously* of nothing. I am sure a wise man will not of opinions which have been held by men, in *other* respects at least, confessedly of more powerful Intellect than himself. 'Tis an assumption of *infallibility*; for if a man were wakefully mindful that what he now thinks foolish, he may himself hereafter think wise, it is not in nature, that he should *despise* those who now believe what it is possible he may himself hereafter believe——& if he deny this possibility, he must *on that point* deem himself infallible & immutable.—Now in your Letter of Yesterday you speak with *contempt* of two things, Old Age & the Christian Religion:—this Religion was believed by Newton, Locke, & Hartley, after intense investigation, which in each had been preceded by unbelief.—This does not *prove* it's truth; but it should save it's followers from *contempt*—even though thro' the infirmities of mortality they should *have lost their teeth*. I call that man a Bigot, Thelwall, whose intemperate Zeal for or against any opinions leads him to contradict himself in the space of half-a-dozen lines. Now this you appear to me to have done.—I will write fully to you now; because I shall never renew the Subject. I shall not be idle in defence of the Religion, I profess; & my books will be the place, not my letters.—You say the Christian is a *mean* Religion: now the Religion, which Christ taught, is simply 1 that there is an Omnipresent Father of infinite power, wisdom, & Goodness, in whom we all of us move, & have our being & 2. That when we appear to men to die, we do not utterly perish; but after this Life shall continue to enjoy or suffer the consequences & [natur]al effects of the Habits, we have formed here, whether good or evil.—This is the Christian *Religion* & all of the Christian *Religion*. That there is *no fancy* in it, I readily grant; but that it is mean, & deficient in *mind*, and *energy*, it were impossible for me to admit, unless I admitted that there *could be* no dignity, intellect, or force in any thing but *atheism*.—But tho' it appeal not, itself, to the fancy, the truths which it teaches, admit the highest exercise of it. Are the 'innumerable multitude of angels & archangels' less splendid beings than the countless Gods & Goddesses of Rome & Greece?—And can you seriously think that Mercury from Jove equals in poetic sublimity 'the mighty Angel that came down from Heaven, whose face was as it were the Sun, and his feet as pillars of fire: Who set his right foot on the sea, and his left upon the earth. And he sent forth a loud voice; and when he had sent it forth, seven Thunders uttered their Voices: and when the seven Thund[ers] had uttered their Voices, the mighty Angel lifted up his hand to Heaven, & sware by Him that liveth for ever & ever, that TIME was no more?[']° Is not Milton a *sublimer* poet than Homer or Virgil? Are not his Personages more sublimely cloathed? And do you not know, that there is not perhaps *one* page in Milton's Paradise Lost, in which he has not borrowed his imagery from the *Scriptures*?—I allow, and rejoice that *Christ* appealed only to the understanding & the affections; but I affirm that, after reading Isaiah, or St Paul's Epistle to the Hebrews, Homer & Virgil are disgustingly *tame* to me, & Milton himself barely tolerable. You and I are very differently organized, if you think that the following (putting serious belief out of the Question) is a mean flight of impassioned Eloquence; in which the Apostle marks the difference between the Mosaic & Christian Dispensations— 'For ye are not come unto the Mount that might be touched' (i.e. a *material* and earthly place) 'and that burned with fire; nor unto Blackness, and Tempest, and the sound of a Trumpet, and the Voice of Words, which voice they who heard it intreated that it should not be spoken to them any more; but ye are come unto Mount Sion, and unto the city of the living God, to an innumerable multitude of Angels, to God the Judge of all, and to the Spirits of just Men made perfect!'°——*You* may prefer to all this the Quarrels of Jupiter & Juno, the whimpering of wounded Venus, & the Jokes of the celestials on the lameness of Vulcan—be it so (The difference in our tastes it would not be difficult to account for from the different feelings which we have associated with these ideas)——I shall continue with Milton to say, that

Sion Hill

Delights *me* more, and Siloa's Brook that flow'd
Fast by the oracle of God!°

'Visions fit for Slobberers.' If infidelity do not lead to Sensuality, which in every case except your's I have observed it to do, it always takes away all respect for those who become unpleasant from the infirmities of Disease or decaying Nature. Exempli gratiâ [e.g.]—The *Aged* are '*Slobberers*'—The *only* Vision, which Christianity holds forth, is indeed peculiarly adapted to these *Slobberers*—Yes! to these lonely & despised, and perishing SLOBBERERS it proclaims, that their 'Corruptible shall put on *Incorruption*, & their Mortal put on *Immorality*.'°

'Morals for the Magdalen & Botany Bay.'° Now, Thelwall! I presume that to preach morals to the virtuous is not quite so requisite, as to preach them to the vicious. 'The Sick need a Physician.'° Are morals, which would make a Prostitute a Wife, & a Sister; which would restore her to inward peace & purity; are morals, which would make Drunkards sober, the ferocious benevolent, & Thieves honest, *mean morals*? Is it a despicable trait in our Religion, that it's professed object is 'to heal the broken-hearted, and give Wisdom to the Poor Man?'°—It preaches *Repentance*—what repentance? Tears, & Sorrow, & a repetition of the same crimes?—No. A 'Repentance unto good works'°—a repentance that completely does away all superstitious terrors by teaching, that the *Past* is nothing in itself; that if the Mind *is* good, that it *was* bad, imports nothing. 'It is a religion for Democrats.' It certainly teaches in the most explicit terms the rights of Man, his right to Wisdom, his right to an equal share in all the blessings of Nature; it commands it's disciples to go every where, & every where to preach these rights; it commands them never to use the arm of flesh, to be perfectly non-resistant; yet to hold the promulgation of *Truth* to be a Law above Law, and in the performance of this office to defy 'Wickedness in high places,'° and cheerfully to endure ignominy, & wretchedness, & torments, & death, rather than *intermit* the performance of it; yet while enduring ignominy, & wretchedness, & torments & death to feel nothing but sorrow, and pity, and love for those who inflicted them; wishing their Oppressors to be altogether such as they, 'excepting these bonds.'°—Here is *truth* in theory; and in practice a union of energetic *action*, and more energetic *Suffering*. For activity amuses; but he, who can *endure* calmly, must possess the seeds of true Greatness. For all his animal

spirits will of necessity fail him; and he has only his *Mind* to
trust to.——These doubtless are morals for all the Lovers of
Mankind, who wish to *act* as well as *speculate*; and that you
should allow this, and yet not three lines before call the same
Morals mean, appears to me a gross self-contradiction, symptomatic of Bigotry.—I write freely, Thelwall! for tho' *personally*
unknown, I really love you, and can count but few human
beings, whose hand I would welcome with a more hearty
Grasp of Friendship. I suspect, Thelwall! that you never read
your Testament since your Understanding was matured,
without carelessness, & previous contempt, & a somewhat
like Hatred—Christianity regards morality as a process—it
finds a man vicious and unsusceptible of noble motives; &
gradually leads him, at least, desires to lead him, to the height
of disinterested Virtue—till in relation & proportion to his
faculties & powers, he is perfect 'even as our Father in Heaven
is perfect.'° There is no resting-place for Morality. Now I will
make one other appeal, and have done for ever with the
subject.—There is a passage in Scripture which comprizes the
whole process, & each component part, of Christian Morals.
Previously, let me explain the word Faith—by Faith I
understand, first, a deduction from experiments in favor of the
existence of something not experienced, and secondly, the
motives which attend such a deduction. Now motives being
selfish are only the beginning & the *foundation*, necessary and
of first-rate importance, yet made of vile materials, and
hidden beneath the splendid Superstructure.——

   'Now giving all diligence, add to your Faith *Fortitude*, and to
Fortitude Knowlege, and to Knowlege Purity, and to
Purity *Patience, and to Patience †Godliness, and to Godliness
Brotherly-kindness, and to Brotherly-kindness Universal Love.'°

   * Patience. Permit me, as a definition of this word to quote one sentence from my
first Address.°—Page 20: 'Accustomed to regard all the affairs of Man, as a Process,
they never hurry & they never pause.' In his not possessing *this* virtue, all the horrible
excesses of Robespierre° did, I believe, originate.
   † Godliness: the belief, the habitual, & efficient belief, that we are always in the
presence of our universal Parent.—I will translate literally a passage from a German
Hexameter Poem°——It is the Speech of a Country clergyman on the birth-day of his
Daughter—The *latter part* fully expresses the Spirit of Godliness, & it's connection
with Brotherly-Kindness. (Pardon the harshness of the Language—for it is translated
totidem verbis [word for word].[)] 'Yes! my beloved Daughter! I am cheerful,
cheerful as the Birds singing in the Wood here, or the Squirrel that hops among the

I hope, whatever you may think of Godliness, you will like the *note* on it.—I need not tell you, that Godliness is God*like*-ness, and is paraphrased by Peter—'that ye may be partakers of the divine nature.'°—i.e. act from a love of order, & happiness, & not from any self-respecting motive—from the *excellency*, into which you have exalted your *nature*, not from the *keenness* of *mere prudence*.

——'add to your faith fortitude, and to fortitude knowlege, and to knowlege purity, and to purity patience, and to patience Godliness, and to Godliness brotherly kindness, and to brotherly kindness universal Love.' Now, Thelwall! Can you after reading this consciously repeat that these words are fit only for Prostitutes & hardened Rogues?—Putting *Faith* out of the Question, (which by the by is not mentioned as a virtue but as the leader to them) can you mention a virtue which is not here enjoined—& supposing the precepts embod[ied] in the practice of any one human being, would not Perfection be personified?—I write these things not with any expectation of making you a Christian—I shou[ld smile] at my own folly, if I conceived it even in a friendly day-dream. But I do wish to see a progression in your *moral* character, & I *hope* to see it—for

aëry branches around it's young in their Nest. To day it is eighteen years since God gave me my Beloved, now my only child, so intelligent, so pious, and so dutiful. How the Time flies away! Eighteen years to come—how far the Space extends itself before us! and how does it vanish when we look back upon it! It was but yesterday, it seems to me, that as I was plucking flowers here, & offering praise, on a sudden the joyful Message came, "A Daughter is born to us". Much since that time has the Almighty imparted to us of Good and of Evil. But the Evil itself was Good; for his Loving-kindness is infinite. Do you recollect (*to his Wife*) as it once had rained after a long Drought, and I (Louisa in my arms) was walking with thee in the freshness of the Garden, how the Child snatched at the rainbow, and kissed me, and said—Papa! there it rains flowers from Heaven! Does the blessed God strew these, that we children may gather them up? Yes! I answered—full-blowing and heavenly Blessings does the Father strew, who stretched out the Bow of his Favor: flowers & fruits that we may gather them with thankfulness & joy. *Whenever I think of that great Father then my Heart lifts itself up, and swells with active impulse towards all his Children, our Brothers who inhabit the Earth around us; differing indeed from one another in powers and understanding, yet all dear Children of the same Parent, nourished by the same Spirit of Animation, and ere long to fall asleep; to fall asleep, and again to wake in the common Morning of the Resurrection; all who have loved their fellow-creatures, all shall rejoice with Peter, and Moses, and Confucius, and Homer, and Zoroaster, with Socrates who died for truth, and also with the noble *Mendlesohn, who teaches that the divine one was never crucified.*' *A German, Jew by parentage, and *Deist* by election. He has written some of the most acute books possible in favor of natural Immortal[ity] and Germany deems him her profoundest Metaphysician, with the exception of the most unintelligible Emanuel Kant.—

while you so frequently appeal to the passions of Terror, & Ill nature & Disgust, in your popular writings, I must be blind not to perceive that you present in your daily & hourly practice the *feelings* of *universal Love*. 'The ardor of undisciplined Benevolence seduces us into malignity.'—And while you accustom yourself to speak so *contemptuously* of Doctrines you do not accede to, and Persons with whom you do not accord, I must doubt whether even your *brotherly-kindness* might not be made more perfect. That is surely *fit* for a man which his mind after sincere examination approves, which animates his conduct, soothes his sorrows, & heightens his Pleasures. Every good & earnest Christian declares that all this is true of the *visions* (as you please to style them, God knows why) of Christianity——Every earnest Christian therefore is on a level with *slobberers*. Do not charge me with dwelling on *one* expression—these expressions are always indicative of the habit of feeling.—You possess fortitude, and purity, & a large portion of brotherly-kindness & universal Love—drink with unquenchable thirst of the two latter virtues, an[d] *acquire* patience; and then, Thelwall! should *your* System be true, all that can be said, is that (if both our Systems should be found to increase our own & our fellow-crea[tures'] happiness)—Here lie or did lie *the all* of John Thelwall & S. T. Coleridge—they were both humane, & happy, but the former was the more knowing: & if my System should prove true, we, I doubt not, shall both meet in the kingdom of Heav[en,] and I with transport in my eye shall say—'I *told* you so, my *dear* fellow.' But seriously, the faulty habit of feeling, which I have endeavoured to point out in you, I have detected in at least as great degree in my own practice & am struggling to subdue it.—

I rejoice, that the Bankrupt Honesty of the Public has paid even the small Dividend—you mention. As to your second part, I will write you about it, in a day or two, when I give you an account how I have disposed of your first.—My dear little Baby is well; and my Wife thinks, that he already begins to flutter the callow wings of his Intellect. O the wise heart & foolish head of a Mother! Kiss your little Girl for me, & tell her, if I knew her, I would love her; and then I hope in your next letter you will convey *her* Love to me and my Sara.—Your dear Boy, I trust, will return with rosy cheeks. Don't you suspect, Thelwall! that the little Atheis[t,] Madam Stella, has an abominable *Christian* kind of a *Heart?*—My Sara is much interested about her; and I should not wonder if they were to be sworn sister-seraphs in the heavenly Jerusalem. Give my Love to her.

I have sent you some loose sheets which Charles Lloyd & I printed together, intending to make a Volume, but I gave it up, & cancelled them.—Item—a Joan of Arc, with only the passage of my writing cut out for the Printers—as I am printing it in my second Edition, with very great alterations & an addition of four hundred lines, so as to make it a complete & independent Poem—entitled The Progress of Liberty—or the Visions of the maid of Orleans.—Item—a sheet of Sonnets collected by me for the use of a few friends, who payed the printing——There you will see my opinion of Sonnets.—Item, Poems by C. Lloyd on the death of one of your 'Slobberers'—a very venerable old Lady, & a Quaker. The Book is drest like a rich Quaker, in costly raiment but unornamented. The loss of her almost killed my poor young friend: for he doted on her from his Infancy.—Item, a Poem of mine on Burns, which was printed to be dispersed among friends. It was addressed to Charles Lamb.—Item—(Shall I give it thee, Blasphemer? No. I won't—but) to thy Stella I do present the poems of my [Bowles] for a keep-sake.——Of this parcel I do intreat thy acceptance. I have another Joan of Arc—so you have a *right* to the one inclosed.—Postscript—Item, a humourous Droll on S. Ireland, of which I have likewi[se a]nother. Item—A strange Poem written by an Astrologer here, who *was* a man of fine Genius, which, at intervals, he still discovers.—But, ah me! Madness smote with her hand, and stamped with her feet and swore that he should be her's—& her's he is.—He is a man of fluent Eloquence & general knowlege, gentle in his manners, warm in his affections; but unfortunately he has received a few rays of supernatural Light thro' a crack in his upper story. I *express* myself unfeelingly; but indeed my heart always achs when I think of him. Item, some Verses of Robert Southey's to a College Cat.—And finally the following Lines by thy affectionate Friend

S. T. Coleridge

Sonnet

to a young man who abandoned himself to a causeless &
indolent Melancholy.

Hence that fantastic Wantonness of Woe,
   O Youth to partial Fortune vainly dear!
To plunder'd Want's half-shelter'd Hovel go,
   Go, and some hunger-bitten Infant hear
   Moan haply in a dying Mother's Ear;
Or seek some Widow's grave, whose dearer Part
   Was slaughter'd, where o'er his uncoffin'd Limbs
The flocking Flesh-birds scream'd! Then, while thy Heart
   Groans, and thine eyes a fiercer Sorrow dims,
Know, and the Truth shall kindle thy young mind,
   What Nature makes thee mourn, she bids thee heal:
O Abject! if to sickly Dreams resign'd
   All effortless thou leave Earth's common weal
A Prey to the thron'd Murderers of Mankind!

After the five first lines these two followed,

Or when the cold & dismal fog-damps brood
O'er the rank Church-yard with sear Elm-leaves strew'd,
Pace round some Widow's grave &c— Were they rightly
   omitted?

I love Sonnets; but *upon my honor* I do not love *my* Sonnets.

N.B. Direct your Letters
   S. T. Coleridge | Mr Cottle's | High Street | Bristol.

To John Thelwall

                                Decemb. 31st. 1796

   Enough, my dear Thelwall, of Theology. In my book on
Godwin° I compare the two Systems—his & Jesus's—& that
book I am sure you will read with attention.—I entirely
accord with your opinion of Southey's Joan—the 9th book is
execrable—and the poem tho' it frequently reach the *sentimental*,

does not display, the *poetical, Sublime*. In language at once natural, perspicuous, & dignified, in manly pathos, in soothing & sonnet-like description, and above all, in character, & *dramatic* dialogue, Southey is unrivalled; but as certainly he does not possess opulence of Imagination, lofty-paced Harmony, or that *toil* of thinking, which is necessary in order to plan *a Whole*. Dismissing mock humility, & hanging your mind as a looking-glass over my Idea-pot, so as to image on the said mind all the bubbles that boil in the said Idea-pot, (there's a damn'd long-winded Metaphor for you) I think, that an admirable Poet might be made by *amalgamating him & me*. I *think* too much for a *Poet*; he too little for a *great* Poet. But he abjures *thinking*—& lays the whole stress of excellence—on *feeling*.—Now (as you say) they must go together.—Between ourselves, the *Enthusiasm* of Friendship is not with S. & me. We quarreled—& the quarrel lasted for a twelvemonth—We are now reconciled; but the cause of the Difference was solemn—& 'the blasted oak puts not forth it's buds anew'°—we are *acquaintances*—& feel *kindliness* towards each other; but I do not *esteem*, or LOVE Southey, as I must esteem & love the man whom I dared call by the holy name of FRIEND!—and vice versâ Southey of me—I say no more—it is a painful subject—& do you say nothing—I mention this, for obvious reasons—but let it go no farther.——It is a painful subject. Southey's direction at present is—R. Southey, No. 8, Westgate Buildings, Bath, but he leaves Bath for London in the course of a week.

You imagine that I know Bowles personally—I never *saw* him but once; & when I was a boy, & in Salisbury *market-place*.

The passage in your letter respecting your Mother affected me greatly.—Well, true or false, Heaven is a less gloomy idea than Annihilation!—Dr Beddoes, & Dr Darwin think that *Life* is utterly inexplicable, writing as Materialists°—You, I understand, have adopted the idea that it is the result of organized matter acted on by external Stimuli.—As likely as any other system; but you *assume* the thing to be proved—the '*capability* of being stimulated into sensation' *as* a *property* of organized matter—now 'the Capab.' &c is *my* definition of *animal Life*——Monro believes in a plastic immaterial Nature —all-pervading—

And what if all of animated Nature
Be but organic harps diversely fram'd
That tremble into *thought* as o'er them sweeps
Plastic & vast &c°—

(by the bye—that is my favorite of *my* poems—do *you* like it?)
Hunter that the *Blood* is the Life—which is saying nothing at
all—for if the blood were *Life*, it could never be otherwise than
Life—and to say, it is *alive*, is saying nothing—& Ferriar
believes in a *Soul*, like an orthodox Churchman—So much for
Physicians & Surgeons—Now as to the Metaphysicians, Plato
says, it is *Harmony*—he might as well have said, a fiddle stick's
end—but I love Plato—his dear *gorgeous* Nonsense! And *I, tho'*
last not least, I do not know what to think about it—on the
whole, I have rather made up my mind that I am a mere
apparition—a naked Spirit!—And that Life is I myself I! which
is a mighty clear account of it. Now I have written all this not
to expose my ignorance (that is an accidental effect, not the
final cause) but to shew you, that I want to see your Essay on
Animal Vitality—of which Bowles, the Surgeon, spoke in high
Terms—Yet *he* believes in a *body* & a *soul*. Any book may be
left at Robinson's for *me*, 'to be put into the next parcel sent to
Joseph Cottle, Bookseller, Bristol.'——Have you received an
Ode of mine from Parsons's? In your next letter tell me what
you think of the *scattered* poems, I sent you—send me any
poems, and I will be minute in Criticism——for, O Thelwall!
even a long-winded Abuse is more consolatory to an *Author's*
feelings than a short-breathed, asthma-lunged Panegyric.——
Joking apart, I would to God we could sit by a fireside & joke
vivâ voce, face to face—Stella & Sara, Jack Thelwall, &
I!——As I once wrote to my dear *friend*, T. Poole, 'repeating'

Such Verse as Bowles, heart-honour'd Poet, sang,
That wakes the Tear yet steals away the Pang,
Then or with Berkley or with Hobbes romance it
Dissecting Truth with metaphysic lancet.
Or drawn from up those dark unfathom'd Wells
In wiser folly clink the Cap & Bells.
How many tales we told! What jokes we made!
Conundrum, Crambo, Rebus, or Charade;

Ænigmas, that had driven the *Theban mad,
And Puns then best when exquisitely bad;
And I, if aught of archer vein I hit,
With my own Laughter stifled my own Wit.°

To Thomas Poole

Feb. 6, 1797 Monday.

My dear Poole

I could inform the dullest author how he might write an interesting book—let him relate the events of his own Life with honesty, not disguising the feelings that accompanied them.—I never yet read even a Methodist's 'Experience' in the Gospel Magazine without receiving instruction & amusement: & I should almost despair of that Man, who could peruse the Life of John Woolman° without an amelioration of Heart.—As to my Life, it has all the charms of variety: high Life, & low Life, Vices & Virtues, great Folly and some Wisdom. However what I am depends on what I have been; and you, MY BEST FRIEND! have a right to the narration.—To me the task will be a useful one; it will renew and deepen *my* reflections on the past; and it will perhaps make you behold with no unforgiving or impatient eye those weaknesses and defects in my character, which so many untoward circumstances have concurred to plant there.——

My family on my Mother's side can be traced up, I know not, how far—The Bowdens inherited a house-stye & a pig-stye in the Exmore Country, in the reign of Elizabeth, as I have been told—& to my own knowlege, they have inherited nothing better since that time.—On my father's side I can rise no higher than my Grandfather, who was dropped, when a child, in the Hundred of Coleridge in the County of Devon; christened, educated, & apprenticed by the parish.—He afterwards became a respectable Woolen-draper in the town of South Molton. / I have mentioned these particulars, as the time may come in which it will be useful to be able to prove

*Œdipus.

myself a genuine Sans culotte,° my veins uncontaminated with one drop of Gentility. My father received a better education than the others of his Family in consequence of his own exertions, not of his superior advantages. When he was not quite 16 years old, my Grandfather became bankrupt; and by a series of misfortunes was reduced to extreme poverty. My father received the half of his last crown & his blessing; and walked off to seek his fortune. After he had proceeded a few miles, he sate him down on the side of the road, so overwhelmed with painful thoughts that he wept audibly. A Gentleman passed by, who knew him: & enquiring into his distresses took my father with him, & settled him in a neighb'ring town as a schoolmaster. His school increased; and he got money & knowlege: for he commenced a severe & ardent student. Here too he married his first wife, by whom he had three daughters; all now alive. While his first wife lived, having scraped up money enough, at the age of 20 he walked to Cambridge, entered at Sidney College, distinguished himself for Hebrew & Mathematics, & might have had a fellowship: if he had not been married.—He returned—his wife died—Judge Buller's Father gave him the living of Ottery St Mary, & put the present Judge to school with him—he married my Mother, by whom he had ten children of whom I am the youngest, born October 20th [21], 1772.

These sketches I received from my mother & Aunt; but I am utterly unable to fill them up by any particularity of times, or places, or names. Here I shall conclude my first Letter, because I cannot pledge myself for the accuracy of the accounts, & I will not therefore mingle them with those, for the accuracy of which in the minutest parts I shall hold myself amenable to the Tribunal of Truth.—You must regard this Letter, as the first chapter of an history; which is devoted to dim traditions of times too remote to be pierced by the eye of investigation.——

Your's affectionately
S. T. Coleridge

To Thomas Poole

Sunday   March 1797

My dear Poole

My Father, (Vicar of, and Schoolmaster at, Ottery St. Mary, Devon) was a profound Mathematician, and well-versed in the Latin, Greek, & Oriental Languages. He published, or rather attempted to publish, several works: 1st, Miscellaneous Dissertations arising from the 17th and 18th Chapters of the Book of Judges; II. Sententiae excerptae [selected sayings], for the use of his own School; 3rd (& his best work) a Critical Latin Grammar; in the preface to which he proposes a bold Innovation in the names of the Cases. My father's new nomenclature was not likely to become popular, altho' it must be allowed to be both sonorous and expressive— exempli gratiâ [e.g.]—he calls the ablative the Quippe-quare-quale-quia-quidditive Case!—My Father made the world his confidant with respect to his Learning & ingenuity: & the world seems to have kept the secret very faithfully.—His various works, uncut, unthumbed, have been preserved free from all pollution, except that of his Family's Tails.—This piece of good-luck promises to be hereditary: for all *my* compositions have the same amiable *home-staying* propensity.— The truth is, My Father was not a first-rate Genius—he was however a first-rate Christian. I need not detain you with his Character—in learning, good-heartedness, absentness of mind, & excessive ignorance of the world, he was a perfect *Parson Adams.*°—My Mother was an admirable Economist, and managed exclusively.—My eldest Brother's name was John: he went over to the East Indies in the Company's Service; he was a successful Officer, & a brave one, I have heard: he died of a consumption there about 8 years ago. My second Brother was called William—he went to Pembroke College, Oxford; and afterwards was assistant to Mr Newcome's School, at Hackney. He died of a putrid fever the year before my Father's death, & just as he was on the eve of marriage with Miss Jane Hart, the eldest Daughter of a very wealthy Druggist in Exeter.—My third Brother, James, has been in the army since the age of sixteen—has married a woman of

fortune—and now lives at Ottery St Mary, a respectable Man.
My Brother Edward, the wit of the Family, went to Pembroke
College; & afterwards, to Salisbury, as assistant to Dr
Skinner: he married a woman 20 years older than his Mother.
She is dead: & he now lives at Ottery St Mary, an idle Parson.
My fifth Brother, George, was educated at Pembroke College,
Oxford; and from thence went to Mr Newcome's, Hackney,
on the death of William. He stayed there fourteen years: when
the living of Ottery St Mary was given him—there he now has
a fine school, and has lately married Miss Jane Hart; who
with beauty, & wealth, had remained a faithful Widow to the
memory of William for 16 years.—My Brother George is a
man of reflective mind & elegant Genius. He possesses
Learning in a greater degree than any of the Family, excepting
myself. His manners are grave, & hued over with a tender
sadness. In his moral character he approaches every way
nearer to Perfection than any man I ever yet knew—indeed,
he is worth the whole family in a Lump. My sixth Brother,
Luke (indeed the seventh, for one Brother, the second, died in
his Infancy, & I had forgot to mention him) was bred as a
medical Man—he married Miss Sara Hart: and died at the
age of 22, leaving one child, a lovely Boy, still alive. My
Brother Luke was a man of uncommon Genius,—a severe
student, & a good man.——The 8th Child was a Sister,
Anne—she died a little after my Brother Luke—aged 21.

> Rest, gentle Shade! & wait thy Maker's will;
> Then rise *unchang'd*, and be an Angel still!°

The 9th Child was called Francis: he went out as a
Midshipman, under Admiral Graves—his Ship lay on the
Bengal Coast—& he accidentally met his Brother John—who
took him to Land, & procured him a Commission in the
Army.—He shot himself (having been left carelessly by his
attendant) in a delirious fever brought on by his excessive
exertions at the siege of Seringapatam: at which his conduct
had been so gallant, that Lord Cornwallis paid him a high
compliment in the presence of the army, & presented him
with a valuable gold Watch, which my Mother now has.—All
my Brothers are remarkably handsome; but they were as
inferior to Francis as I am to them. He went by the name of

'the handsome Coleridge.' The tenth & last Child was S. T. Coleridge, the subject of these Epistles: born (as I told you in my last) October 20th, 1772.

From October 20th, 1772 to October 20th, 1773.——Christened Samuel Taylor Coleridge—my Godfather's name being Samuel Taylor Esq. I had another Godfather, his name was Evans: & two Godmothers; both called 'Monday' [Mundy].—

From October 20th, 1773 to October 20th 1774.——In this year I was carelessly left by my Nurse—ran to the Fire, and pulled out a live coal—burnt myself dreadfully—while my hand was being Drest by a Mr Young, I spoke for the first time (so my Mother informs me) & said—'Nasty Doctor Young'!—The snatching at fire, & the circumstance of my first words expressing hatred to professional men, are they at all *ominous*? This Year, I went to School—My Schoolmistress, the very image of Shenstone's,° was named, Old Dame Key—she was nearly related to Sir Joshua Renyolds.°—

From October 20th 1774 to October 1775. I was inoculated; which I mention, because I distinctly remember it: & that my eyes were bound—at which I manifested so much obstinate indignation, that at last they removed the bandage—and unaffrighted I looked at the lancet & suffered the scratch.—At the close of this Year I could read a Chapter in the Bible.

Here I shall end; because the remaining years of my Life *all* assisted to form *my particular mind*—the three first years had nothing in them that seems to relate to it.

To Joseph Cottle

[April, 1797]

My dearest Cottle

I love & respect you, as a Brother. And my memory deceives me woefully, if I have not evidenced by the animated turn of my conversation, when we have been tête à tête, how much your company interested me.—But when last in Bristol the day I meant to have devoted to you, was such a day of sadness, that I could *do nothing*—On the Saturday, the

Sunday, & the ten days after my arrival at Stowey I felt a
depression too dreadful to be described—

> So much I felt my genial spirits droop!
> My Hopes all flat, Nature within me seem'd
> In all her functions weary of herself.°

Wordsworth's conversation &c rous'd me somewhat; but even
now I am not the man, I have been—& I think, never
shall.—A sort of calm hopelessness diffuses itself over my
heart.—Indeed every mode of life, which has promised me
bread & cheese, has been, one after another, torn away from
me—but God remains! I have no immediate pecuniary
distress, having received ten pound from Lloyd's Father at
Birmingham.—I employ myself now on a book of morals in
answer to Godwin, & on my Tragedy . . .
David Hartley is well & grows—Sara is well, and desires a
Sister's Love to you—
    Tom Poole desires to be kindly remembered to you—I see
they have reviewed Southey's Poems, & my Ode in the
Monthly Review°—Notwithstanding the Reviews, I, who in
the sincerity of my heart am *jealous for* Robert Southey's fame,
regret the publication of that Volume. Wordsworth complains
with justice, that Southey writes *too much at his ease*—that he
too seldom 'feels his burthen'd breast

> Heaving beneath th' incumbent Deity.'°

He certainly will make literature more *profitable to him* from the
fluency with which he writes, & the facility, with which he
pleases himself. But I fear, that to Posterity his Wreath will
look unseemly—here an ever living Amaranth, & close by it's
side some Weed of an hour, sere, yellow, & shapeless—his
exquisite Beauties will lose half their effect from the bad
company, they keep.—Besides, I am fearful that he will begin
to rely too much on *story* & *event* in his poems to the neglect of
those *lofty imaginings*, that are peculiar to, & definitive of, *the*
Poet. The *story* of Milton might be told in *two pages*—it is this
[whic]h distinguishes *an* Epic *Poem* from a *Romance in metre.*
Observe the march of Milton—his severe application, his
laborious polish, his deep metaphysical researches, his *prayers
to God* before he began his great poem—all, that could lift &

swell his intellect, became his daily food.—I should not think of devoting less than 20 years to an Epic Poem. Ten to collect materials, & warm my mind with universal Science—I would be a tolerable mathematician, I would thoroughly know mechanics, hydrostatics, optics, & Astronomy—Botany, Metallurgy, fossillism, chemistry, geology, Anatomy, Medicine —then *the mind of man*—then the *minds of men*—in *all* Travels, Voyages, & Histories. So I would spend ten years—the next five in the composition of the poem—& the five last in the correction of it—So I would write, haply not unhearing of that divine and nightly-whispering Voice, which speaks to mighty Minds of predestinated Garlands starry & unwithering!—

God love you & S. T. Coleridge

To Thomas Poole

October 9th, 1797

My dearest Poole

From March to October—a long silence! but [as] it is possible, that I may have been preparing materials for future letters, the time cannot be considered as altogether subtracted from you.

From October 1775 to October 1778.

These three years I continued at the reading-school—because I was too little to be trusted among my Father's School-boys—.After breakfast I had a halfpenny given me, with which I bought three cakes at the Baker's close by the school of my old mistress—& these were my dinner on every day except Saturday & Sunday—when I used to dine at home, and wallowed in a beef & pudding dinner.—I am remarkably fond of Beans & Bacon—and this fondness I attribute to my father's having given me a penny for having eat a large quantity of beans, one Saturday—for the other boys did not like them, and as it was an economic food, my father thought, that my attachment & penchant for it ought to be encouraged.
——My Father was very fond of me, and I was my mother's darling—in consequence, I was very miserable. For Molly,

who had nursed my Brother Francis, and was immoderately
fond of him, hated me because my mother took more notice of
me than of Frank—and Frank hated me, because my mother
gave me now & then a bit of cake, when he had none—quite
forgetting that for one bit of cake which I had & he had not, he
had twenty sops in the pan & pieces of bread & butter with
sugar on them from Molly, from whom I received only
thumps & ill names.—So I became fretful, & timorous, & a
tell-tale—& the School-boys drove me from play, & were
always tormenting me—& hence I took no pleasure in boyish
sports—but read incessantly. My Father's Sister kept an *everything* Shop at Crediton—and there I read thro' all the gilt-
cover little books that could be had at that time, & likewise all
the uncovered tales of Tom Hickathrift, Jack the Giant-killer,
&c & &c &c &c— / —and I used to lie by the wall, and
mope—and my spirits used to come upon me suddenly, & in a
flood—& then I was accustomed to run up and down the
church-yard, and act over all I had been reading on the docks,
the nettles, and the rank-grass.—At six years old I remember
to have read Belisarius, Robinson Crusoe, & Philip Quarle°—
and then I found the Arabian Nights' entertainments—one
tale of which (the tale of a man who was compelled to seek for
a pure virgin) made so deep an impression on me (I had read
it in the evening while my mother was mending stockings)
that I was haunted by spectres, whenever I was in the
dark—and I distinctly remember the anxious & fearful
eagerness, with which I used to watch the window, in which
the books lay—& whenever the Sun lay upon them, I would
seize it, carry it by the wall, & bask, & read—. My Father
found out the effect, which these books had produced—and
burnt them.—So I became a *dreamer*—and acquired an
indispositon to all bodily activity—and I was fretful, and
inordinately passionate, and as I could not play at any thing,
and was slothful, I was despised & hated by the boys; and
because I could read & spell, & had, I may truly say, a
memory & understanding forced into almost an unnatural
ripeness, I was flattered & wondered at by all the old
women—& so I became very vain, and despised most of the
boys, that were at all near my own age—and before I was
eight years old, I was a *character*—sensibility, imagination,

vanity, sloth, & feelings of deep & bitter contempt for almost all who traversed the orbit of my understanding, were even then prominent & manifest.

From October 1778 to 1779.—That which I began to be from 3 to 6, I continued from 6 to 9.—In this year I was admitted into the grammer school, and soon outstripped all of my age.—I had a dangerous putrid fever this year—My Brother George lay ill of the same fever in the next room.——My poor Brother Francis, I remember, stole up in spite of orders to the contrary, & sate by my bedside, & read Pope's Homer to me—Frank had a violent love of beating me—but whenever that was superseded by any humour or circumstance, he was always very fond of me—& used to regard me with a strange mixture of admiration & contempt —strange it was not—: for he hated books, and loved climbing, fighting, playing, & robbing orchards, to distraction.—

My mother relates a story of me, which I repeat here— because it must be regarded as my first piece of wit.—During my fever I asked why Lady Northcote (our neighbour) did not come & see me.—My mother said, She was afraid of catching the fever—I was piqued & answered—Ah—Mamma! the four Angels round my bed an't afraid of catching it.—I suppose, you know the old prayer—

> Matthew! Mark! Luke! & John!
> God bless the bed which I lie on.
> Four Angels round me spread,
> Two at my foot & two at my bed [head]—

This prayer I said nightly—& most firmly believed the truth of it.—Frequently have I, half-awake & half-asleep, my body diseased & fevered by my imagination, seen armies of ugly Things bursting in upon me, & these four angels keeping them off.—In my next I shall carry on my life to my Father's Death.—

God bless you, my dear Poole! | & your affectionate
S. T. Coleridge.

To Thomas Poole

[Endorsed Octr 16th, 1797]

Dear Poole

From October 1779 to Oct. 1781.——I had asked my
mother one evening to cut my cheese *entire*, so that I might
toast it: this was no easy matter, it being a *crumbly* cheese—My
mother however did it— / I went into the garden for some
thing or other, and in the mean time my Brother Frank *minced*
my cheese, 'to disappoint the favorite'. I returned, saw the
exploit, and in an agony of passion flew at Frank—he
pretended to have been seriously hurt by my blow, flung
himself on the ground, and there lay with outstretched
limbs——I hung over him moaning & in a great fright—he
leaped up, & with a horse-laugh gave me a severe blow in the
face—I seized a knife, and was running at him, when my
Mother came in & took me by the arm—/I expected a
flogging—& struggling from her I ran away, to a hill at the
bottom of which the Otter flows—about one mile from
Ottery.—There I stayed; my rage died away; but my
obstinacy vanquished my fears—& taking out a little shilling
book which had, at the end, morning & evening prayers, I
very devoutly repeated them—thinking *at the same time* with
inward & gloomy satisfaction, how miserable my Mother
must be!—I distinctly remember my feelings when I saw a Mr
Vaughan pass over the Bridge, at about a furlong's distance—
and how I watched the Calves in the fields beyond the river. It
grew dark—& I fell asleep—it was towards the latter end of
October—& it proved a dreadful stormy night— / I felt the
cold in my sleep, and dreamt that I was pulling the blanket
over me, & actually pulled over me a dry thorn bush, which
lay on the hill—in my sleep I had rolled from the top of the hill
to within three yards of the River, which flowed by the
unfenced edge of the bottom.—I awoke several times, and
finding myself wet & stiff, and cold, closed my eyes again that
I might forget it.——In the mean time my Mother waited
about half an hour, expecting my return, when the *Sulks* had
evaporated—I not returning, she sent into the Church-yard,
& round the town—not found!—Several men & all the boys

were sent to ramble about & seek me—in vain! My Mother
was almost distracted—and at ten o'clock at night I was *cry'd*
by the crier in Ottery, and in two villages near it—with a
reward offered for me.—No one went to bed—indeed, I
believe, half the town were up all one night! To return to
myself—About five in the morning or a little after, I was
broad awake; and attempted to get up & walk—but I could
not move—I saw the Shepherds & Workmen at a distance—&
cryed but so faintly, that it was impossible to hear me 30 yards
off——and there I might have lain & died—for I was now
almost given over, the ponds & even the river near which I
was lying, having been dragged.—But by good luck Sir
Stafford Northcote, who had been out all night, resolved to
make one other trial, and came so near that he heard my
crying—He carried me in his arms, for near a quarter of a
mile; when we met my father & Sir Stafford's Servants.—I
remember, & never shall forget, my father's face as he looked
upon me while I lay in the servant's arms—so calm, and the
tears stealing down his face: for I was the child of his old
age.——My Mother, as you may suppose, was outrageous
with joy—in rushed a *young Lady*, crying out—'I hope, you'll
whip him, Mrs Coleridge!'—This woman still lives at
Ottery—& neither Philosophy or Religion have been able to
conquer the antipathy which I *feel* towards her, whenever I
see her.—I was put to bed—& recovered in a day or so—but I
was certainly injured—For I was weakly, & subject to the
ague for many years after—.—

My Father (who had so little of parental ambition in him,
that he had destined his children to be Blacksmiths &c, & had
accomplished his intention but for my Mother's pride & spirit
of aggrandizing her family) my father had however resolved,
that I should be a Parson. I read every book that came in my
way without distinction—and my father was fond of me, &
used to take me on his knee, and hold long conversations with
me. I remember, that at eight years old I walked with him one
winter evening from a farmer's house, a mile from Ottery——
& he told me the names of the stars—and how Jupiter was a
thousand times larger than our world—and that the other
twinkling stars were Suns that had worlds rolling round
them—& when I came home, he shewed me how they rolled

round— / . I heard him with a profound delight &
admiration; but without the least mixture of wonder or
incredulity. For from my early reading of Faery Tales, &
Genii &c &c—my mind had been habituated *to the Vast*——&
I never regarded *my senses* in any way as the criteria of my
belief. I regulated all my creeds by my conceptions not by my
sight—even at that age. Should children be permitted to read
Romances, & Relations of Giants & Magicians, & Genii?——
I know all that has been said against it; but I have formed my
faith in the affirmative.—I know no other way of giving the
mind a love of 'the Great', & 'the Whole'.—Those who have
been led to the same truths step by step thro' the constant
testimony of their senses, seem to me to want a sense which I
possess—They contemplate nothing but *parts*—and all *parts*
are necessarily little—and the Universe to them is but a mass
of *little things*.—It is true, that the mind *may* become credulous
& prone to superstition by the former method—but are not
the Experimentalists credulous even to madness in believing
any absurdity, rather than believe the grandest truths, if they
have not the testimony of their own senses in their favor?—I
have known some who have been *rationally* educated, as it is
styled. They were marked by a microscopic acuteness; but
when they looked at great things, all became a blank & they
saw nothing—and denied (very illogically) that any thing
could be seen; and uniformly put the negation of a power for
the possession of a power—& called the want of imagination
Judgment, & the never being moved to Rapture Philosophy!—
    Towards the latter end of September 1781 my Father went
to Plymouth with my Brother Francis, who was to go as
Midshipman under Admiral Graves; the Admiral was a friend
of my Father's.—My Father settled my Brother; & returned
Oct. 4th, 1781—. He arrived at Exeter about six o'clock—&
was pressed to take a bed there by the Harts—but he
refused—and to avoid their intreaties he told them—that he
had never been superstitious—but that the night before he
had had a dream which had made a deep impression. He
dreamt that Death had appeared to him, as he is commonly
painted, & touched him with his Dart. Well he returned
home—& all his family, I excepted, were up. He told my
mother his dream—; but he was in high health & good

spirits—& there was a bowl of Punch made—& my Father gave a long & particular account of his Travel, and that he had placed Frank under a religious Captain &c—/ At length, he went to bed, very well, & in high Spirit.—A short time after he had lain down he complained of a pain in his bowells, which he was subject to, from the wind—my mother got him some peppermint water—and after a pause, he said—'I am much better now, my dear!'—and lay down again. In a minute my mother heard a noise in his throat—and spoke to him—but he did not answer—and she spoke repeatedly in vain. Her *shriek* awaked me—& I said, 'Papa is dead.'—I did not know [of] my Father's return, but I knew that he was expected. How I came to think of his Death, I cannot tell; but so it was.—Dead he was—some said it was the Gout in the Heart—probably, it was a fit of Apoplexy / —He was an Israelite without guile; simple, generous, and, taking some scripture texts in their literal sense, he was conscientiously indifferent to the good & the evil of this world.—

God love you & S. T. Coleridge

To Thomas Poole

[Endorsed Feby 19th 1798]
From October 1781 to October 1782.

After the death of my father we, of course, changed houses, & I remained with my mother till the spring of 1782, and was a day-scholar to Parson Warren, my Father's successor— / He was a booby, I believe; and I used to delight my poor mother by relating little instances of his deficiency in grammar knowlege—every detraction from his merits seemed an oblation to the memory of my Father, especially as Parson Warren did certainly *pulpitize* much better.—Somewhere, I think, about April 1792 [1782], Judge Buller, who had been educated by my Father, sent for me, having procured a Christ's Hospital Presentation.°—I accordingly went to London, and was received by my mother's Brother, Mr Bowden, a Tobacconist & (at the same [time]) clerk to an Underwriter. My Uncle lived at the corner of the Stock

exchange, & carried on his shop by means of a confidential
Servant, who, I suppose, fleeced him most unmercifully.—He
was a widower, & had one daughter who lived with a Miss
Cabriere, an old Maid of great sensibilities & a taste for
literature——Betsy Bowden had obtained an unlimited influence over her mind, which she still retains—Mrs Holt (for this
is her name now) was, when I knew her, an ugly & an artful
woman & not the kindest of Daughters—but indeed, my poor
Uncle would have wearied the patience & affection of an
Euphrasia.°—He was generous as the air & a man of very
considerable talents—but he was a Sot.—He received me with
great affection, and I stayed ten weeks at his house, during
which time I went occasionally to Judge Buller's. My Uncle
was very proud of me, & used to carry me from Coffee-house
to Coffee-house, and Tavern to Tavern, where I drank, &
talked & disputed, as if I had been a man— /. Nothing was
more common than for a large party to exclaim in my hearing,
that I *was a prodigy*, &c &c &c—so that, while I remained at
my Uncle's, I was most completely spoilt & pampered, both
mind & body. At length the time came, & I donned the *Blue*
coat & yellow stockings, & was sent down to Hertford, a town
20 miles from London, where there are about 300 of the
younger Blue coat boys—At Hertford I was very happy, on
the whole; for I had plenty to eat & drink, & pudding &
vegetables almost every day. I stayed there six weeks; and
then was drafted up to the great school at London, where I
arrived in September, 1792 [1782]—and was placed in the
second ward, then called Jefferies's ward; & in the under
Grammar School. There are twelve Wards, or dormitories, of
unequal sizes, beside the Sick Ward, in the great School—&
they contained, all together, 700 boys; of whom I think nearly
one third were the Sons of Clergymen. There are 5 Schools, a
Mathematical, a Grammar, a drawing, a reading, & a writing
School—all very large Buildings.—When a boy is admitted, if
he read very badly, he is either sent to Hertford or to the
Reading-School—(N.B. Boys are admissible from 7 to 12
years old)—If he learn to read tolerably well before 9, he is
drafted into the lower Grammar-school—if not, into the
writing-school, as having given proof of unfitness for classical
attainment.—If before he is eleven he climbs up to the first

form of the lower Grammar-school, he is drafted into the head
Grammar School—if not, at 11 years old he is sent into the
writing School, where he continues till 14 or 15—and is then
either apprenticed, & articled as clerk, or whatever else his
turn of mind, or of fortune shall have provided for him. Two
or three times a year the Mathematical Master beats up for
recruits for the King's boys, as they are called—and all, who
like the navy, are drafted into the Mathematical & Drawing
Schools—where they continue till 16 or 17, & go out as
Midshipmen & Schoolmasters in the Navy.—The Boys, who
are drafted into the head Grammar School, remain there till
13—& then if not chosen for the university, go into the writing
school. Each dormitory has a Nurse, or Matron—& there is a
head Matron to superintend all these Nurses.—The boys
were, when I was admitted, under excessive subordination to
each other, according to rank in School—& every ward was
governed by four Monitors, (appointed by the *Steward*, who
was the supreme Governor out of School—our Temporal
Lord) and by four *Markers*, who wore silver medals, & were
appointed by the head Grammar Master, who was our
supreme Spiritual Lord. The same boys were commonly both
Monitors & Markers—We read in classes on Sundays to our
Markers, & were catechized by them, & under their sole
authority during prayers, &c—all other authority was in the
monitors; but, as I said, the same boys were ordinarily both
the one & the other.—Our diet was very scanty—Every
morning a bit of dry bread & some bad small beer—every
evening a larger piece of bread, & cheese or butter, whichever
we liked—For dinner—on Sunday, boiled beef & broth—
Monday, Bread & butter, & milk & water—on Tuesday,
roast mutton, Wednesday, bread & butter & rice milk,
Thursday, boiled beef & broth—Friday, boiled mutton &
broth—Saturday, bread & butter, & pease porritch—Our
food was portioned—& excepting on Wednesdays I never had
a belly full. Our appetites were *damped* never satisfied—and we
had no vegetables.—

S. T. Coleridge

To George Coleridge

[*Circa* 10 March 1798]

My dear Brother

An illness, which confined me to my bed, prevented me from returning an immediate answer to your kind & interesting Letter. My indisposition originated in the stump of a tooth over which some matter had formed: this affected my eye, my eye my stomach, my stomach my head; and the consequence was a general fever—and the sum of pain was considerably increased by the vain attempts of our Surgeon to extract the offending stump. Laudanum gave me repose, not sleep: but YOU, I believe, know how divine that repose is—what a spot of inchantment, a green spot of fountains, & flowers & trees, in the very heart of a waste of Sands!—God be praised, the matter has been absorbed; and I am now recovering a pace, and enjoy that *newness* of sensation from the fields, the air, & the Sun, which makes convalescence almost repay one for disease.——I collect from your letter, that our opinions and feelings on political subjects are more nearly alike, than you imagine them to be. Equally with you (& perhaps with a deeper conviction, for my belief is founded on actual experience) equally with you I deprecate the moral & intellectual habits of those men both in England & France, who have modestly assumed to themselves the exclusive title of Philosophers & Friends of Freedom.° I think them at least *as* distant from greatness as from goodness. If I know my own opinions, they are utterly untainted with French Metaphysics, French Politics, French Ethics, & French Theology.—As to THE RULERS of France, I see in their views, speeches, & actions nothing that distinguishes them to their advantage from other animals of the same species. History has taught me, that RULERS are much the same in all ages & under all forms of government: they are as bad as they dare to be. The Vanity of Ruin & the curse of Blindness have clung to them, like an hereditary Leprosy. Of the French Revolution I can give my thoughts the most adequately in the words of Scripture—'A great & strong wind rent the mountains & brake in pieces the rocks *before* the Lord; but the Lord was not

in the wind; and after the wind an earthquake; but the Lord
was not in the earthquake: and after the earthquake a Fire—&
the Lord was not in the fire:' and now (believing that no
calamities are permitted but as the means of Good) I wrap my
face in my mantle & wait with a subdued & patient thought,
expecting to hear 'the still small Voice,'° which is of God.—In
America (I have received my information from unquestionable
authority) the morals & domestic habits of the people are
daily deteriorating: & one good consequence which I expect
from revolutions, is that Individuals will see the necessity of
individual effort; that they will act as kind neighbours & good
Christians, rather than as citizens & electors; and so by
degrees will purge off that error, which to me appears as wild
& more pernicious than the παγχρυσοῦν [pan-chrysoun] and
panacea of the old Alchemists°—the error of attributing to
Governments a talismanic influence over our virtues & our
happiness—as if Governments were not rather effects than
causes. It is true, that all effects react & become causes—& so
it must be in some degree with governments—but there are
other agents which act more powerfully because by a nigher &
more continuous agency, and it remains true that Governments are more the *effect* than the *cause* of that which we
are.—Do not therefore, my Brother! consider me as an enemy
to Governments & Rulers: or as one who say[s] that they are
evil. I do not say so—in my opinion it were a species of
blasphemy. Shall a nation of Drunkards presume to babble
against sickness & the head-ach?—I regard Governments as I
regard the abscesses produced by certain fevers—they are
necessary consequences of the disease, & by their pain they
increase the disease; but yet they are in the wisdom &
goodness of Nature; & not only are they physically necessary
as effects, but also as causes they are *morally* necessary in order
to prevent the utter dissolution of the patient. But what should
we think of the man who expected an absolute *cure* from an
ulcer that only prevented his dying?——Of GUILT I say
nothing; but I believe most stedfastly in original Sin; that from
our mothers' wombs our understandings are darkened; and
even where our understandings are in the Light, that our
organization is depraved, & our volitions imperfect; and we
sometimes see the good without *wishing* to attain it, and

oftener *wish* it without the energy that wills & performs—And
for this inherent depravity, I believe, that the *Spirit* of the
Gospel is the sole cure—but permit me to add, that I look for
the *spirit* of the Gospel 'neither in the mountain, nor at
Jerusalem'°——.

You think, my Brother! that there can be but two *parties* at
present, for the Government & against the Government.—It
may be so—I am of no party. It is true, I think the present
ministry weak & perhaps unprincipled men; but I could not
with a safe conscience vote for their removal; for I could point
out no substitutes. I think very seldom on the subject; but as
far as I have thought, I am inclined to consider the Aristocrats
as the more respectable of our three factions, because they are
more decorous. The Opposition & the Democrats are not only
vicious—they wear the *filthy garments* of vice.

> He that takes
> Deep in his soft credulity the stamp
> Design'd by loud Declaimers on the part
> Of Liberty, themselves the slaves of Lust,
> Incurs derision for his easy faith
> And lack of Knowlege—& with cause enough.
> For when was public Virtue to be found
> Where private was not? Can he love the whole
> Who loves no part? He be a *nation's* friend
> Who is, in truth, the friend of no man there?
> Can he be strenuous in his country's cause
> Who slights the charities, for whose dear sake
> That country, if at all, must be belov'd?
>
> Cowper.°—

I am prepared to suffer without discontent the consequences
of my follies & mistakes—: and unable to conceive how that
which I am, of Good could have been without that which I
have been of Evil, it is withheld from me to regret any thing: I
therefore consent to be deemed a Democrat & a Seditionist. A
man's character follows him long after he has ceased to
deserve it—but I have snapped my squeaking baby-trumpet
of Sedition & the fragments lie scattered in the lumber-room
of Penitence. I wish to be a good man & a Christian—but I
am no Whig, no Reformist, no Republican—and because of

the multitude of these fiery & undisciplined spirits that lie in wait against the public Quiet under these titles, because of them I chiefly accuse the present ministers—to whose folly I attribute, in great measure, their increased & increasing numbers.—You think differently: and if I were called on by you to prove my assertions, altho' I imagine I could make them appear plausible, yet I should feel the insufficiency of my data. The Ministers may have had in their possession facts which may alter the whole state of the argument, and make my syllogisms fall as flat as a baby's card-house—And feeling this, my Brother! I have for some time past withdrawn myself almost totally from the consideration of *immediate* causes, which are infinitely complex & uncertain, to muse on fundamental & general causes—the 'causae causarum [causes of causes].'—I devote myself to such works as encroach not on the antisocial passions—in poetry, to elevate the imagination & set the affections in right tune by the beauty of the inanimate impregnated, as with a living soul, by the presence of Life—in prose, to the seeking with patience & a slow, very slow mind 'Quid sumus, et quidnam victuri gignimur[']—What our faculties are & what they are capable of becoming.—I love fields & woods & mounta[ins] with almost a visionary fondness—and because I have found benevolence & quietness growing within me as that fondness [has] increased, therefore I should wish to be the means of implanting it in others—& to destroy the bad passions not by combating them, but by keeping them in inaction.

> Not useless do I deem
> These shadowy Sympathies with things that hold
> An inarticulate Language: for the Man
> Once taught to love such objects, as excite
> No morbid passions, no disquietude,
> No vengeance & no hatred, needs must feel
> The Joy of that pure principle of Love
> So deeply, that, unsatisfied with aught
> Less pure & exquisite, he cannot chuse
> But seek for objects of a kindred Love
> In fellow-natures, & a kindred Joy.
> Accordingly, he by degrees perceives

His feelings of aversion softened down,
A holy tenderness pervade his frame!
His sanity of reason not impair'd,
Say rather that his thoughts now flowing clear
From a clear fountain flowing, he looks round—
He seeks for Good & finds the Good he seeks.
                                    Wordsworth.°—

I have layed down for myself two maxims—and what is more
I am in the habit of regulating myself by them—With regard
to others, I never controvert opinions except after some
intimacy & when alone with the person, and at the happy
time when we both seem awake to our own fallibility—and
then I rather state *my* reasons than argue against his.—In
general conversation & general company I endeavor to find
out the opinions common to us—or at least the subjects on
which difference of opinion creates no uneasiness—such as
novels, poetry, natural scenery, local anecdotes & (in a serious
mood and with serious men) the general evidences of our
Religion.——With regard to myself, it is my habit, on
whatever subject I think, to endeavour to discover all the good
that has resulted from it, that does result, or that can
result—to this I bind down my mind and after long
meditation in this tract, slowly & gradually make up my
opinions on the quantity & the nature of the Evil.—I consider
this as a most important rule for the regulation of the intellect
& the affections—as the only means of preventing the passions
from turning the Reason into an hired Advocate.——I thank
you for your kindness—& purpose in a short time to walk
down to you —but my Wife must forego the thought, as she is
within 5 or 6 weeks of lying-in.—She & my child (whose name
is David Hartley) are remarkably well.——You will give my
duty to my Mother—& my love to my Brothers, to Mrs J. &
G. Coleridge—. Excuse my desultory style & illegible scrawl:
for I have written you a long letter, you see—& am, in truth,
too weary to write a fair copy, or re-arrange my ideas—and I
am anxious that you should know me as I am——
            God bless you | & your affectionate Brother
                                    S. T. Coleridge

To Thomas Poole

[Poole's last letter had brought Coleridge news of the death of his son
Berkeley on 10 Feb. 1799, and of a plan of the Wedgwoods to buy an
estate near Stowey.]

April 6th, 1799

My dearest Poole

Your two letters, dated, Jan. 24th and March 15th, followed
close on each other. I was still enjoying 'the livelier impulse
and the dance of thought'° which the first had given me, when
I received the second.—At the time, in which I read Sara's
lively account of the miseries which herself and the infant had
undergone, all was over & well—there was nothing to *think*
of—only a mass of Pain was brought suddenly and closely
within the sphere of my perception, and I was made to suffer it
over again. For this bodily frame is an imitative Thing, and
touched by the imagination gives the hour that is past, as
faithfully as a repeating watch.—But Death—the death of an
Infant—of one's own Infant! —I read your letter in calmness,
and walked out into the open fields, oppressed, not by my
feelings, but by the riddles, which the Thought so easily
proposes, and solves—never! A Parent—in the strict and
exclusive sense a *Parent*—! to me it is a *fable* wholly without
meaning except in the *moral* which it suggests—a fable, of
which the Moral is God. Be it so—my dear dear Friend! O let
it be so! La nature (says Pascal) 'La Nature confond les
Pyrrhoniens, et la raison confond les Dogmatistes. Nous avons
une impuissance à prouver, invincible à tout le Dogmatisme:
nous avons une idée de la vérité, invincible à tout le
Pyrrhonisme.'° [Nature confounds the sceptics, and reason
confounds the dogmatists. We have an inability to prove,
which cannot be surmounted by dogmatism. We have a
notion of truth, which cannot be overcome by scepticism.] I
find it wise and human to believe, even on slight evidence,
opinions, the contrary of which cannot be proved, & which
promote our happiness without hampering our Intellect.—My
Baby has not lived in vain—this life has been to him what it is
to all of us, education & developement! Fling yourself forward

into your immortality only a few thousand years, & how small
will not the difference between one year old & sixty years
appear!—Consciousness—! it is no otherwise necessary to our
conceptions of future Continuance than as connecting the
present link of our Being with the one *immediately* preceding it; &
that degree of Consciousness, *that* small portion of *memory*, it
would not only be arrogant, but in the highest degree absurd,
to deny even to a much younger Infant.—'Tis a strange
assertion, that the Essence of Identity lies in *recollective*
Consciousness—'twere scarcely less ridiculous to affirm, that
the 8 miles from Stowey to Bridgewater consist in the 8 mile
stones. Death in a doting old age falls upon my feelings ever as
a more hopeless Phaenomenon than Death in Infancy / ; but
nothing is hopeless.—What if the vital force which I sent from
my arm into the stone, as I flung it in the air & skimm'd it
upon the water—what if even that did not perish!—It was
life—! it was a particle of *Being*—! it was *Power*!—& *how could* it
perish—? *Life, Power, Being!*—organization may [be] &
probably *is*, their *effect*; their *cause* it *cannot* be!—I have
indulged very curious fancies concerning that force, that
swarm of motive Powers which I sent out of my body into that
Stone; & which, one by one, left the untractable or already
possessed Mass, and——but the German Ocean lies between
us.—It is all too far to send you such fancies as these!——
'Grief' indeed,

> Doth love to dally with fantastic thoughts,
> And smiling, like a sickly Moralist,
> Finds some resemblance to her own Concerns
> In the Straws of Chance, & Things Inanimate!°

But I cannot truly say that I grieve—I am perplexed—I am
sad—and a little thing, a very trifle would make me weep; but
for the death of the Baby I have *not* wept!—Oh! this strange,
strange, strange Scene-shifter, Death! that giddies one with
insecurity, & so unsubstantiates the living Things that one
has grasped and handled!—/ Some months ago Wordsworth
transmitted to me a most sublime Epitaph / whether it had any
reality, I cannot say.—Most probably, in some gloomier
moment he had fancied the moment in which his Sister might
die.

Epitaph

A Slumber did my spirit seal,
  I had no human fears:
She seem'd a Thing, that could not feel
  The touch of earthly years.

No motion has she now, no force;
  She neither hears nor sees,
Mov'd round in Earth's diurnal course
  With rocks, & stones, and trees!

April 8th, 1799.

I feel disappointed beyond doubt at the circumstance of which you have half informed me, deeply disappointed; but still we can *hope*. If you live at Stowey, & my moral & intellectual Being grows & purifies, as I would fain believe, that it will—there will be always a motive, a strong one to their coming. In your next letter, I pray you, be more minute.—As to your servants & the people of Stowey in general—Poole, my Beloved! you have been often unwisely fretful with me when I have pressed upon you their depravity.—Without religious joys, and religious terrors nothing can be expected from the *inferior* Classes in society—whether or no any *class* is strong enough to stand firm without them, is to me doubtful.—There are favoured *Individuals*, but not *Classes*. Pray, where is Cruikshanks? & how go his affairs?—and what good Luck has Sam. Chester had?— / —In this hurly burly of unlucky Things, I cannot describe to you how pure & deep Joy I have experienced from thinking of your dear Mother!—O may God Almighty give her after all her agonies now at last a long, rich, yellow Sunset, in this, her evening of Life!—So good, and so virtuous, and with such an untameable Sensibility *to enjoy* the blessings of the Almighty—surely God in heaven never made a Being more capable of enjoying with a deeper Thankfulness of Earth Life & it's Relations!—

With regard to myself I am very busy, very busy indeed!—I attend several Professors, & am getting many kinds of knowlege; but I stick to my Lessing°—The Subject more & more interests me, & I doubt not in the least, that I shall wholly clear my expences by the end of October.—I am sorry to tell you, that I find that work as hard as I may I cannot

collect all the vast quantity of Materials which I must collect,
in less than six weeks—if I would do myself justice; &
perhaps, it may be 8 weeks. — / The materials which I have &
shall have would of themselves make a quarto volume; but I
must not work quite so hard as I have done / it so totally dries
up all my colour.—With regard to the house at Stowey, I must
not disguise from you that to live *in* Stowey, & in that house
which you mention, is to me an exceedingly unpleasant
Thought. Rather than go any where else assuredly I would do
it—& be glad / but the thought is unpleasant to me.—I do not
like to live *in* a Town—still less in Stowey where excepting
yourself & Mother there is no human being attached to us &
few who do not dislike us.—Besides, it [is] a sad Tyranny that
all who live in towns are subject to—that of inoculating all at
once &c &c. And then the impossibility of keeping one's
children free from vice & profaneness—& &c.—

If I do not send off this letter now, I must wait another
week—What must I do?—How you will look, when you see
the blank Page!—My next shall make up for it—

Heaven bless you
& S. T. Coleridge

To James Webbe Tobin

Wednesday, Sept. 17. 1800. Grieta Hall, Keswick.—
My dear [Tobin]

Both Wordsworth and I shall be at home for these six
months at least—& for aught I know to the contrary, for these
six years. I need not say, how happy I shall be to see you &
your friend—we have room for you—. The Miss Speddings°
are very good friends of our's, and are not amiss in their
exteriors, yet nothing remarkable, in minds or bodies. They are
chatty sensible women, republicans in opinion, and just like
other Ladies of their rank, in practice—. You will no doubt see
them. From Davy's long silence I augured that he was doing
something for me—I mean for me inclusive, as a member of
the Universe—God bless him! I feel more than I think wise to
express, from the disappointment in not seeing him—. From

the commencement of November next I give myself exclusively
to the Life of Lessing—till then I occupy myself with a volume
of Letters from Germany°—to the publication of which my
Poverty but not my Will consents.——The delay in Copy has
been owing in part to me, as the writer of Christabel—Every
line has been produced by me with labor-pangs. I abandon
Poetry altogether—I leave the higher & deeper Kinds to
Wordsworth, the delightful, popular & simply dignified to
Southey; & reserve for myself the honorable attempt to make
others feel and understand their writings, as they deserve to be
felt & understood. There is no thought of ever collecting my
Morning Post Essays—they are not worth it. Wordsworth,
after these volumes have been published, will set about
adapting his Tragedy for the Stage—Sheridan has sent to him
about it.° What W. & I have seen of the Farmer's Boy° (only a
few short extracts) pleased us very much.—

When you come, do not by any means *forget* to bring with
you a bottle of Davy's Acid for Wordsworth—. Does not Davy
admire Wordsworth's Ruth? I think it the finest poem in the
collection.—Excuse the brevity of this letter, for I am busied
in writing out a sheet for Biggs.—

Your's with unfeigned Esteem
S. T. Coleridge

P.S. My wife was safely & speedily delivered of a very fine boy
on last Sunday Night—both he & she are as well as it is
possible that Mother & new born Child can be. She dined &
drank Tea *up*, in the parlor with me, this day——and this is
only Wednesday Night!—There's for you.

Wordsworth's Health is but *so so*—Hartley is the same
Animal as ever—he moves & lives,

> As if his Heritage were Joy
> And Pleasure were his Trade.°

I heard from Godwin a few days hence—he is delighted with
Ireland & Curran°——

To William Godwin

Monday, Sept. 22. 1800

Dear Godwin

I received your letter, and with it the inclosed Note, which shall be punctually redelivered to you on the first of October.—

Your Tragedy to be exhibited at Christmas!—I have indeed merely read thro' your letter; so it is not strange, that my heart still continues beating out of time. Indeed, indeed, Godwin! such a stream of hope & fear rushed in on me, when I read the sentence, as you would not permit yourself to feel. If there be any thing yet undreamt of in our philosophy; if it be, or if it be possible, that thought can impel thought out of the visual limit of a man's own scull & heart; if the clusters of ideas, which constitute our identity, do ever connect & unite into a greater Whole; if feelings could ever propagate themselves without the servile ministrations of undulating air or reflected light; I seem to feel within myself a strength & a power of desire, that might dart a modifying, commanding impulse on a whole Theatre. What does all this mean? Alas! that sober sense should know no other way to construe all this except by the tame phrase—I wish you success.—

That which Lamb informed you, is founded in truth. Mr Sheridan sent thro' the medium of Stewart a request to Wordsworth to present a Tragedy to his stage, & to me a declaration that the failure of my piece was owing to my obstinacy in refusing any alteration. I laughed & Wordsworth smiled; but my Tragedy will remain at Keswick, and Wordsworth's is not likely to emigrate from Grasmere.° Wordsworth's Drama is in it's present state not fit for the stage, and he is not well enough to submit to the drudgery of making it so. Mine is fit for nothing except to excite in the minds of good men the hope, that 'the young man is likely to do better.' In the first moments I thought of re-writing it, & sent to Lamb for the copy with this intent—I read an act, & altered my opinion, & with it my wish.—Your feelings respecting Baptism are, I suppose, much like mine! At times I dwell on Man with such reverence, resolve all his follies &

superstitions into such grand primary laws of intellect, & in such wise so contemplate them as ever-varying incarnations of the eternal Life, that the Lama's Dung-pellet, or the Cow-tail which the dying Brahman clutches convulsively, become sanctified & sublime by the feelings which cluster round them. In that mood I exclaim, My boys shall be christened!—But then another fit of moody philosophy attacks me—I look at my doted-on Hartley—he moves, he lives, he finds impulses from within & from without—he is the darling of the Sun and of the Breeze! Nature seems to bless him as a thing of her own! He looks at the clouds, the mountains, the living Beings of the Earth, & vaults & jubilates! Solemn Looks & solemn Words have been hitherto connected in his mind with great & magnificent objects only—with lightning, with thunder, with the waterfall blazing in the Sunset—/—then I say, Shall I suffer the Toad of Priesthood to spurt out his foul juice in this Babe's Face? Shall I suffer him to see grave countenances & hear grave accents, while his face is sprinkled, & while the fat paw of a Parson crosses his Forehead?—Shall I be grave myself, & tell a lie to him? Or shall I laugh, and teach him to insult the feelings of his fellow-men? Besides, are we not all in this present hour fainting beneath the duty of *Hope*? From such thoughts I start up, & vow a book of severe analysis, in which I will tell *all* I believe to be Truth in the nakedest Language in which it can be told.—

My wife is now quite comfortable—Surely, you might come, & spend the very next four weeks not without advantage to both of us. The very Glory of the place is coming on—the local Genius is just arraying himself in his higher Attributes. But above all, I press it, because my mind has been busied with speculations, that are closely connected with those pursuits which have hitherto constituted your utility & importance; and ardently as I wish you success on the stage, I yet cannot frame myself to the thought, that you should cease to appear as a *bold* moral thinker. I wish you to write a book on the power of words, and the processes by which human feelings form affinities with them—in short, I wish you to *philosophize* Horn Tooke's System,° and to solve the great Questions—whether there be reason to hold, that an action bearing all the *semblance* of pre-designing Consciousness may

yet be simply organic, & whether a *series* of such actions are
possible—and close on the heels of this question would follow
the old 'Is Logic the *Essence* of Thinking?' in other words—Is
thinking impossible without arbitrary signs? &—how far is the
word 'arbitrary' a misnomer? Are not words &c parts &
germinations of the Plant? And what is the Law of their
Growth?—In something of this order I would endeavor to
destroy the old antithesis of *Words* & *Things*, elevating, as it
were, words into Things, & living Things too. All the
nonsense of vibrations° etc you would of course dismiss.

If what I have here written appear nonsense to you, or
common-place thoughts in a harlequinade of outré expressions,
suspend your judgement till we see each other.

Your's sincerely,
S. T. Coleridge

I was in the Country when Wallenstein was published.°
Longman sent me down half a dozen—the carriage back the
book was not worth—

To Humphry Davy

Tuesday, Feb. 3. 1801

My dear Davy
    I can scarcely reconcile it to my Conscience to make you
pay postage for another Letter. O what a fine Unveiling of
modern Politics it would be, if there were published a minute
Detail of all the sums received by Government from the Post
Establishment, and of all the outlets, in which the sums so
received, flowed out again—and on the other hand all the
domestic affections that had been stifled, all the intellectual
progress that would have been, but is not, on account of this
heavy Tax, &c &c——The *Letters* of a nation ought to be payed
for, as an article of national expence.——Well—but I did not
take up this paper to flourish away in splenetic Politics.——

    A Gentleman resident here, his name Calvert,° an idle,
good-hearted, and ingenious man, has a great desire to
commence fellow-student with me & Wordsworth in Chemistry.

—He is an intimate friend of Wordsworth's—& he has proposed to Wordsworth to take a house which he (Calvert) has nearly built, called Windy Brow, in a delicious situation, scarce half a mile from Grieta Hall, the residence of S. T. Coleridge Esq. / and so for him (Calvert) to live with them, i.e. Wordsworth & his Sister.—In this case he means to build a little Laboratory &c.—Wordsworth has not quite decided, but is strongly inclined to adopt the scheme, because he and his Sister have before lived with Calvert on the same footing, and are much attached to him; because my Health is so precarious, and so much injured by Wet, and his health too is, like little potatoes, no great things, and therefore Grasmere (13 miles from Keswick) is too great a distance for us to enjoy each other's Society without inconvenience as much as it would be profitable for us both; & likewise because he feels it more & more necessary for him to have some intellectual pursuit less closely connected with deep passion, than Poetry, & is of course desirous too not to be so wholly ignorant of knowleges so exceedingly important—. However whether Wordsworth come or no, Calvert & I have determined to begin & go on. Calvert is a man of sense, and some originality / and is besides what is well called a *handy* man. He is a good practical mechanic &c—and is desirous to lay out any sum of money that may be necessary. You know how long, how ardently I have wished to initiate myself in Chemical science—both for it's own sake, and in no small degree likewise, my beloved friend!—that I may be able to sympathize with *all*, that you do and think.—Sympathize blindly with it all I do even *now*, God knows! from the very middle of my heart's heart—; but I would fain sympathize with you in the Light of Knowlege.—This opportunity therefore is exceedingly precious to me—as on my own account I could not afford any the least additional expence, having been already by long & successive Illnesses thrown behind hand so much, that for the next 4 or five months, I fear, let me work as hard as I can, I shall not be able to do what my heart within me *burns* to do—that is, *concenter* my free mind to the affinities of the Feelings with Words & Ideas under the title of 'Concerning Poetry & the nature of the Pleasures derived from it.'——I have faith, that I do understand this subject / and I am sure,

that if I write what I ought to do on it, the Work would
supersede all the Books of Metaphysics hitherto written / and
all the Books of Morals too.—To whom shall a young man
utter *his Pride*, if not to a young man whom he loves?——

I beg you therefore, my dear Davy! to write to me a long
Letter when you are at leisure, informing me I What Books it
will be well for Mr Calvert to purchase. 2. Directions for a
convenient little Laboratory—and 3rdly—to what amount the
apparatus would run in expence, and whether or no you
would be so good as to superintend it's making at Bristol.—
Fourthly, give me your advice how to *begin*——and fifthly &
lastly & mostly do send a *drop* of hope to my parched Tongue,
that you will, if you can, come & visit me in the Spring.—
Indeed, indeed, you ought to see this Country, this divine
Country—and then the Joy you would send into *me*!

The Shape of this paper will convince you with what
eageress I began this Letter—I really did not see that it was
not a Sheet.

I have been *thinking* vigorously during my Illness—so that I
cannot say, that my long long wakeful nights have been all lost
to me. The subject of my meditations ha[s] been the Relations
of Thoughts to Things, in the language of Hume, of Ideas to
Impressions:° I may be truly described in the words of
Descartes.° I have been 'res cogitans, id est, dubitans,
affirmans, negans, p[auca] intelligens, multa ignorans, volens,
nolens, imaginans etia[m], et sentiens —' [a thing that thinks:
that is, a thing that doubts, affirms, denies, understands a few
things, is ignorant of many things, is willing, is unwilling, and
also which imagines and has sensory perceptions] & I please
myself with believing, that [you] will receive no small pleasure
from the result of [my] broodings, altho' I expect in you (in
some points) [a] determined opponent—but I say of my mind,
in this respect,

'Manet imperterritus ille
Hostem magnanimum opperiens, et mole suâ stat.'°

[He stands firm in all his might, free of all fear, awaiting his great-hearted
enemy.]

Every poor fellow has his proud hour sometimes—& this, I
suppose, is mine.—

I am better in every respect than I was; but am still *very feeble*. The Weather has been woefully against me for the last fortnight, it having rained here almost incessantly—I take large quantities of Bark,° but the effect is (to express myself with the dignity of Science) $X = 0\ 0\ 0\ 0\ 0\ 0\ 0$: and I shall not gather strength or t[hat] suffusion of bloom which belongs to my healthy state, till I can walk out.

God bless you, my dear Davy! & your ever affectionate Friend, S. T. Coleridge.

P.S. An electrical machine & a number of little nick nacks connected with it Mr Calvert has.——*Write*.

To Dorothy Wordsworth

Monday, Feb. 9.   1801

My dearest Rotha

The Hack, Mr Calvert was so kind as to borrow for me, carried me home as pleasantly as the extreme Soreness of my whole frame admitted. I was indeed in the language of Shakespere, not a Man but a Bruise°—I went to bed immediately, & rose on Sunday quite restored.—If I do not hear from you any thing to the contrary, I shall walk half way to Grasmere, on Friday Morning—leaving Keswick at ten o'clock precisely—in the hopes of meeting Sara°—partly to prevent the necessity of William's walking so far, just as he will have begun to tranquillize, & partly to remove from Mrs Coleridge's mind all uncertainty as to the time of her coming, which if it depended on William's mood of Body, might (unless he went to the injury of his health) be a week, or a fortnight hence——But if Sara should have been so fatigued, as not to be able to take so long a walk without discomfort, on Friday / I shall walk on to Grasmere, & return with her the next day—all this however to be understood with the usual Deo Volente of Health & Weather. The Small Pox is in Keswick—& we are anxious, and eddy-minded about Derwent— /

I had a very long conversation with Hartley about Life,

Reality, Pictures, & Thinking, this evening. He sate on my
knee for half an hour at least, & was exceedingly serious. I
wish to God, you had been with us. Much as you would
desire to believe me, I cannot expect that I could communicate
to you all that Mrs C. & I felt from his answers—they were so
very sensible, accurate, & well worded. I am convinced, that
we are under great obligations to Mr Jackson,° who, I have no
doubt, takes every opportunity of making him observe the
differences of Things: for he pointed out without difficulty that
there might be five Hartleys, Real Hartley, Shadow Hartley,
Picture Hartley, Looking Glass Hartley, and Echo Hartley /
and as to the difference between his Shadow & the Reflection
in the Looking Glass, he said, the Shadow was black, and he
could not see his *eyes* in it. One thing, he said, was very
curious—I asked him what he did when he thought of any
thing—he answered—I look at it, and then go to sleep. To
sleep?—said I—you mean, that you *shut your eyes.* Yes, he
replied—I shut my eyes, & put my hands so (covering his
eyes) and go to sleep—then I WAKE again, and away I
run.——That of shutting his eyes, & covering them was a
Recipe I had given him some time ago / but the notion of that
state of mind being Sleep is very striking, & he meant more, I
suspect, than that People when asleep have their eyes
shut—indeed I *know* it from the tone & *leap up* of Voice with
which he uttered the word 'WAKE.' To morrow I am to exert
my genius in making a paper-balloon / the idea of carrying up
a bit of lighted Candle into the clouds makes him almost
insane with Pleasure. As I have given you Hartley's Metaphysics I will now give you a literal Translation of page 49 of
the celebrated Fichte's Uber den Begriff der Wissenschaftslehre°
—if any of *you*, or if either your Host or Hostess, have any
propensity to *Doubts*, it will cure them for ever / for the object
of the author is to attain absolute certainty. So read it aloud.
(N.B. the 'I' means poor Gilbert's° *I—das 'Ich'*—)——'Suppose,
that A in the proposition A = A stands not for the I, but for
something or other different, then from this proposition you
may deduce the condition under which it may be affirmed,
that it is established, and *how* we are authorized to conclude,
that If A is established, then it is established. Namely: the
Proposition, A = A, holds good originally only of the I: it is

abstracted from the Proposition in the Science of absolute Knowlege, I am I—the substance therefore or sum total of every Thing, to which it may be legitimately applied, must lie in the I, and be comprehended under it. No A therefore can be aught else than something established in the I, and now therefore the Proposition may stand thus: What is established in the I, is established—if therefore A is established in the I, then it is established (that is to say in so far as it is established, whether as only possible, or as real, or necessary) and then the Proposition is true without possibility of contradiction, if the I is to be I.—Farther, if the I be established, because it is established, then all, that is established in the I, is established because it is established; and provided only, that A is indeed a something established in the I, then it is established, if it is established; and the second Question likewise is solved.'——Here's a numerous Establishment for you / nothing in Touchstone ever equalled this°—it is not even surpassed by Creech's account of Space in his notes to Lucretius.°—

Remember me & my wife kindly to Mr & Mrs Clarkson°—& give a kiss for me to dear little Tom—God love him!—I gave H. pictures, nuts, & mince pie, all as a Present from Tommy.——Heaven bless you, my dear friends! S. T. C.—

To Josiah Wade

March 6th, 1801

My very dear friend,

I have even now received your letter. My habits of thinking and feeling have not hitherto inclined me to personify commerce in any such shape as could tempt me to turn Pagan, and offer vows to the Goddess of our Isle. But when I read that sentence in your letter, 'The time will come I trust, when I shall be able to pitch my tent in your neighbourhood,' I was most potently tempted to a breach of the second commandment, and on my knees, to entreat the said Goddess, to touch your bank notes and guineas with her magical, multiplying wand. I could offer such a prayer for you, with a better conscience than for most men, because I know that you have never lost that healthy common sense, which regards money only as the means of independence, and that you would sooner than most men cry out, enough! enough! To see one's children secured against want, is doubtless a delightful thing; but to wish to see them begin the world as rich men, is unwise to ourselves, (for it permits no close of our labors) and is pernicious to them; for it leaves no motive to their exertions, none of those sympathies with the industrious and the poor, which form at once the true relish and proper antidote of wealth. . . .

Is not March rather a perilous month for the voyage from Yarmouth to Hamburg? danger there is very little, in the packets, but I know what inconvenience rough weather brings with it; not from my own feelings, for I am never sea sick, but always in exceeding high spirits on board ship, but from what I see in others. But you are now an old sailor. At Hamburg I have not a shadow of acquaintance. My letters of introduction produced for me (with one exception, viz. Klopstock the brother of the poet) no real service, but merely distant and ostentatious civility. And Klopstock will by this time have forgotten my name, (which indeed he never properly knew) for I could speak only English and Latin, and he only French and German. At Ratzeburgh (35 English miles N. E. from Hamburgh on the road to Lubec) I resided four months, and I should hope, was not unbeloved by more than one family, but this is out of your route. At Gottingen I stayed near five months, but here I knew only students, who will have left the place by this time, and the high learned professors, only one of whom could speak English, and they are so wholly engaged in their academical occupations, that they would be of no service to you. Other acquaintance in Germany I have none, and connection I never had any. For though I was much intreated by some of the Literati to correspond with them, yet my natural laziness, with the little value I attach to literary men, as literary men, and with my aversion from those letters, which are to be made up of studied sense, and unfelt compliments, combined to prevent me from availing myself of the offer. Herein and in similar instances, with English authors of repute, I have ill consulted the growth of my reputation and fame. But I have cheerful and confident hopes of myself. If I can hereafter do good to my fellow creatures, as a poet, and as a metaphysician, they will know it; and any other fame than this, I consider as a serious evil, that would only take me from out the number and sympathy of ordinary men, to make a coxcomb of me.

As to the Inns or Hotels at Hamburgh, I should recommend you to some German Inn. Wordsworth and I were at the 'Der Wilde Man,' and dirty as it was, I could not find any Inn in Germany very much cleaner, except at Lubec. But if you go to an English Inn, for heaven's sake, avoid the Shakspeare, at Altona, and the King of England, at Hamburgh. They are houses of plunder, rather than entertainment. The Duke of York's Hotel, kept by Seaman, has a better reputation, and thither I would advise you to repair; and I advise you to pay your bill every morning at breakfast time; it is the only way to escape imposition. What the Hamburgh merchants may be I know not, but the tradesmen are knaves. Scoundrels, with yellow-white phizzes, that bring disgrace on the complexion of a bad tallow candle. Now as to carriage, I know scarcely what to advise; only make up your mind to the very worst vehicles, with the very worst horses, drawn by the very worst postillions, over the very worst roads, (and halting two hours at each time they change horses) at the very worst inns; and you have a fair, unexaggerated picture of travelling in North Germany. The cheapest way is the best; go by the common post waggons, or stage coaches. What are called extraordinaries, or post chaises, are little wicker carts, uncovered, with moveable benches or forms in them, execrable in every respect. And if you buy a vehicle at Hamburgh, you can get none decent under thirty or forty guineas, and very probably it will break to pieces on the infernal roads. The canal boats are delightful, but the porters everywhere in the United Provinces, are an impudent, abominable, and dishonest race. You must carry as little luggage as you well can with you, in the canal boats, and when you land, get recommended to an inn beforehand, and bargain with the porters first of all, and never lose sight of them, or you may never see your portmanteau or baggage again.

My Sarah desires her love to you and yours. God bless your dear little ones! Make haste and get rich, dear friend! and

bring up the little creatures to be playfellows and schoolfellows
with my little ones!

Again and again, sea serve you, wind speed you, all things
turn out good to you!

God bless you,
S. T. Coleridge.

To Thomas Poole

Monday Night. [16 March 1801]
[Endorsed March 16, 1801]

My dear Friend

The interval since my last Letter has been filled up by me in
the most intense Study. If I do not greatly delude myself, I
have not only completely extricated the notions of Time, and
Space; but have overthrown the doctrine of Association, as
taught by Hartley, and with it all the irreligious metaphysics
of modern Infidels—especially, the doctrine of Necessity.°—
This I have *done*; but I trust, that I am about to do
more—namely, that I shall be able to evolve all the five
senses, that is, to deduce them from *one sense*, & to state their
growth, & the causes of their difference——& in this
evolvement to solve the process of Life & Consciousness.——I
write this to you only; & I pray you, mention what I have
written to no one.—At Wordsworth's advice or rather fervent
intreaty I have intermitted the pursuit—the intensity of
thought, & the multitude of minute experiments with Light &
figure, have made me so nervous & feverish, that I cannot
sleep as long as I ought & have been used to do; & the Sleep,
which I have, is made up of Ideas so connected, & so little
different from the operations of Reason, that it does not afford
me the due Refreshment. I shall therefore take a Week's
respite; & make Christabel ready for the Press—which I shall
publish by itself—in order to get rid of all my engagements
with Longman—My German Book I have suffered to remain
suspended, chiefly because the thoughts which had employed
my sleepless nights during my illness were *imperious* over me,
& tho' Poverty was staring me in the face, yet I dared behold

my Image miniatured in the pupil of her hollow eye, so
steadily did I look her in the Face!——for it seemed to me a
Suicide of my very soul to divert my attention from Truths so
important, which came to me almost as a Revelation /
Likewise, I cannot express to you, dear Friend of my
heart!—the loathing, which I once or twice felt, when I
attempted to write, merely for the Bookseller, without any
sense of the moral utility of what I was writing.—I shall
therefore, as I said, immediately publish my CHRISTABEL,
with two Essays annexed to it, on the Praeternatural—and on
Metre. This done I shall propose to Longman instead of my
Travels (which tho' nearly done I am exceedingly anxious not
to publish, because it brings me forward in a *personal* way, as a
man who relates little adventures of himself to *amuse* people—&
thereby exposes me to sarcasm & the malignity of anonymous
Critics, & is besides *beneath me*—I say, *beneath me* / for to whom
should a young man utter the pride of his Heart if not to the
man whom he loves more than all others?) I shall propose to
Longman to accept instead of these Travels a work on the
originality & merits of Locke, Hobbes, & Hume / which work
I mean as a *Pioneer* to my greater work, and as exhibiting a
proof that I have not formed opinions without an attentive
Perusal of the works of my Predecessors from Aristotle to
Kant.—I am *confident*, that I can prove that the Reputation of
these three men has been wholly unmerited, & I have in what
I have already written traced the whole history of the causes
that effected this reputation entirely to Wordsworth's satisfaction.

You have seen, I hope, the lyrical Ballads—In the divine
Poem called Michael, by an infamous Blunder of the Printer
near 20 lines are omitted in page 210, which makes it nearly
unintelligible—Wordsworth means to write to you & to send
them together with a list of the numerous Errata. The
character of the Lyrical Ballads is very great, & will increase
daily. They have *extolled* them in the British Critic.

Ask Chester (to whom I shall write in a week or so
concerning his German Books) for Greenough's Address—&
be so kind as to send it immediately. Indeed, I hope for a *long*
Letter from you—your opinion of the L. B, the preface
&c—You know, I presume, that Davy is appointed Director

of the Laboratory; and Professor at the Royal Institution?—I
received a very affectionate Letter from him on the Occasion.
Love to all—We are all well, except perhaps myself—Write!—
God love you

                               & S T Coleridge

To Thomas Poole

[Coleridge had sent Poole a copy of the first of a series of
'philosophical letters' addressed to Josiah Wedgwood, containing the
results of his study of Descartes and Locke.]

                             Monday Night [23 March 1801]
My dear Friend
I received your kind Letter of the 14th—I was agreeably
disappointed in finding that you had been interested in the
Letter respecting Locke—those which follow are abundantly
more entertaining & important; but I have no one to
transcribe them—nay, three Letters are written which have
not been sent to Mr Wedgewood, because I have no one to
transcribe them for me—& I do not wish to be without
Copies— / of that Letter, which you have, I have no
Copy.—It is somewhat unpleasant to me, that Mr Wedgewood
has never answered my letter requesting his opinion of the
utility of such a work, nor acknowleged the receipt of the long
Letter containing the evidence that the whole of Locke's
system, as far as it was a system, & with the exclusion of those
parts only which have been given up as absurdities by his
warmest admirers, pre-existed in the writings of Des Cartes,
in a far more pure, elegant, & delightful form.——Be not
afraid, that I shall join the party of the *Little-ists°*—I believe,
that I shall delight you by the detection of their artifices—Now
Mr Locke was the founder of this sect, himself a perfect Little-
ist. My opinion is this—that deep Thinking is attainable only
by a man of deep Feeling, and that all Truth is a species of
Revelation. The more I understand of Sir Isaac Newton's
works, the more boldly I dare utter to my own mind &
therefore to *you*, that I believe the Souls of 500 Sir Isaac

Newtons would go to the making up of a Shakspere or a Milton. But if it please the Almighty to grant me health, hope, and a steady mind, (always the 3 clauses of my hourly prayers) before my 30th year I will thoroughly understand the whole of Newton's Works—At present, I must content myself with endeavouring to make myself entire master of his easier work, that on Optics. I am exceedingly delighted with the beauty & neatness of his experiments, & with the accuracy of his *immediate* Deductions from them—but the opinions founded on these Deductions, and indeed his whole Theory is, I am persuaded, so exceedingly superficial as without impropriety to be deemed false. Newton was a mere materialist—*Mind* in his system is always passive—a lazy Looker-on on an external World. If the mind be not *passive*, if it be indeed made in God's Image, & that too in the sublimest sense—the Image of the *Creator*—there is ground for suspicion, that any system built on the passiveness of the mind must be false, as a system. / I need not observe, My dear Friend, how unutterably silly & contemptible these Opinions would be, if written to any but to another Self. I assure you, solemnly assure you, that you & Wordsworth are the only men on Earth to whom I would have uttered a word on this subject—. It is a rule, by which I hope to direct all my literary efforts, to let my Opinions & my Proofs go together. It is *insolent* to *differ* from the public *opinion* in *opinion*, if it be only *opinion*. It is sticking up little *i by itself i* against the whole alphabet. But one *word* with *meaning* in it is worth the whole alphabet together—such is a sound Argument, an incontrovertible Fact.—

O for a lodge in a Land, where human Life was an end, to which Labor was only a Means, instead of being, as it [is] here, a mere means of carrying on Labor.—I am oppressed at times with a true heart-gnawing melancholy when I contemplate the state of my poor oppressed Country.—God knows, it is as much as I can do to put meat & bread on my own table; & hourly some poor starving wretch comes to my door, to put in his claim for part of it.—It fills me with indignation to hear the *croaking* accounts, which the English Emigrants send home of America. The society is so bad—the manners so vulgar—the servants so insolent.—Why then do they not seek out one another, & make a society—? It is arrant ingratitude to talk so

of a Land in which there is no Poverty but as a consequence of
absolute Idleness—and to talk of it too with abuse comparatively with England, with a place where the laborious Poor are
dying with Grass with[in] their Bellies!—It is idle to talk of
the Seasons—as if that country must not needs be miserably
misgoverned in which an unfavorable Season introduces a
famine. No! No! dear Poole! it is our pestilent Commerce, our
unnatural Crowding together of men in Cities, & our
Government by Rich Men, that are bringing about the
manifestations of offended Deity.——I am assured, that such
is the depravity of the public mind, that no literary man can
find bread in England except by misemploying & debasing his
Talents—that nothing of real excellence would be either felt or
understood. The annuity, which I hold, perhaps by a very
precarious Tenure, will shortly from the decreasing value of
money become less than one half of what it was when first
allowed to me—If I were allowed to retain it, I would go &
settle near Priestly, in America°/ I shall, no doubt, get a
certain price for the two or three works, which I shall next
publish—; but I foresee, they will not sell—the Booksellers
finding this will treat me as an unsuccessful Author—i.e. they
will employ me only as an anonymous Translator at a guinea
a sheet—(I will write *across* my other writing in order to finish
what I have to say.) I have no doubt, that I could make 500£ a
year, if I liked. But then I must forego all desire of Truth and
Excellence. I say, I would go to America, if Wordsworth
would go with me, & we could persuade two or three Farmers
of this Country who are exceedingly attached to us, to
accompany us—I would go, if the difficulty of procuring
sustenance in this Country remain in the state & degree, in
which it is at present. Not on any romantic Scheme, but
merely because Society has become a matter of great
Indifference to me—I grow daily more & more attached to
Solitude—but it is a matter of the utmost Importance to be
removed from seeing and suffering *Want*.
    God love you, my dear Friend!—
                                                    S. T. Coleridge.

To William Godwin

Greta Hall, Keswick   Wednesday, March 25, 1801
Dear Godwin
I fear, your Tragedy° will find me in a very unfit state of mind to sit in Judgement on it. I have been, during the last 3 months, undergoing a process of intellectual *exsiccation*. In my long Illness I had compelled into hours of Delight many a sleepless, painful hour of Darkness by chasing down metaphysical Game—and since then I have continued the Hunt, till I found myself unaware at the Root of Pure Mathematics—and up that tall smooth Tree, whose few poor Branches are all at it's very summit, am I climbing by pure adhesive strength of arms and thighs—still slipping down, still renewing my ascent.—You would not know me—! all sounds of similitude keep at such a distance from each other in my mind, that I have *forgotten* how to make a rhyme—I look at the Mountains (that visible God Almighty that looks in at all my windows) I look at the Mountains only for the Curves of their outlines; the Stars, as I behold them, form themselves into Triangles—and my hands are scarred with scratches from a Cat, whose back I was rubbing in the Dark in order to see whether the sparks from it were refrangible by a Prism. The Poet is dead in me—my imagination (or rather the Somewhat that had been imaginative) lies, like a Cold Snuff on the circular Rim of a Brass Candle-stick, without even a stink of Tallow to remind you that it was once cloathed & mitred with Flame. That is past by!—I was once a Volume of Gold Leaf, rising & riding on every breath of Fancy—but I have beaten myself back into weight & density, & now I sink in quicksilver, yea, remain squat and square on the earth amid the hurricane, that makes Oaks and Straws join in one Dance, fifty yards high in the Element.

However, I will do what I can—Taste & Feeling have I none, but what I have, give I unto thee.——But I repeat, that I am unfit to decide on any but works of severe Logic.

I write now to beg, that, if you have not sent your Tragedy, you may remember to send Antonio with it, which I have not yet seen—& likewise my Campbell's Pleasures of Hope, which Wordsworth wishes to see.°

Have you seen the second Volume of the Lyrical Ballads, & the Preface prefixed to the First?——I should judge of a man's Heart, and Intellect precisely according to the degree & intensity of the admiration, with which he read those poems——Perhaps, instead of Heart I should have said Taste, but when I think of The Brothers, of Ruth, and of Michael, I recur to the expression, & am enforced to say *Heart*. If I die, and the Booksellers will give you any thing for my Life, be sure to say—'Wordsworth descended on him, like the Γνῶθι σεαυτόν [Know Thyself] from Heaven;° by shewing to him what true Poetry was, he made him know, that he himself was no Poet.'

In your next Letter you will perhaps give me some hints respecting your prose Plans.—.

God bless you
& S. T. Coleridge

I have inoculated my youngest child, Derwent, with the Cowpox—he passed thro' it without any sickness.—I myself am the Slave of Rheumatism—indeed, tho' in a certain sense I *am recovered* from my Sickness, yet I have by no means *recovered* it. I congratulate you on the settlement of Davy in London.—I hope, that his enchanting manners will not draw too many Idlers round him, to harrass & vex his mornings.—. . .°

P.S.—What is a fair Price—what might an Author of reputation fairly ask from a Bookseller for one Edition, of a 1000 Copies, of a five Shilling Book?—

To Thomas Poole

Saturday, April 18. 1801

My dearest Poole

He must needs be an unthinking or a hard-hearted man who is not often oppressed in his spirits by the present state of the Country. There is a dearth of Wisdom still heavier than that of Corn / the mass of the inhabitants of the country are

growing more & more acquainted with the blackness of the
conspiracy, which the Wealthy have entered into, against
their comforts & independence & intellect. But they perceive
it only thro' the dimness of passions & personal indignation.
The professed Democrats, who on an occasion of uproar
would press forward to be the Leaders, are without knowlege,
talents, or morals. I have conversed with the most celebrated
among them; more gross, ignorant, & perverted men I never
wish to see again!—O it would have made you, my friend! 'a
sadder & a wiser man',° if you had been with me at one of
Horne Tooke's public Dinners!°—I could never discover by
any train of Questions that any of these Lovers of Liberty had
either [a] distinct *object* for their Wishes, or distinct views of
the *means*.—All seemed a quarrel about names!—Taxes—
national Debt—representation—overthrow of Tythes & Church
Establishments—&c &c.——I believe, that it would be easy
to enumerate the causes of the evils of the Country, & to *prove*
that they & they alone were the great & calculable causes; but
I doubt the *possibility* of pointing out a Remedy.—Our
enormous Riches & accompanying Poverty have corrupted
the *Morals* of the nation. All *Principle* is scouted—: by the
Jacobins, because it is the death-blow of vainglorious Scepticism
—by the Aristocrats, because it is visionary & theoretical—
even our most popular Books of Morals, (as Paley's° for
instance) are the corrupters & poisoners of all moral sense &
dignity, without which neither individual or people can stand
& be men.—O believe me, Poole! it is all past by with that
country, in which it is generally believed that Virtue &
Prudence are two words with the same signification—in which
Vice is considered as evil only because it's distant consequences
are more painful than it's immediate enjoyments are pleasurable—and in which the whole human mind is considered as
made up of just four ingredients, Impression, Idea, Pleasure
and Pain.—I said, that I doubted the possibility of pointing
out a Remedy—my reason is this—The Happiness & Misery
of a nation must ultimately be traced to the morals &
understandings of the People. A nation where the Plough is
always in the Hand of the owner, or (better still) where the
Plough, the Horse, and the Ox have no existence, may be a
great & a happy nation; and may be *called* so, relatively to

others less happy, if it has only a manifest *direction* & *tendency*
towards this 'best Hope of the World.'° Now where there is no
possibility of making the number of independent & virtuous
men bear any efficient proportion to the number of the
Tyrants & the Slaves—that country is fallen never to rise
again! There is no instance in the World in which a Country
has ever been regenerated which has had so large a proportion
of it's Inhabitants crowded into it's metropolis, as we in G.
Britain.—I confess, that I have but small Hopes of France;
tho' the proportion there is not nearly so great.—So enormous
a metropolis imposes on the Governors & People the necessity
of Trade & Commerce—these become the Idols—and every
thing that is lovely & honest fall[s] in sacrifice to these
Demons.—It is however consoling to me in some small degree
to find these opinions of the iniquity of Wealth & Commerce
more & more common / especially, among the humbler
Quakers in the North, & the more religious Part of the Day
Labourers in this County. I assure you, they legislate
respecting the Rights & Wrongs of Property with great
Boldness & not without a due sense of the enormous
Difficulties that would attend the Enthronement of Justice &
Truth.—O merciful Heaven! if it were thy good Will to raise
up among us *one* great good man, only *one* man of a
commanding mind, enthusiastic in the *depth* of his Soul, calm
on the *surface*—and devoted to the accomplishment of the *last
End* of human Society by an Oath which no Ear of Flesh ever
heard, but only the omnipresent God!—Even this unhappy
nation might behold what few have the courage to dream of,
and almost as few the goodness to wish.——
   I trust, that your troubles & commotions are now over.°
What well grounded Objection can there be to the fixing the
Minimum of Wages by some article of a *certain real value*? If at
any time there should be so many Candidates for Labor, that,
but for this Law, the Masters could get Labourers at a still
cheaper Rate, then the Parishes might be obliged to employ a
large number in the cultivation of Lands, &c. O there are
ways enough, Poole! to *palliate* our miseries—but there is not
honesty nor public spirit enough to adopt them.—Property is
the bug bear—it stupifies the heads & hardens the hearts of
our Counsellors & Chief Men!—They know nothing better

than Soup-shops—or the boldest of them push forward for an abolition of Tythes!—*Honest Men!*—I trust, that these anti-tythe men will be the occasion of a miracle—they will make even our Priests utter aloud the *very Truth*. It will be a proud Day for me, when the Gentlemen of landed Property set in good earnest about plundering the Clergy——'When Rogues quarrel,'° &c—the proverb is somewhat musty.—

I have written a long Letter & said nothing of myself. In simple verity, I am disgusted with that subject. For the last ten days I have kept my Bed, exceedingly ill. I feel and am certain, that 'I to the Grave go down.'°—My complaint I can scarcely describe / it is a species of irregular Gout which I have not strength of constitution sufficient to ripen into a fair Paroxysm—it flies about me in unsightly swellings of my knees, & dismal affections of my stomach & head. What I suffer in mere *pain* is almost incredible; but that is a trifle compared with the gloom of my Circumstances.—I feel the transition of the Weather even in my bed—at present, the Disease has seized the whole Region of my Back, so that I scream mechanically on the least motion.—If the fine Weather continue, I shall revive—& look round me—& before the Fall of the Year make up my mind to the important Question—Is it better to die or to quit my native Country, & live among Strangers?—Another Winter in England would *do for me*.—Besides, I am rendered useless & wretched—not that my bodily pain afflicts me—God forbid! Were I a single man & independent, I should be ashamed to think myself wretched merely because I suffered Pain / that there is no Evil which may not ultimately be reduced into Pain, is no part of my Creed. I would rather be in Hell, deserving Heaven, than be in Heaven, deserving Hell. It is not my bodily Pain—but the gloom & distresses of those around me for whom I ought to be labouring & cannot.—

Enough of this——It is the last time, I shall ever write you in such a [. . . ?]—you have perplexities enough of your own.—

God love you, & S. T. Coleridge—

To Robert Southey

Oct. 21. 1801.—The day after my Birth day—29 years of age!—Who on earth can say that without a sigh!

[De]ar Southey

You did not stay long enough with us to *love* these mountains & this wonderful vale.° Yesterday the snow fell—and to day—O that you were here—Lodore full—[the] mountains snow-crested—& the dazzling silver of the Lake— this cloudy, sunny, misty, howling Weather!——After your arrival I move southward in the hopes that warm Rooms & deep tranquillity may build me up anew; & that I may be able to return in the Spring without the necessity of going abroad. I propose to go with you & Edith to London—& thence to Stowey or Wedgewood's, as circumstances direct.—My knee is no longer swoln, & this frosty weather agrees with me—but O Friend! I am sadly shattered. The least agitation brings on bowel complaints, & within the last week *twice* with an ugly symptom—namely—of sickness even to vomiting—& Sara— alas! we are not suited to each other. But the months of my absence I devote to *self*-discipline, & to the attempt to draw her nearer to me by a regular developement of all the sources of our unhappiness—then for another Trial, *fair* as I hold the love of good men dear to me—*patient*, as I myself love my own dear children. I will go believing that it will end happily—if not, if our mutual unsuitableness continues, and (as it assuredly will do, if it continue) increases & strengthens, why then, it is better for her & my children, that I should live apart, than that she should be a Widow & they Orphans. Carefully have I *thought thro'* the subject of marriage & deeply am I convinced of it's indissolubleness.—If I separate, I do it in the earnest desire to provide for her & [the]m; that while I live, she may enjoy the comforts of life; & that when I die, something may have been accumulated that may secure her from degrading Dependence. When I least love her, then m[ost] do I feel anxiety for her peace, comfort, & welfare. Is s[he] not the mother of my children? And am I the man not to know & feel this?—Enough of this. But, Southey! much as we differ in our habits, you do indeed possess my esteem & affection in a degree that makes it uncomfortable to me not to tell you what I have told you. I once said—that I *missed* no body—I only enjoyed the *present*. At that moment my heart misgave me, & had no one been present, I should have said to you—that you were the only exception— / for my mind is full of visions, & you had been so long connected with the fairest of all fair dreams, that I feel your absence more than I enjoy your society: tho' that I do not enjoy your society so much, as I anticipated that I should do, is wholly or almost wholly owing to the nature of my domestic feelings, & the fear, or the consciousness, that you did not & could not sympathize with him [them].—Now my heart is a little easy.—God bless you!——

Dear Davy!—If I have not overrated his intellectual Powers, I have little fear for his moral character. Metaphysicians! Do, Southey, keep to your own most excellent word (for the invention of which you deserve a pension far more than Johnson for his Dictionary) & always say—*Metapothecaries*. There does not exist an instance of a *deep* metaphysician who was not led by his speculations to an austere system of morals—. What can be more austere than the Ethics of Aristotle—than the systems of Zeno, St Paul, Spinoza (in the Ethical Books of his Ethics), Hartley, Kant, and Fichte?—As to Hume, was he not—ubi non fur, ibi stultus [stupid except in what he stole from others]—& often thief & blockhead at the same time? It is not *thinking* that will disturb a man's morals, or confound the distinctions, which *to think* makes. But it is *talking—talking—talking—that* is the curse & the poison. I defy Davy to *think* half of what he *talks*: if indeed he talk what has been attributed to him. But I must see with my own eyes, & hear with my own ears. Till then I will be to Davy, what Max was to Wallenstein.° Yet I do agree with you that chemistry tends in it's present state to turn it's Priests into Sacrifices. One way, in which it does it—this however is an opinion, that would make Rickman° laugh at me if you told it him—is this—it prevents or tends to prevent a young man from falling in love. We all have obscure feelings that must be connected with some thing or other—the Miser with a guinea—Lord Nelson with a blue Ribbon°—Wordsworth's old Molly with her washing Tub—Wordsworth with the Hills, Lakes, & Trees— / all men are poets in their way, tho' for the most part their ways are *damned bad ones*. Now Chemistry makes a young man associate these feelings with inanimate objects—& that without any moral revulsion, but on the contrary with complete self-approbation—and his distant views of Benevolence, or his sense of immediate beneficence, attach themselves either to Man as the whole human Race, or to Man, as a sick man, as a painter, as a manufacturer, &c—and in no way to man, as a Husband, Son, Brother, Daughter, Wife, Friend, &c &c—. That to be in love is simply to confine the feelings prospective of animal enjoyment to one woman is a gross mistake—it is to associate a large proportion of all our obscure feelings with a real form—A miser is *in love* with a guinea, & a virtuous young man with a woman, in the same sense, without figure or metaphor. A young poet may do without being in love with a woman—it is enough, if he loves—but to a young chemist it would be salvation to be downright romantically in Love—and unfortunately so far from the Poison & antidote growing together, they are like the Wheat & Barberry.°—

You are not the first person who has sought in vain for Mole & Mulla.°—I shall end this Letter with a prayer for your speedy arrival, & a couple of Sapphic Verses translated *in my way* from Stolberg°—You may take your Oath for it, it was no admiration of the Thought, or the Poetry that made me translate them—

To the Will o/ the Wisps —

But now I think of it—no—I will pursue my first thought——

Lunatic Witch-fires! Ghosts of Light & Motion!
Fearless I see you weave your wanton Dances
Near me, far off me, You that tempt the Trav'ller
                                        Onward & onward,

Wooing, retreating, till the Swamp beneath him
Groans!—And 'tis dark!—This Woman's Wile—I know it!
Learnt it from *thee*, from *thy* perfidious Glances,
                                        Black-ey'd Rebecca!—

It is more poetical than the original, of which this is a literal Translation—Still play, juggling Deceiver! still play thy wanton Dances, Fugitive child of Vapor, that fervently temptest onward the Wanderer's feet, then coyly fleest, at length beguilest into Ruin. These maiden Wiles—I know them—learnt them all out of thy blue eyes, fickle Nais.

Heaven bless you—.—S. T. Coleridge

To William Godwin

Friday Morning, Jan. 22. 1802
King's Street, Covent Garden—

Dear Godwin

I wrote to you yesterday, immediately on my arrival, a few hasty Lines—went to the Lecture at the Royal Institution, & dined with Poole & Davy, in a large party—a sort of anniversary club Dinner, of a club with a long name of which Tobin is a member—Vapidarians,° I think, they call themselves. I returned at 9 o/ clock, went to bed, & this morning

I feel, that I have drunken deep
Of all the Blessedness of Sleep°—

No wonder—I have not slept two hours for the last three nights.—This morning I reperused your Letter—& I write again, because I fear, that in the fretfulness of fatigue & hurry I might not have answered it with the respect & affection due to you.—

I have no other wish, than that you should know 'the Truth, the whole Truth, & (if possible) nothing but the Truth' of me in the sum total of my character, much more in it's immediate relations to you. You date the supposed alteration of my feelings towards you, & consequent conduct, from Midsummer last; & my conduct since my arrival in town from the North you have regarded as an exacerbation of the Disease. My conduct since November I conceived that I have fully explained. You appear to me not to have understood the nature of my body & mind—. Partly from ill-health, & partly from an unhealthy & reverie-like vividness of *Thoughts*, &

(pardon the pedantry of the phrase) a diminished Impressibility from *Things*, my ideas, wishes, & feelings are to a diseased degree disconnected from *motion* & *action*. In plain & natural English, I am a dreaming & therefore an indolent man—. I am a Starling self-incaged, & always in the Moult, & my whole Note is, Tomorrow, & tomorrow, & tomorrow. The same causes, that have robbed me to so great a degree of the self-impelling self-directing Principle, have deprived me too of the due powers of Resistances to Impulses from without. If I might so say, I am, as an *acting* man, a creature of mere Impact. 'I will' & 'I will not' are phrases, both of them equally, of rare occurrence in my dictionary.—This is the Truth—I regret it, & in the consciousness of this Truth I lose a larger portion of Self-estimation than those, who know me imperfectly, would easily believe— / I evade the sentence of my own Conscience by no quibbles of self-adulation; I ask for Mercy indeed on the score of my ill-health; but I confess, that this very ill-health is as much an effect as a cause of this want of steadiness & self-command; and it is for mercy that I ask, not for justice.—To apply all this to the present case—

When you spent the Tuesday Evening with me at my Lodgings, I told you my scheme—i.e. that line of conduct, which I thought it my duty to pursue, & which I *wished* to realize.—If I deviated from it, it was (with the exception of two Saturdays, which I dined out, the one with Mackintosh & the other with Sharp, & which I did from *Principle*)—all the rest, (& I must add in favor of myself, that the whole scarcely amounted to more than half of half a dozen) was from the causes, I have stated. I was *taken* out to *dinner*; & if you had come & fixed a day, you too would have *taken* me.—But indeed, Godwin! you were offended, far too hastily. For a week & more I was exceedingly unwell; & in one instance, when I had fully intended to have met you, I had a hint given to me that it would be *unpleasant* to you, &c.—So much for my apparent or real Neglect of you since my arrival in town.—The altered Tone of my Letters previously, is a different affair. When I wrote to you, that I did not imagine you to be much interested about my personal existence, you think this may be fairly considered as a developement of the state of my feelings towards you.—No.——It developed nothing; but it hinted disappointment, & that my feelings of personal concern respecting you had been starved by the imagined want of correspondent feelings in your mind. I had been really & truly interested in you, & for you; & often in the heat of my spirit I have spoken of your literary Imprudences & Self-delusions with asperity, that if '*the good-natured* Friends'° have conveyed it to you [they] would have conveyed a bare story of the constancy of my friendship—but the truth & the whole Truth, [is] that I have been angry because I have been *vexed*. My letters before Midsummer expressed what I felt——and nothing but what I felt. If I underwent any alteration of feelings, it was in consequence of my appearing to observe in your Letters a want of interest in me, my health, my goings on. This offended my *moral* nature, & (so help me God) not my personal Pride. I considered it as a great Defect in your character, & as I always write from my immedia[te] feelings (with more or less suppression) I suffered the Belief to appear in the tone of my language—I was struggling with sore calamities, with bodily pain, & languor—with pecuniary Difficulties—& worse than all, with domestic Discord, & the heart-withering Conviction—that I could not be happy without my children, & could not but be miserable with the mother of them.—Of all this you knew but a part, & that, no doubt, indistinctly / yet there did appear to me in your letters a sort of indifference—a total want of affectionate Enquiry— pardon me, if I dare express all my meaning in a harsh form—it did appear to me, as if without any attachment to me you were simply gratified by the notion of my attachment to you. But I must repeat (for if I know my own heart, it is the naked Truth) it offended my moral, & not my personal, feelings: for I have purchased Love by Love.—I am boisterous & talkative in general company; & there are those, who have believed that Vanity is my ruling Passion. They do not know me.—As an *Author*, at all events, I have neither Vanity nor ambition—I think meanly of all, that I have done; and if ever I hope proudly of my future Self, this Hot Fit is uniformly followed & punished by Languor, & Despondency—or rather, by lazy & unhoping Indifference.—In the 2nd Volume of Wordsworth's Lyrical Ballads you will find certain *parts*, & *superfices* of me *sketched* truly under the title—'A character in

the antithetical manner.[']°—I have written thus, and thus
prolixly of myself, with far other feelings than those of Self-
love, or of pleasure from the writing about myself—. You
seemed to doubt my regard & esteem for you: to whom but to
a man whom I regarded & esteemed, would I, or could I, have
written this Letter?—Your's, S. T. Coleridge

To William Sotheby

Tuesday, July 13, 1802. Greta Hall, Keswick
My dear Sir
  I had written you a letter, and was about to have walked to
the Post with it, when I received your's from Longnor—it
gave me such lively pleasure, that I threw my Letter into the
Fire / for it related chiefly to the Erste Schiffer of Gesner° /
and I could not endure that my first Letter to you should *begin*
with a subject so little interesting to my Heart or Understanding.—I trust, that you are before this at the end of your
Journey; and that Mrs and Miss Sotheby have so completely
recovered themselves, as to have almost forgotten all the
fatigue, except such instances of it as it may be pleasant to
them to remember. Why need I say, how often I have thought
of you since your departure, & with what Hope & pleasurable
Emotion? I will acknowlege to you, that your very, very kind
Letter was not only a Pleasure to me, but a Relief to my mind
/ for after I had left you on the Road between Ambleside &
Grasmere, I was dejected by the apprehension, that I had
been unpardonably loquacious, and had oppressed you, & still
more Mrs Sotheby, with my many words so impetuously
uttered. But in simple truth you were yourselves in part the
innocent causes of it / for the meeting with you; the manner of
the meeting; your kind attentions to me; the deep & healthful
delight, which every impressive & beautiful object seemed to
pour out upon you; kindred opinions, kindred pursuits,
kindred feelings, in persons whose Habits & as it were *Walk* of
Life, have been so different from my own—; these, and more
than these which I would but cannot say, all flowed in upon
me with unusually strong Impulses of Pleasure / and Pleasure,

in a body & soul such as I happen to possess, 'intoxicates more than strong Wine.'°—However, *I promise to be a much more subdued creature—when you next meet me* / for I had but just recovered from a state of extreme dejection brought on in part by Ill-health, partly by other circumstances / and Solitude and solitary Musings do of themselves impregnate our Thoughts perhaps with more Life & Sensation, than will leave the Balance quite even.—But you, my dear Sir! looked [at a] brother Poet with a Brother's Eyes—O that you were now in my study, & saw what is now before the window, at which I am writing, that rich mulberry-purple which a floating Cloud has thrown on the Lake—& that quiet Boat making it's way thro' it to the Shore!—We have had little else but Rain & squally weather since you left us, till within the last three Days—but showery weather is no evil to us—& even that most oppressive of all weathers, hot small *Drizzle*, exhibits the Mountains the best of any. It produced such new combinations of Ridges in the Lodore & Borrodale Mountains, on Saturday morning, that, I declare, had I been blindfolded & so brought to the Prospect, I should scarcely have known them again. It was a Dream, such as Lovers have—a wild & transfiguring, yet enchantingly lovely, Dream of an Object lying by the side of the Sleeper. Wordsworth, who has walked thro' Switzerland, declared that he never saw any thing superior—perhaps nothing equal—in the Alps.—The latter part of your Letter made me truly happy. Uriel himself should not be half as welcome° / & indeed he, I must admit, was never any great Favorite of mine. I always thought him a Bantling of zoneless Italian Muses which Milton heard cry at the Door of his Imagination, & took in out of charity.—However, come horsed as you may, carus mihi expectatusque venies [you will come as one dear to me and eagerly awaited]. *De ceteris rebus, (si quid agendum est, et quicquià sit agendum) ut quam rectissime agantur, omni meâ curâ, operâ, diligentiâ, providebo.* [About all the other matters—if anything needs to be done—whatever needs to be done—I shall see to it that they are done as correctly as possible with all my care, energy and diligence.°]

On my return to Keswick I reperused the erste Schiffer with great attention; & the result was an increasing Disinclination to the business of translating it / tho' my fancy was not a little

flattered by the idea of seeing my Rhymes in such a gay
Livery—as poor Giordano Bruno says in his strange yet noble
Poem De Immenso et Innumerabili

Quam ganymedeo Cultu, graphiceque Venustus!
Narcissis referam, peramârunt me quoque Nymphae.

[Dressed up like Ganymede, and splendidly attractive! I shall tell every
Narcissus the Nymphs have loved me too.°]

But the Poem was too silly. The first conception is noble—so
very good, that I am spiteful enough to hope that I shall
discover it not to have been original in Gesner—he has so
abominably maltreated it.—First, the story is very inartificially
constructed—we should have been let into the existence of the
Girl & her Mother thro' the young Man, & after *his*
appearance / this however is comparatively a trifle.—But the
machinery is so superlatively contemptible & commonplace—
as if a young man could not dream of a Tale which had deeply
impressed him without Cupid, or have a fair wind all the way
to an Island within sight of the Shore, he quitted, without
Æolus.° Æolus himself is a God devoted & dedicated, I should
have thought, to the Muse of Travestie / his Speech in Gesner
is not defici[ent] in Fancy—but it is a Girlish Fancy—& the
God of the winds exceedingly disquieted with *animal* Love /
ind[uces?] a very ridiculous Figure in my Imagination.—
Besides, it was ill taste to introduce Cupid and Æolus at a
time which we positive[ly] know to have been anterior to the
invention & establishment of the Grecian Mythology—and
the speech of Æolus reminds me perpetually of little Engravings
from the Cut Stones of the Ancients, Seals, & whatever else
they call them.—Again, the Girl's yearnings & conversations
with [her] Mother are something between the Nursery and
the Veneris Volgivagae Templa [Temples of promiscuous
Love°]—et libidinem spirat et subsusurrat, dum innocentiae
loquelam, et virgineae cogitationis dulciter offensantis luctamina
simulat. [She breathes desire and whispers desire, while she
feigns words of innocence and the resistance of a maidenly
way of thinking whose faltering gives her pleasure.]—It is not
the Thoughts that a lonely Girl *could* have; but exactly such as
a Boarding School Miss whose *Imagination*, to say no worse,
had been somewhat stirred & heated by the perusal of French

or German Pastorals, would suppose her to say. But this is indeed general in the German & French Poets. It is easy to cloathe Imaginary Beings with our own Thoughts & Feelings; but to send ourselves out of ourselves, to *think* ourselves in to the Thoughts and Feelings of Beings in circumstances wholly & strangely different from our own / hoc labor, hoc opus [this is the labour, this is the real task°] / and who has atchieved it? Perhaps only Shakespere. Metaphisics is a word, that you, my dear Sir! are no great Friend to / but yet you will agree, that a great Poet must be, implicitè [implicitly] if not explicitè [explicitly], a profound Metaphysician. He may not have it in logical coherence, in his Brain & Tongue; but he must have it by *Tact* / for all sounds, & forms of human nature he must have the *ear* of a wild Arab listening in the silent Desart, the eye of a North American Indian tracing the footsteps of an Enemy upon the Leaves that strew the Forest—; the *Touch* of a Blind Man feeling the face of a darling Child— / and do not think me a Bigot, if I say, that I have read no French or German Writer, who appears to me to have had a *heart* sufficiently pure & simple to be capable of this or any thing like it. / I could say a great deal more in abuse of poor Gesner's Poem; but I have said more than, I fear, will be creditable in your opinion to my good nature. I must tho' tell you the malicious Motto, which I have written on the first page of Klopstock's Messias°—

> Tale tuum carmen nobis, divine Poeta,
> Quale *Sopor!*

[Inspired poet, your verses come upon me like *sleep!*]

Only I would have the words, *divine Poeta*, translated, *Verse-making* DIVINE. I read a great deal of German; but I do dearly dearly dearly love my own Countrymen of old times, and those of my contemporaries who write in their Spirit.

William Wordsworth & his Sister left me Yesterday on their way to Yorkshire / they walked yesterday to the foot of Ulswater, from whence they go to Penrith & take the Coach—I accompanied them as far as the 7th Mile Stone. Among the last things, which he said to me, was—'Do not forget to remember [me] to Mr [So]theby with whatever affectionate terms, so slight an Intercourse may permit—and

how glad we shall all be to see him again.'—I was much
pleased with your description of Wordsworth's character as it
appeared to y[ou—] it is in few words, in half a dozen Strokes,
like s[ome of] Mortimer's° Figures, a fine Portrait—The word
'homoge[neity' gave] me great pleasure, as most accurate &
happily expressi[ve. I must] set you right with regard to my
perfect coinc[idence with] his poetic Creed. It is most certain,
that that P[reface° arose from] the heads of our mutual
Conversations &c—& the f[irst pass]ages were indeed partly
taken from notes of mine / for it was at first intended, that the
Preface should be written by me—and it is likewise true, that I
warmly accord with W. in his abhorrence of these poetic
Licences, as they are called, which are indeed mere tricks of
Convenience & Laziness. *Exemp. Grat.* Drayton has these
Lines—

> Ouse having Ouleney past, as she were waxed mad,
> From her first stayder Course immediately doth gad,
> And in meandred Gyres doth whirl herself about,
> *That, this* way, here and there, back, forward, in and out,
> And like a wanton Girl oft doubling in her Gait
> In labyrinthine Turns & Twinings Intricate &c &c°—

the first poets observing such a stream as this, would say with
truth & beauty—it *strays*—& now every stream shall *stray*
wherever it prattles on it's pebbled *way*—instead of it's bed or
channel / . (I have taken the instance from a Poet, from whom
as few Instances of this vile commonplace trashy Style could
be taken as from any writer—from Bowles's *execrable Translation*
of that lovely Poem of Dean Ogle's, vol. II. p. 27.—° / I am
confident, that Bowles good-naturedly translated it in a hurry,
merely to give him an excuse for printing the admirable
original.)—In my opinion every phrase, every metaphor,
every personification, should have it's justifying cause in some
passion either of the Poet's mind, or of the Characters
described by the poet—But *metre itself* implies a *passion*, i.e. a
state of excitement, both in the Poet's mind, & is expected in
that of the Reader—and tho' I stated this to Wordsworth, &
he has in some sort stated it in his preface, yet he has [not]
done justice to it, nor has he in my opinion sufficiently
answered it. In my opinion, Poetry justifies, as *Poetry*

independent of any other Passion, some new combinations of Language, & *commands* the omission of many others allowable in other compositions / Now Wordsworth, me saltem judice [in my opinion, at least], has in his system not sufficiently admitted the former, & in his practice has too frequently sinned against the latter.—Indeed, we have had lately some little controversy on this subject—& we begin to suspect, that there is, somewhere or other, a *radical* Difference [in our] opinions —Dulce est inter amicos rarissimâ Dissensione condiri plurimas consensiones [It is pleasant for the close harmony of friends to be leavened by an occasional disagreement], saith St Augustine,° who said more good things than any Saint or Sinner, that I ever read in Latin.

Bless me! what a Letter!——And I have yet to make a request to you / I had read your Georgics at a Friend's House in the Neighbourhood—and on sending for the book I find that it belonged to a Book Club, & has been returned. If you have a copy interleaved, or could procure one for me, and will send it to me per Coach with a copy of your original Poems I will return them to you with many thanks in the Autumn° / & will endeavor to improve my own taste by writing in the blank Leaves my feelings both of the Original & your Translation / your poems I want for another purpose—of which hereafter. —Mrs Coleridge & my children are well—she desires to be respectfully remembered to Mrs & Miss Sotheby. Tell Miss Sotheby that I will endeavor to send her soon the completion of the Dark Ladié°—as she was goodnatured [enough] to be pleased with the first part——Let me hear from you soon, my dear Sir!—& believe me with heart-felt wishes for you & your's, in every day phrase, but indeed indeed not with every-day Feeling, your's most sincerely,

S. T. Coleridge.

I long to lead Mrs Sotheby to a Scene that has the grandeur without the Toil or Danger of Scale Force—it is called the White Water Dash.°——

To Sara Hutchinson

August 10, 1802. Tuesday Evening

My dearest Sara

You will this morning, I trust, have received the Letter which I left at the Ambleside Post (the first, I came to) on Sunday Evening. I have half such another, the continuation of my tour, written; but on my arrival yesterday at my home, about 8 o'clock in the evening, I found 7 Letters for me / I opened none for an hour, I was so overglad to see the children again / and the first, I opened, I was forced to answer directly—which was as much as I could do, to save the Post—& to day I have been so busy letter-writing, that I have not time to finish the Great-sheet Letter—so must send a short one, briefly to say that I have received your two Letters, one of Monday, Aug. 2. inclosing the 5£—which I read last night, & had better left it alone, as I did 5 others—for it kept me awake longer than I ought to have been—and one this evening. I am well, & have had a very delightful & feeding Excursion, or rather Circumcursion.—When you did not hear from me, & in answer too to a letter containing a note, you should surely have concluded, my Darling! that I was not at home: for when do I neglect these things to those, I love? Other things, & weighty ones, God help me! I neglect in abundance / for instance / two little Boxes, which Dorothy fears, (& with abundant Reason) are lost— & which contain, besides my cloathes & several very valuable Books, all my written collections made in Germany—which taken merely in a pecuniary point of view are not worth less than 150£ to me.——More Rain coming! I broke off writing to look at the Sky / it was exactly 35 minutes after 7, which [was] 4 minutes after the real Sunset, and long long after the apparent sun-set behind our Vales—& I saw such a sight as I never before saw. Beyond Bassenthwaite at the end of the view was a Sky of bright yellow-green; but over that & extending all over Bassenthwaite, & almost up to Keswick church a Cloud-Sky of the deepest most fiery Orange—Bassenthwaite Lake look'd like a Lake of 'blood-red Wine'°—and the River Greta, in all it's winding, before our house, & the upper part of the

Keswick Lake, were fiery red—even as I once saw the Thames when the huge Albion Mills were burning, amid the Shouts of an exulting Mob—but with one foot upon Walla Crag, and the other foot exactly upon Calvert's House at Windy Brow was one great Rainbow, *red* and *all* red, entirely formed by the Clouds——I have now seen all the Rain-bows, that, I suppose, are possible—the Solar Rainbow, with it's many colors, the grey lunar Rainbow, & a fiery red Rainbow, wholly from the Clouds after sunset!—

I seem, I know not why, to be beating off all Reference to Dorothy & William, & their Letters°—I heard from Sotheby of their meeting—(tho' I did not read his Letter till after I had read your's—) I wish, I wish, they were back!——When I think of them in Lodgings at Calais, Goslar comes back upon me; & of Goslar I never think but with dejection.— Dear little Caroline!—Will she be a ward of Annette?—Was the subject too delicate for a Letter?—I suppose so.——To morrow morning they will leave Calais, if they indeed leave it 10 days after the Date of Dorothy's Letter / so that they will probably be with you, I would fain hope, by Monday next.—I saw old Molly° yesterday / She was weakly, but '*mended*' from what she had been / the Rheumatic Pain & weakness had left her Back, & gone into her arms—I slept at Bratha on Sunday Night—& did not go on to Grasmere, tho' I had time enough, and was not over-fatigued; but tho' I have no objection to sleep in a lonely House, I did not like to sleep in *their* lonely House. I called the next day—went into the garden—pulled some Peas, & shelled & drest them, & eat them for my dinner with one rasher of Bacon boiled—but I did not go up stairs, nor indeed any where but the Kitchen. Partly I was very wet & my boots very dirty—& Molly had set the Pride of her Heart upon it's niceness—& still more—I had small desire to go up!

It was very kind in you, my Darlings! to send the 5£; (which I have now sent back) but it was not very wise. I could have easily procured 3 or 4£ from Mr Jackson / but I gave up the Residence at St Bees,° because I began to reflect that in the present state of my finances I ought not to *spend* so much money. Thomas Ashburner's call was the *occasion* of my resolve not to go to St Bees; but my own after reflections were the

cause.—In the course of my Tour (& I was absent 9 days) I
gave away to Bairns, & foot-sore Wayfarers four shillings, &
some odd pence; & I *spent* nine shillings—sum total, £0" 13s
0D—but to this must be added the wear & tear of my Boots,
which are gone to be mended; & sixpence for a great knee-
patch for my Pantaloons, which will not however be worn an
hour the shorter time for the said large knee-patch. I have now
*no clothes but what are patched at the elbows, & knees, & in the
seat*—& I am determined to wear them *out & out*—& to have
none till after Christmas.——Hartley is in good spirits; but he
does not look well. Derwent too looks less rosy than usual—for
we cannot keep him from the Gooseberries—Hartley says—
[']He is far over wicked; but it's all owing to Adam, who did
the same thing in Paradise.'—Derwent can *repeat* all the
Letters; & can point out six or seven / O! that you could see
his Darling mouth, when he shouts out Q.—But notwithstanding his *erudition*, he is very backward in his Tongue.—
Lloyd's children° are nice fair Babies; but there is nothing
lovely in their countenances or manners.—I have seldom seen
children, I was so little inclined to caress—fair & clean, as
they were. O how many a cottage Bairn have I kissed or
long'd to kiss, whose Cheeks I could scarce see for the healthy
dirt—but these I had no wish to kiss!—There is a something
in children that makes Love flow out upon them, distinct from
beauty, & still more distinct from good-behaviour / I cannot
say, God knows! that our children are even decently well-
behaved—& Hartley is no beauty—& yet it has been the Lot
of the two children to be beloved. They are the general
Darlings of the whole Town: & wherever they go, Love is their
natural Heritage.

Mrs Coleridge is now pretty well.—

God bless my darling Sara!—& thee, dear Mary! I will
finish my long Letter, as soon as possible / but for the next 3 or
4 days I shall be exceedingly busy. Write immediately. Kind
Remembrances to Tom & Joanna.—Bless you, my Darling! |
&

S. T. Coleridge

I have received a large Wedgewood Jug, & a large Cup,
finely embossed with figures, & thick-rimmed with silver, as a

present, from—*Lady Rush!*° with a *kind Note.*—I had a shrewd
suspicion, that I was a favorite.——
   Inclosed is the £5, 5s note.—

To William Sotheby

                    Friday, Sept. 10, 1802. Greta Hall, Keswick
My dear Sir
   The Books have not yet arrived, and I am wholly unable to
account for the Delay. I suspect, that the cause of it may be
Mr Faulder's mistake in sending them by the Carlisle Waggon
—they should have been sent by the Kendal & Whitehaven
Waggon. A person is going to Carlisle on Monday from this
place—& will make diligent enquiry—& if he succeed, still I
cannot have them in less than a week—as they must return to
Penrith, & there wait for the next Tuesday's Carrier. I ought
perhaps to be ashamed of my weakness / but I must confess,
I have been downright *vexed* by the Business—every Cart,
every return-Chaise from Penrith, has renewed my Hopes,
till I begin to play tricks with my own Impatience—&
say—Well—I take it for granted, that I sha'n't get [them]
for these 7 days, &c &c—with other of those Half-lies,
that Fear begets upon Hope.—You have imposed a pleasing
task on me in requesting the minutiae of my opinions
concerning your Orestes°—whatever these opinions may be,
the disclosure of them will be a sort of *map* of my mind, as a
Poet & Reasoner—& my curiosity is strongly excited. I feel
you a man of Genius in the choice of the subject. It is my
Faith, that the 'Genus irritabile' [touchy race (of poets)] is a
phrase applicable only to *bad* poets—Men of great Genius
have indeed, as an essential of their composition, great
sensibility, but they have likewise great confidence in their
own powers—and Fear must always precede anger, in the
human mind. I can with truth say, that from those, I love,
mere general praise of any thing, I have written, is as far from
giving me pleasure, as mere general censure—in any thing, I
mean, to which I have devoted much time or effort. 'Be
minute, & assign your Reasons often, & your first impressions

always—& then blame or praise—I care not which—I shall
be gratified'—These are *my* sentiments, & I assuredly believe,
that they are the sentiments of all, who have indeed felt *a true
Call* to the Ministry of *Song*. Of course, I too 'will act on the
golden rule of doing to others, what I wish others to do unto
me.'—But while I think of it, let me say that I should be much
concerned, if you applied this to the First Navigator°—It
would absolutely mortify me, if you did more than look over
it—& when a correction suggested itself to you, take your pen,
& make it—& then let the copy go to Tomkyns°—What they
have been, I shall know when I see the Thing in Print—for it
must please the present times, if it please any—and you have
been far more in the fashionable World, than I, & must needs
have a finer & surer Tact of that which will offend or disgust
in the higher circles of Life.——Yet it is not what I should
have advised Tomkyns to do—& that is one reason why I *can
not* & *will not* except more than a brace of copies, from him. I
do not like to be associated in a man's mind with his
Losses—if he have the Translation gratis, he must take it on
his own judgment—but when a man pays for a thing, & he
loses by it, the Idea will creep in, spite of himself, that the
Failure was, in part, owing to the badness of the Translation.
While I was translating the Wallenstein, I told Longman, it
would never answer—when I had finished it, I wrote to him /
& foretold that it would be waste paper on his Shelves, & the
dullness charitably layed upon my Shoulders. It happened, as
I said—Longman lost 250£ by the work / 50£ of which had
been payed to me—poor pay, Heaven knows! for a thick
Octavo volume of blank Verse—& yet I am sure, that
Longman never thinks of me but Wallenstein & the Ghosts of
his departed Guineas dance an ugly Waltz round my
Idea.—This would not disturb me a tittle, if I thought well of
the work myself—I should feel a confidence, that it would win
it's way at last / but this is not the case with Gesner's Der erste
Schiffer.—It may as well lie here, till Tomkins wants it—let
him only give me a week's notice, and I will transmit it to you
with a large margin.—Bowles's Stanzas on Navigation are
among the best in that second Volume° / but the whole
volume is woefully inferior to it's Predecessor. There reigns
thro' all the blank verse poems such a perpetual trick of

moralizing every thing—which is very well, occasionally—but
never to see or describe any interesting appearance in nature,
without connecting it by dim analogies with the moral world,
proves faintness of Impression. Nature has her proper
interest; & he will know what it is, who believes & feels, that
every Thing has a Life of it's own, & that we are all *one Life*. A
Poet's *Heart* & *Intellect* should be *combined, intimately* combined
& *unified*, with the great appearances in Nature—& not merely
held in solution & loose mixture with them, in the shape of
formal Similies. I do not mean to *exclude* these formal
Similies—there are moods of mind, in which they are
natural—pleasing moods of mind, & such as a Poet will often
have, & sometimes express; but they are not his highest, &
most appropriate moods. They are 'Sermoni propiora' which
I once translated—'*Properer for a Sermon.*'° The truth is—Bowles
has indeed the *sensibility* of a poet; but he has not the *Passion* of
a great Poet. His latter Writings all want *native* Passion—Milton
here & there supplies him with an appearance of it—but he
has no native Passion, because he is not a Thinker—& has
probably weakened his Intellect by the haunting Fear of
becoming extravagant / Young somewhere in one of his prose
works remarks that there is as profound a Logic in the most
daring & dithyrambic parts of Pindar, as in the Ὄργανον
[*Organon*] of Aristotle°—the remark is a valuable one /

> Poetic Feelings, like the flexuous Boughs
> Of mighty Oakes, yield homage to the Gale,
> Toss in the strong winds, drive before the Gust,
> Themselves one giddy storm of fluttering Leaves;
> Yet all the while, self-limited, remain
> Equally near the fix'd and parent Trunk
> Of Truth & Nature, in the howling Blast
> As in the Calm that stills the Aspen Grove.°—

That this is deep in our Nature, I felt when I was on Sca'
fell—. I involuntarily poured forth a Hymn in the manner of
the *Psalms*, tho' afterwards I thought the Ideas &c disproportionate to our humble mountains—& accidentally lighting on
a short Note in some swiss Poems, concerning the Vale of
Chamouny, & it's Mountain, I transferred myself thither, in
the Spirit, & adapted my former feelings to these grander

external objects.° You will soon see it in the Morning Post—&
I should be glad to know whether & how far it pleased
you.—It has struck [me] with great force lately, that the
Psalms afford a most compleat answer to those, who state the
Jehovah of the Jews, as a personal & national God—& the
Jews, as differing from the Greeks, only in calling the minor
Gods, Cherubim & Seraphim—& confining the word God to
their Jupiter. It must occur to every Reader that the Greeks in
their religious poems address always the Numina Loci, the
Genii, the Dryads, the Naiads, &c &c°—All natural Objects
were *dead*—mere hollow Statues—but there was a Godkin or
Goddessling *included* in each—In the Hebrew Poetry you find
nothing of this poor Stuff—as poor in genuine Imagination, as
it is mean in Intellect— / At best, it is but Fancy, or the
aggregating Faculty of the mind—not *Imagination*, or the
modifying, and *co-adunating* Faculty. This the Hebrew Poets
appear to me to have possessed beyond all others—& next to
them the English. In the Hebrew Poets each Thing has a Life
of it's own, & yet they are all one Life. In God they move &
live, & *have* their Being—not *had*, as the cold System of
Newtonian Theology represents / but *have*. Great pleasure
indeed, my dear Sir! did I receive from the latter part of your
Letter. If there be any two subjects which have in the very
depth of my Nature interested me, it has been the Hebrew &
Christian Theology, & the Theology of Plato. Last winter I
read the Parmenides & the Timaeus with great care—and O!
that you were here, even in this howling Rain-Storm that
dashes itself against my windows, on the other side of my
blazing Fire, in that great Arm Chair there—I guess, we
should encroach on the morning before we parted. How little
the Commentators of Milton have availed themselves of the
writings of Plato / Milton's Darling! But alas! commentators
only hunt out verbal Parallelisms—*numen abest* [the spirit is
wanting]. I was much impressed with this in all the many
Notes on that beautiful Passage in Comus from l. 629 to 641
—all the puzzle is to find out what Plant Haemony is—which
they discover to be the English Spleenwort—& decked out, as
a mere play & licence of poetic Fancy, with all the strange
properties suited to the purpose of the Drama—They thought
little of Milton's platonizing Spirit—who wrote nothing

without an interior meaning. 'Where more is meant, than meets the ear'° is true of himself beyond all writers. He was so great a Man, that he seems to have considered Fiction as profane, unless where it is consecrated by being emblematic of some Truth / What an unthinking & ignorant man we must have supposed Milton to be, if without any hidden meaning, he had described [it] as growing in such abundance that the dull Swain treads on it daily—& yet as never *flowering*—Such blunders Milton, of all others, was least likely to commit—Do look at the passage—apply it as an Allegory of Christianity, or to speak more precisely of the Redemption by the Cross—every syllable is full of Light!—['|a *small unsightly Root* [']—to the Greeks Folly, to the Jews a stumbling Block—[']The leaf was darkish & had prickles on it[']—If in this Life only we have hope, we are of all men the most miserable / & [a] score of other Texts—[']But in another country, as he said, Bore a bright golden Flower'—the exceeding weight of Glory prepared for us hereafter / —[']but [not] in this soil, unknown, & like esteem'd & the dull Swain treads on it daily with his clouted shoon['] / The Promises of Redemption offered daily & hourly & to all, but accepted scarcely by any—[']He called it Haemony[']—Now what is Haemony? Αιμα-οινος—Blood-wine.—And he took the wine & blessed it, & said—This is my Blood— / the great Symbol of the Death on the Cross.°—There is a general Ridicule cast on all allegorizers of Poets—read Milton's prose works, & observe whether he was one of those who joined in this Ridicule.—There is a very curious Passage in Josephus—De Bello Jud. L. 7. cap. 25 (al. vi. §§ 3) which is, in it's literal meaning, more wild, & fantastically absurd than the passage in Milton—so much so that Lardner quotes it in exultation, & asks triumphantly—Can any man who reads it think it any disparagement to the Christian Religion, that it was not embraced 'by a man who could believe such stuff as this?—God forbid! that it should affect Christianity, that it is not believed by the learned of this world.'°—But the passage in Josephus I have no doubt, [is] wholly allegorical.— ῞Εστησε signifies—*He hath stood*—which in these times of apostacy from the principles of Freedom, or of Religion in this country, & from both by the same persons in France, is no unmeaning Signature, if subscribed with humility, & in the remembrance of, Let him that stands take heed lest he fall—. However, it is in truth no more than S. T. C. written in Greek. *Es tee see°*—

Pocklington will not sell his House—but he is ill—& perhaps, it may be to be sold—but it is sunless all winter. God bless you, & [your's,] & S. T. Coleridge

Mrs Coleridge joins me in most respectful remembrances to Mrs & Miss Sotheby.—

To Mrs S. T. Coleridge

[Coleridge was away from home on a visit to Tom Wedgwood, with the possibility that he might be invited to accompany Wedgwood on a journey to France and Italy. On his way, he had spent some time at Penrith with Sara Hutchinson, and there had followed an angry exchange of letters, Mrs Coleridge resenting his attention to the Wordsworths and Sara Hutchinson, and Coleridge demanding that she try to be friendly towards them. Mrs Coleridge was pregnant, and their daughter Sara would be born on Dec. 23.]

St Clear's, Carmarthen.
Tuesday MORNING, ½ past 5!! Nov. 22 [23]. 1802
My dear Love

We left this place some two hours before your Letter arrived; & returned hither yesterday Afternoon, ½ past I—half an hour too late for me to answer your Letter by yesterday's Post. I know, that this will be a Morning of Bustle: & the desire of writing you lay so heavy on my mind, that I awoke at 4 o/clock this morning. The fires here in every room keep in all day & all night; & yet they do not use as much coal on the whole, as we do. It burns like a Brick-kiln Fire—is never touched—& never goes out, till the last cinder falls out of the Grate. Would to Heaven! you had only a few Waggon loads of them for the next 3 or 4 months!—A little after the Clock struck 5, I rose & lit my Candle, found the untended Fire in the parlour bright & clear; & am sitting by it, writing to you—to tell you, how very much I was & am affected by the tidings of your Fainting—& to beg you, INSTANTLY to get a Nurse. If Mary's Aunt cannot come, do write immediately to

Mrs Clarkson, & try to get Mrs Railton. To be sure, there is a mawkish '*so-vāry-good*'-ness about her character, & her Face & Dress have far too much of the Smug-doleful in them, for *my* Taste; but I believe, she is really a well-intentioned honest woman, & she is certainly an excellent Nurse.—At all events, get somebody immediately—have a fire in your Bedroom—& have nothing to do with Derwent, either to mind or to dress him. If you are seriously ill, or unhappy at my absence, I will return at all Hazards: for I know, you would not *will* it, tho' you might *wish* it, except for a serious cause.

I shall write to Mr Estlin for my Letter. You speak too of a Letter from Mr Dennis. Where is it? I have received none. If I want the Old Man of the Alps,° I will write for it.—

Indeed, my dear Love! I did not write to you that Letter from the Passage without much pain, & many Struggles of mind, Resolves, & Counter-resolves. Had there been nothing but your Feelings concerning Penrith I should have passed it over—as merely a little tiny Fretfulness—but there was one whole sentence of a very, very different cast. It immediately disordered my Heart, and Bowels. If it had not, I should not have written you; but it is necessary, absolutely necessary for you to know, how such things do affect me. My bodily Feelings are linked in so peculiar a way with my Ideas, that you cannot *enter into* a state of Health so utterly different from your own natural Constitution—you can only see & know, that so it is. Now, what we know only by the outward fact, & not by sympathy & inward experience of the same, we are ALL of us too apt to forget; & incur the necessity of being *reminded* of it by others. And this is one among the many causes, which render the marriage of unequal & unlike Understandings & Dispositions so exceedingly miserable. Heaven bear me witness, I often say inly—in the words of Christ—Father forgive her! she knows not what she does°—Be assured, my dear Love! that I shall never write otherwise than *most* kindly to you, except after great *Aggressions* on your part: & not then, unless my reason convinces me, that some good end will be answered by my Reprehensions.—My dear Love! let me in the spirit of love say two things / 1. I owe duties, & solemn ones, to you, as my wife; but I owe equally solemn ones to Myself, to my Children, to my Friends, and to Society. Where Duties are

at variance, dreadful as the case may be, there must be a
Choice. I can neither retain my Happiness nor my Faculties,
unless I move, live, & love, in perfect Freedom, limited only
by my own purity & self-respect, & by my incapability of
loving any person, man or woman, unless I at the same time
honor & esteem them. My Love is made up 9/10ths of fervent
wishes for the permanent *Peace* of mind of those, whom I love,
be it man or woman; & for their Progression in purity,
goodness, & true Knowlege. Such being the nature of my
Love, no human Being can have a right to be jealous. My
nature is quick to love, & retentive. Of those, who are within
the immediate sphere of my daily agency, & bound to me by
bonds of Nature or Neighbourhood, I shall love each, as they
appear to me to deserve my Love, & to be capable of returning
it. More is not in my power. If I would do it, I could not. That
we can love but one person, is a miserable mistake, & the
cause of abundant unhappiness. I can & do love many people,
dearly—so dearly, that I really scarcely know, which I love
the best. Is it not so with every good mother who has a large
number of Children—& with many, many Brothers & Sisters
in large & affectionate Families?—Why should it be otherwise
with Friends? Would any good & wise man, any warm & wide
hearted man marry at all, if it were part of the Contract—
Henceforth this Woman is your only friend, your sole beloved!
all the rest of mankind, however amiable & akin to you, must
be only your *acquaintance*!—? It were well, if every woman
wrote down before her marriage all, she thought, she had a
right to, from her Husband—& to examine each in this
form—By what *Law* of God, of Man, or of general reason, do I
claim *this* Right?—I suspect, that this Process would make a
ludicrous Quantity of Blots and Erasures in most of the first
rude Draughts of these Rights of Wives—infinitely however to
their own Advantage, & to the security of their true & genuine
Rights. 2.—Permit me, my dear Sara! without offence to you,
as Heaven knows! it is without any feeling of Pride in myself,
to say—that in sex, acquirements, and in the quantity and
quality of natural endowments whether of Feeling, or of
Intellect, you are the Inferior. Therefore it would be preposterous to expect that I should see with your eyes, & dismiss
my Friends from *my* heart, only because you have not chosen

to give them any Share of *your* Heart; but it is not preposterous, in me, on the contrary I have a *right* to expect & demand, that you should to a certain degree love, & act kindly to, those whom I deem worthy of my Love.—If you read this Letter with half the Tenderness, with which it is written, it will do you & both of us, GOOD; & contribute it's share to the turning of a mere Cat-hole into a Dove's nest! You know, Sally Pally! I must have a Joke—or it would not be me!

Over frightful Roads we at last arrived at Crescelly, about 3 o/clock—found a Captain & Mrs Tyler there (a stupid Brace) Jessica, Emma, & Frances Allen—all simple, good, kind-hearted Lasses—& Jesse, the eldest, uncommonly so. We dined at ½ past 4—just after dinner down came Old Allen°—O Christ! Old Nightmair! An ancient Incubus! Every face was saddened, every mouth pursed up!—Most solemnly civil, like the Lord of a stately Castle 500 years ago! Doleful & plaintive eke: for I believe, that the Devil *is* twitching him home. After Tea he left us, & went again to Bed—& the whole party recovered their Spirits. I drank nothing; but I eat sweet meats, & cream, & some fruit, & talked a great deal, and sate up till 12, & did not go to sleep till near 2. In consequence of which I arose sickish, at ½ past 7—my breakfast brought me about—& all the way from Crescelly I was in a very pleasurable state of feeling; but my feelings too tender, my thoughts too vivid—I was *deliciously* unwell. On my arrival at St Clear's I received your Letter, & had scarcely read it, before a fluttering of the Heart came on, which ended (as usual) in a sudden & violent Diarrhoea / I could scarcely touch my Dinner, & was obliged at last to take 20 drops of Laudanum—which now that I have for 10 days left off all stimulus of all kinds, excepting ⅓rd of a grain of opium, at night, acted upon me more [pow]erfully than 80 or 100 drops would have done at Keswick.—I slept sound what I did sleep; but I am not *quite* well this morning; but I shall get round again in the course of the Day.—You must see by this, what absolute necessity I am under of *dieting* myself—& if possible, the still greater Importance of *Tranquillity* to me.—All the Woodcocks seem to have left the Country; T. Wedgewood's hopes & schemes are again all afloat; to day we leave this place for Narbarth, 12 miles from hence—shall probably

return to Crescelly—& then—God knows, where! Cornwall
perhaps—Ireland perhaps—perhaps, Cumberland—possibly,
Naples, or Madeira, or Teneriffe. I don't see any likelihood of
our going to the Moon, or to either of the Planets, or fixed
Stars—& that is all, I can say. Write immediately, my dear
Love! & direct to me—where?—That's the Puzzle—to be left
at the Post Office, Carmarthen.—God bless you, my dear
Love! & speed me back to you & our dear H. & D, & *etc*. Mr
T. Wedgewood desires his best respects to you—he is just
come down.—God bless you again & S. T. Coleridge

Best respects to Colonel Moore—& his Lady & Miss
D'arcy—& always remember me affectionately to Mr Jackson,
& Hartley's other Mother.——

To Thomas Wedgwood

Greta Hall, Keswick. Sept. 16. [1803.] Friday
My dear Wedgwood
   I reached home on yesterday noon; & it was not a Post
Day.—William Hazlitt is a thinking, observant, original man,
of great power as a Painter of Character Portraits, & far more
in the manner of the old Painters, than any living Artist, but
the Object must be *before* him / he has no imaginative
memory. So much for his Intellectuals.—His manners are to
99 in 100 singularly repulsive—: brow-hanging, shoe-contem-
plative, *strange* / Sharp° seemed to like him / but Sharp saw
him only for half an hour, & that walking—he is, I verily
believe, kindly-natured—is very fond of, attentive to, &
patient with, children / but he is jealous, gloomy, & of an
irritable Pride—& addicted to women, as objects of sexual
Indulgence. With all this, there is much good in him—he is
disinterested, an enthusiastic Lover of the great men, who
have been before us—he says things that are his own in a
way of his own—& tho' from habitual Shyness & the Outside
& bearskin at least of misanthropy, he is strangely confused &
dark in his conversation & delivers himself of almost all his
conceptions with a Forceps, yet he says more than any man, I
ever knew, yourself only excepted, that is his own in a

way of his own—& oftentimes when he has warmed his mind, & the synovial juice has come out & spread over his joints he will gallop for half an hour together with real Eloquence. He sends well-headed & well-feathered Thoughts straight forwards to the mark with a Twang of the Bow-string.—If you could recommend him, as a Portrait-painter, I should be glad. To be your Companion he is, in my opinion, utterly unfit. His own Health is fitful.—I have written, as I ought to do, to you most freely imo ex corde [from the bottom of my heart] / you know me, both head & heart, & will make what deductions, your reason will dictate to you. I can think of no other person. What wonder? For the last years I have been shy of all mere acquaintances—

> To live belov'd is all, I need,
> And whom I love, I love indeed.°

I never had any ambition; & now, I trust, I have almost as little Vanity.—

For 5 months past my mind has been strangely shut up. I have taken the paper with an intention to write to you many times / but it has been all one blank Feeling, one blank idealess Feeling. I had nothing to say, I could say nothing. How deeply I love you, my very Dreams make known to me.—I will not trouble you with the gloomy Tale of my Health. While I am awake, by patience, employment, effort of mind, & walking I can keep the fiend at Arm's length; but the Night is my Hell, Sleep my tormenting Angel. Three Nights out of four I fall asleeep, struggling to lie awake—& my frequent Night-screams have almost made me a nuisance in my own House. Dreams with me are no Shadows, but the very Substances & foot-thick Calamities of my Life. Beddoes, who has been to me ever a very kind man, suspects that my Stomach 'brews Vinegar'—it may be so—but I have no other symptom but that of Flatulence / shewing itself by an asthmatic Puffing, & transient paralytic Affections / this Flatulence has never any acid Taste in my mouth / I have now no bowel-rumblings. I am too careful of my Diet—the supercarbonated Kali does me no service, nor magnesia— neither have I any headach. But I am grown hysterical.—Mean-time my Looks & Strength have improved. I myself fully

believe it to be either atonic, hypochondriacal Gout, or a
scrophulous affection of the mesenteric Glands. In the hope of
driving the Gout, if Gout it should be, into the feet, I walked,
previously to my getting into the Coach at Perth, 263 miles in
eight Days, with no unpleasant fatigue: & if I could do you
any service by coming to town, & there were no Coaches, I
would undertake to be with you, on foot, in 7 days.—I must
have strength somewhere / My head is indefatigably strong,
my limbs too are strong—but acid or not acid, Gout or
Scrofula, Something there is [in] my stomach or Guts that
transubstantiates my Bread & Wine into the Body & Blood of
the Devil— Meat & Drink I should say—for I eat but little
bread, & take nothing, in any form, spirituous or narcotic,
stronger than Table Beer.—I am about to try the new Gout
Medicine / & if it cures me, I will turn Preacher, form a new
Sect in honor of the Discoverer, & make a greater clamour *in
his Favor*, as the Anti-podagra, 'that was to come & is already
in the world',° than ever the Puritans did *against* the poor
Pope, as Anti-christ.—All my Family are well. Southey, his
Wife & Mrs Lovell are with us. He has lost his little Girl, the
unexpected Gift of a long marriage, & stricken to the very
Heart is come hither for such poor comforts as my society can
afford him.——To diversify this dusky Letter I will write in a
Post-script an Epitaph, which I composed in my Sleep for
myself, while dreaming that I was dying. To the best of my
recollection I have not altered a word—Your's, dear Wedgwood, and of all, that are dear to you at Gunville,° gratefully
& most affectionately, S. T. Coleridge

Epitaph

Here sleeps at length poor Col, & without Screaming,
Who died, as he had always liv'd, a dreaming:
Shot dead, while sleeping, by the Gout within,
Alone, and all unknown, at E'nbro' in an Inn.

It was on Tuesday Night last at the Black Bull, Edinburgh—

To Thomas Poole

[Returning from a visit to the Wedgwoods at Gunville, Poole had spoken to Coleridge about John Leslie (1766–1832), a scientist whom Tom Wedgwood had assisted—as he did Coleridge—with an annuity. Finding apparently that his opinion of Leslie was known to the Wedgwoods, Poole had written to Coleridge, asking, 'Did you ever mention to T.W. that I disliked Leslie?']

Friday, Oct. 14. 1803. Greta Hall, Keswick
My dearest Poole
I received your letter this evening, thank you for your kindness in answering it immediately, and will prove my thankfulness by doing the same. In answer to your Question respecting Leslie & T. Wedgwood, I say—to the best of my Knowlege, *Not a word, at any time.* I have examined & cross-examined my recollective Faculty with no common earnestness; and I cannot produce in myself even the dimmest *Feeling* of any such conversation. Yet I talk so much & so variously, that doubtless I say a thousand Things that exist in the minds of others, when to my own consciousness they are as if they had never been. I lay too many Eggs in the hot Sands with Ostrich Carelessness & Ostrich oblivion—And tho' many are luckily trod on & smashed; as many crawl forth into Life, some to furnish Feathers for the Caps of others, and more alas! to plume the Shafts in the Quivers of my Enemies and of them 'that lie in wait against my Soul.'° But in the present instance, if I had mentioned any thing of the Kind, T. Wedgwood has so great a Love for you, as well as respect & affectionate Regard for Leslie, that he would have both suffered & expressed great Pain / I should have instantly felt that I had done wrong—& events of this sort I *never forget.* Likewise, I admire Leslie, & cherish high Hopes of him; & thought at the time, that part of your Dislike had been ill-founded, & that you had disliked him for a cause which had made you more than once treat me very harshly—namely, a supposed disposition in me to detract from the merits of two or three, whom you from childhood had been taught to contemplate with religious awe; but whom I thought very second rate Men / not sufficiently considering, that for one man whom Leslie or

myself might *lower* in the Symposium of Genius, there are 10
faces unknown at present to you, whom we should place at the
head of the Table & in the places of Honor—in other words,
that there is perhaps a larger mass (& a more frequent calling
of it into activity) of awe & love of the great departed in my
mind than in your's—This was in my Heart—for I suffered a
great deal from your Expressions between Blandford &
Gunville—& would of itself, have restrained me from making
your Dislike a subject of Conversation / & as *to the other* cause
of your Dislike, it is so very serious a Thing, that I should have
thought myself downright a Rogue if I had mentioned it.—I
think therefore, that without the least rashness I may *assert* at
once, that I never did speak to T. W. on the subject. If any
thing of this nature have come to his ears from me, it must
have been thro' some third or fourth Person—Tobin for
instance, who is an exceeding mischiefmaker, his Blindness,
poor Fellow! making this sort of Gossip a high Treat to him /
but I do not recollect having mentioned it to him—or to any
one, but, I believe, to Wordsworth / and I hope therefore, that
it will not have originated in me at all. It would be very, very
painful to me. But I cannot be as confident of this, as of the
former. Since I finished the Letter, I seem to have some *dim*,
very *dim*, Feeling of having mentioned it once to *Davy*. I seem
to feel, as if I had not mentioned it to Wordsworth—but that *it
was Davy*. But this is very likely to be all the mere straining of
the memory—colours in the eyes from staring in the Dusk &
rubbing them. Whoever mentioned [it] to T. W. acted a very
unwise part—to use the mildest phrase. If I mentioned your
Dislike of Leslie to T. W., it would have been assuredly
mentioned as common to myself & to Leslie [you?]—and as
arising from the same Cause—tho' the Dislike in my instance
was only for the moment, a bubble broken by the agitation
that gave it Birth.—O deeply, deeply do I detest this rage for
Personality: & it is among the clamours of my Conscience,
that I have so long delayed the Essay, which for so many years
I have planned & promised!——

Wordsworth is in good health, & all his family. He has one
LARGE Boy, christened John. He has made a Beginning to his
Recluse. He was here on Sunday last: his Wife's Sister,° who is
on a visit at Grasmere, was in a bad hysterical way, & he rode

in to consult our excellent medical men. I now see very little of Wordsworth: my own Health makes it inconvenient & unfit for me to go thither one third as often, as I used to do—and Wordsworth's Indolence, &c keeps him at home. Indeed, were I an irritable man, and an unthinking one, I should probably have considered myself as having been very unkindly used by him in this respect—for I was at one time confined for two months, & he never came in to see me / me, who had ever payed such unremitting attentions to him. But we must take the good & the ill together; & by seriously & habitually reflecting on our own faults & endeavouring to amend them we shall then find little difficulty in confining our attention as far as it acts on our Friends' characters, to their good Qualities.—Indeed, I owe it to Truth & Justice as well as to myself to say, that the concern, which I have felt in this instance, and one or two other more *crying* instances, of Self-involution in Wordsworth, has been almost wholly a Feeling of friendly Regret, & disinterested Apprehension—I saw him more & more benetted in hypochondriacal Fancies, living wholly among *Devotees*—having every the minutest Thing, almost his very Eating & Drinking, done for him by his Sister, or Wife—& I trembled, lest a Film should rise, and thicken on his moral Eye.—The habit too of writing such a multitude of small Poems was in this instance hurtful to him—such Things as that Sonnet of his in Monday's Morning Post, about Simonides & the Ghost°— / I rejoice therefore with a deep & true Joy, that he has at length yielded to my urgent & repeated—almost unremitting—requests & remonstrances— & will go on with the Recluse exclusively.—A Great Work, in which he will sail; on an open Ocean, & a steady wind; unfretted by short tacks, reefing, & hawling & disentangling the ropes—great work necessarily comprehending his attention & Feelings within the circle of great objects & elevated Conceptions—this is his natural Element—the having been out of it has been his Disease—to return into it is the specific Remedy, both Remedy & Health. It is what Food is to Famine. I have seen enough, positively to give me feelings of hostility towards the plan of several of the Poems in the L. Ballads: & I really consider it as a misfortune, that Wordsworth ever deserted his former mountain Track to wander in Lanes

& allies; tho' in the event it may prove to have been a great
Benefit to him. He will steer, I trust, the middle course.—But
he found himself to be, or rather to be called, the Head &
founder of a *Sect* in Poetry: & assuredly he has written—&
published in the M. Post, as W. L. D. & sometimes with no
signature—poems written with a *sectarian* spirit, & in a sort of
Bravado.—I know, my dear Poole, that you are in the habit of
keeping my Letters; but I must request of you, & do *rely* on it,
that you will be so good as to destroy this Letter—& likewise,
if it be not already done, that Letter which in the ebulliency of
indistinct Conceptions I wrote to you respecting Sir Isaac
Newton's Optics°—& which to my *Horror* & Shame I saw that
Ward had transcribed—a Letter which if I were to die & it
should ever see the *Light* would damn me forever, as a man
mad with Presumption.—

Hartley is what he always was—a strange strange Boy—
'*exquisitely wild*'!° An utter Visionary! like the Moon among thin
Clouds, he moves in a circle of Light of his own making—he
alone, in a Light of his own. Of all human Beings I never yet
saw one so utterly naked of *Self*—he has no Vanity, no Pride,
no Resentment / and tho' *very passionate*, I never yet saw him
angry with any body. He is, tho' now 7 years old, the merest
Child, you can conceive—and yet Southey says, that the Boy
keeps him in perpetual Wonderment—his Thoughts are so
truly his own. [He is] not generally speaking an *affectionate*
Child / but his Dispositions are very sweet. A great Lover of
Truth, and of the finest moral nicety of Feeling—apprehension
all over—& yet always Dreaming. He said very prettily about
half a year ago—on my reproving him for some inattention, &
asking him if he did not see something—[']My Father![']
quoth he with flute-like Voice—'I see it—I saw it—I see it
now—& tomorrow I shall see it when I shut my eyes, and
when my eyes are open & I am looking at other Things; but
Father! it's a sad pity—but it can't be helped, you know—but I
am always being a bad Boy, because I am always *thinking of my
Thoughts*.'—He is troubled with Worms—& to night has had a
clyster of oil & Lime water, which never fails to set him to
rights for a month or two—. If God preserve his Life for me, it
will be interesting to know what he will be—for it is not my
opinion, or the opinion of two or of three—but all who have

been with him, talk of him as of a thing that cannot be forgotten / Derwent, & my meek little Sara, the former is just recovering of a very bad epidemic Intermittent Fever, with tearing cough—& the other sweet Baby is even now suffering under it—. He is a fat large lovely Boy—in all things but his Voice very unlike Hartley—very vain, & much more fond & affectionate—none of his Feelings so profound—in short, he is just what a sensible Father ought to wish for—a fine, healthy, strong, beautiful child, with all his senses & faculties as they ought to be—with no chance, as to his person, of being more than a good-looking man, & as to his mind, no prospect of being more or less than a man of good sense & tolerably *quick parts.*—Sara is a remarkably interesting Baby, with the finest possible Skin & large blue eyes—& she smiles, as if she were basking in a sunshine, as mild as moonlight, of her own quiet Happiness. She has had the Cow-pock. Mrs Coleridge enjoys her old state of excellent Health. We go on, as usual—except that tho' I do not love her a bit better, I quarrel with her much less. We cannot be said to live at all as Husband & Wife / but we are peaceable Housemates.—Mrs Lovell & Mrs Southey have miserable Health; but Mrs Southey, I hope, is breeding —& Mrs Lovell never can be well, while there exist in the world such Things as Tea, and Lavender & Hartshorn Slops, & the absence of religious, & the presence of depressing, Passions.—Southey I like more & more / he is a good man / & his Industry stupendous! Take him all in all, his regularity & domestic virtues, Genius, Talents, Acquirements, & Knowlege —& he stands by himself.—But Mrs S. & Mrs Lovell are a large, a very large Bolus!—but it is astonishing, how one's Swallow is enlarged by the sense of doing one's Duty—at least where the Pill is to pass off some time or other—& the Medicine to be discontinued.—But scarcely can even the sense of Duty reconcile one to taking Jalap regularly instead of Breakfast, Ipecacuanha for one's Dinner, Glauber's salt in hot water for one's Tea, & the whole of the foregoing in their different Metempsychoses after having passed back again thro' the mouth, or onwards thro' the Bowels, in a grand Maw-wallop for one's Supper.—My own Health is certainly improved by this new Gout medicine / I cannot however get delivered in a full natural way of this child of Darkness &

Discomfort—always threatening & bullying—but the swelling
never inflames sufficiently & all is commonly carried off in a
violent Sweat—a long sudden soaking Sweat. But God be
praised! my Nights since I last wrote have been astonishingly
improved & I am confident now that my Complaint is nothing
but flying Gout with a little Gravel.°—This Letter I meant to
be about myself—O that I could but be in London with you.
It seems to me that you are entering on the porch of a Temple,
for which Nature has made & destined you to be the Priest.
But more of this hereafter.——

   I have been, to use a mild word, agitated by two INFAMOUS
atrocious Paragraphs in the Morning Post of Thursday &
Friday last—I believe them to be Mackintosh's°—*O that they
were*! I would hunt him into Infamy.—I am now exerting
myself to the utmost on this Subject. Do write me *instantly what*
you think of them / or rather, what you thought, what you felt,
what you said!—

                                        S. T. Coleridge

Many articles in the M.P. not mine are attributed to me. Very
probably, those infamous articles may—Stuart has sold the
paper for 15000£—he netted 8000£ a year—it was scarcely 2
years' purchase.—Do write instantly on the subject of this *No
Quarter!*——I have written twice to Stuart who still, I believe,
superintends the paper in part—& can get no answer from
him.—Ever & for ever, dearest Friend, gratefully & with
affectionate Esteem your's—

To Robert Southey

2nd Feby. 1805. Sat. Morning, 4 o/clock. Treasury, Malta.
Dear Southey
   A Privateer is to leave this Port to day at Noon, for
Gibraltar / and it chancing that an Officer of Rank takes his
passage in her, Sir A. Ball trusts his Dispatches, with due
precautions, to this unusual mode of conveyance, and I must
inclose a Letter to you in the government parcel. I pray, that
the Lead attached to it will not be ominous of it's tardy

voyage, much less of it's making a diving-tour whither the spirit of Shakespere went under the name of the dreaming Clarence.° Certain it is, that I awoke about some half hour ago, from so vivid a dream, that the work of Sleep had completely destroyed all Sleepiness—I got up, went to my Office-room, rekindled the wood-fire, for the purpose of writing to you, having been so employed from morn to eve in writing public Letters, some as long as memorials, from the hour that this opportunity was first announced to me, that, for once in my life at least, I can with strict truth affirm that I have had *no time* to write to you / if by time be understood the moments of Life, in which our powers are alive.—I am well—at least, till within the last fortnight. I WAS perfectly so—till the news of the Sale of my blessed House played the 'foe intestine'° with me. But of that hereafter.——My dear Southey! the longer I live, and the more I see, know, and think, the more deeply do I seem to feel your Goodness / and why at this distance may I not allow myself to utter forth my whole thought by adding—your greatness. 'Thy Kingdom come' will have been a petition already granted, when in the minds and hearts of all men both words mean the same—or (to shake off a state of feeling deeper than may be serviceable to me) when, gulielmosartorially speaking (i.e. Williamtayloricè°) the latter word shall have become an incurable Synonime, a lumberly Duplicate, thrown into the kennel of the Lethe-lapping Chronos Anubioeides,° as a carriony bare-ribbed Tautology. O me! it will not do! You, my children, the Wordsworths, are at Keswick and Grasmere—and I am at Malta—and it is silly hypocrisy to *pretend* to joke, when I am heavy at heart. By the accident of the sale of a dead Colonel's Effects, who arrived in this healing Climate too late to be healed, I procured the perusal of the second Volume of the Annual Review. I was suddenly and strangely affected by the marked attention, which you had payed to my few Hints, by the insertion of my Joke on Booker, but more, far more than all, by the affection for me which peeped forth in that 'William Brown of Ottery.'° I knew, you stopt, before, and after, you had written the words. But I am to speak of your Reviews in general. I am confident, for I have carefully reperused almost the whole Volume, & what I knew or detected to be your's, I have read

over and over again, with as much quiet care and as little
Warping of Partiality, as if it had been a manuscript of my
own, going to the Press / I can say confidently, that in my best
judgment they are models of good sense, and correct style—of
high and honest feeling intermingled with a sort of Wit, which
(I now translate as truly, tho' not as verbally as I can the
sense of an observation, which a literary Venetian who resides
here as the editor of a political Journal, made to me after
having read your review of Clarke's Mar. Dis.) unites that
happy *turn* of words, which is the essence of French Wit, with
those comic picture-making combinations of Fancy, that
characterizes the old wit of old England. If I can find time to
copy off what in the hurry of the moment I wrote on loose
papers that cannot be made up into a letter without subjecting
you to an expence utterly disproportionate to their value, I
shall prove to you that I have been watchful in marking what
appeared to me false, or *better-not*, or *better-otherwise*, parts, no
less than what I felt to be excellent. It is enough to say at
present, that seldom in my course of reading have I been more
deeply impressed than by the sense of the diffused Good, they
were likely to effect. At the same time I could not help feeling,
to how many false and pernicious principles both in Taste and
in Politics they were likely by their excellence to give a non-
natural circulation. W. Taylor grows worse and worse. As to
his political dogmata, concerning Egypt &c, God forgive him!
he knows not what he does! But as to his Spawn about Milton,
and Tasso—nay, Heaven forbid! it should be *Spawn* / it is pure
Toad's spit, not as Toad spit is, but as it is vulgarly believ'd to
be. *See too his Art: in the Crit. Rev.*°

Now for your feelings respecting Madoc, I regard them as
all nerve- and stomach-work, you having too recently quitted
the business—Genius too has it's intoxication, which however
divine, leaves it's headaches and it's nauseas. Of the very best
of the few bad, good, and indifferent things I have written, I
have had the same sensations.—Concerning the immediate
chrysopoetic [gold-making] powers of Madoc° I can only fear
somewhat and hope somewhat—Midas and Apollo are as
little Cronies as Marsyas and Apollo°; but of it's great and
lasting effects on your Fame, if I doubted, I should then doubt
all things, in which I had hitherto had firm faith / neither am I

without cheerful Belief respecting it's *ultimate* effects on your worldly Fortune. O dear Southey! when I see *this* Booby with his ten pound a day, as Mr Commissary X, and *that* thorough-Rogue two doors off him, with his 15£ a day, as Mr General Pay Master YZ, it stirs up a little Bile from the Liver, & gives my poor stomach a pinch, when I hear you talk of having to look forward for an 100 or 150£. But cheerily! what do we complain of? would *we* be either of those men? O had I domestic Happiness, and an Assurance even of the Health, I now possess, continuing to me in England, what a blessed Creature should I be, tho' I found it necessary to feed me and mine on roast Potatoes for 2 days in each week in order to make ends meet, and to awake my Beloved with a Kiss on the first of every Janry—Well, my best Darling! we owe nobody a farthing!—and I have you, my children, two or three friends, and a thousand Books!——

I have written very lately to Mrs Coleridge. If my Letter reach her, as I have quoted in it a part of your's of Oct. 19th, she will wonder that I took no notice of the House and the *Bellygerent*.° / From Mrs C. I have received no letter by the last Convoy. In truth, I am, and have reason to be, ashamed to own to what a diseased excess my sensibility has worsened into. I was so agitated by the receipt of Letters, that I did not bring myself to open them for 2 or 3 days, half-dreaming that from there being no Letter from Mrs C., some one of the Children had died, or that she herself had been ill or——for so help me God! most ill-starred as our marriage has been, there is perhaps nothing that would so frightfully affect me as any change respecting her Health or Life. And when I had read about a 3rd of your Letter, I walked up & down, & then out, & much business intervening, I wrote to her before I had read the remainder, or my other Letters. I grieve exceedingly at the event, & my having foreseen it does not diminish the Shock. My dear Study! and that House in which such persons have been! where my Hartley has made his first love-commune with Nature / to belong to White! Oh how could Mr Jackson have the heart to do it! As to the Climate, I am fully convinced, that to an Invalid all parts of England are so much alike, that no disadvantages on that score can overbalance any marked Advantages from other causes. Mr J. well knows that but for

my absolute confidence in him I should have taken the House
for a long Lease—but, poor Man! I am rather to soothe than
to reproach him. When will he ever again have lovi[ng]
Friends & Housemates like to us—? and dear good Mrs
Wilson! Surely M[rs] Coleridge must have written to me tho'
no Letter has arrived.

Now for myself—I am anxiously expecting the arrival of Mr
Chapman from Smyrna, who is (by the last ministry, if that
should hold valid) appointed Successor to Mr Macauley, as
Public Secretary of Malta, the second in rank to the Governor.
Mr M. an old man of 80, died on the 18th of last month, calm
as a sleeping Baby, in a tremendous Thunder & Lightning
Storm / In the interim, I am and some 50 times a day
subscribe myself, Segretario Publico dell' Isole di Malta,
Gozo, e delle loro dipendenze [Public Secretary of the Islands
of Malta, Gozo, and their dependencies]. I live in a perfect
Palace, & have all my meals with the Governor; but my
profits will be much less, than if I had employed my time &
efforts in my own literary pursuits. However, I gain new
Insights / & if (as I doubt not, I shall) I return, having
expended nothing, having paid all my prior debts as well as
interim expences, [(] of the which debts I consider the 100£
borrowed by me from Sotheby, on the firm of W. Wordsworth,
the heaviest) with health, & some additional Knowlege both
in Things & Languages, I surely shall not have lost a year.
My intention is assuredly to leave this place at the farthest in
the latter end of next month, whether by the Convoy, or
overland by Trieste, Vienna, Berlin, Embden, & Denmark, I
must be guided by circumstances—At all events it will be well
if a Letter should be left for me, at the Courier office in
London, by the first of May, informing me of all which is
necessary for me to know / But of one thing I am most
anxious, namely, that my Assurance money should be paid—I
pray you, look to that / You will have heard long before this
Letter reaches you that the French Fleet have escaped from
Toulon / I have no Heart for Politics—Else I could tell you
how for the last 9 months I have been working in memorials
concerning Egypt, Sicily, & the Coast of Africa / Could
France once possess these, she would be in a far grander sense
than the Roman, an Empire of the World—& what would

remain to England? England & that which our miserable Diplomatists affect, now to despise, & now to consider as a misfortune, our language & institutions in America?—France is blest by nature / for in possessing Africa she would have a magnificent Outlet for her Population as near her own Coasts as Ireland to our's—an America, that must forever be an integral part of the Mother Country. Egypt is eager for France—only more, far more eager for G. Britain. The universal cry there / I have seen translations of 20 at least mercantile Letters in the Court of Admiralty here, (in which I have made a speech with a Wig & Gown, a true Jack of all Trades) all stating that the vox populi [voice of the people] is—English, English, if we can! But *Hats*, at all events!—('*Hats*' means Europeans in contradistinction to Turbans!)—God bless you, Southey!—I wish earnestly to kiss your child—and all whom you love, I love, as far as I can, for your sake——

S. T. C.

To George Coleridge

[Coleridge and his family were on their way to Ottery St Mary, where there was a prospect of Coleridge's teaching in his brother's school; George Coleridge's response to this letter, however, was to insist that the visit be put off, and to inform Coleridge that he was giving up the school.]

2 April, 1806 [1807].—

My dear Brother

The omniscience of the supreme Being has always appeared to me among the most tremendous thoughts, of which an imperfect rational Being is capable; and to the very best of men one of the most awful attributes of God is, the Searcher of Hearts. As he knows us, we are not capable of knowing ourselves—it is not impossible, that this perfect (as far as in a creature can be) Self-knowlege may be among the spiritual punishments of the abandoned, as among the joys of the redeemed Spirits. Yet there are occasions, when it would be both a comfort and advantage to us, if with regard to a particular conduct & the feelings & impulses connected with

it, we could make known to another and with the same degree
of vividness the state of our own Hearts, even as it exists in our
own consciousness. Sure am I at least, that I should rejoice if
without the pain & struggles of communication (pain referent
not to any delicacy or self-reproach of my own) there could be
conveyed to you a fair Abstract of all that has passed within
me, concerning yourself and Ottery, and the place of my
future residence, & the nature of my future employments (all
more or less connected with you)—but after I have been with
you awhile, in proportion as I gain your confidence &
confident esteem, so I shall be able to pour my whole Heart
into you—I leave this place (a seat of Sir G. Beaumont's) on
Saturday, March [April] the 4th—& proceed to Bristol—
where I am to meet Mrs Coleridge, & the two children (for
Hartley is with me) and immediately proceed to Ottery. —If
you find reason to believe, that I should be an assistance or a
comfort to you by settling there in any connection with you, I
am prepared to strike root in my native place; and if you knew
the depth of the friendship, I have now for ten years (without
the least fluctuation amid the tenderest and yet always
respectful Intimacy) felt toward, and enjoyed from, Mr W.
Wordsworth, as well as the mutual Love between me and his
immediate House-hold, you would not think the less of my
affection and sense of duty towards you, my paternal Brother,
when I confess that the resolution to settle myself at so great a
distance from him has occasioned one among the two or three
very severe struggles of my life. Previously however to my
meeting you, and at the time of thus communicating to you
my resolve, provided it should be satisfactory to you—it is
absolutely necessary that I should put you in possession of the
true state of my domestic Affairs—the agony, which I feel on
the very thought of the subject and the very attempt to write
concerning it, has been a principal cause not only of the
infrequency & omission of my correspondence with you, but
of the distraction of all settled pursuits hitherto—

   In short, with many excellent qualities, of strict modesty,
attention to her children, and economy, Mrs Coleridge has a
temper & general tone of feeling, which after a long—& for six
years at least—a patient Trial I have found wholly incompatible with even an endurable Life, & such as to preclude all

chance of my ever developing the talents, which my Maker has entrusted to me—or of applying the acquirements, which I have been making one after the other, because I could not be doing nothing, & was too sick at heart to exert myself in drawing from the sources of my own mind to any perseverance in any regular plan. The few friends, who have been Witnesses of my domestic Life, have long advised separation, as the necessary condition of every thing desirable for me—nor does Mrs Coleridge herself state or pretend to any objection on the score of attachment to me;—that it will not look *respectable* for her, is the sum into which all her objections resolve themselves.—At length however, it is settled (indeed, the state of my Health joined with that of my circumstances, and the duty of providing what I can, for my three Children, would of themselves dictate the measure, tho' we were only indifferent to each other) but Mrs Coleridge wishes—& very naturally— to accompany me into Devonshire, that our separation may appear free from all shadow of suspicion of any other cause than that of unfitness & unconquerable difference of Temper. O that those, who have been Witnesses of the Truth, could but add for me that commentary on my last Words, which my very respect for Mrs Coleridge's many estimable qualities would make it little less than torture to me to attempt.— However, we part as Friends—the boys of course will be with me. What more need be said, I shall have an opportunity of saying when we are together.—If you wish to write to me, before my arrival, my address will be—Mr Wade's, Aggs' Printing-office, St Augustin's Back, Bristol.

Make my apologies to my dear Nephews; and assure them, that it will be a great Joy to me to endeavor to compensate for my epistolary neglect by my conversation with them—and that any valuable Knowlege, which it should be in my power to communicate to them, will on their account become more valuable to me.—My Love & my Duty to all, who have to claim it from me. I am, my dear Brother, with grateful & affectionate esteem

your friend & brother,
S. T. Coleridge

To Daniel Stuart

[*Circa* 18 April 1808]

Dear Friend—

I feel myself impelled to write to you some ten Sentences on a subject so full of anxious Hope to you, so full of regretful Anguish to me.° Exclusive of Health, Virtue, and respectable Connections, there seem to me to be just four points, on which a wise man ought to make calm and most deliberate questions—and unless he can answer *all* four queries in the affirmative, he has no chance to be happy—and if he be a man of feeling, no possibility even of being comfortable. I. Is A a woman of plain good sense, as manifested by sound judgment as to common occurrences of Life, and common persons, and either possessing information enough, or with an understanding susceptible of acquiring it, enough, I say, to be and to become a companion? In few words, has she good sense with average quickness of understanding? 2. Is she of a sympathizing disposition, in *general*—does she possess the sensibility, that a good man expects in an amiable Woman?—3. Has she that steadiness of moral feeling, that simplicity undebauched by lust of admiration, that sense of duty joined with a constancy of nature, which enables her to concentrate her affections to their proper Objects in their proper proportions and relations —to her Sisters, Brothers, Parents, *as* Sisters, Brothers, Parents, to her children as her Children, to her Husband as her Husband?—N.B. The second & third Query by no means supersede each other. I know a woman of great sensibility, quick & eager to sympathize, yet ever carried away by the present object—a wholly uncentering Being. This Woman is a pleasant companion, a lively Housemate, but O! she would *starve* the Heart, and wound the pride as well as affections, of a Husband—she cannot be a *Wife*.—Again, Mrs Southey is a woman answering tolerably well in affirmative to the third query—She loves her Husband almost too exclusively, & has a great constancy of affection, such as it is. But she sympathizes with nothing, she enters into none of his peculiar pursuits—she only loves *him*;—she is therefore a respectable Wife, but not a Companion. Dreary, dreary, would be the

Hours, passed with her—amusement, and all the detail of whatever cheers or supports the spirits, must be sought elsewhere. Southey finds them in unceasing Authorship, never interrupted from morning to night but by sleep & eating.—

4 and lastly. Are all these 3 classes of necessary qualities combined with such manners & such a person, as is striking to you—as suits your feelings, & coalesces with your old associations, as a man, as both a *bodily* and *intellectual* man?—

I feel a deep conviction, that any man looking soberly & watching patiently, might obtain a full solution to all these queries, with scarce the possibility of being deluded. He will see too, whether she is highly esteemed & deeply beloved by her Sister, Brother, oldest Friends, &c—. If there be an atmosphere of true affection & domestic feelings in her family, he cannot help himself breathing it, & perceiving that he breathes it. But alas! alas! is it because it is the most important step of human Life, that therefore it so often happens, that it is the only one, in which even wise men have acted foolishly—from haste, or passion, or inquietude from singleness, or mistaken notions of Honor leading them to walk into the Gulph with their eyes open! God preserve my friend from this worst of miseries! God guide my friend to that best of earthly goods, which makes us better by making us happier, & again happier by making us better!—

To Sir George Beaumont

[*Circa* 30 December 1808]

Dear Sir George

There is not a sentence in your kind Letter, to which I do not assent with my whole head and heart.° To deny the *fitness* of motives from a future state to *any* class of men, or the urgent *need* of such motives for *very many* men, I deem not only unpsychological but pernicious. Nay, the most exalted finite Being must need the Faith in Immortality as giving to Virtue an adequate *Object* and *Consequence*, altho' in the very *Idea* of Virtue it should have found a sufficient *Impulse*, an adequate *ground* of Action.—But, dear Sir George! as natural and necessary as motives of Hope and Fear (indefinite) are to vicious men, in the process of leading them to a nobler state, even so necessary is it for all men, the bad as well as the Good, that the *Idea* of Virtue should exist, and a Faith in it's Reality. Else we sacrifice the End to the Means.—But I shall more clearly convey my meaning when I have in my first Essay° shewn the nature & evinced the power, of *Principles*—. Are we not a union of Reason, Understanding, and Sense (i.e. the Senses)? As necessary as *Perceptions* are to the Senses, so necessary are *Rules* to the Understanding; and as necessary as *Rules* to the Understanding, so necessary are *Principles* to the Reason. For our sensuous nature would give us only Instinct, our Understanding could only superadd Cunning, or Prudence —in REASON lies the possibility of Virtue. The habit of realizing, as far as we can, the practical *Ideas* of Reason by availing ourselves of the powers of the *Understanding* & the *Sense* is human Wisdom.—In my Essay these Thoughts will be developed *popularly*. This is my definition of a *just popular* Style: when the Author has had his own eye fixed steadily on the *abstract*, yet permits his Readers to see only the *Concrete*.

It is a Whim of modern Date to consider Christianity as a mere Code of Ethics. This seems to me a degradation of the New Testament. It is an offer of Redemption from Moral Evil and it's Consequences, with a declaration of the conditions of acceptance. This indeed contains all the great principles of morality, but only as a *part*—it contains *medicines* too for those incapable of immediate Virtue—not only Rules to walk *well*, but means by which the Lame & the Palsied Spirit, may regain the possibility of walking *at all*. But be it remembered, that tho' the vessel must be cleansed before the new wine be poured in, yet the act of washing out the Cup is not the Infusion of the Wine! be it remembered, that the WORD of God did not exclusively bid men avoid the *wrath* to come—*He* likewise said—Be ye *perfect*, even as your Father in Heaven is perfect. And we are assured, that unless that *Fear*, which is the *Beginning* of Wisdom, shall proceed to LOVE, there can be no Union with God: for God is Love. To the *Diseased* Christ says, Love yourselves so as to leave your *Vices*; but to the *Convalescent*, Love your Neighbour as yourselves; and God *above all*. What then do I blame? Him who *couches* the blind Eye?°

God forbid! Whom then? Him who lets the Light in on the couched Eye slowly and gradually?—As little. But those I blame, who would convert the temporary Curtain before the window into a windowless Wall—a perpetual exclusion of Light. Those who, with Dr Paley in his Chapter on Moral Obligation,° annihilate the *Idea* of Virtue by placing it's *essence* in Selfishness: and say *implicitly*—*Obey* God, *benefit* your Neighbour; but *love* YOURSELVES above all. One more observation—a very important one—and I conclude. I more than doubt whether a *mere* feeling of Selfishness would ever be called into action by Christ, or considered as a possible means of leading vicious men to the Capability of Virtue—I recollect no instance in the *New* Testament, in which it is said—Be temperate & chaste, in order that you may enjoy the keen pleasures, of which Health is the necessary Condition—still less any passage which says—Be honest—and God will make you rich.—But I recollect many passages, in which Rewards are offered in a Future State, & Punishments threatened.—Wherein lies the Difference?—In this: that in the belief of the Latter there is *implied* a FAITH, a submission of the fleshly Sense to the Moral Being, which is verily and indeed the *Beginning* of Wisdom; the *ground* & *condition*, of Virtue. Besides, it is not only the shadowiness of all Prospects beyond the Grave, and the uncertainty accompanying them in the bodily Feelings and Imagination, that remove these Hopes & Fears from mere Selfishness; this removal is further affected by the *generic* nature of these Consequences—What I hope for myself, I hope for all men—I cannot hope Heaven for myself as myself, but for all good men in the number of which *I* may be included. No act of Thought or Feeling necessarily *social* can be absolutely *selfish*—not therefore the *Insisting* on Heaven and the place of Death do I object to, but to such representations of Reward & Punishment as tend to take away the virtuous Leaven, to make them more selfish than they are in their own nature—. Now this bad Process is carried on in two ways, first, by giving the vulgarest & most material Images, not as Images, but as the Truth & the Reality—thus by a most perverse Alchemy transmuting Spirit into grossest Body, instead of leading thro' the Body to the Spirit—secondly, by excluding from Reality & Belief all *nobler* Prospects, and

presenting an Image of Christianity, with no *Crown* on the
Head, no Sceptre in the Hand. There are fewer men than is
generally supposed, so utterly denaturalized as to have no
Dawning at all of the Truth & the true Idea, of Goodness: and
where ever there does exist even a Dawn of that Idea, it lends
a *force* to the selfish motives, which we more often underrate
than exaggerate. From opposites (say the Logicians) non
datur Transitus nisi per intermedium [there is no crossing
(from one to the other) except by way of what lies between].
Now that State, which is selfish, yet not wholly selfish, not
virtuous yet not wholly without virtue, is the Intermedium
that makes it possible to pass from Vice to Holiness—that
state therefore Christianity attempts to produce in the *first*
instance—and he who would preach as a Christian dare
deprive it of *neither* of it's constituent parts.—Finally, dear Sir
George! this is my Faith—that Christianity is a divine *Religion*,
which acknowleges the *existing* state of human nature with
more than all the *Historic* Truth of the Epicurean Philosophy,
and yet establishes an *Ideal* of Virtue in all the severity of the
Stoic—at once avoiding the baseness of the one, and the
bloating visionariness of the other.—This is a very dull Letter;
but even it's prolixity tho' it may tire you, yet will not be
unpleasing, as an evidence of the Value, I set on your
Esteem.—With affectionate & respectful mind,

                                        S. T. Coleridge

Miss Wordsworth will write to Lady B. in a few days.

To Thomas Poole

                                    28 Jan. 1810.
                                    Grasmere, Kendal.
My dear Friend
    My 'Man-traps and Spring-guns in this garden'° have
hitherto existed only on the painted Board, in terrorem [to
provoke fear]. Of course, I have received and thank you for
both your letters. What Wordsworth may do, I do not know;
but I think it highly probable, that I shall settle in or near

London. Of the fate of THE FRIEND I remain in the same ignorance nearly as at the publication of the 20th No.—It would make you sick were I to waste my paper by detailing the numerous instances of meanness in the mode of payment & discontinuance, especially among the Quakers. So just was the answer, I once made in the presence of some '*Friends*'° to the ? What is genuine Quakerism? Answer. The Antithesis of the present Quakers.—I have received this evening together with your's one as a Specimen—N.B. Three days after the publication of the 21st No.—and 16 days after the publication of the Supernumerary—A Bill upon a post master—an order of discontinuance and information that any others, that may come, will not be paid for—: as if I had been gifted with prophecy—and this precious Epistle directed—To Thomas Coleridge, of Grazemar.—And yet this Mr Newman would think himself libelled, if he were called a dishonest man. There is one important subject, on which I mean shortly to write—on the influence of the Laws of the Land on the practice and moral feelings of men.—We will take for granted, that the Friend can be continued. On this supposition, I have lately *studied* the Spectator°—& with increasing pleasure & admiration. Yet it must be evident to you, that there is a class of Thoughts & Feelings, and these too the most important, even practicably, which it would be impossible to convey in the manner of Addison: and which if Addison had possessed, he would not have been Addison. Read for instance Milton's prose tracts, and only *try* to conceive them translated into the style of the Spectator—or the finest parts of Wordsworth's pamphlet. It would be less absurd to wish, that the serious Odes of Horace had been written in the same style, as his Satires & Epistles.—Consider too the very different Objects of the Friend & of the Spectator: & above all, do not forget, that these are AWEFUL TIMES!—that the love of Reading, as a refined pleasure weaning the mind from grosser enjoyments, which it was one of the Spectator's chief Objects to awaken, has by that work, & those that followed (Connoisseur, World, Mirror &c) but still more, by Newspapers, Magazines, and Novels, been carried into excess: and the Spectator itself has innocently contributed to the general taste for unconnected writing—just as if 'Reading made easy' should act to give men

an aversion to words of more than two syllables, instead of
drawing them *thro'* those words into the power of reading
Books in general.—In the present age, whatever flatters the
mind in it's ignorance of it's ignorance, tends to aggravate
that ignorance—and I apprehend, does on the whole do more
harm than good.—Have you read the Debate on the
Address?° What a melancholy picture of the intellectual
feebleness of this Country!—So much on the one side of the
Question. On the other, 1. I will preparatory to writing on any
chosen Subject consider whether it *can* be treated popularly,
and with that lightness & variety of illustration which form
the charm of the Spectator—if it can, I will do my best. If not,
next whether yet there may not be furnished by the *results* of
such an Essay Thoughts & Truths that may be so treated, &
form a second Essay—3rdly. I shall always, *besides* this, have
at least one No. in 4, of rational entertainment, such as were
Satyrane's Letters:° as instructive as I can, but yet making
entertainment the chief Object in my own mind—. But lastly,
in the Supplement of the Friend I shall endeavor to include
whatever of higher & more abstruse meditation may be
needed as the foundations of all the Work after it—and the
difference between those, who will read & master that
Supplement, & those who decline the toil, will be simply
this—that what to the former will be *demonstrated Conclusions*,
the latter must start from as from *Postulates* and (to all whose
minds have not been sophisticated by a Half Philosophy)
Axioms. For no two things, that are yet different, can be in
closer harmony than the deductions of a profound Philosophy,
and the dictates of plain Common-sense—Whatever tenets
are obscure in the one, and requiring the greatest powers of
abstraction to reconcile, are the same which are held, tho' in
manifest contradiction, by the common sense, and yet held
and firmly believed, without sacrificing A to −A, or −A to A.
There is a beautiful remark on this in Beattie's Immutability,
concerning the faith of Sailors in Predestination, & yet equally
in their free-agency & moral responsibility.°—After this work,
I shall endeavor to pitch my note to the Idea of a common
well-educated thoughtful man, of ordinary talents; and the
exceptions to this rule shall not form more than one fifth of the
work—. If with all this it will not do, well! And *well* it will be,

in it's noblest sense: for *I* shall have done my best.—Of Parentheses I may be too fond—and will be on my guard in this respect—. But I am certain that no work of empassioned & eloquent reasoning ever did or could subsist without them—They are the *drama* of Reason—& present the thought growing, instead of a mere Hortus siccus. The aversion to them is one of the numberless symptoms of a feeble Frenchified Public.—One other observation—I have reason to *hope* for contributions from Strangers—some from *you* I *rely* on—& these will give a variety which is highly desirable—so much so, that it would weigh with me even to the admission of many things from unknown Correspondents tho' but little above mediocrity—if they were proportionally short, and on subjects which I should not myself treat.

The Supernumerary was printed before I received Ward's third letter. The account of Fourdrinier,° which I sent you, was transcribed from Fourdrinier's Letter, stating my Debt, & the manner in which it had been paid.—I daresay, it will be found accurate—but if not, it must surely be, that Mr Purkis has sent down paper since that account, which yet is not likely—For F. says, 'I have this day presented your whole account as finally settled to Mr Sharp &c'—.

You once asked me, what I thought of Grenville Sharpe's Greek Articles.° My old School-fellow, & the first Friend, I ever had, the Revd Mr Middleton, has written a thick Octavo on this Subject, deeply interesting—& with some few exceptions, most accurate—It is evident even from *him*, tho' a sort of Advocate, that the rule must be so modified, & so hemm'd in by exceptions, anticipations of mind, &c, as to render it of little practical value. On the first appearance of Christopher Wordsworth's Book on the Subject I studied the matter seriously; [and] but for accidents should have published on it—One fact I *suspected* at [first], and on research found my suspicion right—viz. that admitting G. Sharp['s] Rule, it is altogether nugatory in the case to which it is applied—He *states* the rule as not applying to Proper names—Now I can prove by a multitude of Instances that from the earliest Ages of Christianity the word Κύριος, = Lord equally with Θεός, Χριστός [God, Christ], &c was used as a proper name—the characteristic of which in the Greek Language is, that you may use it indifferently with or without the article—Δημοσθέ-νης [Demosthenes], or o [the] Demosthenes, just as we say—Siddons or *the* Siddons—except that what is significant and of course rare in English is common & evidently of perfect indifference in the Greek—*exactly* as in English, Almighty God, or *the* Almighty God—The English is superior to the Greek in point of Articles—The Greek can say—Θεός, which means *a* God, or ὁ Θεός, = *the* God, it depending on the context whether *the* God means some God who was spoken of before, as Apollo for instance, or the Supreme Being—& they have no other way of avoiding this equivocation but by using the neuter adjective, and instead of ὁ Θεός [the God] writing το Θεῖον = the divine nature. Now in English we say—*a* God (not a man) *the* God (he of whom we spoke last) and *God*. Consider too, my dear Poole! how little an argument derived from any strict grammatical rule of pure Greek can apply by the Christian Scriptures, when Origen & all the Greek Fathers without exception appeal to the impurity, grammatical barbarisms, & Hebraisms as a proof [of] their authenticity—What becomes of their *Idiōtai*, = illiterate men, applied to them even to St John & to St Paul?—But consult common sense & the philosophy common to all languages, & you will find that even admitting such a rule, it's observation must depend on the ideas connected with the words to which the article is or is not prefixed—that is, in order to apply it, you must first know the very thing which was to be proved by it. For instance, I met in the Lane yesterday the Plumber and Glazier—here *we* know that one person only is meant—I met yesterday the Parson and Clerk—Here are two. Doubtless, it would be better & more accurate to say, the Parson and the Clerk—but where there can be no mistake, what nation even in their common language, even their common writing, is scrupulous in observing such an accuracy? Now, I could produce 20 instances like these of the Plumber & Glazier, and the Parson & Clerk out of the purest Greek Authors—how little then can the Rule be applicable to the Syro-Greek of the New Testament?—Thank God! the doctrine does not want tali auxilio [such help]—& I feel convinced, that after a fair perusal of my Supplement you will perceive that Socinianism has not a pin's point to ground itself upon: and that No

Trinity, no God—is a matter of natural Religion as well as of Christianity, of profound Philosophy no less than of Faith.

May God bless you, and your affectionate
S. T. Coleridge.

To William Wordsworth

[This letter, occasioned by the publication of Walter Scott's narrative poem *The Lady of the Lake* in May 1810, airs some of Coleridge's feelings about the popularity of Scott's poems—including *The Lay of the Last Minstrel* (1805) and *Marmion* (1808)—written in a mode widely known to have been influenced by Coleridge's as yet unpublished *Christabel*.]

[Early October 1810]

I am reading Scott's Lady of the Lake, having had it on my table week after week till it cried shame to me for not opening it. But truly as far as I can judge from the first 98 pages, my reluctance was not unprophetic. Merciful Apollo!—what an easy pace dost thou jog on with thy unspurred yet unpinioned Pegasus!—The movement of the Poem (which is written with exception of a multitude of Songs in regular 8 syllable Iambics) is between a sleeping Canter and a Marketwoman's trot—but it is endless—I seem never to have made any way—I never remember a narrative poem in which I felt the sense of Progress so languid—. There are (speaking of the first 90 pages) two or three pleasing Images—that of the Swan, p. 25.—is the best—the following seems to me to demand something more for it's introduction than a mere description for description's sake supplies—

> With boughs that *quaked** at every breath   *!
> Gray Birch and Aspen wept beneath;
> Aloft, the ash and warrior Oak
> Cast anchor in the rifted Rock—

I wish, there were more faults of this kind—if it be a fault—yet I think, if it had been a beauty, it would not have instantly struck a perplexed feeling in my mind—as it did, & continues

to do—a *doubt*—I seem to feel, that I could have used the
metaphor; but not in that way, or without other images or
feelings in tune with it.—That the Lady of the Lake is not
without it's peccadillos against the 8th Commandment a la
mode [in the manner] of Messieurs Scott & Campbell, this
may suffice—

> Some feelings are to mortals *given*
> *With less* of Earth in them than *Heaven*.
>   Vide Ruth, p. 110.°—

In short, what I felt in Marmion, I feel still more in the Lady
of the Lake—viz. that a man accustomed to cast words in
metre and familiar with descriptive Poets & Tourists, himself
a Picturesque Tourist, must be troubled with a mental
Strangury, if he could not lift up his leg six times at six
different Corners, and each time p—— a canto.°—I should
imagine that even Scott's warmest admirers must acknowlege
& complain of the number of prosaic lines—PROSE IN
POLYSYLLABLES, surely the worst of all prose for chivalrous
Poetry—not to mention the liberty taken with our Articles, &
pron. relatives such as—

> And Malcolm heard his Ellen's Scream
> *As faultered thro' terrific Dream.*
> Then Roderick plunged *in sheath* his sword
> And veiled his wrath *in scornful word*
> 'Rest safe, till morning! Pity, 'twere
> Such cheek should feel the midnight air.
> Then may'st thou to James Stuart tell
> Roderick will keep the Lake & Fell
> Nor lackey, with his free-born Clan,
> *The pageant pomp of earthly man!—
> More would he of Clan Alpine know,
> Thou canst our Strength & Passes shew.
> Malise, what ho!'—his henchman came;
> 'Give our safe conduct to the Graeme!'
> Young Malcolm answered, calm and bold,
> [']Fear nothing for thy favourite hold.

* Vide Wesley's Hymns for the Arminian Methodist chapel.—

> The Spot, *an Angel deigned to grace,
> Is blessed, tho' *robbers* HAUNT THE PLACE;
> Thy churlish Courtesy for those
> Reserve, who fear to be thy foes.
> As safe to me the mountain way
> At midnight, as in blaze of Day,
> !!!Tho', with his boldest at his back,
> Even Roderick Dhu *beset the Track*!†
> Brave Douglas—lovely Ellen—nay—
> Nought here of parting will I say.
> Earth does not hold a lonesome glen
> So secret,‡ but we meet agen.
> Chieftain! we too shall find an hour.'
> He said, and left the sylvan Bower.—

On my word, I have not *selected* this Stanza—I do not say, that there are not many better, but I do affirm, that there are some worse, and that it is a fair specimen of the general style.—But that you may not rely on my Judgment I will transcribe the next Stanza likewise, the 36th—

> Old Alan§ followed to the Strand
> (Such was the Douglas's Command)
> And anxious told, how, on the morn,
> The stern Sir Roderick *deep had sworn*,
> The fiery Cross should circle o'er
> Dale, Glen, & Valley, Down, & Moor.
> Much were the Peril to the Graeme
> From those, who to the signal came;
> Far up the Lake 'twere *safest land*,
> Himself would row him to the Strand.
> He gave his Counsel to the wind,
> While Malcom did, unheeding, bind,

* Ellen: an Angel means a beautiful young Lady. I think, I have met with the same thought *elsewhere*! and 'deigned to grace'—N.B. She was residing there by compulsion, her father being under the wrath of '*King James*.'
† What a thumping Braggadocio this youthful Lover is!
‡ S. has been called the Caledonian Comet; but Comets move in ellipses—and this is doubtless a most eccentric Ellipse, which would frighten Priscian.°—
§ A miserable copy of Bracy the Bard—Allan too has a *prophetic Dream*; and what is it? The very ancient Story to be met with in all books of second Sight, that a Gentleman travelling found a dinner prepared for him at a place where he had never been before (as related in Humphrey Clinker, et passim)!°—

Round Dir, & Pouch and broad-sword roll'd,
His ample Plaid in tightened *fold*,
And stripped his Limbs *to such array*
As best might suit the watery way.

37

Then spoke abrupt: 'Farewell to thee,
Pattern of old Fidelity!'
The Minstrel's hand he kindly prest,—
'O! could I *point a place* of rest!
My Sovereign holds in ward my land,
My Uncle leads my vassal band;
To tame his foes, his friends to aid,
Poor Malcolm has but heart & blade.[']

Poor Malcolm! a hearty Blade, that I will say for him!—
    The Poem commences with the poorest Paraphrase-Parody
of the Hart Leap Well°—.
    I will add but one extract more, as an instance of the Poet's
ear for lyric harmony—Observe, this a poem of the dark Ages,
& admire with me the felicity of aiding the imagination in it's
flight into the Ages past, & oblivion of the present by—God
save the King! & other savory Descants.

Boat Song. (Canto 2. *19.* p. 69)

Hail to the Chief who in triumph advances,
Honour'd & blest be the evergreen Pine!
Long may the Tree in his banner that glances,
Flourish, the Shelter and grace of our line!
    Heaven send it happy dew,
    Earth lend it sap anew,
Gayly to bourgeon and *broadly to grow,*
    While every highland Glen
    Sends our shouts back agen,
'Roderigh Vich Alpine dhu, ho! ieroe!'

Now, that will tell! that last Gaelic Line is 'a damn'd hard
Hit'—as Renyolds said of a passage in King Lear°—I
suppose, there is some untranslatable Beauty in the Gaelic
words, which has preserved this one line in each stanza
unenglished—even as the old Popish Translators left the

Latin Words & Phrases of the Vulgate sticking, like raisins in a pudding, in the English Text.—

In short, my dear William!—it is time to write a Recipe for Poems of this sort—I amused myself a day or two ago on reading a Romance in Mrs Radcliff's style° with making out a scheme, which was to serve for all romances a priori—only varying the proportions——A Baron or Baroness ignorant of their Birth, and in some dependent situation—Castle—on a Rock—a Sepulchre—at some distance from the Rock—Deserted Rooms—Underground Passages—Pictures—A ghost, so believed—or—a written record—blood on it!—A wonderful Cut throat— &c &c &c—Now I say, it is time to make out the component parts of the Scottish Minstrelsy—The first Business must be, a vast string of patronymics, and names of Mountains, Rivers, &c—the most commonplace imagery the Bard gars look almaist as well as new,° by the introduction of Benvoirlich, Uam Var,

> on copse-wood gray
> That *waved & wept* on *Loch Achray*,
> And mingled with the pine trees *blue*
> On the bold Cliffs of Benvenue —
>
> How should the Poet e'er give o'er,
> With his eye fix'd on Cambus-More—
> Need reins be tighten'd in Despair,
> When rose Benledi's ridge *in air*
> Tho' not one image grace the Heath,
> It gain such charm from flooded Teith—
> Besides, you need not travel far,
> To reach the Lake of Vennachar—
> Or *ponder refuge* from your Toil
> By far Lochard or Aberfoil!°—

Secondly, all the nomenclature of Gothic Architecture, of Heraldry, of Arms, of Hunting, & Falconry—these possess the same power of reviving the caput mortuum° & rust of old imagery—besides, they will stand by themselves, Stout Substantives, if only they are strung together, and some attention is paid to the sound of the words—for no one attempts to understand the meaning, which indeed would snap the charm—3—some pathetic moralizing on old times, or any thing else, for the head & tail pieces—with a *Bard* (that is absolutely necessary) and Songs of course— For the rest, whatever suits Mrs Radcliff, i.e. in the Fable, and the Dramatis Personae, will do for the Poem—with this advantage, that however thread-bare in the Romance Shelves of the circulating Library it is to be taken as quite new as soon as told in rhyme—it need not be half as interesting—& the Ghost may be a Ghost, or may be explained—or both may take place in the same poem—Item—the Poet not only may but must mix all dialects *of all ages*—and all styles from Dr Robertson's° to the Babes in the wood—

I have read only two Cantos out of six—it is not that it would be any act of self-denial to send you the Poem, neither is it for the pain, which, I own, I should feel, and shrink *at* but not *from*, of asking Southey to permit me to send it—that I do not send you the Poem to day—but because I think, you would not wish me to ask Southey, who perhaps would refuse, and certainly would grant it with reluctance & fear—& because I take for granted, that you will have a copy sent you shortly—

I send the Brazil which has entertained & instructed me. The Kehama is expected.°

May God bless you!—I am curious to see the Babe; but long more anxiously to see little Catherine—

S. T. Coleridge—

To Henry Crabb Robinson

34, Southampton Buldings—
[12 March 1811]

I have to thank you, my dear Robinson! for the pleasure, I have enjoyed in the perusal of Anton Wall's delightful Tale.° I read it first with my eyes only, & only for myself—but the second time aloud & to two amiable Women—& both times I felt myself in the embrace of the Fairy Amatonda. The German *Recensent* [Review] has noticed as a defect and an oversight what I regard as one of the capital Beauties of the

Work; & thus convinced me that for Reviewers the world over & for Readers whose Intellects are commensurate with their's, an Author must write under his best conceptions, This is excellent & I mean so & so by it: even as to the *bodily* dim-sighted, Apelles himself° might be under the necessity of saying, This is a Sheep—& this is a Woman. I allude to the omission of Murad.° I recollect no fairy tale with so just and fair Moral as this of Anton Wall's—Virtue itself, tho' joined with outward competence, cannot give that happiness which *contents* the human heart, without Love; but *Love* is impossible without Virtue.—Love, true human Love—i.e. two hearts, like two correspondent concave mirrors, having a common focus, while each reflects and magnifies the other, and in the other itself, is an endless reduplication, by sweet Thoughts & Sympathies.—Now Hassan finds content at the outset—in Beneficence, (the emanciption of his Slaves) the social sense (his household henceforward contains only affectionate friends & fellow-labourers), local attachment, chearful Industry—& lastly, virtuous *Love. Him* Amatonda kisses thrice in the first week of his pursuit.—Solmar & Selim wander ten years in the pursuit; they are, however, OFTEN most *honorably,* ALWAYS *innocently* employed—their hearts remain pure—and they *merit* their Biribi and Tabuna.—But Murad sets out on a vile pursuit, & continues it by vile means—He marries a woman, he does not love—neglects her—is a debauchee & a systematic flatterer—he would 'die of ennui' at Beitul Salam—but cuique sua praemia [each has his own reward]—*his* industry was to wealth, as means to their material ends—& such pleasures, as Wealth & a city Life can confer, let Murad enjoy! What a frightful Incongruity would it not have been, if an Amina had been awarded to the ministerial [Shelter?] of the governing Sultanas!—Defects however there must be in all mortal works.—From Hassan's watching of Algol's countenance we of necessity anticipate some wicked purpose—as well as from the magician's desertion of Bator in his adversity—but no such Thing appears—the fairy Amatonda meets those who deserve her. Algol allegorizes the Hopes & Wishes of the youthful Imagination, which, like Dreams, betoken or betray the innate moral character, out of which they proceed. For all prophecies are the first effects of some Agent, whose presence

is not yet seen: as I have heard a friend calling to me by the
echoes of his voice among our rocks in Cumberland, before I
heard the voice itself or saw *him*.—Perhaps, I may be as dull in
this as the Reviewer was in his Objection; but I cannot help
conjecturing, that Wall in the first floating plan of his Work
had intended to have introduced Algol again—& his not
having done so seems to me almost as great a fault, as if a
character of consequence were to disappear in the first Act of a
Tragedy.—

Secondly, instead of admiring the scanty portion of the
supernatural in the Tale, I think this the only important Fault
in it's construction—Neither the Hair Girdle, the Ring, the
Sword, or the gold pin do any thing which might not have
been done without them, or in any way carry on the Story.
Nay, in Solmar's case, it is worse than nothing—it is *privative*
& not merely negative—for as far as it is recollected, it
detracts from Solmar's Courage—& like enchanted armour,
which the Knights of Chivalry forswore, blends cowardice
with valour. The best of it is, that one does not recollect it.

Thirdly (bless us! here's one of James the first's subdividing
chaplains resurgent in the shape of a Reviewer!) Thirdly—and
(O word of comfort!) *Lastly*—I do not understand the meaning
of the four Houris, & the untasted Banquet in the magician's
Palace. I have tried, over and over again, to make out some
allegorical Substrate; but really have been able to find nothing
but a French Hamiltono-Voltairish Cantharadine,° grossly
inconsistent with the character of Hassan, whose Love for
Amina is beautifully described as having had a *foundation* from
early Childhood—and this I many years ago planned as the
subject-matter of a poem, viz—long & deep Affection suddenly,
in one moment, flash-transmuted into *Love*. In short, I believe,
that *Love* (as distinguished both from Lust and from that
habitual attachment which may include many Objects,
diversifying itself by *degrees* only), that that *Feeling* (or
whatever it may be more aptly called), that specific mode of
Being, which one Object only can possess, & possesses totally,
is always the abrupt creation of a moment—tho' years of
Dawning may have preceded. I said, *Dawning*—for often as I
have watched the Sun-rising, from the thinning, diluting Blue
to the Whitening, to the fawn-coloured, the pink, the crimson,

the glory, yet still the Sun itself has always *started* up, out of the Horizon—! between the brightest Hues of the Dawn and the first Rim of the Sun itself there is a *chasm*—all before were Diff[er]ences of Degrees, passing & dissolving into each other—but this is a difference of *Kind*—a chasm of Kind in a continuity of Time.—And as no man who had never watched for the rise of the Sun, could understand what I mean, so can no man who has not been in Love, understand what Love is—tho' he will be sure to imagine & believe, that he does.—Thus, Wordsworth is by nature incapable of being in Love, tho' no man more tenderly attached—hence he ridicules the existence of any other passion, than a compound of Lust with Esteem & Friendship, confined to one Object, first by accidents of Association, and permanently, by the force of Habit & a sense of Duty. Now this will do very well—it will suffice to make a good Husband—it may be even desirable (if the largest sum of easy & pleasurable sensations in this Life be the right aim & end of human Wisdom) that we should have this, & no more—but still it is not *Love*—& there is such a passion, as Love—which is no more a compound, than Oxygen, tho' like Oxygen, it has an almost universal affinity, and a long & finely graduated Scale of elective Attractions. It combines with Lust—but how?—Does Lust call forth or occasion Love?—Just as much as the reek of the Marsh calls up the Sun. The sun calls up the vapor—attenuates it, lifts it—it becomes a cloud—and now it is the Veil of the Divinity—the Divinity transpiercing it at once hides & declares his presence—We *see*, we are conscious of, *Light* alone; but it is Light embodied in the earthly nature, which that Light itself awoke & sublimated. What is the Body, but the fixture of the mind? the stereotype Impression? Arbitrary are the Symbols—yet Symbols they are.—Is Terror in my Soul—my Heart beats against my side—Is Grief? *Tears* form in my eyes. In her homely way the Body tries to interpret all the movements of the Soul. Shall it not then imitate & symbolize that divinest movement of a FINITE Spirit—the yearning to compleat itself by Union?—Is there not a Sex in Souls? We have all eyes, Cheeks, Lips—but in a lovely Woman are not the eyes womanly—yea, every form, every motion, of her whole frame *womanly*? Were there not an Identity in the

Substance, man & woman might *join*, but they could never *unify*—were there not throughout, in body & in soul, a corresponding and adapted Difference, there might be addition, but there could be no combination. One *and one* = 2; but one cannot be multiplied into one. $1 \times 1 = 1$—At best, it would be an idle echo, the same thing needlessly repeated—as the Ideot told the Clock—one, one, one, one &c—.

It has just come into my head, that this Scrawl is very much in the Style of Jean Paul.° I have not however as yet looked into the Books, you were so kind as to leave with me—further than to see the Title page. If you do not want it, for some time, I should be glad to keep it by me—while I read the original works themselves—.I pray you, procure them for me—work by work—and I will promise you most carefully to return them, you allowing me three days for two Volumes. I am very anxious to have them—& shall fill one volume of the Omniana with the extracts, quoting your criticism as my Introduction —only instead of the *shelves* or steps I must put the Ladder of a Library—or whatever name those moveable Steps are called which one meets with in all well-furnitured Libraries —

I have been extremely unwell—& am indeed—tho' rather better.

George Burnet's Death, told too abruptly, & in truth exaggerated, overset my dear, most dear & most excellent Friend & Heart's Sister, Mary Lamb—& her Illness has almost overset me—Troubles, God knows! have thronged upon me—Alas! alas! all my dearest Friends I have of late either suffered *from*, or suffered *for*. 'Tis a cruel sort of World we live in!—

God bless you | & | Your's with affectionate Esteem,
                                    S. T. Coleridge

P.S. I began with the Scrap of Paper—meaning only to write half a score Lines—And now I have written enough for half a dozen Letters, unnecessarily—when to have written to half a dozen Claimants is a moral (would it were, a physical) necessity. But moral obligation is to me so very strong a Stimulant, that in 9 cases out of ten it acts as a Narcotic. The Blow that should rouse, *stuns* me.

Do not forget whenever you write to Bury, to recall my

name to Mrs Clarkson.° May God eternally bless her! To feel, not only how *much*, but *how* I love and esteem her, reconciles me to my own nature, when I am least contented with it. Had she been my Sister, I should have been a great man. (Excuse a Vanity which struggles forth out of the pangs of Humility.) But I have never had any one, in whose Heart and House I could be an Inmate, who loved me enough to take pride & joy in the efforts of my power, being at the same time so by me beloved as to have an influence over my mind. And I am too weak to do my Duty for the Duty's Sake. All honorable Things would be dear to me, if they were only lovely—as reputation, fame, competence, Health of Mind & Body—but then in order to become lovely to me, I must be able to think of them as adding to the happiness of some other Being who found her happiness in mine—and under whatever name that might be, with all the duties belonging to that name, Wife or Sister, I *know* that I could not only be content, but be happy. I never saw a woman yet, whom I could so imagine to have [been] born of one parent with me at one Birth, as Catharine Clarkson—She has all, that is good in me, and all that is innocent in the peculiarizing parts of my nature—Would to God! I had what she has besides—& which I have not—her sacred *magnanimity*!

To Daniel Stuart

Sunday Morning. [28 April 1811]

Dear Stuart

I arrived safe at my lodgings, about ½ past 12; but I have suffered, as I deserved, most severely for my Intemperance. So well too as I was becoming, I can scarce pardon myself for my Incaution—the ground of it all is that vile custom of drinking to each other during dinner, which not only makes a modest or heedless man's inclinations dependent on the habits, or intended civilities & complimentary respects of every one of his fellow-guests, but is, I am persuaded, absolute poison to the whole digestive System. How indeed should Nature withstand two violent actions at the same time, that of the

Food on the secretory vessels and that of hot diffusive Stimuli
on all the nerves of the Stomach! Besides, how much more
cheerful, with what cool and broad-awake Hilarity, our
Fathers used to take their first bumper of Port, after the Cloth
was removed! The presence of the women too for the first half
hour made the bottle circulate very slowly: so that the
primitiae [first course] and most important part of digestion
was performed under the assistance of two or three glasses &
of easy leisurely chat & mirth, before the Drinking set in.
Whereas now, a man is flustered by the violent processes
going on in his stomach; and tho' we drink less wine than
formerly, what we drink, injures us more. 'When the Devil,
was sick'°—he amused himself with writing sermons. And the
fact is, that till yesterday I have not been able to keep any
thing on my Stomach, with such confusion in the feeling of my
Skull and Forehead, tho' not in my thoughts, whenever I bent
down to write, as rendered me incapable of writing any thing
to any purpose. I vow to God, and I pray, God help me to
keep the vow, that I never hereafter will drink a single Glass of
Wine during dinner, except in case of sudden faintness when I
should have drank it as a medicine at any other time. Perfect
Health I do not expect ever to have; but Experience has
convinced me, and I shall act most criminally if I rebel against
it, that by getting up early, by an entire abstinence from
Spirits on all ordinary occasions, and by living in a family
where my social affections are kept alive, that I may
henceforward and for some years enjoy such a portion of
Health as will enable me to perform all my literary Duties
quietly and systematically. The quickness, with which I pass
from Illness into my best state of Health, is astonishing, &
makes many think it impossible, that I should have been so ill,
the day or two before; but this child-like suddenness of
convalescence is, I believe, symptomatic of those whose
complaints arise from weakness and irritability of the Bowels,
and who have at the same time more power of the nervous,
than strength of the muscular, system.

So much for the Past. For the present and future I wish
most anxiously to have your advice & assistance. I must
commence by telling you, great a weakness as it must appear,
that so deep and so rankling is the wound, which Wordsworth

has wantonly and without the slightest provocation inflicted in return for a 15 years' most enthusiastic, self-despising & alas! self-injuring Friendship, (for as to his wretched Agents, the Montagus, Carlisles, Knapps, &c, I despise them too much to be seriously hurt by any thing, they for themselves can say or do) that I cannot return to Grasmere or it's vicinity—where I must often see & always be reminded of him. Every man must take the measure of his own strength. I may, I do, regret my want of fortitude; but so it is, that incurable depression of Spirits, Brooding, Indolence, Despondence, thence Pains & nightly Horrors, & thence the Devil & all his Imps to get rid of them or rather to keep them just at arm's length, would be infallibly the result. Even to have only thought of Wordsworth, while writing these Lines, has, I feel, fluttered & disordered my whole Inside. On the other hand, to live by myself would be almost equally dangerous.—I have however an alternative in my power: if only I can procure any regular situation, which might employ me & my pen from 9 to 2, 5 or even 6 days a week—in this case, I could settle myself with comfort to my own feelings & with perfect propriety, as a member of Morgan's Family.—In this letter I address you, dear Stuart! in a twofold character—first, as my Friend, & secondly, as I would any other person, Perry or Walter—as the former, I am sure you will give me the best advice in your power, but in the latter character I wish nothing but the mere fact of advantage or disadvantage, convenience or inconvenience, relatively to yourself. But it struck me, that by devoting myself for the next half year to the Courier, as a regular Duty, I might prove useful to the Paper: as, if it were desirable, I could be at the office every morning by ½ past 9, to read over all the Morning Papers &c, & point out whatever seemed noticeable to Mr Street,°—that I might occasionally write the leading Paragraph when he might wish to go into the City or to the Public offices—and besides this, I would carry on a series of articles, a column and a half or two columns each, independent of small paragraphs, poems etc, as would fill whatever room there was in the Courier whenever there was room. In short, I would regularly furnish six Columns to Mr Street, which [he] might suffer to accumulate in busy times—. I have thought, that this might perhaps be pleasing to Street:

as I should have no pretence to any controll or Intermeddle-
ment; but merely during a certain space of Time be in part,
his Assistant, and in part, a political Writer in the service of
the Paper—. Should the Plan seem feasible to you in itself,
and your objections rest chiefly on your fears as to my
steadiness, I can only say—Give me a month's Trial.

I am very uneasy about the payment of my Annuity
Assurance—even in London there is far more owing to me
than that amounts to—and this I doubt not, I shall be able to
collect as soon as my mind is once at ease, and any thing is but
settled. Besides, as soon as Southey brings up my Manuscripts, I
am sure of being able to sell them for more or less.—But I am
interrupted—I hope to see you tomorrow morning, either at
Brompton or at the Courier office—God bless you &

S. T. Coleridge.

To an unknown correspondent

[This letter is a reply to an enquiry about Walter Scott's indebtedness
to Coleridge's *Christabel* in *The Lay of the Last Minstrel* (1805). Although
Coleridge did not publish *Christabel* until 1816, he had frequently
recited it in company, and a few manuscript copies existed. Both
Scott and Byron admired it, and Scott generously ackowledged its
influence. Coleridge discusses the same issue in an earlier letter,
pp. 146–51.]

[Circa 15–21 December 1811]

Sir

As I am bound to thank you for your good-will and the high
opinion, you have been pleased to express of my Genius, so I
ask in return that you should give me credit for perfect
sincerity in the motives and feelings, which I shall assign for
my inability to comply with your request.

Excuse me, if I say that I have ever held parallelisms
adduced in proof of plagiarism or even of intentional
imitation, in the utmost contempt. There are two Kinds of
Heads in the world of Literature. The one I would call,
SPRINGS: the other TANKS. The latter class habituated to
receiving only, full or low, according to the state of it's

Feeders, attach[es] no distinct notion to living production as contra-distinguished from mechanical formation. If they find a fine passage in Thomson, they refer it to Milton; if in Milton to Euripides or Homer; and if in Homer, they take for granted it's pre-existence in the lost works of Linus or Musaeus. It would seem as if it was a part of their Creed, that all Thoughts are traditional, and that not only the Alphabet was revealed to Adam but all that was ever written in it that was worth writing.—But I come to the point. I can scarcely call myself an Acquaintance of Mr Walter Scott's; but I have met him twice or thrice in company. Those who hold that a Man's nature is shewn in his Countenance would not need the confident assurance, which all his Friends & Acquaintance so unanimously give, that he is of the most frank and generous disposition, incapable of trick or concealment.—The mere expression of his Features, and the Tones of his Voice in conversation, independent of the matter, sufficiently attest the fervor & activity of his mind.—The Proofs must be strong indeed, Sir! which could convince me that such a man could consciously make an unfair and selfish use of *any* Manuscript that came by accident into his possession—least of all, one of a known Contemporary.—What then are they the Facts that are to weaken this presumption?—First, that the Fragment, entitled Christabel, was composed many *years*, and known & openly admired by Mr Scott some time, before the *publication* of the Lay of the Last Minstrel. (For be pleased to observe, it is no part of the known *Fact* that the Lay of the Last Minstrel was not composed in part at least or at least *planned*, before Mr S. had seen the Fragment in question.[)]

Secondly, that of those who had seen or heard the Fragment a large proportion were struck with certain lines the same or nearly the same in the L.L.M., with similar movements in the manner of narration and the arrangement of the Imagery, and lastly with that general resemblance which is exprest by the words—the one still reminded them of the other.—Before I proceed to the arguments on the other side, I will examine these, and if I can rely on my own feelings at the present moment, exactly as I would wish a friend of mine to do if I had been the fortunate Author of the Lay of the last Minstrel and the Marmion, & Mr W. S. the earlier Writer of the Christabel.

Now it must be obvious on the first calm reflection, that Mr
W. S. could have had no previous intention of using the
Christabel—from the very fact which has furnished the main
strength of the contrary presumption—For before the appearance of the Lay of the L. M. he not only mentioned the
Christabel repeatedly to persons who had never before heard
of it, not only praised it with warmth, but *recited* it.—In order
to evade or weaken this fact, we must make the arbitrary
supposition, that he had not at that time planned his Poem as
it now appears: and that the purpose was formed in his mind
afterwards, & while he was composing.—A purpose, of
course, implies consciousness.—Now this again is rendered in
the highest degree improbable by another of the Facts above
stated, & by one too that has assuredly had no small share in
occasioning the suspicion—the existence, I mean, of a number
of Lines the same or nearly the same in both Authors. I have
not the Poems by me; but I distinctly remember, that the
greater part consisted of Phrases, such as Jesu Maria! shield
thee well, &c—which might have occurred to a score of
Writers who had been previously familiar with Poems &
Romances written before the Reformation or translated from
the Spanish—and the small remainder contain nothing
remarkable either in language, thought, feeling or imagery.
From long disuse I cannot have the tenth part of the fluency in
versification as Mr Scott or Southey have: & yet I would
undertake in a couple of Hours to alter every one of these
Lines or Couplets, without the least injury to the context, to
retain the same meaning in words equally poetical & suitable,
& yet entirely remove all the *appearance* of Likeness.—And
this, Sir! is what an intentional Plagiarist would have
done—He would have *translated*, not transcribed.

If then there be any just ground for the Charge of 'stolen
feathers' (say rather, for an imitation of the mode of flying), it
must be found in the supposed close likeness of the metre, the
movements, the way of relating an event, in short, in the general
resemblance of the great Features, which have given to the
Physiognomy of Mr W. S.'s late Poems their marked
originality, in the public Feeling. Now that several persons,
and these too persons of education, and liberal minds, at
several times, and without any knowlege of each other's

opinions have been struck with this general resemblance, &
have expressed themselves more or less strongly on the
subject, I do not pretend to deny: for it is a fact of my own
knowlege. But it would be most dishonorable in me if I did not
add, that *if* I had framed my expectations exclusively by the
opinions & assertions of others, those whose expressions were
most limited would have excited anticipations, which my own
after Perusal of the Lay of the Last Minstrel were [was?] far
from veriyfing [verifying?] to my own mind. But I will admit
that of this neither I or Mr S. are or can be the proper Judges.
A Poet may be able to appreciate the merit of each particular
Part of his own Poem as well, or (if he have a well-disciplined
mind) better than any other can do; but of the *effect* of the
Whole as a Whole he cannot from the very nature of Things
(from the foreknowlege of each following part, from the parts
having been written at different times, from the blending of
the pleasures & disgusts of Composing with the Composition
itself, &c) have the same sensation, as the Reader or auditor
to whom the whole is new & simultaneous.—The Case must
then be thus stated. Put aside the fact of the previous
acquaintance with the Christabel—suppose that no circumstances were known, that rendered it probable—Would the
resemblances in and of themselves have enforced, or at least
have generally suggested, the suspicion that [the] later Poem
was an intentional Imitation of the elder? In other words, is
the general Likeness, or are the particular resemblances, such
as a liberal and enlightened Reader could not with any
probability consider as the result of mere Coincidence
between two Writers of similar Pursuits, and (argumenti
causâ loquor [I speak for the sake of argument]) of nearly
equal Talent? Coincidence is here used as a negative—not as
implying that the Likeness between two Works is merely
accidental, the effect of chance, but as asserting that it is not
the effect of imitation. Now how far Coincidence in this sense
and under the supposed Conditions is possible, I can myself
supply an instance, which happened at my Lectures in Flower
de Luce Court only last week, and the accuracy of which does
not rely on *my* evidence only, but can be proved by the
separate testimony of some hundred Individuals—that is, by
as many as have attended & retained any distinct recollection

of my Lectures at the Royal Institution or at Fetter Lane. After the close of my Lecture on Romeo and Juliet a German Gentleman, a Mr Bernard Krusve, introduced himself to me, and after some courteous Compliments said, Were it not almost impossible, I must have believed that you had either heard or read my Countryman Schlegel's Lecture on this play, given at Vienna: the principles, thought, and the very illustrations are so nearly the same—But the Lectures were but just published as I left Germany, scarcely more than a week since—& the only two Copies of the Work in England I have reason to think, that I myself have brought over. One I retain: the other is at Mr Boosy's—I replied that I had not even heard of these Lectures, nor had indeed seen any work of Schlegel's except a volume of Translations from Spanish Poetry, which the Baron Von Humboldt had lent me when I was at Rome—one piece of which, a Translation of a Play of Calderon I had compared with the original, & formed in consequence a high Opinion of Schlegel's Taste & Genius.— A Friend standing by me added—This cannot be a question of Dates, Sir! for if the gentleman, whose name you have mentioned, first gave his Lectures at Vienna in 1810 I can myself bear witness, that I heard Mr Coleridge deliver all the *substance* of to night's Lecture at the Royal Institution some years before.—The next morning Mr Krusve called on me & made me a present of the Work; and as much as the Resemblance of the L. of L.M. fell below the anticipations which the accounts of others were calculated to excite, so much did this Work transcend.—Not in one Lecture, but in all the Lectures that related to Shakespear, or to Poetry in general, the Grounds, Train of Reasoning, &c were different in language only—& often not even in that—. The Thoughts too were so far peculiar, that to the best of my knowlege they did not exist in any prior work of Criticism—Yet I was far more flattered, or to speak more truly, I was more confirmed, than surprize[d]. For Schlegel & myself had both studied deeply & perseverantly the philosophy of Kant, the distin- guishing feature of which [is] to treat every subject in reference to the operation of the mental Faculties, to which it specially appertains—& to commence by the cautious dis- crimination of what is essential, i.e. explicable by mere consideration of the Faculties in themselves, from what is empirical—i.e. the modifying or disturbing Forces of Time, Place, and Circumstances. Suppose myself & Schlegel (my argument not my vanity leads to these seeming Self-flatteries) nearly equal in natural powers, of similar pursuits & acquirements, and it is only necessary for both to have mastered the spirit of Kant's Critique of the Judgment to render it morally certain, that writing on the same Subject we should draw the same conclusions by the same trains [of reasoning] from the same principles, write to one purpose & with one spirit.

Now, Sir! apply this to Mr W. Scott. If his Poem had been in any sense a borrowed thing, it's Elements likewise would surely be assumed, not native. But no insect was ever more like in the color of it's skin & juices to the Leaf, it fed on, than Scott's Muse is to Scott himself—Habitually conversant with the antiquities of his Country, & of all Europe during the ruder periods of Society, living as it were, in whatever is found in them imposing either to the Fancy or interesting to the Feelings, passionately fond of natural Scenery, abundant in local Anecdote, and besides learned in

> all the antique Scrolls of Faery Land,
> Processions, Tournaments, Spells, Chivalry°—

in all languages from Apuleius to Tam o' Shanter°—how else or what else could he have been expected to write? If I dared prophecy, I would say that Posterity will blame him, if at all, for being totus [in toto, all in all]. —His Poems are evidently the indigenous Products of his Mind & Habits.—

But I have wearied myself, & shall weary you.—I will only add, that I have a volume of Poems now before me, compleatly made up of gross plagiarisms from Akenside, Thomson, Bowles, Southey, & the Lyrical Ballads—it is curious to observe how many artifices the poor Author has used to disguise the theft, transpositions, dilutions, substitutions of Synonimes, &c &c—and yet not the least resemblance to any one of the Poets whom he has pillaged.—He who can catch the Spirit of an original, has it already. It will not [be] by Dates, that Posterity will judge of the originality of a Poem; but by the original spirit itself. This is to be found neither in a

Tale however interesting, which is but the Canvass, no nor yet in the Fancy or the Imagery—which are but Forms & Colors—it is a subtle Spirit, all in each part, reconciling & unifying all— Passion and Imagination are it's *most* appropriate names; but even these say little—for it must be not merely Passion but poetic Passion, poetic Imagination.—

To Charles Lamb

[In October 1810 a mutual acquaintance, Basil Montagu, caused a permanent rift between Wordsworth and Coleridge by telling Coleridge that Wordsworth had 'commissioned' him to say that he had no hope of Coleridge, that he had been 'an absolute nuisance' in the household, and that he was a 'rotten drunkard'. Coleridge immediately broke with both Wordsworth and Montagu, and went to live with John Morgan and his family. As rumours spread, however, Wordsworth came to feel that something must be done, and in 1812 he arrived in London seeking an explanation. The quarrel was eventually patched up through the mediation of Crabb Robinson.]

2 May, 1812

My dear Charles

I should almost deserve what I have suffered, if I refused even to put my Life in Hazard in defence of my own Honor & Veracity, and in satisfaction of the Honor of a Friend. I say, *Honor*, in the latter instance, singly: because I never felt as a matter of serious Complaint, *what* was stated to have been said—(for this, tho' painfully aggravated, was yet substantially true(—but *by* WHOM it was said, and *to* whom, & *how* & *when*.—Grievously unseasonable therefore as it is, that I should again be overtaken & hurried back by the Surge, just as I had begun to feel the firm Ground under my feet—just as I had flattered myself, & given reason to my hospitable Friends to flatter themselves, that I had regained Tranquillity, & had become quite myself—at the time too, when every Thought should be given to my Lectures, on the success or failure of my efforts in which no small part of my reputation & future Prospects will depend —yet if Wordsworth, upon reflection, adheres to the Plan proposed, *I* will not draw back.—It is right, however, that I should state one or two things—First, that it has been my constant desire that evil should not propagate evil—or the unhappy accident become the means of *spreading* Dissension.—2—that I never quarreled with Mr Montagu—say rather, for that is the real truth, that Mr Montagu never was, or appeared to me, a man with whom I could without self-contempt allow myself to quarrel.—And lastly, that in the present Business there are but three possible cases—either, 1, Mr. Wordsworth said what I solemnly aver that I most distinctly recollect Mr Montagu's representing him as having said, and which *I* understood not merely as great unkindness & even cruelty but as an intentional mean of putting an end to our long Friendship, or to the terms at least under which it had for so long a period subsisted—or, 2, Mr Montagu has grossly mispresented Wordsworth & most cruelly & wantoned [wantonly ?] injured me—or (3) I have wantonly invented & deliberately persevered in atrocious falsehoods, which place me in the same relation to Mr. Montagu, as (in the second case) Mr Montagu would stand in to me. If therefore Mr Montagu declares to my face that he did not say what I solemnly aver that he did—what must be the consequence, unless I am a more abject Coward than I have hitherto suspected, I need not say.°—

Be the consequences, *what* they may, however, I will not shrink from doing my Duty; but previously to the meeting I should very much wish to transmit to Wordsworth a statement which I long ago begun with the intention of sending it to Mrs Wordsworth's Sister—but desisted in consequence of understanding that she had already decided the matter against me—. My reason for wishing this is that I think it right that Wordsworth should know & have the means of ascertaining, some conversations which yet I could not publicly bring forward without hazarding great disquiet in a family, known (tho' slightly) to Wordsworth—2. because common Humanity would embarrass me in stating before a Man what I and others think of his Wife—& lastly, certain other points which my own delicacy and that due to Wordsworth himself & his family preclude from being talked of —for Wordsworth ought not to forget that whatever influence old associations may have on his mind respecting

Montagu, yet that *I* never respected or liked him—for if I had
ever in a *common* degree done so, I should have quarreled with
him long before we arrived in London.—Yet all these facts
ought to be known—because supposing Montagu to affirm
what I am led to suppose, he has—then nothing remains but
the comparative Probability of our two accounts—& for this
the state of my feelings towards Wordsworth & his family, my
opinion of Mr & Mrs Montagu, and my previous intention not
to lodge with them in town, are important documents as far as
they do not rely on my own present assertions.—Woe is me,
that a friendship of 15 years should come to this!—and such a
friendship, in which, I call God Almighty to be my witness, as
I ever thought it no more than my Duty, so did I ever feel a
readiness to prefer him to myself, yea, even if Life & outward
Reputation itself had been the pledge required—But this is
now vain talking—Be it, however, remembered that I have
never wandered beyond the one single complaint, that I had
been cruelly & unkindly treated—I made no charge against
my friend's Veracity, even in respect to his charges against
me—that I have explained the circumstance to those only,
who had already more or less perfectly become acquainted
with our difference or were certain to hear of it from
others—& that except on this one point no word of reproach,
or even of subtraction from his good name, as a good man, or
from his merits as a great man, ever escaped me—May God
bless you, my dear Charles! &

S. T. Coleridge—

To William Wordsworth

Monday, 4 May 1812.
71, Berners' Street.

I will divide my statement, which I will endeavor to send
you tomorrow, into two Parts, in separate Letters. The latter
commencing from Sunday Night, 28 October 1810, i.e. that on
which the communication was made to me, and which will
contain my solemn avowal of what was said by Mr & Mrs
Montagu, you will make what use of, you please—but the

former I write to you, and in *confidence*—yet only as far as to your own heart it shall appear evident, that in desiring it I am actuated by no wish to shrink personally from any Test, not involving an acknowlegement of my own degradation, & so to become a false witness against myself, but only by delicacy towards the feelings of others, and the dread of spreading the curse of Dissention. But, Wordsworth! the very message, you sent by Lamb & which *Lamb* did not deliver to me from the anxiety not to add fuel to the flame, sufficiently proves what I had learnt on my first arrival at Keswick, & which alone prevented my going to Grasmere—namely, that you had prejudged the case. As soon as I was informed, that you had denied having used certain expressions, I did not hesitate a moment (nor was it in my power to do so) to give you my fullest faith, and approve to my own consciousness the truth of my declaration, that I should have felt it as a blessing, tho' my Life had the same instant been hazarded as the pledge, could I with firm conviction have given Montagu the Lie at the conclusion of his Story, even as at the very first sentence I exclaimed—'Impossible! It is impossible!'—The expressions denied were indeed only the most offensive part to the feelings—but at the same time I learnt that you did not hesitate instantly to express your conviction, that Montagu never said those words & that I had invented them—or (to use your own words) 'had forgotten myself.' Grievously indeed, if I know aught of my nature, must I have forgotten both myself & common Honesty, could I have been villain enough to have invented & persevered in such atrocious falsehoods.—Your message was that 'if I declined an explanation, you begged I would no longer continue to talk about the affair.'—When, Wordsworth, did I ever decline an explanation? From you I expected one, & had a right to expect it: for let Montagu have added what he may, still that which remained was most unkind & what I had little deserved from you who might by a single question have learnt from me that I never made up my mind to lodge with Montagu and had tacitly acquiesced in it at Keswick to tranquillize Mrs Coleridge to whom Mrs Montagu had made the earnest professions of watching & nursing me, & for whom this & her extreme repugnance to my original, & much wiser, resolution

of going to Edingburgh & placing myself in the House, and
under the constant eye, of some medical man, were the sole
grounds of her assent that I should leave the North at
all.—Yet at least a score of times have I begun to write a
detailed account, to Wales & afterwards to Grasmere, & gave
it up from excess of agitation,—till finally I learnt that *all* of
your family had decided against me unheard.—*And that I
would no longer talk about it*—If, Wordsworth, you had but done
me the common justice of asking those with whom I have been
most intimate & confidential since my first arrival in Town in
Oct. 1810, you would have received either negative or positive
proofs how little I needed the admonition, or deserved the
sarcasm. Talk about it? O God! it *has* been talked about—! &
that it had, was the sole occasion of my disclosing it even to
Mary Lamb, the first person who heard of it from me—and
that not voluntarily—but that morning a Friend met me, &
communicated what so agitated me that then having previously
meant to call at Lamb's I was compelled to do so from
faintness & universal Trembling, in order to sit down.—Even
to her I did not intend to mention it; but alarmed by the
wildness & paleness of my Countenance & agitation I had no
power to conceal, she entreated me to tell her what was the
matter. In the first attempt to speak, my feelings overpowered
me, an agony of weeping followed, & then alarmed at my own
imprudence and conscious of the possible effect on her health
& mind if I left her in that state of suspense, I brought out
convulsively some such words as—Wordsworth—Wordsworth
has given me up. *He* has no hope of me—I have been an
absolute Nuisance in his family—And when long Weeping
had relieved me, & I was able to relate the occurrence
connectedly, she can bear witness for me, that disgraceful, as
it was, that I should be made the Topic of vulgar Gossip, yet
that 'had the whole & ten times worse, been proclaimed by a
Speaking Trumpet from the Chimneys, I should have smiled
at it—or indulged indignation only as far as it excited me to
pleasurable activity—; —but that *you* had said it, this & this
only, was the Sting! the Scorpion-tooth!'—Mr Morgan &
afterwards his Wife & her Sister were made acquainted with
the whole Case—& Why? Not merely that I owed it to their
ardent Friendship, which has continued to be my main

comfort and my only support, but because they had already heard of it, in part—because a most intimate & dear Friend of Mr & Mrs Montagu's had urged Mr Morgan to call at the Montagues in order to be put on his guard against me. He came to me instantly, told me that I had enemies at work against my character, & pressed me to leave the Hotel & to come home with him—with whom I have been ever since, with exception of a few Intervals when from the bitter consciousness of my own infirmities & increasing inequality of Temper I took lodgings against his will & was always by his zealous friendship brought back again. If it be allowed to call any one on earth Saviour, Morgan & his Family have been my Saviours, Body and Soul. For my moral Will was, & I fear is, so weakened relatively to my Duties to myself, that I cannot act, as I ought to do, except under the influencing knowlege of it's effects on those I love & believe myself loved by. To him likewise I explained the affair: but neither from him or his family has one word ever escaped concerning it.—Last Autumn Mr & Mrs Southey came to town and at Mr May's at Richmond, as we were walking alone in the Garden, the Subject was introduced—& it became my Duty to state the whole affair to them, even as the means of transmitting it to you.—With these exceptions I do not remember ever to have made any one my Confidant—tho' in two or three instances I have alluded to the suspension of our familiar Intercourse without explanation, but even here only where I knew or fully believed the persons to have already heard of it.—Such was Mrs Clarkson, who wrote to me in consequence of one sentence in a Letter to her—yet even to her I entered into no Detail, & disclosed nothing that was not necessary to my own defence in not continuing my former correspondence.—In short, the one only thing which I have to blame in myself was that in my first Letter to Sir G. Beaumont I had concluded with a desponding remark allusive to the Breach between us, not in the slightest degree suspecting that he was ignorant of it—In the Letters, which followed, I was compelled to say more (tho' I never detailed the words which had been uttered to me) in consequence of Lady Beaumont's expressed apprehension & alarm lest in the advertisement for my Lectures the sentence 'concerning the Living Poets' contained

an intention on my part to attack your literary merits.—The
very Thought, that I could be imagined capable of feeling
vindictively toward you at all, much more of gratifying the
passion in so despicable as well as detestable manner, agitated
me—I sent her Ladyship the verses composed after your
recitation of the great Poem at Cole-orton & desired her to
judge whether it was possible that a man, who had written
that Poem, could be capable of such an act°—and in a Letter
to Sir G. B. anxious to remove from his mind the assumption,
that I had been agitated by the disclosure of any till then
unknown actions of mine or parts of conduct, I endeavored to
impress him with the real truth: that not the facts disclosed,
but the manner & time & the person by whom & the persons
to whom they had been disclosed, formed the whole ground of
the Breach.—And writing in great agitation I once again used
the same words which had venially burst from me the
moment, Montagu had ended his account—O this is cruel!
this is *base*!—I did not reflect on it till it was irrevocable—&
for that one word, the only word of positive reproach that ever
escaped from me, I feel sorrow—& assure you, that there is no
permanent feeling in my heart which corresponds to it.—Talk
about it?—Those who have seen me & been with me, day after
day, for so many many months could have told you, how
anxiously every allusion to the Subject was avoided—and
with abundant reason—for immediate & palpable derangement of Body as well as Spirits regularly followed it.—Besides
had there not existed in your mind—let me rather say, if ever
there had existed any portion of Esteem & Regard for me
since the Autumn of 1810, would it have been possible that
your quick and powerful Judgement could have overlooked
the gross improbability, that I should first invent & then
scatter abroad for Talk at Public Tables the phrases, which
(Mr Robinson yesterday informed me) Mr Sharon Turner
was indelicate enough to trumpet abroad at Longman's
Table?°—I at least will call on Mr Sharon and demand his
authority. —It is my full conviction, that in no one of the
hundred Tables at which any *particulars* of our Breach have
been mentioned, could the Authority be traced back to those
who had received the account from myself.
It seemed unnatural to me, nay, it was unnatural to me to

write to you or to any of your family with a cold exclusion of
the feelings which almost [over]power me even at this
moment—& I therefore write this preparatory Letter, to
disburthen my heart, as it were, before I sit down to detail my
recollections simply, and unmixed with the anguish which
spite of my best efforts accompany them.

But one thing more—the last Complaint that you will hear
from me, perhaps. When without my knowlege dear Mary
Lamb, just then on the very verge of a Relapse, wrote to
Grasmere, was it kind or even humane to have returned such
an answer, as Lamb deemed it unadvisable to shew me; but
which I learnt from the only other person, who saw the
answer, amounted in Substance to a Sneer on my reported
high Spirits & my wearing Powder? —When & to whom did I
ever make a merit of my Sufferings?—Is it consistent *now* to
charge me with going about complaining to every body, & *now*
with my high Spirits?—Was I to carry a gloomy face into
every society? or ought I not rather to be grateful, that in the
natural activity of my Intellect God had given me a
counteracting principle to the intensity of my feelings, & a
means of escaping from a part of the Pressure?—But for this I
had been driven mad—& yet for how many months was there
a continual Brooding & going on of the one gnawing
Recollection behind the curtain of my outward Being even
when I was most exerting myself—and exerting myself more
in order the more to benumb it! I might have truly said, with
Desdemona,

> I am not merry, but I do beguile
> The Thing, I am, by seeming otherwise.°

And as to the Powder, it was first put in to prevent my taking
Cold after my Hair had been thinned, & I was advised to
continue it till I became wholly grey—as in it's then state it
looked as if I had dirty powder in my hair, & even when
known to be only the everywhere intermixed grey, yet
contrasting with a face even younger than my real age gave a
queer & contradictory character to my whole appearance.—
Whatever be the result of this long delayed explanation, I
have loved you & your's too long & too deeply to have it in my
own power to cease to do so.   S. T. Coleridge.

To Joseph Cottle

[Cottle had written to Coleridge exhorting him to pull himself together, abandon opium, return to his family, and make use of 'the ample abilities which God has given you'.]

April 26, 1814

You have poured oil in the raw and festering Wound of an old friend's Conscience, Cottle! but it is oil of Vitriol!° I but barely glanced at the middle of the first page of your Letter, & have seen no more of it—not from resentment (God forbid!) but from the state of my bodily & mental sufferings, that scarcely permitted human fortitude to let in a new visitor of affliction. The object of my present reply is to state the case just as it is—first, that for years the anguish of my spirit has been indescribable, the sense of my danger *staring*, but the conscience of my GUILT worse, far far worse than all!—I have prayed with drops of agony on my Brow, trembling not only before the Justice of my Maker, but even before the Mercy of my Redeemer. 'I gave thee so many Talents. What hast thou done with them'?°—Secondly—that it is false & cruel to say, (overwhelmed as I am with the sense of my direful Infirmity) that I attempt or ever have attempted to *disguise* or conceal the cause. On the contrary, not only to friends have I stated the whole Case with tears & the very bitterness of shame; but in two instances I have warned young men, mere acquaintances who had spoken of having taken Laudanum, of the direful Consequences, by an ample exposition of it's tremendous effects on myself—Thirdly, tho' before God I dare not lift up my eyelids, & only do not despair of his Mercy because to despair would be adding crime to crime; yet to my fellow-men I may say, that I was seduced into the ACCURSED Habit ignorantly.—I had been almost bed-ridden for many months with swellings in my knees—in a medical Journal I unhappily met with an account of a cure performed in a similar case (or what to me appeared so) by rubbing in of Laudanum, at the same time taking a given dose internally—It acted like a charm, like a miracle! I recovered the use of my Limbs, of my appetite, of my Spirits—& this continued for near a fortnight

—At length, the unusual Stimulus subsided—the complaint returned—the supposed remedy was recurred to——but I can not go thro' the dreary history—suffice it to say, that effects were produced, which acted on me by *Terror* & *Cowardice* of PAIN & sudden Death, not (so help me God!) by any temptation of Pleasure, or expectation or desire of exciting pleasurable Sensations. On the very contrary, Mrs Morgan & her Sister will bear witness so far, as to say that the longer I abstained, the higher my spirits were, the keener my enjoyments—till the moment, the direful moment, arrived, when my pulse began to fluctuate, my Heart to palpitate, & such a dreadful *falling-abroad*, as it were, of my whole frame, such intolerable Restlessness & incipient Bewilderment, that in the last of my several attempts to abandon the dire poison, I exclaimed in agony, what I now repeat in seriousness & solemnity—'I am too poor to hazard this! Had I but a few hundred Pounds, but 200£, half to send to Mrs Coleridge, & half to place myself in a private madhouse, where I could procure nothing but what a Physician thought proper, & where a medical attendant could be constantly with me for two or three months (in less than that time Life or Death would be determined) then there might be Hope. Now there is none!'—O God! how willingly would I place myself under Dr Fox in his Establishment—for my Case is a species of madness, only that it is a derangement, an utter impotence of the *Volition*, & not of the intellectual Faculties—You bid me rouse myself—go, bid a man paralytic in both arms rub them briskly together, & that will cure him. Alas! (he would reply) that I cannot move my arms is my Complaint & my misery.—

My friend, Wade, is not at home—& I sent off all the little money, I had—or I would with this have inclosed the 10£ received from you.—

May God bless you | & | Your affectionate & | most afflicted
S. T. Coleridge.—

Dr Estlin, I found, is raising the city against me, as far as he & his friends can, for having stated a mere matter of fact, . . . —viz—that Milton had represented Satan as a sceptical Socinian°—which is the case, & I could not have explained the excellence of the sublimest single Passage in all his

Writings had I not previously informed the Audience, that
Milton had represented Satan as knowing the prophetic &
Messianic Character of Christ, but sceptical as to any higher
Claims—& what other definition could Dr E. himself give of a
sceptical Socinian?—Now that M. has done so, please to
consult, Par. Regained, Book IV. from line 196.—& then the
same Book from line 500.—

To J. J. Morgan

14 May, Saturday [1814]
2. Queen's Square—

My dear Morgan

If it could be said with as little *appearance* of profaneness, as
there is feeling or intention in my mind, I might affirm; that I
had been crucified, dead, and buried, descended into *Hell*, and
am now, I humbly trust, rising again, tho' slowly and
gradually.° I thank you from my heart for your far too kind
Letter to Mr Hood—so much of it is true that such as you
described I always wished to be. I know, it will be vain to
attempt to persuade Mrs Morgan or Charlotte, that a man,
whose moral feelings, reason, understanding, and senses are
perfectly sane and vigorous, may yet have been *mad*—And yet
nothing is more true. By the long long Habit of the accursed
Poison my Volition (by which I mean the faculty *instrumental*
to the Will, and by which alone the Will can realize itself—it's
Hands, Legs, & Feet, as it were) was compleatly deranged, at
times frenzied, dissevered itself from the Will, & became an
independent faculty: so that I was perpetually in the state, in
which you may have seen paralytic Persons, who attempting
to push a step forward in one direction are violently forced
round to the opposite. I was sure that no ease, much less
pleasure, would ensue: nay, was certain of an accumulation of
pain. But tho' there was no prospect, no gleam of Light before,
an indefinite indescribable Terror as with a scourge of ever
restless, ever coiling and uncoiling Serpents, drove me on from
behind.—The worst was, that in *exact proportion* to the
importance and *urgency* of any Duty was it, as of a fatal necessity,

sure to be neglected: because it added to the Terror above described. In exact proportion, as I *loved* any person or persons more than others, & would have sacrificed my Life for them, were *they* sure to be the most barbarously mistreated by silence, absence, or breach of promise.—I used to think St James's Text, 'He who offendeth in one point of the Law, offendeth in all',° very harsh; but my own sad experience has taught me it's aweful, dreadful Truth.—What crime is there scarcely which has not been included in or followed from the one guilt of taking opium? Not to speak of ingratitude to my maker for the wasted Talents; of ingratitude to so many friends who have loved me I know not why; of barbarous neglect of my family; excess of cruelty to Mary & Charlotte, when at Box, and both ill—(a vision of Hell to me when I think of it!) I have in this one dirty business of Laudanum an hundred times deceived, tricked, nay, actually & consciously LIED.—And yet *all* these vices are so opposite to my nature, that but for this *free-agency-annihilating* Poison, I verily believe that I should have suffered myself to have been cut to pieces rather than have committed any one of them.

At length, it became too bad. I used to take [from] 4 to 5 ounces a day of Laudanum, once . . . [ou]nces, i.e. near a Pint—besides great quantities [of liquo]r. From the Sole of my foot to the Crown of [my h]eart° there was not an Inch in which I was not [contin]ually in torture: for more than a fortnight no [sleep] ever visited my Eye lids—but the agonies of [remor]se were far worse than all!—Letters past between Cottle, Hood, & myself—& our kind Friend, Hood, sent Mr Daniel to me. At his second Call I told him plainly (for I had sculked out the night before & got Laudanum) that while I was in my own power, all would be in vain—I should inevitably cheat & trick *him*, just as I had done Dr Tuthill —that I must either be removed to a place of confinement, or at all events have a Keeper.—Daniel saw the truth of my observations, & my most faithful excellent friend, Wade, procured a strong-bodied, but decent, meek, elderly man, to superintend me, under the name of my Valet—All in the House were forbidden to fetch any thing but by the Doctor's order.—Daniel generally spends two or three hours a day with me—and already from 4 & 5 ounces has brought me down to four tea-spoonfuls in the 24 Hours—The terror & the indefinite craving are gone—& he expects to drop it altogether by the middle of next week—Till a day or two after that I would rather not see you.

To J. J. Morgan

Sunday, 15 May, 1814.
2. Queen's Square.

My dear Morgan

To continue from my last—Such was the direful state of my mind, that (I tell it you with horror) the razors, penknife, & every possible instrument of Suicide it was found necessary to remove from my room! My faithful, my *inexhaustibly patient* Friend, WADE, has caused a person to sleep by my bed side, on a bed on the floor: so that I might never be altogether alone—O Good God! why do such good men love me! At times, it would be more delightful to me to lie in the Kennel,° & (as Southey said) 'unfit to be pulled out by any honest man except with a pair of Tongs.'—What *he* then said (perhaps) rather unkindly of me, was prophetically true! Often have I wished to have been thus trodden & spit upon, if by any means it might be an atonement for the direful guilt, that (like all others) first *smiled* on me, like Innocence! then crept closer, & yet closer, till it had thrown it's serpent folds round & round me, and I was no longer in my own power!—*Something* even the most wretched of Beings (*human* Beings at least) owes to himself—& this I *will* say & *dare* with truth say—that never was I led to this wicked direful practice of taking Opium or Laudanum by any desire or expectation of exciting *pleasurable* sensations; but purely by *terror*, by cowardice of pain, first of mental pain, & afterwards as my System became weakened, even of bodily Pain.

My Prayers have been fervent, in agony of Spirit, and for hours together, incessant! still ending, O! only for the merits, for the agonies, for the cross of my blessed Redeemer! For I am nothing, but evil—I can do nothing, but evil! Help, Help!—I believe! help thou my unbelief!°—

Mr Daniel has been the wisest of physicians to me. I cannot say, how much I am indebted both to his Skill and Kindness. But he is one of the few rare men, who can make even their Kindness Skill, & the best and most unaffected Virtues of their Hearts *professionally* useful.

Anxious as I am to see you, yet I would wish to delay it till some 3 days after the total abandonment of the Poison. I expect, that this will commence on Tuesday next.—

Dr Estlin has contrived not only to pick a gratuitous quarrel with me, but by his female agents to rouse men who should be ashamed of such folly, for my saying in a Lecture on the Paradise Regained, that Milton had been pleased to represent the Devil as a sceptical Socinian.° Alas! if I *should* get well—wo! to the poor Doctor, & to his Unitarians! They have treated me so ungenerously, that I am by the allowance of all my friends let loose from all bands of delicacy. Estlin has behaved downright cruel & brutal to me.—

I scarce know what to say or to bid you say to Mary or to Charlotte°—for I cannot, of course, address myself to the reason of Women—& all that their common sense, their experience, & their feelings, suggest to them, must be irreversably against me. Nevertheless, strange as it must appear to them & perhaps incredible, it is still true, that I not only have loved ever, and still do *love* them; but that there never was a moment, in which I would not have shed my very blood for their sakes—At the very worst, I never neglected them but when in an hundred fold degree I was injuring myself. But this I cannot expect women to understand or believe—& must take the alienation of Mary's & Charlotte's esteem & affection among the due punishments of my Crime—

I am as much pleased as it is possible I can be at present in the present state of my body & mind at the improving state of your Affairs. Nothing would give me truer delight, than being recovered, to be able by my exertions to aid you: and assuredly, either this will [be] the case, or my Death.

I ought to say, that Mr Daniel is *sanguine* respecting my total recovery: tho' he admits, that after the Laudanum has been totally discontinued, there must be a long process to remedy the ravages in my constitution, which it has caused, &

to bring down my carcase to something like a bulk proportionate to my years—

Allston has altogether forgot me: but I have not forgot
him!—but I am an Englishman, & he is an American!—I was
in my bitterest affliction glad to hear that his Picture had been
noticed, however unworthily & by such a scurvy set of Judges.
I intreated Bird to call on him and intreat him to write to me,
tho' but *two* Lines—But I fear, Allston, tho' the very best &
prime, is an American!

I dare not ask you to give my Love to Mary—it is sufficient,
that she has it.—As soon as I am better, if I do not come over,
I will write & ask you to come over hither after Miss Brent's
Return from London—

Your affectionate Friend
S. T. Coleridge

To Joseph Cottle

Friday, 27 May 1814

My dear Cottle

Gladness be with you for your convalescence, and equally
at the Hope which has sustained and tranquillized you thro'
your imminent Peril. Far otherwise is & hath been my
state—yet I too am grateful, tho' I can not rejoice. I feel, with
an intensity unfathomable by words, my utter nothingness,
impotence, & worthlessness, in and for myself—I have learnt
what a sin is against an infinite imperishable Being, such as is
the Soul of Man—I have had more than a Glimpse of what is
meant by Death, & utter Darkness, & the Worm that dieth
not°—and that all the Hell of the Reprobate is no more
inconsistent with the Love of God, than the Blindness of one
who has occasioned loathsome and guilty Diseases to eat out
his eyes, is inconsistent with the Light of the Sun. But the
consolations, at least the *sensible* sweetness, of Hope, I do *not*
possess. On the contrary, the Temptation, which I have
constantly to fight up against, is a fear that if Annihilation &
the *possibility* of Heaven were offered to my choice, I should
choose the former.

This is, perhaps, in part, a constitutional Idiosyncrasy: for when a *mere Boy* I wrote these Lines—

> O what a wonder seems the fear of Death,
> Seeing, how gladly we all sink to Sleep,
> Babes, children, Youths, & Men,
> Night following Night for threescore years & ten!°

And in my early manhood in lines, descriptive of a gloomy solitude, I disguised my own sensations in the following words—

> Here Wisdom might abide, & here Remorse!
> Here too the woe-worn Man, who weak in Soul,
> And of this busy human Heart aweary,
> Worships the spirit of *unconscious Life*
> In Tree or Wild-flower.—Gentle Lunatic!
> If so he might not *wholly cease* to BE,
> He would far rather not be that, he is;
> But would be something, that he knows not of,
> In Woods or Waters or among the Rocks.°—

My main Comfort therefore consists in what the Divines call, *the Faith of Adherence*—and no spiritual Effort appears to benefit me so much, as the one, earnest, importunate, & often for hours momently [repeated], Prayer: 'I believe! Lord, help my Unbelief! Give me Faith but as a mustard Seed: & I shall remove this mountain! Faith! Faith! Faith! I believe—O give me Faith! O for my Redeemer's sake give me Faith in my Redeemer.'

In all this I justify God: for I was accustomed to oppose the preaching of the Terrors of the Gospel, & to represent it as debasing Virtue by admixture of slavish Selfishness. I now see that what is spiritual can only be spiritually *apprehended*—comprehended It cannot be.

Mr Eden gave you a too flattering account of me. It is true, I am restored as much beyond my expectations almost, as my Deserts; but I am *exceedingly* weak, & need for myself solace & refocillation° of animal spirits, instead of being in a condition of offering it to others.—Yet as soon as I can, I will call on you.

S. T. Coleridge

P.S. It is no small gratification to me, that I have seen &
conversed with Mrs H. More°—She is indisputably the *first*
literary female, I ever met with—In part, no doubt, because
she is a Christian.—Make my best respects when you write—

To Josiah Wade

Bristol, June 26th, 1814

Dear Sir,

For I am unworthy to call any good man friend—much less
you, whose hospitality and love I have abused; accept,
however, my intreaties for your forgiveness, and for your
prayers.

Conceive a poor miserable wretch, who for many years has
been attempting to beat off pain, by a constant recurrence to
the vice that reproduces it. Conceive a spirit in hell, employed
in tracing out for others the road to that heaven, from which
his crimes exclude him! In short, conceive whatever is most
wretched, helpless, and hopeless, and you will form as
tolerable a notion of my state, as it is possible for a good man
to have.

I used to think the text in St. James that 'he who offended in
one point, offends in all,' very harsh;° but I now feel the awful,
the tremendous truth of it. In the one crime of OPIUM, what
crime have I not made myself guilty of!—Ingratitude to my
Maker! and to my benefactors—injustice! *and unnatural cruelty
to my poor children!*—self-contempt for my repeated promise—
breach, nay, too often, actual falsehood!

After my death, I earnestly entreat, that a full and
unqualified narration of my wretchedness, and of its guilty
cause, may be made public, that at least some little good may
be effected by the direful example!

May God Almighty bless you, and have mercy on your still
affectionate, and in his heart, grateful—

S. T. Coleridge.

To Joseph Cottle

March 7—1815

My dear Cottle

I received by means of Mr Wade's Son your 'Messiah'° a few days ago: or by Mr Hood, I do not remember which. I have read about one half; and tho' I myself see your plan, yet I find it difficult to explain it to the Public, so as to make it consistent with the received conception of a Poem, call it epic, heroic, divine or what you like. The common end of all *narrative*, nay, of *all*, Poems is to convert a *series* into a *Whole*: to make those events, which in real or imagined History move on in a *strait* Line, assume to our Understandings a *circular* motion—the snake with it's Tail in it's Mouth. Hence indeed the almost flattering and yet appropriate Term, Poesy—i.e. poiēsis = *making*. Doubtless, to *his* eye, which alone comprehends all Past and all Future in one eternal Present, what to our short sight appears strait is but a part of the great Cycle—just as the calm Sea to us *appears* level, tho' it be indeed only a part of a *globe*. Now what the Globe is in Geography, *miniaturing* in order to *manifest* the Truth, such is a Poem to that Image of God, which we were created into, and which still seeks that Unity, or Revelation of the *One* in and by the *Many*, which reminds it, that tho' in order to be an individual Being it must go forth *from* God, yet as the *re*ceding from *him* is to *pro*ceed towards Nothingness and Privation, it must still at every step turn back toward him in order to *be* at all—Now a straight Line, continuously retracted forms of necessity a circular orbit. Now God's Will and Word CANNOT be frustrated. His aweful *Fiat* was with ineffable awefulness applied to Man, when all things and all living Things, Man himself (as a mere animal) included, were called forth by the Universal—*Let there be*—and then the Breath of the Eternal superadded to make an *immortal* Spirit—immortality being, as the author of the 'Wisdom of Solomon' profoundly expresses it, the only possible Reflex or Image of Eternity.° The Immortal Finite is the contracted Shadow of the Eternal Infinite.—Therefore *nothingness* or *Death*, to which we move as we recede from God & the Word, *cannot* be nothing; but that tremendous Medium between Nothing and true Being, which Scripture & inmost Reason present as most, most horrible! I have said this to shew you the connection between things in themselves comparatively trifling, and things the most important, by their derivation from common sources.—

The addition of Fiction, such as that of the Quarrel between Satan & Beelzebub, could not have been blamed (unless we blame the Paradise Lost) had it been written before the Paradise Lost. But as all your Readers have learnt from Milton alone, that Satan & Beelzebub were different Persons (in the Scriptures they are different names of the same Evil Being) it produces an effect too light, too much savoring of capricious Invention, for the exceeding Solemnity of the Subject. These are the two faults of your Poem. I do not say, these appear to me: because, my dear Cottle, if I am not *sure* of this, I have no sense of Surety: and I must write to you in *sincerity*—i.e. sine cerâ, without *wax*, entire, unrivetted.—But with the same sincerity I can and will say, and that forthwith, thro' the best channel, I can procure (alas! I have no interest in the Edingburgh or Quarterly Reviews; but in the Eclectic or the Christian Observer I hope to have my Review inserted) that all exclusive of the Plan is most praise-worthy—that the Plan, as it is, is well executed—that the fine passages capable of quotation as separate Flowers are many—and that the metre and language rise in simplicity, dignity, & variety, above some of the very *Idols* of the Age.—

You will wish to know something of myself. In Health, I am not worse than when at Bristol I was best—yet fluctuating, yet unhappy—in circumstances [. . .] poor indeed! I have collected my scattered & my Manuscript Poems sufficient to make one volume—Enough I have to make another. But till the latter is finished, I cannot, without great Loss of character, publish the former—on account of the arrangement—besides the necessity of corrections. For instance, I earnestly wish to begin the Volumes with what has never been seen by any, however few—such as a series of Odes on the different Sentences of the Lord's Prayer—and more than all this, to finish my greater Work on Christianity, considered as Philosophy and as the only Philosophy. All the materials I have—no small part reduced to form, & written—but O me!

what can I do, when I am so poor that in having to turn off every week from these to some mean Subject for the Newspapers I distress myself, & at last neglect the greater wholly to do *little* of the Less. If it were in your power to receive my manuscripts (for instance, what I have ready for the Press of my Poems) & by setting me forward with 30 or 40£, taking care that what I send & would make over to you, would more than secure you from Loss—I am sure, you would do it—But I would die, after my recent experience of the cruel & insolent Spirit of Calumny, rather than subject myself as a slave to a Club of Subscribers to my Poverty.° If I were to say, I am easy in my Conscience, I should add to it's pains by a Lie; but this I can truly say, that my embarrassments have not been occasioned by the bad parts, or selfish indulgences, of my nature. I am at present five and twenty Pounds in arrear, my expences being at 2£, 10s, per week. You will say, I ought to live for less—and doubtless, I might, if I were to alienate myself from all social affections, and from all Conversation with persons of the same education—. Those, who so severely blame me, never ask whether at any time in my Life I had *for myself* & *my family's* wants, 50£ before hand—God knows, of the 300£ received thro' you *what went to myself*. No, bowed down under manifold infirmities, I yet dare appeal to you for the truth of what I say—that I have remained poor by always having been poor, and incapable of pursuing any one great work for want of a competence before hand—

S. T. Coleridge.

My best regards to your Sisters—Let me, I pray you, at least hear from you & immediately.—

To William Wordsworth

[Wordsworth had written to seek an explanation of the comparatively unenthusiastic opinion of his *Excursion* (1814) expressed by Coleridge in a letter to the Beaumonts.]

30 May 1815

My honored Friend
On my return from Devizes, whither I had gone to procure

some Vaccine matter (the Small Pox having appeared in Calne, and Mrs M's Sister believing herself never to have had it) I found your Letter: and I will answer it immediately, tho' to answer it as I could wish to do would require more recollection and arrangement of Thought than is always to be commanded on the Instant. But I dare not trust my own habit of procrastination—and do what I would, it would be impossible in a single Letter to give more than *general* convictions. But even after a tenth or twentieth Letter I should still be disquieted as knowing how poor a substitute must Letters be for a vivâ voce [oral] examination of a Work with it's Author, Line by Line. It is most uncomfortable from many, many Causes, to express anything but sympathy, and gratulation to an absent friend, to whom for the more substantial Third of a Life we have been habituated to look up: especially, where our Love, tho' increased by many and different influences, yet begun and throve and knit it's Joints in the perception of his Superiority. It is not in *written words*, but by the hundred modifications that Looks make, and Tone, and denial of the FULL sense of the very words used, that one can reconcile the struggle between sincerity and diffidence, between the Persuasion, that I am in the Right, and that as deep tho' not so vivid conviction, that it may be the positiveness of Ignorance rather than the Certainty of Insight. Then come the Human Frailties—the dread of giving pain, or exciting suspicions of alteration and Dyspathy—in short, the almost inevitable Insincerities between imperfect Beings, however sincerely attached to each other. It is hard (and I am *Protestant* enough to doubt whether it is right) to confess the whole Truth even of one's Self—Human Nature scarce endures it even *to* one's Self!—but to me it is still harder to do this of and to a revered Friend.—

But to your Letter. First, I had never determined to print the Lines addressed to you—I lent them to L. Beaumont on her promise that they should be copied and returned—& not knowing of any copy in my own possession I sent for them, because I was making a *Mss* Collection of *all* my poems, publishable or unpublishable—& still more perhaps, for the Handwriting of the only perfect Copy, that entrusted to her Ladyship.°—Most assuredly, I never once thought of printing them without having consulted you—and since I lit on the first rude draught, and corrected it as well as I could, I wanted no additional reason for it's not being published in my Life Time, than it's *personality* respecting myself—After the opinions, I had given publicly, for the preference of the Lycidas (moral no less than poetical) to Cowley's Monody,° I could not have printed it consistently—. It is for the Biographer, not the Poet, to give the *accidents* of *individual* Life. Whatever is not representative, generic, may be indeed most poetically exprest, but is not Poetry. Otherwise, I confess, your prudential Reasons would not have weighed with me, except as far as my name might haply injure your reputation —for there is nothing in the Lines as far [as] your Powers are concerned, which I have not as fully expressed elsewhere— and I hold it a miserable cowardice to withhold a deliberate opinion only because the Man is alive.

2ndly. for the EXCURSION. I feared that had I been silent concerning the Excursion, Lady B. would have drawn some strange inference—& yet I had scarcely sent off the Letter before I repented that I had not run that risk rather than have approach to Dispraise communicated to you by a third person—. But what did my criticism amount to, reduced to it's full and naked Sense?—This: that *comparatively* with the *former* Poem° the excursion, as far as it was new to me, had disappointed my expectations—that the Excellences were so many and of so high a class, that it was impossible to attribute the inferiority, if any such really existed, to any flagging of the Writer's own genius—and that I conjectured that it might have been occasioned by the influence of self-established Convictions having given to certain Thoughts and Expressions a depth & force which they had not for readers in general.—In order therefore to explain the *disappointment* I must recall to your mind what my *expectations* were: and as these again were founded on the supposition, that (in whatever order it might be published) the Poem on the growth of your own mind was as the ground-plat and the Roots, out of which the Recluse was to have sprung up as the Tree—as far as the same Sap in both, I expected them doubtless to have formed one compleat Whole, but in matter, form, and product to be different, each

not only a distinct but a different Work.—In the first I had
found 'themes by thee first sung aright'—

Of Smiles spontaneous and mysterious fears
(The first-born they of Reason and Twin-birth),
Of Tides obedient to external force,
And Currents self-determin'd, as might seem,
Or by some central Breath; of moments aweful,
Now in thy inner Life, and now abroad,
When Power stream'd from thee, and thy Soul received
The Light reflected as a Light bestow'd!—
Of Fancies fair, and milder Hours of Youth,
Hyblaean murmurs of poetic Thought
Industrious in it's Joy, in vales and Glens
Native or outland, Lakes and famous Hills!
Or on the lonely High-road, when the stars
Were rising; or by secret mountain streams,
The Guides and the Companions of thy Way.

Of more than *Fancy*—of the *social sense*
Distending wide and man beloved as man:
Where France in all her towns lay vibrating
Ev'n as a Bark becalm'd beneath the Burst
Of Heaven's immediate Thunder, when no Cloud
Is visible, or Shadow on the Main!—
For Thou wert there, thy own Brows garlanded,
Amid the tremor of a realm aglow,
Amid a mighty Nation jubilant,
When from the general Heart of Human Kind
HOPE sprang forth, like a full-born Deity!
Of that dear Hope afflicted, and amaz'd,
So homeward summon'd! thenceforth calm & sure
From the dread Watch tower of man's absolute Self
With Light unwaning on her Eyes, to look
Far on!—herself a Glory to behold,
The Angel of the Vision!—Then (last strain!)
Of Duty! Chosen Laws controlling choice!
Action and Joy!—AN ORPHIC SONG INDEED,
A SONG DIVINE OF HIGH AND PASSIONATE TRUTHS
TO THEIR OWN MUSIC CHAUNTED!

Indeed thro' the whole of that Poem 'με Αὖρα τις εἰσέπνευσε μυστικωτάτη [a most mystical breeze blew upon me].'° *This* I considered as 'the EXCURSION'; and the second as 'THE RECLUSE' I had (from what I had at different times gathered from your conversation on the Plan) anticipated as commencing with you set down and settled in an abiding Home, and that with the Description of that Home you were to begin a *Philosophical Poem*, the result and fruits of a Spirit so fram'd & so disciplin'd, as had been told in the former. Whatever in Lucretius is Poetry is not philosophical, whatever is philosophical is not Poetry: and in the very Pride of confident Hope I looked forward to the Recluse, as the *first* and *only* true Phil. Poem in existence. Of course, I expected the Colors, Music, imaginative Life, and Passion of *Poetry*; but the matter and arrangement of *Philosophy*—not doubting from the advantages of the Subject that the Totality of a System was not only capable of being harmonized with, but even calculated to aid, the unity (Beginning, Middle, and End) of a *Poem*. Thus, whatever the Length of the Work might be, still it was a *determinate* Length: of the subjects announced each would have it's own appointed place, and excluding repetitions each would relieve & rise in interest above the other—. I supposed you first to have meditated the faculties of Man in the abstract, in their correspondence with his Sphere of action, and first, in the Feeling, Touch, and Taste, then in the Eye, & last in the Ear, to have laid a solid and immoveable foundation for the Edifice by removing the sandy Sophisms of Locke, and the Mechanic Dogmatists, and demonstrating that the Senses were living growths and developements of the Mind & Spirit in a much juster as well as higher sense, than the mind can be said to be formed by the Senses°—. Next, I understood that you would take the Human Race in the concrete, have exploded the absurd notion of Pope's Essay on Man, Darwin, and all the countless Believers—even (strange to say) among Xtians [Christians] of Man's having progressed from an Ouran Outang state°—so contrary to all History, to all Religion, nay, to all Possibility—to have affirmed a Fall in some sense, as a fact, the possibility of which cannot be understood from the nature of the Will, but the reality of which is attested by Experience & Conscience—Fallen men contemplated in the different ages of the World, and in the different states—Savage—Barbarous—Civilized—the lonely Cot, or Borderer's Wigwam—the Village—the Manufacturing Town—Sea-port—City—Universities—and not disguising the sore evils, under which the whole Creation groans, to point out however a manifest Scheme of Redemption from this Slavery, of Reconciliation from this Enmity with Nature— what are the Obstacles, the *Antichrist* that must be & already is—and to conclude by a grand didactic swell on the necessary identity of a true Philosophy with true Religion, agreeing in the results and differing only as the analytic and synthetic process, as discursive from intuitive, the former chiefly useful as perfecting the latter—in short, the necessity of a general revolution in the modes of developing & disciplining the human mind by the substitution of Life, and Intelligence (considered in it's different powers from the Plant up to that state in which the difference of Degree becomes a new kind (man, self-consciousness) but yet not by essential opposition) for the philosophy of mechanism which in every thing that is most worthy of the human Intellect strikes *Death*, and cheats itself by mistaking clear Images for distinct conceptions, and which idly demands Conceptions where Intuitions alone are possible or adequate to the majesty of the Truth.—In short, Facts elevated into Theory—Theory into Laws—& Laws into living & intelligent Powers—true Idealism necessarily perfecting itself in Realism, & Realism refining itself into Idealism.—

Such or something like this was the Plan, I had supposed that you were engaged on—. Your own words will therefore explain my feelings—viz—that your object 'was not to convey recondite or refined truths but to place commonplace Truths in an interesting point of View.'° Now this I supposed to have been in your two Volumes of Poems, as far as was desirable, or p[ossible,] without an insight into the whole Truth—. How can common [trut]hs be made permanently interesting but by being *bottomed* in our common nature—it is only by the profoundest Insight into Numbers and Quantity that a sublimity & even religious Wonder become attached to the simplest operations of Arithmetic, the most evident properties of the Circle or Triangle—.

I have only to finish a Preface which I shall have done in

two or at farthest three days—and I will then, dismissing all comparison either with the Poem on the Growth of your own Support [*sic*], or with the imagined Plan of the Recluse, state fairly my main Objections to the Excursion as it is —But it would have been alike unjust both to you and to myself, if I had led you to suppose that any disappointment, I may have felt, arose wholly or chiefly from the Passages, I do not like—or from the Poem considered irrelatively.—

Allston lives at 8, Buckingham Place, Fitzroy Square—He has lost his wife—& been most unkindly treated—& most unfortunate—I hope, you will call on him.—Good God! to think of such a Grub as *Daw*[*e*] with more than he can do—and such a Genius as Allston, without a Single Patron!°

God bless you!—I am & never have been other than your |

most affectionate

S. T. Coleridge.—

Mr and Mrs Morgan desire to be affectionately remembered to you—& they would be highly gratified if you could make a little Tour & spend a short time at Calne—there is an admirable collection of Pictures at Corsham—. Bowles left Bremhill (2 miles from us where he has [a] perfect Paradise of a Place) for town yesterday morning—

To R. H. Brabant

Saturday, 29 July 1815—

My dear Sir

The necessity of extending, what I first intended as a preface, to an Autobiographia literaria, or Sketches of my literary Life & opinions, as far as Poetry and *poetical* Criticism is [are] concerned, has confined me to my Study from 11 to 4, and from 6 to 10, since I last left you.—I have just finished it, having only the correction of the *Mss.* to go thro'.—I have given a full account (raisonné [reasoned out]) of the Controversy concerning Wordsworth's Poems & Theory, in which my name has been so constantly included°—I have no doubt, that Wordsworth will be displeased—but I have done my

Duty to myself and to the Public, in (as I believe) compleatly subverting the Theory & in proving that the Poet hmself has never acted on it except in particular Stanzas which are the Blots of his Compositions.—One long passage—a disquisition on the powers of association, with the History of the Opinions on this subject from Aristotle to Hartley, and on the generic difference between the faculties of Fancy and Imagination—I did not indeed altogether insert, but I certainly extended and elaborated, with a view to your perusal—as laying the foundation Stones of the Constructive or Dynamic Philosophy in opposition to the merely mechanic°—. But I am running on as usual and shall not leave space enough for the purpose of this note if I do not, like a Skaiter, strike a Stop with my Heel.—

I have just received a polite Invitation from the Marquis & Marchioness of Lansdown to dine with them on Monday: & in Calne I cannot procure a pair of black silk Stockings worth having. I therefore take the Liberty of requesting Mrs Brabant to purchase a pair for me at Devizes, of the larger size *and* weight—from 17 to 20 Shillings: should this note reach you in time, and an opportunity be likely to occur for sending them to Calne, so that I might receive them before 4 o/clock on Monday Afternoon—and at the same time, I would thank you to procure for me at Anstey's a quarter of a Pound of plain Rappee with half an Ounce of Maccaba intermixed°—

As soon after next week as you and Mrs Brabant should find it convenient, I propose to spend two or three days with you—should William not have been sent off to School—& bringing my papers with me endeavor to put Mrs Brabant & her Sister in full possession of my plan for the elementary Instruction of children in the Latin or Greek—& at that time I will thank & settle with Mrs Brabant for the commissions, with which I have taken the liberty to trouble her—.

Believe me, my dear Sir, | with great & affectionate Esteem |
your's
S. T. Coleridge

P.S. Should it be convenient to you for me to pay you a visit the week after next, might I venture to request that it might be entirely to *you*, and *your Family*?—

To James Gillman

42, Norfolk St. Strand—
Saturday Noon. [13 April 1816]

My dear Sir

The first half hour, I was with you, convinced me that I should owe my reception into your family exclusively to motives not less flattering to me than honorable to yourself. I trust, we shall ever in matters of intellect be reciprocally serviceable to cach other. Men of sense generally come to the same conclusions; but they are likely to contribute to each other's enlargement of View in proportion to the distance, or even opposition of the points from which they set out. Travel and the strange variety of situations and employments on which Chance has thrown me in the course of my Life might have made me a mere man of Observation, if Pain and Sorrow and Self-miscomplacence° had not forced my mind in on itself, and so formed habits of *meditation*. It is now as much my nature to evolve the *fact* from the *Law*, as that of a practical man to deduce the Law from the Fact.

[With regard to the Terms] permit me to say, [that I offer them as proportioned to my *present* ability; and least of all things] to my sense of the service. But that indeed cannot be [*payed*] for: it must be returned in kind by esteem and grateful affection. —

And now of myself. My ever-wakeful Reason, and the keenness of my moral feelings will secure you from all unpleasant circumstances connected with me save only one: viz.—*Evasion*, and the cunning of a specific madness. You will never *hear* any thing but truth from me—Prior Habits render it out of my power to *tell* a falsehood, but unless watched carefully, I dare not promise that I should not with regard to this detested Poison be capable of *acting* a Lie.—No sixty hours *have yet passed* without my having taking [taken?] Laudunum—tho' for the last week comparatively trifling doses. I have full belief, that your *anxiety* will not need to be extended beyond the first week: and for the first week I shall not, I *must not be permitted* to leave your House, unless I should walk out with you.—Delicately or indelicately, this *must* be done: and both the Servant and the young Man must receive absolute commands from you on no account to fetch any thing for me. The stimulus of Conversation suspends the terror that haunts my mind; but when I am alone, the horrors, I have suffered from Laudanum, the degradation, the blighted Utility, almost overwhelm me—. If (as I feel for *the first time* a soothing Confidence it will prove) I should leave you restored to my moral and bodily Health, it is not myself only that will love and honor you—Every friend, I have (and thank God! spite of this wretched vice I have many & warm ones who were friends of my Youth & have never deserted me) will think of you with reverence.

I have taken no notice of your kind apologies—if I could not be comfortable in your House & with your family, I should deserve to be miserable.

I presume, there will be no Objection to Mr Morgan coming to me, as my literary Counsellor and Amanuensis at ½ past 11 every morning & staying with me till ½ past 3. I have been for so many years accustomed to dicta[te] while he writes that I now cannot compose without him—. He is an old acquaintance of Dr Adams's: and has kindly left his family for a month at Calne in order to be with me during such hours, as I should be otherwise alone.

If you could make it convenient, I should wish to be with you by Monday Evening: as it would prevent the necessity of my taking fresh Lodgings in Town.

With respectful Compliments to Mrs Gillman & her Sister I
remain, dear Sir, | your much obliged
S. T. Coleridge

To Thomas Boosey

4 Septr. 1816
Highgate

Dear Sir

I forgot to desire young Mr Boosey to add the work of Dr Stieglitz on animal Magnetism to the List, and all the works of the *Philosopher*, Jacobi, *except* his Briefe über die Lehre des

Spinoza, which I have.—I beg it as a particular Favor that you would entrust me with all the numbers, you happen to possess of the Allgemeine Literatur-Zeitung, for a few weeks—I think, I may venture to promise that the result will be of equal advantage to yourself as to me. All the Articles respecting Medicine, Chemistry, Magnetismus, and the Natur-philosophie with it's opponents in general, are my sole present Object; but it would take too much of your Son's Time to select these numbers—and I cannot afford to purchase them for years back (From the beginning of the *present* year I have ordered them.)—tho' if you could bring a German Literary Reading and Book Society to bear, I should propose the employing of some Friend in Germany to pick up at the Book sales as compleat a set from the year 1800, as could be purchased at half price, in order to be kept among the Books of Reference.—It might appear presumptuous and arrogant if I should say that *I* know no literary man but myself fitted for the conduct of a periodical Work, the Object of which should be to create an enlightened Taste for the genuine productions of German Genius in Science, and the Belles Lettres; but the arrogance would disappear on a closer view.—There may be, or rather, there *are, many* who have a much more extensive knowlege of German Literature than myself; but that is only one of the Requisites. It is an indispensable Condition, that the person should be equally familiar with the past History and the present State of the Taste and Philosophy of Great Britain, not only or chiefly as it appears in books, but as it exists in the minds, and is manifested in the conversations, of our eminent men, Authors or not Authors, and in the pursuits and prepossessions of our young Gentlemen at the two Universities. Not therefore in Learning or Talent do I claim the least superiority; but in the united knowlege of German and English Literature, without over or under valuing either.—The four great characteristics by the predominance of one or the other of which the Nations of Europe are intellectually distinguished, are 1. Genius, or the originating, intuitive and combining Power: 2. Talent, or the power of acquiring, arranging, illustrating, and applying the knowlege learnt from others. 3. Good Sense. 4. Cleverness or the faculty of means & instruments—the *handiness* of the mind.—Now the

French have their national characteristic eminence in *Talent* and *cleverness*—; but good sense, or the *balance* of the faculties, = *instinctive* rectitude of practical Judgement, is rare among them, and if found at all, found only in old French men; and as to *Genius*, from the latter half of the reign of Louis the 14th to the present day, the instances are so few & so equivocal, that the appearance of it always suggests to my mind the suspicion of plagiarism or assistance from German or Italian Writers— (So *ex. gr.* [e.g.] whatever is solid and original in Mad. de Stahl° was given her by Schlegel, & other Germans.)—The English possess Genius occasionally (that is, Men of Genius *have been numerous* and *are* so, in proportion to the small number that in any age or country have been thus gifted)—but good sense *diffusedly*. The former is the national honor; but the latter is the national *Character*. Germany in proportion to it's population is on a par with England in the frequency of Genius; but as greatly excels us in *Talent*, as it is inferior in sobriety of intellect, in *good sense*.—Thus then:

Talent Cleverness	{ France	Detail (Experimental) Wit	{ France
Genius Talent	{ Germany	Theory Encyclopaedic Breadth	{ Germany
Genius Good sense	{ England	Selection Humour	{ England—.

The Scotch appear to me dull Frenchmen, and superficial Germans.—They have no *Inside*. Of course, individual exceptions are not rare, in either of the Countries mentioned.—

I have written this on the supposition, that you may some time or other have occasion to speak with literary Germans, and the English Students of German Literature on the plan of a Reading Room & Book Society, as introductory to some central *Anglo-german* Magazine & Review.—To such persons it might be interesting to know beforehand the general Taste and Principles of the Proposer.—I have only to add that *if* you can oblige me with the numbers of the Jena Allgem. Lit. Zeit., the sooner the better—and that I am anxious to have the Books, which I ordered yesterday as soon as possible—to which I would annex any *answer* (if such there be) of *Fichte* to Schelling's Darstellung der Verhältness &c, or of *Jacobi* to Schelling's Denkmal: & remain &c

S. T. Coleridge

To Hugh J. Rose

25th Septr 1816
Mudiford, Christchurch.

Dear Sir,

I have received THE FRIEND, which waits only for your instructions, and of which I intreat your acceptance as corrected by myself. You are quite in the right. It is idle to attempt the service of God and Mammon at the same altar. Instead of popularizing therefore I shall do my best to improve the style, which is sometimes more intangled and parenthetic than need is: tho' a book of reasoning without parentheses must be the work either of adeptship or of a *friable* intellect. The acquaintance with so many languages has likewise made me too often *polysyllabic*—for these are the words which are possessed in common by the English with the Latin and its south European offspring, & those into which, with the least *looking round about*, one can translate the *full* words of the Greek, German &c. Still there are not so many as the work has been charged with, if it be judged by what I have tried to impose on myself as the ordeal—that is, to reject whatever can be translated into other words of the same language without loss of any meaning—i.e. without change either in the conception or the feeling appropriate to it—under which latter head I do *not* place the feeling of self-importance on the part of the Author or that of *wonderment* on the part of the Readers.

Dr Johnson's

Let Observation with extensive view
Survey mankind from China to Peru

i.e. Let Observation with extensive observation observe mankind extensively (besides this ἀναιμόσαρκος ἀπαθής

[bloodless, unfeeling] printer's devil's *Person*—OBSERVATION—)
contrasted with Dryden's 'Look round the world'—is a good
instance. Compare this with Milton's 'Yet Virgin of Proserpina
from Jove'°—which you may indeed easily translate into
simple English as far as the *Thought* is concerned, or Image,
but not without loss of the *delicacy*, the sublimation of the
ethereal part of the Thought with a compleat detachment
from the grosser caput mortuum.°

As to Hazlitt, I shall take no notice of him or his libels°—at
least with reference to myself. What could I say to readers
who could believe that I believed in *Astrology* but not in the
Newtonian Astronomy, and had an enthusiastic faith in the
Athanasian Creed and the 39 Articles, but no faith at all in the
existence of the Supreme Being? The last time I had the
misfortune of being in this man's company I distinctly
remember that I pointed out the *causes* of the Ath. Creed
having been adopted by the compilers of our Liturgy, and at
the same time enumerated the weighty reasons for wishing it
to be removed. Among others, that it must either be
interpreted laxly under the superior authority of the Nicene
Creed, or it could not be cleared of a very dangerous approach
to Tritheism in its omission of the Subordination of the Son to
the Father, not as Man merely, but as the Eternal Logos.

But enough of this.—Hazlitt possesses considerable Talent;
but it is diseased by a morbid hatred of the Beautiful, and
killed by the absence of Imagination, & alas! by a wicked
Heart of embruted Appetites. Poor wretch! he is a melancholy
instance of the awful Truth—that man cannot be on a Level
with the Beasts—he must be above them or below them.
Almost all the *sparkles* & *originalities* of his Essays are, however,
echoes from poor Charles Lamb—and in his last libel the
image of the Angel without hands or feet was stolen from a
Letter of my own to Charles Lamb, which had been quoted to
him.

I have no other objection to the re-publication of the
Character of the late Mr Pitt with *a comment* (for I have never
altered my political *principles*) but the dislike to give pain, &
not to any one party—for from the same motive I feel
reluctant to re-publish the 2 Letters to Mr Fox written during
his residence at the Court of Napoleon. Of this latter

gentleman I shall certainly write a Character—the Hint towards it you will see in the third article of the Appendix to the Lay Sermon now printing.°—

Should it please the Almighty to restore me to an adequate state of Health, and prolong my years enough, my aspirations are toward the concentring my powers in 3 Works. The first (for I am convinced that a true System of Philosophy (= the Science of Life) is *best* taught in Poetry as well as most safely) Seven Hymns with a large preface or prose commentary to each—1. to the Sun. 2. Moon. 3. Earth. 4. Air. 5. Water. 6. Fire. 7. God.—The second work, 5 Treatises on the Logos,° or communicative and communicable Intellect, in God and man. 1. Λόγος προπαιδευτικός [propaideutic (preparatory) logic] or Organum verè organum [an instrument of discovery that is truly an instrument of discovery]. 2. Λόγος ἀρχιτεκτονικός [architectonic logic], or the principles of the Dynamic or Constructive Philosophy as opposed to the Mechanic. 3. Commentary in detail on the Gospel of St John—or Λόγος θεάνθρωπος [the god–man (incarnate) logos]. 4. Λόγος ἀγωνιστής [the struggling logos] Biography and Critique on the Systems of Giordano Bruno, Behmen, and Spinoza.° 5. Λόγος ἄλογος [illogical logos] or the Sources and Consequences of modern *Unicism* absurdly called Unitarianism.°

The third, an Epic Poem on the Destruction of Jerusalem under Titus.

I hope that the volumes of my literary work [and] Sibylline Leaves will be out by the end of October.

I am very weak; but the Sea air agrees with me, & I exclaimed again at the first sight of it—

> God be with thee—gladsome ocean!
> How gladly greet I thee once more!
> Ships and waves and endless motion,
> And men rejoicing on thy shore!°

I mean to stay 5 weeks longer at least—but O dear Sir! it is a hard hard thing to be compelled to turn away from such subjects to scribble Essays for Newspapers—too good to answer one purpose, and not good enough for another—But so it is! and God's will be done! Should you leave Cambridge at Christmas I shall be very glad to see you if you will take the trouble of writing to Highgate—at J. Gillman's Esqre, Surgeon, Highgate.

I remain mean time | with unfeigned anticipations of regard |

Your obliged

S. T. Coleridge

To C. A. Tulk

Thursday Evening [12 February 1818]
Highgate.

Dear Sir

As an innocent female often blushes not at any image which had risen in her own mind but from a confused apprehension of some x y z that might be attributed to her by others: so did I feel uncomfortable at the odd co-incidence of my commending to you the late Swedenborgian advertisement—. But when I came home, I simply asked Mrs G. if she remembered my having read to her such an address. She instantly replied not only in the affirmative but mentioned the circumstance of my having expressed a sort of half-inclination, half-intention of addressing a letter to the Chairman mentioning my receipt of a Book of which I highly approved, and requesting him to transmit my acknowlegements, if as was probable the author was known to him or any of the Gentlemen with him.—I asked her then: If she had herself read the advertisement? 'Yes, and I carried it to Mr Gillman, saying how much you had been pleased with the style and the freedom from the sectarian spirit'—And do you recollect the name of the Chairman? 'No!—why, bless me!—could it be Mr Tulk?'— Very nearly the same conversation took place with Mr Gillman afterwards.—I can readily account for the fact in myself: for first—I never recollect any persons by their names, and have fallen into some laughable perplexities by the specific catalepsy of memory, such as accepting an invitation in the Streets from a face perfectly familiar to me, & being afterwards unable to attach the name and habitat thereto—and secondly, that the impression made by a conversation that appeared to me altogether accidental and by your voice and person had been compleated before I heard your name—and lastly, the more habitual thinking is to any one, the larger share has the relation of Cause and effect in producing recognition—But it is strange that neither Mrs or Mr Gillman should have recollected the name, tho' probably the accidentality of having made your Acquaintance, and its being at Little Hampton and associated with our having at the same time and by a similar accidental rencontre become acquainted with the Revd. Mr Cary and his family, *overlayed* any former relique of a man's name in Mrs G. as well as myself.

I return you Blake's poesies, metrical and graphic, with thanks.° With this and the Book I have sent a rude scrawl as to the order in which I was pleased by the several poems.

With respectful Compliments to Mrs Tulk | I remain, dear Sir, | Your obliged
S. T. Coleridge

Blake's Poems.

I begin with my Dyspathies that I may forget them: and have uninterrupted space for Loves and Sympathies. Title page and the following emblem contain all the faults of the Drawings with as few beauties as could be in the compositions of a man who was capable of such faults + such beauties.—The faults—despotism in symbols, amounting in the Title page to the μισητόν [hateful], and occasionally, irregular unmodified Lines of the Inanimate, sometimes as the effect of rigidity and sometimes of exossation—like a wet tendon. So likewise the ambiguity of the Drapery. Is it a garment—or the body incised and scored out? The *Limpness* (= the effect of Vinegar on an egg) in the upper one of the two prostrate figures in the Title page, and the *eye*-likeness of the twig posteriorly on the second—and the strait line down the waist-coat of pinky gold-beater's skin° in the next drawing, with the I don't know whatness of the countenance, as if the mouth had been formed by the habit of placing the tongue, not contemptuously, but stupidly, between the lower gums and the lower jaw—these are the only *repulsive* faults I have noticed. The figure, however, of the second leaf (abstracted from the *expression* of the countenance given it by something about the mouth and

the interspace from the lower lip to the chin) is such as only a
Master learned in his art could produce.

N.B. I signifies, It gave me pleasure. I̶, still greater—I̶I̶, and
greater still. Θ, in the highest degree, o, in the lowest.*

Shepherd I. Spring I (last Stanza I̶). Holy Thursday I̶I̶.
Laughing Song I̶. Nurse's Song I. The Divine Image Θ. The
Lamb I̶. The little Black Boy Θ: yea Θ + Θ! Infant Joy I̶I̶.
(N. b. for the 3 last lines I should wish—When wilt thou
smile, or—O smile, O smile! I'll sing the while—For a Babe
two days old does not, cannot *smile*—and innocence and the
very truth of Nature must go together. Infancy is too holy a
thing to be ornamented.)—Echoing Green I (the figures I̶, and
of the second leaf I̶I̶). The Cradle Song I. The School boy I̶I̶.
Night Θ. On another's Sorrow I. A Dream?—The little Boy
lost I (the drawing I̶). The little boy found I. The Blossom o.
The Chimney Sweeper o. The Voice of the ancient Bard o.

Introduction I̶. Earth's Answer I̶. Infant Sorrow I. The
Clod and the Pebble I. The Garden of Love I̶. The Fly I. The
Tyger I̶. A little Boy lost I̶. Holy Thursday I. P. 13, o. Nurse's
Song o. The little girl lost and found (the ornaments most
exquisite, the poem I). Chimney Sweeper in the Snow o. To
Tirzah—and The Poison Tree I and yet o. A little girl lost o (I
would have had it omitted—not for the want of innocence in
the poem, but from the too probable want of it in many
readers). London I. The sick Rose I. *The little Vagabond*—Tho'
I cannot approve altogether of this last poem and have been
inclined to think that the error which is most *likely* to beset the
scholars of Emanuel Swedenborg is that of utterly demerging
the tremendous incompatibilities with an evil will that arise
out of the essential Holiness of the abysmal Aseity in the Love
of the eternal *Person*—and thus giving temptation to weak
minds to sink this Love itself into *good nature*, & yet still I
disapprove the mood of mind in this wild poem so much less
than I do the servile, blind worm, wrap-rascal scurf-coat of
FEAR of the *modern Saints* (whose whole being is a Lie, to
themselves as well as to their Brethren), that I should laugh
with good conscience in watching a Saint of the new stamp,
one of the Fixt Stars of our eleemosynary Advertisements,

---

* o means that I am perplexed and have no opinion.

groaning in wind-pipe! and with the whites of his Eyes upraised at the *audacity* of this poem!°—Any thing rather than *this* degradation* of Humanity, and therein of the Incarnate Divinity!

S.T.C.

To Robert Southey

[31 January 1819]

Dear Southey

I do not remember whether or no you are acquainted with, have seen or heard of Mr Kenyon. He is a man of fortune, highly educated, a particular friend of our friend, Mr Thomas Poole, who while I was in the West shewed me *particular* kindness. He has been some years abroad with Mrs Kenyon. Last Thursday Evening just before my Lecture a Letter from him was delivered to me, earnestly requesting that I would give his friend, Mr Ticknor, an American Gentleman, an introduction to you and Mr Wordsworth. Mr Kenyon speaks highly of Mr Ticknor—both as a man and a man of liberal principles—I owe it to the memory of dear Allston to have no incredulity on this point. After the Lecture I saw him for a few seconds, and find that he leaves London tomorrow Morning for the North. I could not hesitate therefore in promising and in thus fulfilling my promise that I would give him a letter to you—and any little attentions, that your time will permit, will be put in part to my account by Mr Kenyon, and yet without lessening the sense of your kindness.

On Wednesday Night, just before 12, I was seized with a sort of ague-fit as I was sitting by a good fire—and tho' I got to bed as soon as possible, yet it kept not only me but the bedstead in bed-and body quake till past 4 in the morning—It then made way for a hot fit, with pains on my limbs & across my chest and with sharp *cry-out* stitches whenever I attempted to draw my breath freely. With great Effort I contrived to get thro' the Thursday's Lecture as successfully as the subject

---

* with which how can we utter 'Our Father'?

(Lear) would allow me—but by Mr Gillman's and Mr Green's medical commands I announced a week's intermission. On Friday and Yester evening I had a relapse, but of brief continuance, ending after a short but rather alarming spasm with violent sickness. I trust, however, that by aid of Calomel, Senna+Epsom Salts = Black Dose, Pediluvia,° and as much repose as my circumstances will suffer me to give my mind, I shall be re-established in a few days.

As soon as I have sent off this letter to Mr Ticknor, I shall devote the remainder of the day to Letters to Mrs Coleridge and to Derwent, with some books for Derwent—in which Hartley, who leaves me tomorrow for Oxford, will inclose a letter.

I was as much delighted as I could be, being still more affected, by Mr Collins's exquisite Sketch-picture of Sara—and Hartley assures me, that it is not less faithful as a *portrait*.

You of course have read Antar.° I have merely seen it, having read about ten pages only to Lady Errol°—tho' Mr Hamilton apologized at the Lecture for not having sent me a Copy of his Brother's work. Every one, I find, has regretted the same defect—the mixture of modern phrases in pages, two thirds of the sentences of which read exactly like the Book of Kings—especially as the modernisms might be corrected currente calamo [with running pen, i.e. quickly]. I am anxious to read the whole—it seems to prove, as the Editor I believe has noticed, that the Arab. Nights are originally Persian—perhaps Graeco-persian.—

A Brahmin has, I hear, arisen to attempt what we have both so often wished—viz. to be the Luther of Brahmanism°—and with all the effect, that could be wished—considering the times.

Mr Frere *at a heavy expence* (I was astonished to learn thro' Mr Gillman from the Scribe himself, at how heavy an expence!) has had my Lectures taken down in short-hand. It will be of service to me: tho' the Publication must of course contain much that could not be delivered to a public Audience who, respectable as they have been (scanty, I am sorry to add), expect to be kept awake.—I shall however, God granting me the continuance of the power and the strength, bring them out—first, because a History of *Philosophy*, as the gradual evolution of the instinct of Man to enquire into *the Origin* by the efforts of his own reason, is a desideratum in Literature—and secondly, because it is almost a necessary Introduction to my *magnum opus* [great work], in which I had been making regular and considerable progress till my Lectures—and shall resume, immediately after.—I give 4 and oftener five hours twice a week, and Mr Green (Cline's Nephew and Lecturer & Demonstrating Surgeon at Guy's and Thomas's, a most amiable man, deeply studied in all the physiology and philosophy of the German Schools, and equally dissatisfied with them as myself) writes down what I say—so that we have already compassed a good handsome Volume—and hitherto we have neither of us been able to detect any unfaithfulness to the four Postulates, with which I commenced—1. That the System should be *grounded*. 2. That it should not be grounded in an *abstraction*, nor in a *Thing*. 3. That there be no chasm or saltus [leap] in the deduction or rather production. 4. That it should be bonâ fide [genuinely] progressive, not in circulo [circular]—productive not barren.—

Some Genius in a pamphlet entitled Hypocrisy unveiled written against Mr Wilson has pronounced poor Christabel 'the most obscene Poem in the English Lan[gua]ge.' It seems that Hazlitt from pure malignity had spread about the Report that Geraldine was a man in disguise—I saw an old book at Coleorton in which the Paradise Lost was described as 'an obscene Poem'—so I am in good company.—

God bless you and
S. T. Coleridge.

P.S. All remembrances &c *understood*—& all else deferred to my parcel letter—

To James Gooden

[Gooden, a new acquaintance, had sent Coleridge information about
a club (the 'Harmony') in which he thought he might be interested.
Coleridge does not, however, appear to have become a member.]

14 Jany 1814 [1820]—
Highgate—

Dear Sir

The matrimonial Goddess, & Boreas in conjunction have
imposed so many *Labors* in expectation on our medical
Hercules,° & the latter Divinity growled so many threats to
the poor Invalid, his unworthy Friend, your humble Servant,
in addition to an accumulation of literary engagements to be
fulfilled, that we are compelled to defer the pleasure of passing
an Attic Evening° with you, in pursuance of your kind
invitation, to a more favorable conjunction of Planets.—Accept
my thanks for the Rules of the Harmony. I perceive, that the
members are chiefly Merchants; but yet it were to be wished,
that such an enlargement of the Society could be brought
about, as retaining all it's present purposes might add to them
the groundwork of a Library of Northern Literature, and by
bringing together the many Gentlemen who are attached to it
be the means of eventually making both countries better
acquainted with the valuable part of each other—especially,
the English with the German: for our most sensible men look
at the German Muses thro' a film of prejudice & utter
misconception.

With regard to Philosophy, there are half a dozen things,
good & bad that in this country are so nick-named, but in the
only accurate sense of the term, there neither are, have been,
or ever will be but two essentially different Schools of
Philosophy: the Platonic, and the Aristotelean. To the latter,
but with a somewhat nearer approach to the Platonic,
Emanuel Kant belonged; to the former Bacon and Leibnitz &
in his riper and better years Berkley—And to this I must
profess myself an adherent—nihil novum, vel inauditum
audemus [nothing we undertake is new, or has not been heard
before]: tho' as every man has a face of his own, without being

more or less than a man, so is every true Philosopher an original, without ceasing to be an Inmate of Academus or of the Lyceum.°—But as to caution, I will just tell you how I proceeded myself, 20 years & more ago when I first felt a curiosity about Kant, & was fully aware that to master his meaning, as a system, would be a work of gret Labor & long Time—. First, I asked myself, have I the Labor & the Time in my power? Secondly, if so & if it would be of adequate importance to me if true, by what means can I arrive at a rational presumption for or against?—I enquired after all the more popular writings of Kant—read them with delight.—I then read the Prefaces to several of his systematic works, as the Prolegomena &c°—here too every part, I understood, & that was nearly the whole, was replete with sound & plain tho' bold and novel truths to me—& I followed Socrates's Adage respecting Heraclitus—all I understand is excellent; and I am bound to presume that the rest is at least worth the trouble of trying whether it be not equally so. —In other words, until I understand a writer's Ignorance, I presume myself ignorant of his understanding. Permit me to refer you to a chapter on this subject in my Literary Life.°—Yet I by no means recommend to you an extension of your philosophic researches beyond Kant. In him is contained all that can be *learnt*—& as to the results, you have a firm faith in God, the responsible Will of Man, and Immortality—& Kant will demonstrate to you, that this Faith is acquiesced in, indeed, nay, confirmed by the Reason & Understanding, but grounded on Postulates authorized & substantiated solely by the *Moral* Being—These are likewise *mine*: & whether the *Ideas* are regulative only, as Aristotle & Kant teach, or constitutive & actual as Pythagoras & Plato, is of living Interest to the Philosopher by Profession alone. Both systems are equally true, if only the former abstain from denying *universally* what is denied individually. He for whom Ideas are constitutive, will in effect be a Platonist—and in those, for whom they are regulative only, Platonism is but a hollow affectation. Dryden *could* not have been a Platonist—Shakespear, Milton, Dante, Michael Angelo, & Rafael could not have been other than Platonists. Lord Bacon, who never read Plato's works, taught pure Platonism in his *great* Work, the Novum Organum, and abuses his divine

Predecessor for fantastic nonsense, which he had been the first to explode. —

Accept my best respects as, dear Sir, | Your's most sincerely,
S. T. Coleridge

To Thomas Allsop

Thursday Afternoon [30 March 1820]
My dear young Friend

The only impression left by you on my mind, of which I am aware, is an increased desire to see you again and at shorter intervals. Were you my son by nature, I could not hold you dearer or more earnestly desire to retain you the adopted of whatever within me will remain when the dross and alloy of infirmity shall have been purged away. I feel the most entire confidence, that no prosperous change of my outward circumstances would add to *your* faith in the sincerity of this assurance: still, however, the average of men being what it is, and it being neither possible nor desirable to be fully conscious in our understanding of the habits of thinking and judging in the world around us, and yet to be wholly impassive and unaffected by them in our feelings, it would endear, and give a new value to, an honorable competence, that I should be able to evince the true nature and degree of my esteem and attachment, beyond the suspicion even of the sordid, and separate from all that is accidental and adventitious. But yet the gratitude, I feel to you, is so genial a Warmth, and blends so undistinguishably with my affections, is so perfectly one of the family in the Household of Love, that I would not be otherwise than obliged and indebted to you: and God is my witness, that my wish for an easier and less embarrassed lot is *chiefly* (I think, I might have said, *exclusively*) grounded in the deep conviction, that exposed to a less bleak aspect I should bring forth flowers and fruits, both more abundant and more worthy of the unexampled kindness of your *faith* in me.—Interpreting the '*wine*' and the 'ivy garland'

as figures of poetry signifying competence & the removal of
the petty needs of the body that plug up the pipes of the
playing Fountain (and such, it is too well known, was the
intent and meaning of the hardly used Poet)—and O! how
often, when my heart has begun to swell from the genial
warmth of thought as our northern Lakes from the (so called)
bottom-winds when all above and around is Stillness and
Sunshine—how often have I repeated in my own name the
sweet Stanza of Edmund Spenser—

> Thou kenst not, Percie, how the rhyme should rage
> O! if my temples were bedew'd with wine,
> And girt in garlands of wild ivy twine—
> How I could rear the Muse on stately stage
> And teach her tread aloft in buskin fine
> With queint Bellona in her equipage!

Read this as you would a note at the bottom of a page.

> But ah! Mecaenas is ywrapt in clay
> And great Augustus long ago is dead—

this is a natural sigh, & natural too is the reflection that
follows—

> And if that any buddes of Poesy
> Yet of the old stock gin to shoot again,
> 'Tis or *self*-lost the worldling's meed to gain,
> And with the rest to breathe it's ribauldry:
> Or as it sprung, it wither must again—
> Tom Piper makes them better melody.°

but tho' natural, the complaint is not equally philosophical,
were it only on this account, that I know of no age in which
the same has not been advanced, & with the same grounds.
Nay, I retract. There never was a time, in which the *complaint*
would be so little wise, tho' perhaps none in which the *fact* is
more *prominent*. Neither Philosophy or Poetry ever did, nor as
long as they are terms of comparative excellence & contra-
distinction, ever can be *popular*, nor honored with the praise
and favor of Contemporaries. But on the other hand, there
never was a time, in which either books, that were *held* for
excellent as poetic or philosophic, had so extensive and rapid

a sale, or men reputed Poets and Philosophers of a high rank
were so much *looked up to* in Society or so munificently, almost
profusely, rewarded.—Walter Scott's Poems & Novels (except
only the two wretched Abortions, Ivanhoe & the Bride of
Ravensmuir° or whatever it's name be) supply both instance
& solution of the *present* conditions & components of popularity
—viz—to amuse without requiring any effort of thought, &
without exciting any deep emotion. The age seems *sore* from
excess of stimulation, just as a day or two after a thorough
Debauch & long sustained Drinking-match a man feels all
over like a Bruise. Even to *admire* otherwise than *on the whole*
and where 'I admire' is but a synonyme for 'I remember, I
liked it very much *when I was reading it*', is too much an effort,
would be too disquieting an emotion! Compare Waverley,
Guy Mannering, &c with works that had an *immediate run* in
the last generation—Tristram Shandy, Roderick Random, Sir
Ch. Grandison, Clarissa Harlow, & Tom Jones (all which
became popular as soon as published & therefore instances
fairly in point) and you will be convinced, that the difference
of Taste is real & not any fancy or croaking of my own.

But enough of these Generals. It was my purpose to open
myself out to you in detail.—My health, I have reason to
believe, is so intimately connected with the state of my Spirits,
and these again so dependent on my thoughts, prospective
and retrospective, that I should not doubt the being favored
with a sufficiency for my noblest undertakings, had I the ease
of heart requisite for the necessary abstraction of the
Thoughts, and such a reprieve from the goading of the
immediate exigencies as might make tranquillity possible. But
alas! I know by experience (and this knowlege is not the less,
because the regret is not unmixed with self-blame and the
consciousness of want of exertion and fortitude) that my
health will continue to decline, as long as the pain from
reviewing the barrenness of the Past is great in an inverse
proportion to any rational anticipations of the Future. As I
now am, however, from 5 to 6 hours devoted to actual writing
and composition in the day is the utmost, that my strength,
not to speak of my nervous system, will permit: and the
invasions on this portion of my time from applications, often
of the most senseless kind, are such and so many, as to be

almost as ludicrous even to myself as they are vexatious. In less than a week I have not seldom received half a dozen packets or parcels, of works printed or manuscript, urgently requesting my *candid judgement*, or my correcting hand—add to these Letters from Lords & Ladies urging me to write reviews & puffs of heaven-born Geniuses, whose whole merit consists in their being Ploughmen or Shoemakers—Ditto from Actors —Ditto, Intreaties—for money or recommendations to Publishers from Ushers out of place, &c &c—and to *me*, who have neither influence, interest, or money—and what is still more apropos, can neither bring myself to tell smooth falsehoods or harsh truths, and in the struggle too often do both in the anxiety to do neither—. I have already the *written* materials and contents, requiring only to be put together, from the loose papers and numerous Common-place or Memorandum Books, & needing no other change whether of omission, addition, or correction, than the mere act of arranging & the opportunity of seeing the whole collectively, bring with them of course—the following Works. I. Characteristics of Shakespear's Dramatic Works, with a critical Review of each Play—together with a relative and comparative Critique on the kind and degree of the merits & demerits of the Dramatic Works of Ben Jonson, Beaumont & Fletcher, and Massinger. The history of the English Drama, the accidental advantages, it afforded to Shakespear, without in the least detracting from the perfect originality, or proper creation of the Shakspearian Drama; the contra-distinction of the Latter from the Greek Drama, and it's still remaining *Uniqueness*, with the causes of this from the combined influences of Shakespear himself, as Man, Poet, Philosopher, and finally, by conjunction of all these, *Dramatic Poet*; and of the age, events, manners and state of the English Language. This work, with every art of compression, amounts to three Volumes Oct. of about 500 pages each.—II. Philosophical analysis of the Genius and Works of Dante, Spenser, Milton, Cervantes, and Calderon—with similar but more compressed Criticisms of Chaucer, Ariosto, Donne, Rabelais, and others, during the predominance of the romantic Poesy.—In one large Volume.—These two works will, I flatter myself, form a complete Code of the Principles of Judgement & Feeling applied to Works of Taste—and not of

Poetry only, but of *Poesy* in all it's forms, Painting, Statuary, Music &c. —

III. The History of Philosophy, considered as a tendency of the Human Mind to exhibit the powers of the Human Reason—to discover by it's own strength the origin & laws of Man and the world, from Pythagoras to Locke & Condilliac— 2 Volumes.

IV. Letters on the Old and New Testament, and on the doctrines and principles held in common by the Fathers and Founders of the Reformation, addressed to a Candidate for Holy Orders—including advice on the plan and subjects of Preaching, proper to a Minister of the Established Church.

To the completion of these four Works I have literally nothing more to do, than *to transcribe*; but, as I before hinted, from so many scraps & *sibylline* leaves, including Margins of Books & blank Pages, that unfortunately I must be my own Scribe—& not done by myself, they will be all but lost—or perhaps (as has been too often the case already) furnish feathers for the Caps of others—some for this purpose, and some to plume the arrows of detraction to be let fly against the luckless Bird, from whom they had been plucked or moulted!

In addition to these,—of my GREAT WORK, to the preparation of which more than twenty years of my life have been devoted, and on which my hopes of extensive and permanent Utility, of Fame in the noblest* sense of the word, mainly rest—that, by which I might

> As now by thee, by all the Good be known,
> When this weak frame lies moulder'd in it's grave,
> Which self-surviving I might call my own,
> Which Folly can not mar, nor Hate deprave—
> The Incense of those Powers which risen in flame
> Might make me dear to Him from whom they came!°

of this work, to which all my other writings (unless I except my poems, and these I can exclude in part only) are introductory and preparative; and the result of which (if the premises be, as I with the most tranquil assurance am

---

* Turn to Milton's Lycidas, with Stanza—'Alas! what boots it with incessant care' to the end of that paragraph.° The sweetest music does not fall sweeter on my ear, than this Stanza on both mind & ear as often as I repeat it aloud.

convinced, they are—insubvertible, the deductions legitimate, and the conclusions commensurate & only commensurate with both) must finally be a revolution of all that has been called *Philosophy* or Metaphysics in England and France since the aera of the commencing predominance of the mechanical system at the Restoration of our second Charles, and with this the present fashionable Views not only of Religion, Morals and Politics but even of the modern Physics and Physiology— You will not blame the earnestness of my expressions or the high importance which I attach to this work: for how with less noble objects & less faith in their attainment could I stand acquitted of folly and abuse of Time, Talent, and Learning in a Labor of 3 fourths of my *intellectual* Life?—of this work something more than a Volume has been dictated by me, so as to exist fit for the Press, to my friend and enlightened Pupil, Mr Green—and more than as much again would have been evolved & delivered to paper, but that for the last six or 8 months I have been compelled to break off our weekly Meetings from the necessity of writing (alas! alas! of *attempting* to write) for purposes and on the subjects of the passing Day.—Of my poetic works I would fain finish the Christabel —Alas! for the proud times when I planned, when I had present to my mind the materials as well as the Scheme of the Hymns, entitled Spirit, Sun, Earth, Air, Water, Fire, and Man: and the Epic Poem on what still appears to me the one only fit subject remaining for an Epic Poem, Jerusalem besieged & destroyed by Titus. —

And here comes, my dear Allsop!—here comes my sorrow and my weakness, my grievance and my confession. Anxious to perform the duties of the day arising out of the wants of the day, these wants too presenting themselves in the most painful of all forms, that of a debt owing to those who will not exact and yet need it's payment—and the delay, the long (not live-long but *death*-long) BEHINDHAND of my accounts to Friends whose utmost care and frugality on the one side and industry on the other, the wife's Management & the Husband's assiduity, are put in requisition to make both ends meet, I am at once forbidden to attempt and too perplext effectually to pursue, the *accomplishment* of the works worthy of me, those I mean above enumerated—even if, savagely as I have been injured by one of the two influencive Reviews & with more effective enmity undermined by the utter silence or occasional detractive compliments of the other,* I had the probable chance of disposing of them to the Booksellers so as even to liquidate my mere *Boarding* accounts during the time expended in the transcription, arrangement, and Proof-correction—and yet on the other hand my Heart & Mind are for ever recurring to them—Yes! my Conscience forces me to plead guilty—I have only by fits and starts even prayed, I have not even prevailed on myself to pray to God in sincerity and entireness, for the fortitude that might enable me to resign myself to the abandonment of all my Life's best Hopes—to say boldly to myself—'Gifted with powers confessedly above mediocrity, aided by an Education of which no less from almost unexampled Hardships & Sufferings than from manifold & peculiar advantages I have never yet found a Parallel, I have devoted myself to a Life of unintermitted Reading, Thinking, Meditating and Observing—I have not only sacrificed all wor[l]dly prospects of wealth & advancement but have in my inmost soul stood aloof even from temporary Reputation—in consequence of these toils & this self-dedication I possess a calm & clear consciousness that in many & most important departments of Truth & Beauty I have outstrode my Contemporaries, those at least of highest name—that the number of my printed works bears witness that I have not been idle, and the seldom acknowleged but yet strictly *proveable* effects of my labors appropriated to the immediate welfare of my Age, in the Morning Post before, and during the Peace of Amiens, in the Courier afterwards, and in the series & various subjects of my Lectures, at Bristol, and at the Royal, & Surry Institutions; in Fetter Lane; in Willis's Rooms; at the Crown & Anchor &c (add to which the unlimited freedom of my communications in colloquial life) may surely be allowed as evidence that I have not been useless in my generation; but from circumstances the *main* portion of my Harvest is still on the ground, ripe indeed and only waiting, a few for the sickle, but a large part only for the

* Neither my Literary Life (2 Vol.) nor Sibylline Leaves (1 Vol.) nor Friend (3 Vol.) nor Lay-Sermons, nor Zapolya, nor Christabel, have ever been noticed by the Quarterly Review, of which Southey is yet the main support.—

sheaving, and carting and housing—but from all this I must turn away, must let them rot as they lie, & be as tho' they never had been: for I must go to gather Blackberries, and Earth Nuts, or pick mushrooms & gild Oak-Apples for the Palates & Fancies of chance Customers.—I must abrogate the name of Philosopher, and Poet, and scribble as fast as I can & with as little thought as I can for Blackwood's Magazine, or as I have been employed for the last days, in writing MSS sermons for lazy Clergymen who stipulate that the composition must not be *more* than respectable, for fear they should be desired to publish the Visitation Sermon!'—This I have not yet had courage to do—My soul sickens & my Heart sinks—& thus oscillating between both I do neither—neither as it ought to be done, or to any profitable end. If I were to detail only the various, I might say, capricious interruptions that have prevented the finishing of this very scrawl, begun on the very day I received your last kind letter with the Hare, you would need no other illustrations—

Now I see but one possible plan of rescuing my permanent Utility. It is briefly this & plainly. For what we struggle with inwardly, we find at least easiest to *bolt out*—namely, that of engaging from the circle of those who think respectfully & hope highly of my powers & attainments a yearly sum, for three or four years, adequate to my actual Support with such comforts and decencies of appearance as my Health & Habits have made necessaries, so that my mind may be unanxious as far as the Present Time is concerned—that thus I should stand both enabled and pledged to begin with some one work of those above mentioned, and for two thirds of my whole Time to devote myself to this *exclusively* till finished—to take the chance of it's success by the best mode of publication that would involve me in no risk—then to proceed with the next, & so on till the works above mentioned as already in full material existence should be reduced into *formal* and actual Being—while in the remaining third of my Time I might go on, maturing & compleating my great work, &—for if but easy in mind I have no doubt either of the re-awakening power or of the kindling inclination, my Christabel & what else the happier Hour might inspire—& without inspiration a Barrel organ may be played right deftly; but

All otherwise the state of *Poet* stands:
For lordly Want is such a tyrant fell,
That where he rules, all power he doth expel.
The vaunted verse a vacant head demands,
Ne wont with crabbed Care the Muses dwell:
Unwisely weaves, who takes two webs IN HAND!°

Now Mr Green has offered to contribute from 30 to 40£ yearly for 3 or 4 years; my young Friend & Pupil, the Son of one of my dearest old friends, 50£; and I think that from 10 to 20£ I could rely on from another—the sum required would be about 250£—to be repaid, of course, should the disposal or sale & as far as the disposal & sale of my writings produce the means.—

I have thus placed before you at large & wanderingly as well as diffusely, the statement which I am inclined to send in a compressed form to a few of those, of whose kind dispositions towards me I have received assurances—& to their interest & influence I must leave it—anxious, however, before I do this, to learn from you your very very inmost feeling & judgement, as to the previous questions—Am I entitled, have I earned *a right*, to do this? Can I do it without *Moral* degradation? and lastly—Can it be done without loss of character in the eyes of my acquaintance & of my friends' acquaintance who may become informed of the circumstances? —That if attempted at all, it will be attempted in such a way and that such persons only will be spoken to, as will not expose me to indelicate rebuffs to be afterwards matter of Gossip, I know those, to whom I shall intrust the statement, too well, to be much alarmed about.—

Pray let me either see or hear from You as soon as possible. For indeed and indeed, it is no inconsiderable accession to the pleasure, I anticipate from disembarrassment, that *you* would have to contemplate in a more gracious form & in a more ebullient play of the inward Fountain, the mind & manners of,

My dear Allsop, | Your obliged & very affectionate Friend
                                    S. T. Coleridge

To Thomas Allsop

Saturday [8 April 1820]
Highgate—

My dear Friend

It is not the least advantage of Friendship, that by communicating our thoughts to another we render them distinct to themselves [ourselves?], and reduce the subjects of our sorrow and anxiety to their just magnitude for our own contemplation. As long as we inly brood over a misfortune (there being no divisions or separate circumscriptions in things of mind, no proper beginning nor ending to any Thought, on the one hand; and on the other, the confluence of our recollections being determined far more by sameness or similarity of the Feelings that had been produced by them than by any positive resemblance or connection between the things themselves that are thus recalled to our attention) we establish a center as it were or sort of nucleus in the reservoir of the soul, and toward this needle shoots after needle, cluster-points on cluster-points, from all parts of the contained Fluid and in all directions, till the mind with it's best faculties is locked up in one ungenial Frost. I cannot adequately express the state of confused feeling, in which I wrote my last letter: the letter itself, I doubt not, bore evidence of it's *nest* and mode of incubation, as certain Birds & Lizards drag along with them part of the egg-shells from which they had forced their way. Still one good end was answered—I had made a clearance so far as to have my Head in Light & my Eyes open: and your answer, every way worthy of you, has removed the rest.—

But before I enter on this subject, permit [me] to refer to some points of *comparative* indifference lest I should forget them altogether.—I occasioned you to misconceive me respecting Sir W. Scott°—My purpose was to bring proofs of the inergetic, or inenergetic state of the minds of men induced by the excess and unintermitted action of stimulating events and circumstances, revolutions, battles, Newspapers, Mobs, Sedition & Treason Trials, public Harangues, Meetings, Dinners, the necessity in every individual of ever increasing activity &

anxiety in the improvement of Estate, Trade, &c in proportion
to the decrease of the actual value of money, to the
multiplication of competitors, and to the almost compulsory
expedience of Expence & Prominence even as the means of
obtaining or retaining competence;—the consequent craving
after amusement as proper *relaxation*, as *rest* freed from the
tedium of vacancy, and again after such knowlege & such
acquirements as are ready coin, that will pass *at once*,
unweighed and unassayed; & the unexampled Facilities
afforded for this end by Reviews, Magazines, &c &c—The
Theatres, to which few go to see *a Play* but to see Master
Betty, or Mr Kean, or some one Individual in some *one* Part;
& the single Fact, that our Neighbor, Matthews, night after
night has taken more, than both the regular Theatres
conjointly, & when the best Comedies or whole Plays have
been acted at each House and those by excellent Comedians;
would have yielded a striking instance & illustration of my
position.° But I chose an example in literature as more in
point for the subject of my particular remarks, & because
every Man of Genius, who is born for his age & capable of
acting *immediately* and widely on that age, must of necessity
reflect the age in the first instance, tho' as far as he is a man of
Genius, he will doubtless be himself *reflected* by it reciprocally.
—Now I selected Scott for the very reason, that I do hold him
for a man of *very extraordinary* powers; & when I say, that I
have read the far greater part of his Novels twice, & several
three times, over with undiminished pleasure and interest;
and that in my reprobation of the Bride of Lammar Muir
(with exception, however, of the almost Shakspearian old
Witch-wives at the Funeral) and of the Ivanhoe, I meant to
imply the grounds of my admiration of the others, and the
permanent nature of the Interest, which they excite. In a word, I
am far from thinking, that Old Mortality or Guy Mannering
would have been less admired in the age of Sterne, Fielding &
Richardson, than they are in the present times; but only that
Sterne &c would not have had the same *immediate* popularity
in the present day as in their own less stimulated & therefore
less languid Reading-World. Of W. Scott's *poems* I cannot
speak so highly; still less of the Poetry in his Poems: tho' even
in these the Power of presenting the most numerous Figures &

Figures with the most complex movements & under rapid succession in *true picturesque Unity*, attests true and peculiar Genius.—You cannot imagine, with how much pain I used, many years ago, to hear Wordsworth's contemptuous Assertions respecting Scott—& if I mistake not, I have yet the fragments of the rough Draught of a Letter written by me on this subject so long back as my first Lectures at the Lond. Phil. Society, Fetter Lane, and on the backs of the unused admission Tickets. —One more remark. My criticism was *confined* to the *one* point of the higher degree of intellectual Activity implied in the reading and admiration of Fielding, Richardson & Sterne—in moral, or if that be too high and inwardly a word, in *mannerly* manliness of Taste the present age and it's writers have the decided advantage, and I sincerely trust that Walter Scott's readers would be as little disposed to relish the stupid letchery of the courtship of Widow Wadham [Wadman] as Scott himself would be capable of presenting it. Add, that tho' I cannot pretend to have found in any of these Novels a character that even approaches in Genius, in truth of conception or boldness & freshness of execution, to Parson Adams, Blifil, Strap, Lieutenant Bowling, Mr Shandy, Uncle Toby, & Trim, Lovelace; and tho' Scott's *female* characters will not, even the very best, bear a comparison with Miss Byron, Emily, Clementina in Sir C. Grandison; nor the comic ones with Tabitha Bramble, or with Betty (in Mrs Bennett's Beggar-girl°)—and tho' by the use of the Scotch Dialect, by Ossianic Mock-Highland Motley Heroic, & by extracts from the printed Sermons, Memoirs, &c of the Fanatic Preachers, there is a good deal of *false Effect*, & Stage trick; still the number of characters *so good* produced by one man & in so rapid a succession, must ever remain an illustrious phaeno-menon in Literature, after all the subtractions for those borrowed from English & German Sources, or compounded by blending two or three of the Old Drama into one—ex. gr. [e.g.] the Caleb in the Bride of Lammarmuir.—Scott's great merit, and at the same [time] his *felicity*, and the true solution of the long-sustained *interest* that Novel after novel excited, lie in the nature of the subject—not merely, or even chiefly, because the struggle between the Stuarts & the Presbyterians & Sectaries is still in lively memory, & the passions of the adherency to the former if not the adherency itself, extant in our own Fathers' or Grandfathers' times; nor yet (tho' this is of great weight) because the language, manners, &c introduced are sufficiently different from our own for *poignancy* & yet sufficiently near & similar for sympathy; nor yet because, for the same reason, the Author speaking, reflecting, & describing in his own person remains still (to adopt a painter's phrase) in sufficient *keeping* with his subject matter, while his characters can both talk and feel interestingly to *us* as men without recourse to *antiquarian* Interest, & nevertheless without moral anachronism (—in all which points the Ivanhoe is so wofully the contrary—for what Englishman cares for Saxon or Norman, both brutal Invaders, more than for Chinese & Cochin-chinese?)—yet great as all these causes are, the essential wisdom & happiness of the Subject consists in this: that the contest between the Loyalists & their opponents can never be *obsolete*, for it is the contest between the two great moving Principles of social Humanity—religious adherence to the Past and the Ancient, the Desire & the admiration of Permanence, on the one hand; and the Passion for increase of Knowlege, for Truth as the offspring of Reason, in short, the mighty Instincts of *Progression* and *Free-agency*, on the other. In all subjects of deep and lasting Interest you will detect a struggle between two opposites, two polar Forces, both of which are alike necessary to our human Well-being, & necessary each to the continued existence of the other—Well therefore may we contemplate with intense feelings those whirlwinds which are, for free-agents, the appointed means & only possible condition of that *equi-librium*, in which our moral Being subsists: while the disturbance of the same constitutes our sense of Life. Thus in the ancient Tragedy the lofty Struggle between irresistible Fate & unconquerable Free Will, which founds it's equilibrium in the Providence & the Future Retribution of Christianity—. If instead of a contest between Saxons & Normans, or the Fantees & Ashantees,° a mere contest of Indifferents! of minim Surges in a boiling Fish-kettle! Walter Scott had taken the struggle between the Men of Arts & the Men of arms in the time of Becket, & made us feel how much to claim our well-wishing there was in the cause & character of the Priestly & Papal Party no less than in those of Henry & his Knights, he would have opened a new mine—instead of translating into Leadenhall Street Minerva Library Sentences a cento of the most common incidents of the stately, self-congruous Romances of D'Urfé, Scudéri &c°—N.B. I have not read the Monastery; but I suspect that the Thought or Element of the Faery Work is from the German. I perceive from that passage in the Old Mortality where Morton is discovered by old Alice in consequence of calling his Dog, Elphin, that W.S. has been reading Tiek's Phantasus° (a collection of Faery or Witch Tales) from which both the incident & name is borrowed.—I forget whether I ever mentioned to you that some 18 months ago I had planned & half-collected, half-manufactured & invented a work, to be entitled: THE WEATHER-BOUND TRAVELLERS: or Histories, Lays, Legends, Incidents, Anecdotes and Remarks contributed during a detention in one of the Hebrides—recorded by their Secretary, Lory McHaroldson, Senachy in the Isle of——. The *principle* of the work I had thus exprest in the first chapter—'tho' not *fact*, must it needs be *false*? These things have a truth of their own, if we but knew how to look for it. There is a *humanity* (meaning by this word whatever contra-distinguishes *man*)—there is a humanity common to all periods of Life, which each period from childhood to Age has it's own way of representing. Hence in whatever layed firm hold of us in early Life there lurks an interest and a charm for our maturest years; but which *He* will never draw forth who content with mimicking the unessential tho' natural defects of thought and expression has not the skill to remove the *childish*, yet leave the *childlike* untouched. Let each of us then relate that which has left the deepest impression on his mind, at whatever period of his life he may have seen, heard or read it; but let him tell it in accordance with the present state of his Intellect and Feelings, even as he has, perhaps, (Alnaschar-like°) acted it over again by the parlour Fireside of a rustic Inn, with the Fire & the Candle for his only Companions.'— On the hope of my Lectures answering, I had intended to have done this work out of hand, dedicating the most genial Hours to the completion of Christabel, in the belief that in the former I should be rekindling the feeling, and recalling the state of mind, suitable to the latter.—But the Hope was vain.—

In stating the names and probable size of my Works, I by no means meant any reference to the mode of their publication. I merely wished to communicate to you the amount of my labours.—In two moderate Volumes it was my intention to comprize all those more prominent and systematic parts of my lucubrations on Shakspeare as should be published (in the first instance, at least) in the form of Books—& having selected & arranged these to send the more particular illustrations, and analyses to some respectable Magazine.—In like manner, I proposed to include the philosophical critiques on Dante, Milton, Cervantes &c in a series of Letters entitled, The Reviewer in Exile: or Critic confined to an old Library—. Provided, the Truths (which are, I dare affirm, original & all tending to the same principles & proving the endless fertility of true Principle, & the decision and power of growth which it communicates to all the faculties of the mind) are but in existence, & to be read by such as might wish to read—I have no vanity as to the mode—nay, should prefer that mode which most multiplied the chances—So too as to the order—For *many* reasons it has been my wish to commence with the theological Letters: one & not the least is the strong desire I have, to put you & Hartley & Derwent Coleridge in full possession of my whole Christian Creed, with the grounds of reason and Authority on which it rests; but especially to unfold the true 'glorious Liberty of the Gospel'° by shewing the distinction between Doctrinal Faith & it's Sources, and Historical Belief, with their reciprocal action on each other; and thus on the one hand to do away the servile superstition, which makes men *Bibliolaters* & yet hides from them the proper excellencies, the one continued revelation, of the Bible-documents which they idolize, & on the other hand to expose in it's native Worthlessness the so-called evidences of Christi-anity first brought into *toleration* by Arminius, and into fashion by Grotius and the Socinian Divines. For as such I consider all those who preach & teach in the Spirit of Socinianism, tho' even in the outward form of a Defence of the 39 Articles.°—

I have been interrupted by the arrival of my Sons, Hartley

and Derwent, the latter of whom I had not seen for so dreary a time —I promise myself great pleasure in introducing him to you—Hartley, I seem to remember, you have already met. Indeed, I am so desirous of this, that I will defer what I have to add that I may put this letter in the post, time enough for you to receive it this evening—saying only, that it was not my purpose to have had any further communication on the subject but with Mr Frere—& with *him* only as with a counsellor—. Let me see you as soon as you can, & as often. I shall be better able hereafter to talk with you than to write to you, on the contents of your last. Enough at present, that I trust that much less than the sacrifices, you are disposed to make but which I could not see my way of duty at all clear in permitting, will suffice for the realizing of such wishes as Duty prescribes or authorizes in your

very affectionate & obliged Friend,
S. T. Coleridge

To Thomas Allsop

Highgate
31 [1] July 1820.—

My very dear Friend

Before I opened your Letter—or rather gave it to my best Sister and under God best Comforter° to open—a heavy, a very heavy Affliction came upon me, with all the aggravations of surprize—sudden as a peal of Thunder from a cloudless Sky.—Derwent set off for Oxford yester afternoon—& till he returns, I can tell you only that Hartley has so conducted himself as to have given deep offence to the Master and Fellows of Oriel—& that there is the greatest possible danger that he will not be elected at the close of his probationary Year, i.e. in October next. He is neither charged with, nor suspected of, any criminal act, nor are any instances of intoxication urged against him—but irregularity & neglect of College Rules & Duties, Carelessness of Dress, low Company in contempt of the exprest warnings as well as wishes of the Master & Fellows, & *fondness for Wine*—the term by which the

last Charge is expressed is the only one too mortifying for me
to transcribe. I am convinced that this last is owing, *in great
part*, to his habit almost constitutional (for it characterized his
earliest Childhood) of eagerly *snatching* without knowing what
he is doing, & whatever happens to be before him—bread,
fruit, or Wine—pouring glass after glass, with a kind of St
Vitus' nervousness—not exactly in the same way as my dear
& excellent-hearted c. l. [Charles Lamb], but similarly. Alas!
both Mr and Mrs Gillman had spoken to him with all the
earnestness of the fondest Parents—his cousins had warned
him—& I (long ago) had written to him, conjuring him to
reflect with what a poisoned dagger it would arm his Father's
enemies—yea, and the Phantoms that half-counterfeiting,
half-expounding the Conscience, would persecute his Father's
Sleep.—My Conscience indeed bears me witness, that from
the time I quitted Cambridge no human Being was more
indifferent to the pleasures of the Table than myself, or less
needed any stimulation to my spirits: and that by a most
unhappy Quackery after having been almost bed-rid for six
months with swoln knees & other distressing symptoms of
disordered digestive Functions, & thro' that most pernicious
form of Ignorance, medical half-knowlege, I was *seduced* into
the use of narcotics, not secretly but (such was my ignorance)
openly & exultingly as one who had discovered & was never
weary of recommending a grand Panacaea—& saw not the
truth, till my *Body* had contracted a habit & a necessity —and
that even to the latest my responsibility is for cowardice &
defect of fortitude; not for the least craving after gratification
or pleasurable sensation of any sort, but for yielding to Pain,
Terror, & haunting Bewilderment—but this I say to *Man*
only, who knows only what has been yielded not what has
been resisted. Before God, I have but one voice—Mercy!
Mercy!—. Woe is me!—the Root of all Hartley's faults is Self-
willedness—this was the Sin of his nature, & this has been
fostered by culpable indulgence, at least, non-interference on
my part, while in a different quarter, Contempt of the Self-
interest, he saw, seduced him unconsciously into *Selfishness*.—Pray
for me, my dear Allsop! that I may not pass such another
night as the last. While I am awake & retain my reasoning
powers, the pang is gnawing but I am—except for a fitful

moment or two—tranquil—It is the howling Wilderness of
Sleep that I dread.—

I am most reluctant thus to transplant the thorns from my
own pillow to your's—but sooner or later you must know
it—And how else could I explain to you the incapability, I am
under, of answering your letter, of which I know no more than
that it is so kind as that at another time it's contents would
have inspired me with alarm & perplexity of mind, whether I
have sufficient grounds of assurance that you are not
wronging yourself?—But this would be superseded for the
present (my late visitation & sorrow out of the question) by
my anxiety respecting your Health.—Mr Gillman feels
satisfied that there is nothing in your case symptomatic of
aught more dangerous than irritable & at present disordered
organs of digestion, requiring indeed great & systematic care
but (with prudence, & *sensible* medical aid) by no means
incompatible with longevity & comfortable Health on the
whole. Would to God! that your uncle lived near Highgate, or
that we were settled near Clapham—Most anxious am I (for I
am sure, I do not *over*–rate Gillman's medical skill & sound
medical good sense, & I have had every possible opportunity
of satisfying myself on this head *comparatively* as well as
positively from my intimate acquaintance with so many
medical men, in the course of my life) I am most anxious, that
you should not apply to any medical Practitioner at Clapham,
till you have consulted some Physician recommended by
Gillman & with whom our Friend might have some confidential
Conversation, either going with you or otherwise—so that you
might have from some man of high medical character, as a
Physician, a general Outline of the Treatment, Diet, &c,
which would be a *guide* to a *judicious* Apothecary, should you
have any occasion to apply while at Clapham, & a sort of
inoffensive Moderator on the other supposition—in both an
Index for yourself, to judge of him by.—The next earnest
petition I make to you—for should I lose *you* from this world, I
fear that religious Terrors would shake my strength of mind,
& to how many are you, must you be, very dear—is that you
would stay in the country as long as is *morally* practicable—Let
nothing but *coercive* motives have weight with you—A month's
tranquillity in pure Air (O that I could spend that month with

you with no greater efforts of mental or bodily exercise than would exhilarate both body & mind) might save you many months' interrupted & half-effective Labor.—If any thoughts occur to you at Clapham, on which it would amuse or gratify you to have my notions—write to me, & I shall be served by having something to think & write about not connected with myself.—But at all events write—tho' but two lines—as often as you can, & as much as (but not a syllable more than) you ought—Need I say how unspeakably dear you are to your—you must not refuse me to say, *in-heart*-obliged

S. T. Coleridge

To Hartley Coleridge

[August 1820?]

Yester morning, my dear Hartley! you appeared to agree with me on the truth of the first universal principle of the Polar Logic, as far as it is *Logic*, i.e. confined to the Objects of the Sense and the Understanding, or (what is the same) to the Finite, the Creaturely. You agreed with me, that *One* could not manifest itself or be wittingly distinguished as One, but by the co-existence of an *Other*: or that A could not be affirmed to be A but by the perception that it is *not* B; and that this again implies the perception that B *is* as well as A. We can become CONSCIOUS of *Being* only by means of *Existence*, tho' having thus become conscious thereof, we are in the same moment conscious, that Being must be prior (in thought) to Existence: as without seeing, we should never *know* (i.e. know ourselves to have known) that we had Eyes; but having learnt this, we know that Eyes must be anterior to the act of seeing. With equal evidence we understand that Existence supposes *relation* —for it is, Sisto me *ad extra* [I place myself on the outside], and thereby distinguished from Being. Well then. We know A by B: and B by A. We know, that between A and B there is, first, a something peculiar to each, *that*, namely, by which A is A and *not* B, and B is B and *not* A: and secondly, a something common to them, a one in both; namely, that which is expressed by the copula, *is*: and thirdly, that the latter, =

Being, is in order of thought presupposed in the former. What is last in Reflection, is first in the *genesis*, or order of causation.

We proceed—(at a tortoise or pedicular Crawl, you will say—but believe me, dear Boy! there is no other way of attaining a clear and productive Insight, and that all impatience is an infallible Symptom that the Inquirer is not seeking *the* Truth for Truth's sake, but only *a* truth or something that may pass for such, in order to some alien *End*. And this may be right: the End may be justifiable. I may ask, what 9 × 9 ÷ 4 makes, in order to pay a Bill—or to understand the result of some statement given in proof of the accuracy of some deduction from a chemical experiment. I want the *fact* only, & it is indifferent to my purpose whether I get it from Archimedes or a Carpenter's Ruler. But then you must not affect to be studying *Arithmetic*: nor must an Egyptian who has no wish but to mark off his three Acres and a Half of Tillage Ground, after the overflow of the Nile, inveigh against Euclid for the lumbriciform (*wormy*) proserpence° of his Elements of Geometry. There is no way of arriving at any sciential End but by finding it at every step. The End is in the Means: or the adequacy of each Mean is already it's end. Southey once said to me: You are nosing every nettle along the Hedge, while the Greyhound (meaning himself, I presume) wants only to get sight of the Hare, & FLASH!—strait as a line!—he has it in his mouth!—Even so, I replied, might a Cannibal say to an Anatomist, whom he had watched dissecting a body. But the fact is—I do not care twopence for the *Hare*; but I value most highly the excellencies of scent, patience, discrimination, free Activity; and find a Hare in every Nettle, I make myself acquainted with. I follow the Chamois-Hunters, and seem to set out with the same Object. But I am no Hunter of *that* Chamois Goat; but avail myself of the Chace in order to a nobler purpose—that of making a road across the Mountains, on which Common Sense may hereafter pass backward and forward, without desperate Leaps or Balloons that soar indeed but do not improve the chance of getting onward.—)

A blessing, I say, on the inventors of Notes! You have only to imagine the lines between the ( ) to be printed in smaller type at the bottom of the page—& the Writer may digress, like

Harris, the Historian, from Dan to Barsheba & from Barsheba in hunt after the last Comet, without any breach of continuity.°

Digress? or not digress? That's now no question.
Do it! Yet do it *not*! See Note* below.

Well! to proceed. What is affirmed of A is equally affirmed of B: and what is true of A relatively to B, is no less true of B relatively to C. In other words, Alterity leads to *Plurality*.— 'Mora' is the term used by the Italian Philosophers, as when they define Beauty by Uno nel Più ['The One in the Many' (Coleridge's version)]: but our 'The many' or 'Multeity' has this preference that it seems more naturally to include both *the more* and *the less*. Whether it be above the Unit in the progression of Integrals, or below it in the regression of Fractions

$$\begin{array}{c} 4 \\ 3 \\ 2 \\ \hline 1 \\ \hline \frac{1}{2} \\ \frac{1}{3} \\ \frac{1}{4} \end{array}$$

it is alike in both cases *the Many* as distinguished from One—tho' as One can never be *known* but as it is revealed in and by the Many, so neither can the Many be *known* (i.e. reflected on) but by it's relation to a *One*, and ultimately therefore, *Ones* being=Many, only by reference to THE ONE, which includes instead of excluding the Alter. The Aleph, say the Rabbinical Philologists, is no Letter; but that in and with which all Letters are or become. Even so, there is a higher than 1. or the 1. is an equivocal for two most disparate senses: in the nobler of which it is equivalent to the O positive, which is no *thing* because it is the ground and sufficient cause of *all* things, and no *number* because it is the Numerorum omnium Fons et Numerus [fount and number of all numbers].—N.B. No man can *be*, or can *understand*, a Philosopher, till he has acquired the power and the habit of attaching to words the *generic* sense purely and unmixed with the accidents of comparative *degrees*. It is this which constitutes the difference between the *proper* Nomenclature of Science and the inevitable language of ordinary life. The latter speaks only of *degrees*. With *quantity* and quality it is familiar; but knows nothing of *quiddity* but as a synonyme for worthless subtleties: and only grins wider and with more intense self-complacency when it hears the former speak of invisible *Light*, the *Heat* of Ice, &c. The *Uno* nel *Più* of the philosophic Saint & Bishop of Geneva (Francesco Sales°) would be as senseless to a common Italian, as my 'Multeity in Unity' or 'The One in the Many' could be to a Mr Wheatley of Oriel or the *'cute* Isaacs of the Stock Exchange.—

To C. A. Tulk

[The distinction between reason, defined as the organ of intuitive knowledge, and the understanding, or faculty of knowledge acquired by experience, was crucial to Coleridge's thinking. The argument sketched here is more fully developed in *The Friend* (1818) and *Aids to Reflection* (1825).]

[12 February 1821]

My dear Sir

'They say, Coleridge! that you are a Swedenborgian!' Would to God! (I replied fervently) that *they* were *any thing*. I was writing a brief essay on the prospects of a country, where it has become the *mind* of the Nation to appreciate the evil of public acts and measures by their next consequences or immediate occasions, while the *principle* violated, or that *a* Principle is thereby violated, is either wholly dropt out of the consideration, or is introduced but as a Garnish or ornamental Common-place in the peroration of a Speech! The deep interest was present to my thoughts—of that distinction between the *Reason*, as the source of Principles, the true celestial influx and porta Dei in hominem internum [God's means of entry into the inner man], and the *Understanding*, with the clearness of the proof, by which this distinction is evinced—viz. that vital or zoo-organic Power, Instinct, and Understanding fall all three under the same definition *in genere* [in kind], and the very additions by which the definition is applied from the first to the second, and from the second to the third, are themselves expressive of degrees only and in *degree* only deniable of the preceding—(Ex. gr. [e.g.] 1. Reflect on the *selective* power exercised by the stomach of the Caterpillar on the undigested miscellany of food—the same power exercised by the Caterpillar on the outward Plants—& you will see the order of the conceptions.) 1. Vital power=the power, by which *means are adapted* to proximate ends. 2. Instinct, the power, *which adapts* means to proximate ends. 3. Understanding=the power which adapts means to proximate ends according *to varying circumstances*. May I not safely challenge any man to peruse Huber's Treatise on Ants,° and yet deny their claim to be included in the last definition? — But try to apply the same definition, with any extension of degree, to the Reason—the absurdity will flash upon the conviction. First, in Reason there is and can be no *degree*. Deus introit aut non introit [God either enters or he does not].—Secondly, in Reason there are no *means* nor ends: Reason itself being one with the ultimate end, of which it is the manifestation. Thirdly, Reason has no concern with *things* (i.e. the impermanent flux of particulars) but with the permanent *Relations*; & is to be defined, even in it's lowest or theoretical attribute, as the Power which enables man to draw *necessary* and *universal* conclusions from particular facts or forms—ex. gr. from any 3 cornered thing that the 2 sides of a Triangle are & must be greater than the third.—From the Understanding to the Reason there is no continuous *ascent* possible, it is a metabasis εἰς ἄλλο γένος [crossing-over into another kind], even as from the air to the Light. The true essential peculiarity of the Human Understanding consists in it's capability of being irradiated by the reason—in it's recipiency—& even this is *given* to it by the presence of a higher power than itself. What then must be [the] fate of a nation that substitutes Locke for Logic, and Paley for Morality,° and one or the other for Polity and Theology, according to the predominance of Whig or Tory predilection?—Slavery: or a commotion is at hand!—But if the Gentry and *Clerisy*° (including all the learned & educated) do this, then the nation does it—*or* a commotion is at hand. *Acephalum* enim, aurâ quamvis et calore vitali potiatur, *morientem* rectius dicimus quam quod vivit [For if a man's brain shows no vital signs, we more correctly say that he is dying than that he is living, although he has the breath and warmth of life].—With these thoughts was I occupied when I received your very kind and most acceptable present—& the results I must defer to the next post.—With best regards to Mrs Tulk

    believe me, in the brief interval, | Your obliged & grateful
                                  S. T. Coleridge

To Thomas De Quincey

[When Coleridge badly needed money in 1807, De Quincey had proposed through a friend an anonymous gift of £300. Coleridge accepted it as a loan, but had never been able to repay it. De Quincey was now in need himself, and wrote to Coleridge to remind him of his debt.]

Highgate
Wednesday Noon. [8 August 1821]

Believe me, I *intreat* you, my dear De Quincey! there was no need to remind me of a generous Act, which during the long interval I have never ceased to think of, for the former and better half of the time with cordial satisfaction as of an obligation only less honorable to the Receiver than to you who had so nobly and in so truly delicate a manner conferred the same—but of late years with an unquiet and *aching* gratitude, which has often checked my enquiries after you from a pang of fear, a foreboding that I should hear of something that would make me feel my poverty as a *humiliation*—would turn an ever-recurring *Wish* of the Heart into an absolute *Want*, which not now for the first time I have anxiously looked about for some means of gratifying, and still baffled sink under a Regret that almost seems to border on Remorse. Few and transient have been the spots of Sunshine on my 'Way of Life', and these almost always on the distant land-scape; but whenever a

brighter prospect has dawned on me, the recollections
connected with your name took a foremost part in every
scheme, that I proposed to myself.

I feel that I am lingering on the brink—and what to say, my
dear Sir! I know not! Distressing—and in relation to you and
the circumstances under which you have written to me—doubly
distressing as the disclosure will be—nothing else is left me,
but to lay before you the naked truth—the real state of my
affairs. There are now in my drawer unanswered three
menacing Letters for three several debts, amounting collectively
to about 50£. Even to the House, from which you write, I am
indebted four or five pounds, for books for Hartley when he
was at Oxford, which I cannot think of without a sense of
shame—which I have repeatedly been on the point of settling
and the money snatched from me by some still more urgent
necessity.—The fact is, that I came hither embarrassed—the
successive Losses and increasing Distress of poor Morgan and
his family while I was domesticated with them—and which
being before my eyes, scarcely left me the power of asking
myself concerning the Right or Wrong—absorbed and—but
poor fellow! he is gone, and (I am persuaded) gone where his
many excellent qualities, which never suffered any eclipse in
his prosperous days, will greatly outweigh the one or two
faulty acts done in the confused and feverish dream of
Embarrassment—absorbed and anticipated my resources,
even to the leaving of my own small debts unpaid.—Meantime,
the Christabel, which I should never have consented to
publish, a mere fragment as it was, but for his goading wants,
the 80£ received for it from Murray going to make up the last
sum, I was able to raise for him, fell almost dead-born from
the Press—and it became evident that a powerful and utterly
unprovoked yet immitigable Party, at Edingburgh and
elsewhere, had determined to rail or ridicule down every thing
I should publish, and as much as possible (and with works so
little popular as mine are & ever must be, it was to a very
great extent not only possible but easy) to prevent their
sale—and (which likewise they effected) to discourage *the
Trade* from purchasing them.—Still, however, what by literary
Job-work and what by Lecturing—tho' the latter sadly fell off,
in consequence of my supposed political and religious

apostacy, while the party in power gave me no support, nor did the Writers of the Quarterly Review condescend to notice my Works, except by one or two occasional and vague sentences—I made a shift to get thro' the first and tho' imperfectly the second year of my residence at Highgate. But now came the storm. I had Hartley's expences during his long vacations—as I have since had Derwent's—with other minor calls on their accounts—and last, the unparall[el]ed profligacy of my bankrupt Publishers, of which I will spare you the detail. Sufficient to inform you, that after printing double, and in one instance quadruple the number of Copies contracted for, for each Edition—and tho' the Bankruptcy took place within a *fortnight* after the Publication of the Friend in three Volumes —still from the number sold in that fortnight, and from the sale of the Literary Life, the Sibylline Leaves, the two Lay-sermons and the Zapolya, a sum of 1200£ remained due to me—every farthing of which I lost—the ——, Curtis, a real partner but pretended Creditor of Fennor's, and who had carried on the Printing for the Concern, clapt a *lien* on 500 copies of the Friend—of which the *Trade* Price was a guinea each—and which, tho' a proveable fraud, can only be removed by a Chancery suit—and after all, I was obliged to borrow 120£ in order to buy-up the Halfcopy Rights of all my Works, which would have gone for trifles to Booksellers of no repute, and to prevent the unsold Copies from going for waste paper—perhaps, I had better have let them go—but I was in hope of better times, and that some more successful Work might occasion a call for them—till when I was advised to withdraw them from sale altogether.—Then came Hartley's cruel and most calumnious persecution and the loss of his fellow-ship—and for almost a year I have had him on my hands—& even this a less Loss than the necessity of writing and writing on this infamous business, and the effect on my health and spirits, which one with another incapacitated me from doing any thing for myself continuously—that would fetch money, I mean.—

I declare solemnly, that I must have wanted the necessities of Life, but for the almost unprecedented friendship of Mr and Mrs Gillman, under whose roof I live. Tho' the nominal sum, which I am engaged to contribute towards the expences of the

House, is barely adequate to the first-cost of my actual
maintenance—and tho' medicine, & medical attendance are
not put down at all—yet so many sums have been paid by Mr
G. on my account—that at this moment I stand indebted to
him for 500£—of which, but a short time back, he struck off
120£, as incurred for Derwent and Hartley, as if they had been
his Visitors.—You will understand my feelings when I add
that Mr G. has only his professional income—& that with a
highly respectable practice indeed but from the nature &
circumstances of the place, a practice of very limited extent—
and that he has himself two Sons and an Angel of a Wife.—So
help me God! for months past I have not [had] a shilling in my
pocket—nor do I know how or where to procure a guinea—. I
am endeavoring to make up a parcel for Blackwood's
Magazine —but even this has in part been paid for—

Dear De Quincey! I conjure you to feel convinced that were
it in my power—let what would come the next week—to raise
the money, you should not have received this melancholy
History as an answer—Were you to see me at this moment,
you would know with what anguish & sickness of soul I
subscribe myself your *obliged* & grateful

S. T. Coleridge.

To Derwent Coleridge

11 Jany. 1822.

My dear Derwent

I sit with my pen not only touching the paper, and my head
hanging over it; but *what* to write and with what purpose I
write at all, I know not. What can I urge that would not be the
mere repetition of counsels already urged with all the weight
that my earnest intreaties could add to them, so often both
before you went to Cambridge and since? What that would
not be the echo of echoes, which of late have *volleyed* round you
in a circle—admonitions which Friends of all ages, of your
own & even your Juniors have given you—and I trust, that
wisest and most faithful of all Friends, your own Conscience?
To study to the injury of your health, and the undermining of

your Constitution—was *this* required of you? You have long known both my judgment and my wishes in this respect: that a Senior Wranglership with the first Classical Medal as it's Appendage would be a poor compensation to *me* and in *my* thoughts for shattered nerves and diseased digestive organs. You cannot do without intermissions of Study, without recreation and such as society only can afford you—?—Be it so! But is dissipation of mind and spirit the fit recreation of a Student? Or not rather the fever fit, of which your Studies are like to be the cold, feeble and languid Intermittents? 'I have known instances of Drinkers and Whore-mongers', said Mr Montague to me a few weeks [ago]; 'but in all my long experience of Cambridge never did I see or hear of any one instance of a high Wrangler with or without classical honors, who was a man of Pleasure, Dress, and Family Visiting.' Even extra-collegiate Society, by preference & in a larger proportion than that of his own college, and the flaring about with distinguished Graduates &c; never yet made even if it left a man friends in his own College—who are after all from obvious causes the friends most likely to stick by us. But extra-academic Society, Concerts, Balls—Dressing, and an hour and a half or two Hours not seldom devoted to so respectable a purpose—O God!—even the disappointment as to your success in the University, mortifying as I feel it, arising from such causes and morally ominous, as it becomes in your particular case & with the claims, that *you* must recognize on your exertions, is not the worst. This accursed Coxcombry, like Dacianira's gift,° sends a ferment into the very Life-blood of a Young man's Sense and Genius—and ends in a schirrus of the Heart.—I know by experience what the social recreation is that does an undergraduate good. In my first Term, and from October till March, I read hard, and systematically. I had no acquaintance, much less suitable, (i.e.) studious, Companion in my own College. Six nights out of seven, as soon as chapel was over, I went to Pembroke, to Middleton's (the present B. of Calcutta) Rooms—opened the door without speaking, made and poured out the Tea and placed his cup beside his Book—went on with my Æschylus or Thucydides, as he with his Mathematics, in silence till ½ past 9—then closed our books at the same moment—the size and college Ale came

in—& till 12 we had true Noctes atticae° which I cannot to
this hour think of without a strong emotion—. With what
delight did I not resume my reading in my own Rooms at
Jesus each following Morning. Think you a Ball or a Concert
or a Lady Party, or a Literary Club, would have left me in the
same state—and your studies mathematical? Were it possible
even that it could be otherwise—yet your character must
suffer. If from Ill-health or any other cause, should your (I
quote Middleton's sweet Sonnet to me)°

young Ambition feel the wound
Of blighted Hope and Laurels sought in vain—

what sort of *solution* will be the one current? He *trifled* away his
success!—Can you not controll your Love of appearance and
Showing off for two or three years? At the end of that time the
very qualities that indulged in the interval will stamp you a
trifler &, with such claims on you, far worse! would be
construed into merit by the major part of the world—as not
too learned to be agreeable &c &c—There was a passage in
your letter to Mrs Chisholm° which shocked & wounded me
so much that I could not speak of it to you at the time.—Mr
J. H. Frere used these words to me—That you are above the
run of Readers, and cannot be remunerated by the Press,
increases not lessens the obligations of those who are
conscious of having been especially benefited by you. It is not
in my power to prove to you how much [I] feel this to [have]
been my own case—but I can spare a certain sum which is
[at] your service, & which I consider as your's—and then he
asked me, whether the enabling me to send you to College
would be the most agreeable to me—. Wrangham and
Caldwell were my old—the latter my oldest, Friends.—Suppose
that a Bookseller had given me 300£ for my Lectures, instead
of Mr Frere—would you think the sum more earned by me?
Mr Southey received an annuity from his old Schoolfellow,
Charles Wynne—which on Wynne's Marriage was commuted
for a Pension—Had Southey used this for his Son's university
education—would *Southey's* Son, think you, speak of himself as
a mere poor child of charity, a dependent on the I know not
what—and *contrast* his state with those, who are maintained by
their Fathers?—Had it been as true as it is false—should a Son

have placed his Father in so degrading a point of view—and this in a letter to a vulgar tattling Woman?—But if such be your notions respecting me & yourself (and how little you have been taught or are in the habit of attributing to or connecting with me, as the Source, I mourn to see, chiefly for your sake & because too many others see & notice it)—if you are this mere Almsman, how preposterous must your present conduct be?—I was even hugging myself with a letter from Prof. Calvert to Mr Caldwell—& wondered that Mr Gillman read it with so blank a face. Worship too has twice sent us a present —without a single line—I suppose, because he will not send ill-tidings.—But from different Quarters these ill-tidings have flowed in on me in a head. Even Henry C. has written to his Brother John 'in great grief and indignation' respecting you°—and as to your not writing to Mr Gillman (except as you make use of him) or to me, especially since your examination —'When did you hear from your Son, (says Mr Wells to me) my Son stands third on the List?'—And Mr G. has been so kind to you! not only striking of[f] the 50£ I was engaged to pay for your six months—but at this very time undertaking a serious responsibility for you. O Derwent! would to God you would so act as to permit you to attribute all the kindness shewn you to your own account, with some plausibility at least.—

I am not angry, Derwent!—but it is calamitous that you do not know how anxiously & affectionately I am your *Father*—
S. T. Coleridge

P.S. I hear that you are Premier or Secretary of a Literary Club—about old books.—If such things did not dissipate your time & thoughts, they *dissipate* and perplex your *character*—They are well enough for B.A.s & M.A.s—

To John Dawes

[Late May 1822]

. . . any presumptuous reliance even on efforts of indisputable propriety and duty. Too often the best result will be the consciousness of having done our best.) These are questions,

my dear Sir! into which I shall not enter at present—. But I
can not help questioning the *special* applicability of the remark
or regret to myself or to either of my Sons—least of all, to
Hartley. Giving no trouble to any one—to no one opposing
himself—happy from his earliest infancy, 'a spirit of Joy
dancing on an aspen Leaf'°—to what better can I appeal than
to Mr Wordsworth's own beautiful lines addressed to H. C.
six years old?°—From the hour, he left the Nurse's Arm, Love
followed him like his Shadow. All, all, among whom he lived,
all who saw him themselves, were delighted with him—in
nothing requisite for his age, was he backward—and what was
my fault? That I did not, unadvised & without a hint from any
one of my friends or acquaintances, interrupt his quiet
untroublesome enjoyment by forcing him to *sit still*, and
inventing occasions of trying his obedience—that I did not
without and against all *present* reason, and at the certainty of
appearing cruel, and arbitrary not only to the child but to all
with whom he lived, interrupt his little comforts, and sting
him into a will of resistance to my will, in order that I might
make opportunities of crushing it?—Whether after all that has
occurred, which surely it was no crime not to have fore-seen at
a time when a Foreboding of a less sombre character was
passionately retracted, as 'too [industrious] folly', as 'vain and
causeless Melancholy'°—whether I should act thus, were it all
to come over again, I am more than doubtful. Can I help
remembering that so far from having fractious, disobedient or
indulged children, I could count the times on the fingers of one
hand, in which I had ever occasion to compel their obedience
or punish their disobedience by a *blow* or a harsh sound? If I
but lowered my voice, Hartley would say—Pray, don't speak
low, Father!—and did or ceased to do as he was told.—Can I
forget, how often, when I had expressed myself sorry to see such
or such a child so indulged, and referred to the effects on it's
Temper, I was told—that I could not expect that all children
should be like mine?—At the ordinary time my Boys were sent
to school, and found a Father under the name of a Master in
You. You, dear Sir! can best say, whether they were backward
for their age, or gave proofs of having been neglected either in
moral principles or in good dispositions—whether they were
beyond boys in general undisciplined and disobedient. As

soon as I was informed of Hartley's passionateness & misconduct towards his Brother, you will do me the justice to answer for me, whether I was not even more agitated and interested than in your opinion the case warranted—and whether I left any means untried to bring Hartley to a sense of his error.—A sad sad interval followed for me from the ill-fated hour, I left the North with Mr Montague, speedily as I supposed to return, and Hartley's first Vacation which he spent with me at Calne—Whatever else has been said—how far truly, and how far calumniously, I humbly leave it to my merciful God and Redeemer to determine for me—it will not surely be said, that the two Lads were left friendless, or under the protection of Friends incompetent, or whom I dared believe myself permitted to apprehend unwilling, to observe their goings-on, during their holidays or holiday-tides—. Since the time of Hartley's first arrival at Calne to the present day I am not conscious of having failed in any point of duty, of admonition, persuasion, intreaty, warning, or even (tho' ever reluctantly, I grant) of parental injunction—and of repeating the same whenever it could be done without the almost certain consequence of baffling the end in view. I noticed, and with concern, in Hartley and afterwards in Derwent a pugnacity in self-opinion, which ever had been alien from my own character, the weakness of which consisted in the opposite fault of facility, a readiness to believe others my superiors and to surrender my own judgement to their's—but in part, this appeared to me the fault of the[ir] ages, and in part, I could not refuse an inward assent, tho' I mourned over it in silence, to the complaint made by others—both at Calne and at Highgate—of impressions made on their minds with regard to myself, not more unjust in themselves than unfortunate for them—. As far as the *opinions* & suppositions went, they indeed speedily underwent a revolution, soon after they had been with me & had compared them with those of the respectable Persons, who had known me day & night uninterruptedly year after year—And in Hartley, at least, the revolution was compleat. But the habit of feeling remained—I appeal to God & to their own consciences and to all good men who have observed my conduct towards them whether I have aught to condemn myself for, except perhaps a too delicate

manner of applying to their affections and understandings and
moral sense—and by which, it is to be feared, I have in
Hartley's case unwittingly fostered that cowardice as to
mental pain which forms the one of the two calamitous defects
in his disposition.

For to whatever extent the 'indoles pervicax et reluctatrix'
[stubborn and recalcitrant disposition] betrayed itself during
his sojourn at Calne, and afterwards on his first arrival at
Highgate, I have the testimony of our sensible and exemplary
Minister, the Revd. S. Mence, formerly Tutor at Exeter
[Trinity] College, and who took a lively interest in both my
sons, that it was less & less apparent at each successive visit,
and but a few months before the unhappy fall-out at Oriel he
had, in common with my excellent Friends, Mr and Mrs
Gillman, warmly congratulated me on the striking improvement in Hartley's manners, above all in the points of Docility
and Self-control.

But let it be, that I am rightly reproached for my negligence
in withstanding and taming his Self-will—is this the main
Root of the Evil? I could almost say—Would to God, it were!
for then I should have more Hope. But alas! it is the absence
of a Self, it is the want or torpor of Will, that is the mortal
Sickness of Hartley's Being, and has been, for good & for evil,
his character—his moral *Idiocy*—from his earliest Childhood
—Yea, & hard it is for me to determine which is the worse,
morally considered, I mean: the selfishness from the want or
defect of a manly Self-love, or the selfishness that springs out
of the excess of a worldly Self-interest. In the eye of a
Christian and a Philosopher, it is difficult to say, which of the
two appears the greater deformity, the relationless, uncon-
jugated, and intransitive Verb Impersonal with neither
Subject nor Object, neither governed or governing, or the
narrow proud Egotism, with neither Thou or They except as
it's Instruments or Involutes. *Prudentially*, however, and in
regard to the supposed good and evil of this Life, the balance
is woefully against the former, both because the Individuals so
characterized are beyond comparison the smaller number,
and because they are sure to meet with their bitterest enemies
in the latter. Especially, if the poor dreamy Mortals chance to
be amiable in other respects and to be distinguished by more

than usual Talents and Acquirements. Now this, my dear Sir! is precisely the case with poor Hartley. He has neither the resentment, the ambition, nor the Self-love of a man—and for this very reason he is too often as selfish as a Beast—and as unwitting of his own selfishness. With this is connected his want of a salient point, a self-acting principle of Volition—and from this, again, arise his shrinking from, *his shurking*, whatever requires and demands the exertion of this inward power, his cowardice as to mental pain, and the procrastination consequent on these. His occasional Wilfulness results from his weakness of will aided indeed, now and then, by the sense of his intellectual superiority and by the sophistry which his ingenuity supplies and which is in fact the brief valiancy of Self-despondence.—

Such is the truth & the fact as to Hartley—a truth, I have neither extenuated nor sought to palliate. But equally true it is, that he is innocent, most kindly natured, exceedingly good-tempered, in the management & instruction of Children excels any young man, I ever knew; and before God I say it, he has not to my knowlege a single vicious inclination—tho' from absence & nervousness he needs to be guarded against filling his wine-glass too often—. But this temptation *at present* besets him only under the stimulus of society and eager conversation—just as was the case with his Grandfather, one of the most temperate men alive in his ordinary practice.—His Cousin, the Revd W. Hart Coleridge, assured me that nothing could be more correct, or manageable than Hartley was during the two or three weeks, that he lately passed under his eye—that what he wanted, & what was indispensable, was Kindness without too much Delicacy, Kindness without any regard to his immediate feelings of pain.—Whatever else is to be done or prevented, London he must not live in—the number of young men who will seek his company *to be amused*, his own want of pride, & the opportunity of living or imagining rather that he can live from hand to mouth by writing for Magazines &c—these are Ruin for him.—I have but one other remark to make—that of all the *Waifs*, I ever knew, Hartley is the least likely and the least calculated to lead any human Being astray by his example. He may exhibit a Warning—but assuredly he never will afford an inducement.—

I could not think of his proceeding to the North in acceptance of your kind invitation, without putting you in possession of my inmost convictions. In opening out my heart I may, I fear, have betrayed Symptoms of a wounded Spirit. But the errors of a wounded Spirit are what you, my dear Sir! will be least inclined to judge with harshness.

One assurance I dare give—namely, that at present my Son earnestly looks forward to the hope of making himself agreeable & that he would be most happy should it be in his power to become in any way aidant or serviceable. Under all events I must ever feel and profess myself,

my dear Sir, | with unfeigned respect & regard | Your
obliged & grateful
S. T. Coleridge

To John Taylor Coleridge

[J. T. Coleridge had written a letter of introduction to Coleridge for a German visitor, asking his uncle to use his influence with publishers to get him work.]

Friday [8 April 1825]
Grove, Highgate—

My dear Nephew
I need not tell you, that no attention, in my power to offer, shall be wanting to Dr Reich. As a foreigner and a man of letters, he might claim this in his own right; and that he came from you would have ensured it, even tho' he had been a frenchman. But that he is a German, and that you think him a worthy and deserving man, and that his lot, like my own, has been cast on the bleak North Side of the Mountain, make me reflect with pain on the little influence, I possess, and the all but *zero* of my direct means, to serve or to assist him. The prejudices excited against me by Jeffray, combining with the mistaken notion of my German Metaphysics to which (I am told) some passages in some biographical Gossip-book about Lord Byron have given fresh currency,° have rendered my authority with the TRADE worse than nothing. Of the three

schemes of Philosophy, Kant's, Fichte's and Schelling's (as diverse each from the other as those of Aristotle, Zeno and Plotinus, tho' all crushed together under the name, *Kantean* Philosophy, in the English Talk) I should find it difficult to select the one from which I *differed* the most—tho' perfectly easy to determine which of the three *Men* I hold in highest honor. And Immanuel Kant I assuredly do value most highly; not, however, as a Metaphysician but as a Logician, who has completed and systematized what Lord Bacon had boldly designed and loosely sketched out in the miscellany of Aphorisms, his Novum Organum—In Kant's Critique of the Pure Reason there is more than one fundamental error; but the main fault lies in the Title-page, which to the manifold advantage of the Work might be exchanged for—An Inquisition respecting the constitution and limits of the Human Under-standing.—I can not only honestly assert but I can satisfactorily prove by reference to Writings (Letters, Marginal Notes and those in books that have never been in my possession since I first left England for Hamburgh, &c) that all the elements, the *differentials* as the Algebraists say, of my present Opinions existed for me before I had even seen a book of German Metaphysics, later than Wolff and Leibnitz,° or could have read it, if I had.—But what will this avail? A High German Transcendentalist I must be content to remain—and a young American Painter, Lesly, (the pupil & friend of a very dear friend of mine, Allston) to whom I have been in the habit for ten years and more of shewing as cordial regards as I could to a near relation, has, I find, introduced a portrait of me in a picture from Sir W. Scott's Antiquary as Dr Dusterswevil, or whatever the name is.°—Still however, I will make any attempt to serve Dr Reich, which he may point out and which, I am not sure, would *dis*serve him. I do not, of course, know what command he has over the English Language—If he wrote it fluently, I should think that it would answer to any one of our great Publishers to engage him in the translation of the best and cheapest Natural History in existence—viz. Oken's in three thick Octavo Volumes, containing the inorganic world, and the Animals from the Πρωτόζωα, (Animalcula of Infusions) to Man°—. The Botany was not published, two years ago: whether it is now, I do not know—there is one thin Quarto of Plates. It is by far the most entertaining as well as instructive Book of the Kind, I ever saw; and with a few Notes, and the Omission (or Castigation) of one or two of Oken's adventurous Whimsies, would be a valuable addition to our English Literature.—So much for this.—

I will not disguise from you, my dearest Nephew! that the first certain information of your having taken the Quarterly gave me a pain, which it required all my confidence in the soundness of your Judgement to counteract. I had long before by conversation with experienced Barristers got rid of all apprehension of it's being likely to injure you professionally. My fears were directed to the *invidiousness* of the situation, it being the notion of Publishers that without satire and sarcasm no Review can obtain or keep up a Sale—. Perhaps, pride had some concern in it. *For* myself, I have none—probably becuse I had time out of mind given it up as a lost case, given myself over, I mean, as a predestined Author, tho' without a drop of true *Author* Blood in my veins—But a pride in & for the Name of my Father's House I have—and those, with whom I live, know that it is never more than in *dog-sleep*, and apt to *start up* on slight alarms. Now, tho' very sillily, I felt pain at the notion of any *comparisons* being drawn between *you* (to whom with your Sister my heart pulls the strongest) and Mr Gifford—even tho' they should be to your advantage: and still more, the Thought that so thorough a—— (supply the rest!) —— as Murray, should be or hold himself entitled to have and express an opinion on the subject.° The insolence of one of his proposals to me, viz. that he would publish an edition of my Poems, on the condition that a Gentleman in his confidence (Mr Millman!° I understood) was to select, and make such omissions and corrections as should be thought advisable—this, which offered to myself excited only a smile in which there was nothing sardonic, might very possibly have rendered me sorer and more sensitive when I boded even an infinitesimal ejusdem farinae ['of the same kind', i.e. kinship] in connection with you.

But henceforward I shall look at the thing in a sunnier mood—Mr G. Frere is strongly impressed with the importance and even dignity of the Trust—and on the power, you have, of gradually giving a steadier and manlier tone to the feelings and principles of the higher classes. But I hope very soon to converse with you on this Subject—as soon as I have finished my Essay for the Literary Society,° in which, I flatter myself, I have thrown some light on the passages in Herodotus respecting the derivation of the Greek Mythology from Egypt—and in what sense that paragraph respecting Homer & Hesiod are to be understood—and when I have likewise got my 'Aids to Reflection' out of the Press—. But I have more to do—for the necessities of the day & which are *Nos*—non nobis [we (work), not for ourselves]—than I can well manage so as to go on with my own works—tho' I work from Morning to Night, as far as my health admits and the loss of my friendly Amanuensis.° For the slowness, with which I get on with the pen in my own hand contrasts most strangely with the rapidity with which I dictate.

Your kind letter of invitation did not reach me—but there was one, which I ought to have answered long ago, which came while I was at Ramsgate.—We have had a continued succession of Illness in our family here—at one time six persons confined to their beds. I have been sadly afraid that we should lose Mrs Gillman, who would be a loss indeed to the whole Neighborhood—young and old. But she seems, thank God! to recover strength, tho' slowly.—As I hope to write again in a few days, with my Book, I shall now desire my cordial regards to Mrs J. Coleridge, and with my affectionate Love to the little ones—& assure you that

with the warmest interest of affection and | esteem I am, my
dear John, | your sincere Friend
S. T. Coleridge

To James Gillman

9 Octr 1825
8 Plains of Waterloo
Ramsgate—

My dear Friend
It is a flat'ning Thought, that the more we have seen, the less we have to say. In Youth and early Manhood the Mind

and Nature are, as it were, two rival Artists, both potent
Magicians, and engaged, like the King's Daughter and the
rebel Genie in the Arabian Nights' Enternts., in sharp
conflict of Conjuration—each having for it's object to turn the
other into Canvas to paint on, Clay to mould, or Cabinet to
contain. For a while the Mind seems to have the better in the
contest, and makes of Nature what it likes; takes her Lichens
and Weather-stains for Types & Printer's Ink and prints
Maps & Fac Similes of Arabic and Sanscrit Mss. on her rocks;
composes Country-Dances on her moon-shiny Ripples, Fan-
dangos on her Waves and Walzes on her Eddy-pools;
transforms her Summer Gales into Harps and Harpers,
Lovers' Sighs and sighing Lovers, and her Winter Blasts into
Pindaric Odes, Christabels & Ancient Mariners set to music
by Beethoven, and in the insolence of triumph conjures her
Clouds into Whales and Walrusses with Palanquins on their
Backs, and chaces the dodging Stars in a Sky-hunt!—But alas!
alas! that Nature is a wary wily long-breathed old Witch,
tough-lived as a Turtle and divisible as the Polyp, repullulative
in a thousand Snips and Cuttings, integra et in toto [whole
and entire]! She is sure to get the better of Lady MIND in the
long run, and to take her revenge too—transforms our To Day
into a Canvass dead-colored to receive the dull featureless
Portrait of Yesterday; not alone turns the mimic Mind, the ci-
devant Sculptress with all her kaleidoscopic freaks and
symmetries! into clay, but *leaves* it such a *clay*, to cast dumps or
bullets in; and lastly (to end with that which suggested the
beginning—) she mocks the mind with it's own metaphors,
metamorphosing the Memory into a lignum vitae Escrutoire
[a writing-desk made of living wood] to keep unpaid Bills &
Dun's Letters in, with Outlines that had never been filled up,
MSS that never went farther than the Title-pages, and Proof-
Sheets & Foul Copies of Watchmen, Friends, Aids to
Reflection & other *Stationary* Wares that have kissed the
Publisher's Shelf with gluey Lips with all the tender intimacy
of inosculation!—Finis!—And what is all this about? Why,
verily, my dear Friend! the thought forced itself on me, as I
was beginning to put down the first sentence of this letter, how
impossible it would have been 15 or even ten years ago for me
to have travelled & voyaged by Land, River, and Sea a

hundred and twenty miles, with fire and water blending their souls for my propulsion, as if I had been riding on a Centaur with a Sopha for a Saddle°—& yet to have nothing more to tell of it than that we had a very fine day, and ran aside the steps in Ramsgate Pier at ½ past 4 exactly, all having been well except poor Harriet, who during the middle Third of the Voyage fell into a reflecting melancholy, in the contemplation of successive specimens of her inner woman in a Wash-hand Basin. She looked pathetic; but I cannot affirm, that I observed any thing sympathetic in the countenances of her Fellow-passengers—which drew forth a sigh from me & a sage remark, how many of our virtues originate in the fear of Death—& that while we flatter ourselves that we are melting in Christian Sensibility over the sorrows of our human Brethren and Sisteren, we are in fact, tho' perhaps unconsciously, moved at the prospect of our own End—for who ever sincerely pities Sea-sickness, Toothache, or a fit of the Gout in a lusty Good-liver of 50?—

What have I to say?—We have received the Snuff—for which I thank your providential memory.—There are no one here, that we know—saving & excepting the Joneses—. Mrs Gillman bathed yesterday—and sends her Love—& will write in a day or two.—We went to Margate—(Susan° just this moment comes up close to my ear, just as I was saying to Mrs G.—Is there any thing, Ma'am! that you wish me to say?—with—'Sir! will you give *my* kind love to Mr Gillman?' —Bless her!—She is a darling of a Girl. It is impossible not to love her.)—to Margate, & saw the Caverns, as likewise smelt the same—called on Mr Bailey & got the Novum Organum. In my hurry I scrambled up the Blackwood instead of a Volume of Giambattista Vico which I left on the Table in my Room, & forgot my Sponge & Sponge-Bag of oiled Silk.—But perhaps when I sit down to work, I may have to request something to be sent, which may come with them. I therefore defer it till then—

The Steels enjoy themselves, and are happy. Remember me kindly to Susan.—

I would be remembered to Hutton & Anderson: for they are House-mates. Heart-mates, I fear, they will never seek to be.—

My kind love to Eliza Nixon, and to Amelia, & to
Anne—and my kind regards to Mr Nixon—& my best
possible respects to Mrs Nixon, the Tree-Clip[per.] And pray,
do not forget to mention me affection[ately] & cordially to Mr
and to Mrs Chance—
God bless you, my dear Friend!—You will soon hear again
from

S. T. Coleridge

To James Gillman

[Coleridge wrote from Windsor, where he had gone—interrupting his
holiday—upon reports of the misconduct of the Gillmans' younger
son, Henry, at Eton. Coleridge's nephew Edward Coleridge was the
master chiefly responsible for the boy, and Dr Keate the headmaster.
Henry was eventually withdrawn from the school.]

Saturday Noon. [22 October 1825]
My dear Friend
Tho' I have barely seen Henry, and till I have talked with
him tête à tête can form no decisive judgement, and tho' there
is no Post till tomorrow evening, I yet commence the
Letter—chiefly that I may have more *time* for the writing of
what is to come, when I have that only to write; but likewise
that you may know the process of my mind as well as it's
ultimate decision. I had, of course, a cordial reception from
Edward—and after clearing a plate of mutton kidneys & half
an hour's earnest conversation, I accompanied my Nephew to
Dr Keates who is confined by indisposition, & tho' recovering,
still very weak from a sort of bilious fever. I never remember a
more perfect confirmation, than several of the facts gave, of
your conjectures, tho' the most striking I obtained from Sally.
It was evident (N.B. not to herself: who had drawn no such
conclusion, having mentioned them only as instances of
Henry's simplicity and entire confidence in her, as his
comforter) that the Floggings had gratified his Vanity, &
almost perhaps so as to be an object of his aspiration. What a
strange child he is!—But this is an anticipation.—Edward

began by entreating me to understand one thing—that *he* did not wish the Boy to be removed, on account of any trouble or the like, that he occasioned *him* (Edward) personally—that there were other Boys that gave him far more trouble—that as far as his Letter originated in any motive relating to himself, it was exclusively this—to put you & Mrs Gillman in full possession of what he could & of what he could *not*, henceforward hold himself *responsible* for.—'If his moral Being should receive a stain, more than superficial; and if his classical education should make no advance, or none, that for a moment would be considered by you as compensation for the loss of innocence, in it's two great points, Veracity and Purity; I must not be held responsible for the result. I will do all in my power to prevent it, I will spare no trouble or circumspection to bring about the contrary; but I must not be held responsible for the One, and I cannot promise the other.' No one (he continued) 'can be more thoroughly aware, than I am, that a bare six weeks, and for a *Nestling* too, could not in any ordinary case be considered even a tolerably fair Trial—and especially, when so large a part of his Faults and Failures might, as appears from the Letters you have shewn me, be rationally attributed to the paroxysm of Home-sickness and the Exhaustion consequent both on this and on the previous state of Excitement and the Straining of his Faculties beyond their natural strength. And were the *moral* Risk out of the question, even now tho' this is *not* an ordinary case, I should think that this consideration ought to decide in favor of his remaining here—for a time, at least, sufficient to ascertain what he can or will do, when his mind is at ease, & his feelings reconciled to the change, and familiarized to the ways &c of the School & College. But he does seem to me so little capable of withstanding temptation, and still less, far far less of repelling Seduction—his facility in giving way to any impudent Boy who laughs at or scoffs him for hesitating to follow his example is so extreme—that I do feel that there is a serious *moral* Risk—both respecting his Purity of mind & act, and his *Veracity*. Hitherto, his Honesty and Adherence to the Truth have been exemplary & in some instances affecting. But how long with such childishness, and want of *Sense* (I use the word *practically* & in distinction from Talent or intellectual Capa-

bility) may this continue? I can not remove Temptation—&
there are many bad Boys, from whose intimacy I can warn
him but from whose neighborhood I cannot remove him.—How
long, I say? Let the following Instance shew, how far my
fears are or are not groundless. A bad vulgar-minded bold Boy
asked Henry to go down with him into a Butcher's yard near
the College, instead of going on (as he was going) to the
College. Henry resisted—did not want to go—refused—& on
being again asked or bullied, went—to see a Bullock killed &
cut up—& to receive certain anatomical demonstrations from
the Butcher's Boys, as the little Rascal's (his Seducer's)
premature fancy had anticipated. Poor Henry had either no,
or very indistinct, notions what it was, he was to see.
However, the Bullock *had* been killed & cut up before they
arrived: but one of the Butcher's Lads asked Medsum (or
some such name) whether he had been flogged that day—the
little Vagabond answered, Yes!—"Let us see"—and he
consented & let down his Trousers to shew the[m. (There]
were two Butcher's Lads & a Butcher's man as the Spectators.)
T[hen the] question was put to, & received the same answer
from, Henry. And he too was called on, & desired to do the
same, that they might compare the Floggings. Henry hesitated,
&, I doubt not, was very unwilling—but on the other Boy's
threatening him, that the Butchers would spurt some blood on
him, he consented, and exposed his person & the marks of
Shame to these Ruffians!'—

Other cases have occurred, not indeed (thank God!) of this
sort but yet sad proofs of his incapability to stand out in any
resolve that his own better mind would dictate.—I do think,
my dear Gillman! that the preceding Anecdote suggests a
strong additional Ground of Objection to the practice, &
above all to the frequency of Flogging in the Public Schools. It
can not but weaken the Boys' sense of Self-respect in one of it's
most efficient Supports and Consequents, reverential Modesty
to their own person—& deaden the *human* instinct of proud
Shame, and the connection of Shame with Nakedness.—(+ +)

Of Henry's goings on in point of *Learning*, & of the
Symptoms of Ability or Inability to go through with the Tasks
imposed on him, & which in a short period will increase in
number & difficulty, I can say nothing which has not been

already communicated in my Nephew's Letter to you.—Here then I conclude, for the present, the one side of the Question. Now audi alteram partem [I have heard the other side].— Henry came in, while we were breakfasting. Whether Sally had prepared him, I don't know—Probably she had. He did not appear at all agitated—so very little, that I could not help asking him—if he was not glad to see me? Yes! very glad.—And by his manners & conversation it was plain that he felt under no restraint or awe from his Tutor's Presence. He looked plump & well—& tolerably neat, according to *my* preconceptions of School-boys. He drank a basin or large Cup of Tea & eat a roll & butter—& was obliged (he said) to go off to attend his Master.—At + + of this letter he came to me in Edward's Study, according to my desire: and I have had about an hour's Talk with him.—The result may be conveyed in few words. The neglect of his person in washing & change of line[n] he in part denied—it was a false charge which his Dame's Servant had made to Sally & which his Tutor over-heard—She had said, he neglected washing because he did not wash at his Dame's, where they stole his Soap, but washed at Mother Stevens's where he could do it comfortably; and in part, he laid the fault on his Dame, whom he dislikes, and her Servants whom he detests. But that since the Time, his Tutor had talked to him, he had given no cause of complaint, that he was aware of, in this respect.—When I spoke to him of the Act of Indecency, he was silent. And when I told him, I must tell you of it but would not for the world that his Mother should ever know the particulars, & pointed out the shocking-ness of the degradation as it would appear to every pure mind, he wept. When I charged him with the frightful silliness, the almost ideotic childishness of being vain of his Floggings & boasting almost of them to a Woman-servant, he was silent.—But over and over again, he said, he was happy, very happy—was never happier any where—wished very much to *stay* & said, his greatest difficulty & the chief occasion of his being flogged, was his inability to learn by heart, which he had never been accustomed to—that he could learn Greek far easier than Latin, and Long Ovid (i.e. the Metamorphoses) tho' 40 lines, easier than Short Ovid (i.e. Epistles) tho' but 24—but that he thought, he should get over it—& tho' he could not say much of his Progress hitherto, yet he did think that now he was quite comfortable, he should make way. He talked rationally. It was one of his sensible days, at least. I gave him a Shilling: & bid him come to me [again a]fter Church, i.e. at 4 o'clock. It is now 3. These are the Facts [on both] sides.—

I shall decide, I thin[k, in favor of his s]taying—unless you think no—

On the other hand, he does not seem to have any better reason for believing that he shall be equal to his Tasks & Rank in the School but his *feelings*. I will try to see Pattison.° One bad thing is that the Boys are all possessed with the notion of his silliness & absurdity.

P.S. Edward expects his Brother Henry to pass by Egham on his road from Devon to Town, and has written an urgent letter to stop him & bring him here for a day; & has intreated me so strongly to stay over Monday, that I have given a half-promise to do so—the more readily, that I may have a few lines from you in answer to this, if you write by return of Post. I never was so perplexed & irresolute before. The main argument for his staying till Christmas, at least, is the ill effect, it may have on the Boy's own mind, to think that he has been hardly used, and not allowed to have a fair Trial: when he was eager to do so—Perhaps, too, on his Mother's mind, & might strengthen her desire to repeat the Experiment at the Charter House.—I will again consult Dr Keates.—

God bless you & your ever faithful S.T.C.—

To James Gillman, Jr.

[22 October 1826]

My dear James

There was a time—and indeed for the Many it still continues—when all the different departments of Literature and Science were regarded as so many different Plants, each springing up from a separate root, and requiring it's own particular soil and aspect: and Mathematics and Classics, Philology, Philosophy, and Experimental Science, were treated as *indigenae* [natives] of different Minds—or of minds differently predisposed by their original constitution. Under this belief it was natural, that great stress was laid on the Student's having a *Turn*, or *Taste*, for this or that sort of Knowlege; and it was a valid excuse for reluctance in the study, and want of progress in the attainment, of any particular Branch, that the Individual had no *turn* that way.—But it is the Boast of genuine Philosophy to present a very different and far more hopeful View of the Subject. Without denying the importance or even the necessity of an original Tendency, or what is called a *Genius*, for the attainment of *Excellence* in any one Art or Science, but likewise without forgetting that even among the liberally educated Classes the fewest can or need be eminent Poets, Painters, or Naturalists—but that all ought to be well-informed and right-principled *Men*—the Philosopher considers the several knowleges and attainments, which it is the Object of a liberal Education to communicate or prepare for, as springing from one Root, and rising into one common Trunk, from the summit of which it diverges into the different Branches, and ramifies without losing it's original unity into the minutest Twigs and Sprays of practical application: and so that in all alike it is but the same Principles unfolding into different Rules, and assuming different names & modifications, according to the different Objects, in which these Principles are to be realized. Now as in the present stage of your Studies, & indeed for the next two years of your life, you are engaged in forming the *Trunk* of the Tree of Knowlege, which *Trunk* belongs entire to each and every Branch of the Tree, singly as well as collectively—(the Clergyman must have the *whole*, the Lawyer the whole, the Physician the whole, yea, even the naval and the Military *Officer* must possess the *whole*, if either of these is to be more than a mere Tradesman and *Routinier*,° a *hack* Parson, a *hack* Lawyer, &c, in short, a sapless *Stick*—for that is the right name for a Branch, in which the juices elaborated by the common trunk do not circulate—and for all the uses, that a stick can be applied to, such a man is good for—and good for nothing else!) it must be evident to you, that to have no *Taste*, no *Turn*, no Liking for *this* or for *that* is to confess an unfitness or dislike to a liberal Education *in toto* [altogether]—And what is a liberal Education? That which

draws forth and trains up the germ of free-agency in the
Individual—Educatio, quae *liberum* facit [education, which
makes one *free*]: and the man, who has mastered all the
conditions of *freedom*, is *Homo Liberalis*[a freed man]—the
classical rendering of the modern term, *Gentle*man—because
under the feudal system the *men of family* (Gentiles, generosi,
quibus *gens* erat, et *gen*us [men of family, well-born, who
belong to a particular tribe and birth]) alone possessed these
conditions. I do not undervalue *Wealth*, but even if by descent
or by Lottery (& since Mr Bish mourns in large Capitals, red,
blue, and black, in every—corner over the Last, the downright
Last,° you have but small chance, I suspect, of a snug £30,000
from this latter source, and your dear Father is too rational &
upright a Practitioner and Highgate too healthy a Place for
you to expect any one of the nine Cyphers as the Nominative
of 000£ from the former)—but even if you had an independent
fortune, it would not of itself suffice to make you an
independent man, a free man, or a Gentleman. For believe
me, my dear young Friend! it is no musty old Saw but a Maxim
of Life, a medicinal Herb from the Garden of Experience that
grows amid Sage, Thyme* and Heart's Ease, that He alone is
free & entitled to the name of a Gentleman, who knows himself
and walks in the light of his own consciousness.—

But for this reason, nothing can be rightly taken in, as a
part of a liberal Education, that is not a Mean of acquainting
the Learner with the nature and laws of his own Mind—as far
as it is the representative of the Human Mind generally—. By
knowing what it ought to be, it gradually becomes what it
ought to be—and *this*, the Man's *ideal* Mind, serves for a
Chronometer by which he can set his own pocket Watch and
judge of his Neighbour's.—Most willingly, however, do I
admit, that the far greater part of the process, which is called
Education, and a classical, a liberal Education, corresponds
most vilely to the character here given!—But that all
knowlege, not merely mechanical and like a Carpenter's
Ruler, having it's whole value in the immediate outward use
to which it is applied, without implying any portion of the
science in the user himself, and which instead of re-acting on

---

* This word reminds me of an Ode to PUNNING which I wrote at School, when I was
of your age—& which began with 'SPELLING, avaunt'!

the mind tends to keep it in it's original ignorance—all knowlege, I say, that enlightens and liberalizes, is a form and a means of Self-knowlege, whether it be grammar, or geometry, logical or classical. For such knowlege must be founded on *Principles*: and those Principles can be found only in the Laws of the Mind itself. Thus: the whole of Euclid's Elements is but a History and graphic Exposition of the powers and processes of the Intuitive Faculty—or a Code of the Laws, Acts and ideal Products of the pure Sense. We learn to *construe* our own perceptive power, while we *educe* into distinct consciousness it's inexhaustible *constructive* energies. Every Diagram is a Construction of *Space*: and what is Space, but the universal antecedent Form and ground of all Seeing? Now that *Space* belongs to the mind itself, i.e. that it is but a *way* of contemplating objects, you may easily convince yourself by trying to imagine an outward space. You will immediately find that you imagine a space for *that* Space to exist in—in other words, that you turn this first space into a *thing* in space: or if you could succeed in abstracting from all thought of Color and Substance, & then shutting your eyes try to imagine it—it will be a mere Diagram, and no longer a construction *in* space but a construction *of* Space.—Not less certain and even more evident, is this position, in it's application to *words* and language—to Grammar, Logic, Rhetoric, or the Art of Composition. For (as I have long ago observed to you) it is the fundamental Mistake of Grammarians and Writers on the philosophy of Grammar and Language [to assume] that words and their syntaxis are the immediate representatives of *Things*, or that they correspond to *Things*. Words correspond to Thoughts; and the legitimate Order & Connection of words to the *Laws* of Thinking and to the acts and affections of the Thinker's mind.

In addition to the universal grounds on which I might rest the immense superiority of this method—i.e. Instruction by *insight*, and by the reduction of all Rules to their sources in the mind itself—over the ordinary plan (for *method that* cannot be called, in which there is no μέθοδος [*methodos*, a following after], no intelligible guiding principle of Transition and Progress) I recommend it to *you* as the most efficacious corroborant of the active Memory and the best Substitute for any defect or deficiency of the passive Memory.—Let us indulge our fancy for a moment and suppose that you or I or Sir Humphry Davy had discovered an easy and ready way of decomposing, rapidly and on a great scale, the Water of the Sea into it's component Elements of Oxygen and Hydrogen, with a portion of Carbonic gas: so as to procure by an extemporaneous process a Fuel to any desirable extent, capable of boiling the undecompounded Water—How poor a thing would the most capacious Hold that ever Steam-Frigate could boast of, and the most abundantly stocked with Wood or Coal, and with the largest reservoirs to boot established at different Points, which the Vessel might stop at in the course of the Voyage from London to Bombay or Van Dieman's Land—how poor an affair would it all be, compared with the facilities given us by this discovery! The only danger would be, that the Colliers, Pitmen and Coal Merchants might waylay the Discoverer, and cut his throat.—Now, my dear James! not much unlike this is the difference between the reproductive power consequent on the full, clear and distinct Comprehension of PRINCIPLES, and a familiar acquaintance with the Rules of Involution and Evolution of Particulars in Generals, and the memory that results spontaneously from the impressions left on the Brain & Senses, and may be destroyed by a fit of Sickness, or be suspended at the very moment, you want it, by a Flutter or a dyspeptic Qualm, in favor of the former. In this Memory, to which we trust whatever we learn by rote and all insulated knowleges, seen each for itself without it's relations and dependencies, the recollections stick together like the Dots in Frog-spawn by accidents of Place, Time, and Circumstance (Vide Essays on Method, FRIEND, Vol. III: Essay the First°) or like the eggs in a Caterpillar's Web, by threads of capricious and arbitrary Associations. At the best, the several knowleges are in the Mind as in a Lumber-garret: while *Principles* with the Laws, by which they are unfolded into their consequences, when they are once thoroughly mastered, become the mind itself and are living and constituent parts of it. We know what we want: and what we want, we reproduce—just as a neat-fingered Girl reconstructs the various figures on a Cat cradle. That this is no mere fancy, you have a proof in my own instance. In the gifts of passive or spontaneous Memory I am singularly deficient. Even of my own Poems I should be at a loss to repeat fifty lines. But then I make a point of speaking only on subjects, I understand on *principle* and *with insight*: and on these I set my Logic-engine and spinning jennies a going, and my friends, I suspect, more often complain of a superabundant, than of a deficient, supply of the Article in requisition.

To exemplify this method of instruction by applying it to the principal points of an academic or classical Education—and in the first instance, to the analysis (= parsing), hermeneusis (= construing) and synthesis (= composition) of the Learned Languages—the Greek in comparison and collation with our Mother Tongue affords, I think, the greatest facilities.—The Latin, at all events, is least suited to the experiment—both as being only a very scanty Dialect of the oldest and rudest Greek, and the derivation of it's significant prefixes and affixes (or cases and tenses) requiring all the arts of the veteran Etymologist, τὰς γραμμάτων καὶ συλλαβῶν μεταμορφώσεις [the changes of letters and syllables].—Accordingly, with the Greek I have already begun with you, tho' but in a fragmentary way hitherto, and rather for the purpose of breaking down the *chevaux de frize* [impediments], which the *newness* & strangeness of the Subject throws round it, than in the expectation of leaving any distinct impression of the particular truths. For there is a state of mind the direct opposite to that which takes place in making an Irish *Bull*.° Miss Edgeworth has published a long Essay on *Bulls*—without understanding the precise meaning of the word which she makes synonimous with *Blunders*. But tho' all Bulls are Blunders, every Blunder is not a Bull. In a Bull there is always a *sensation* without a *sense* of connection between two incompatible thoughts.—The thoughts being incompatible, there cannot of course be any *sense* of—i.e. insight into—their connection or compatibility. But a *sensation*, a *feeling*, as if there was a connection, may exist, from various causes: as when for instance, the right order of the Thoughts would be thus— a b c d e f, of which *b* and *e* are incompatible ideas, tho' b is in just connection with c, c with d, and d with *e*—Now if from any heat & hurry of mind and temper such an extreme and undue vividness is given to b and c, as to bedim and practically extinguish the consciousness of (or distract the attention from) c and d, in this case b and c will appear next door neighbors, while the actual, tho' unconscious intervention of c and d, produces a *sensation* of the connection—just as in forgetting a name that was quite familiar to you—you have a *feeling* of remembering it, tho' the recollection is suspended.—Read this over till you understand it.—Now the opposite of this [stat]e is when we have the sense of the connection between any given series of Thoughts, but from their entire strangeness to the mind not the wonted, & therefore craved for, sensation. You understand them, & yet have the feeling of not understanding. The philosophy of the dead Languages I propose therefore to recommence systematically with you, beginning with the Greek Alphabet—then to the significant sounds or elementary *positions*, the Helms & Rudders of words, rather than *words*—and then to the different sorts of words. But for my present purpose, viz. of helping you to write Latin, I shall suppose all this done—& begin by pointing out the characteristic difference between Latin Sentences & English—& from this deduce the Rules & the Helps—This I defer to the next Post but one.—God bless you &

S. T. Coleridge.

P.S. Your Mama has not got over the *shock* of this Morning's Letters—for Mr Stanley wrote a very kind & considerate Letter to me.° What *might* have been the result keeps your mamma's imagination & feelings at work. She thanks you for your letter—& sends her kind love, & will write tomorrow or next day.—Till this shock, your Mama's Health & Looks had improved far beyond what I had dared anticipate—Susan Steele seems Hygeia° herself—& I am pretty well, all but——

To Mrs Gillman

3 May 1827.

My dear Friend
    I received and acknowlege your this morning's Present, both as Plant and Symbol, each with appropriate thanks and

correspondent feeling. The Rose is the Pride of Summer, the Delight and the Beauty of our Gardens; the Eglantine, the Honey-suckle and the Jasmin if not so bright or so ambrosial, are less transient, creep nearer to us, clothe our walls, twine over our porch, and haply peep in at our Chamber window, with the nested Wren or Linnet within the tufts warbling good morning to us.—Lastly, the Geranium passes the door, and in it's hundred varieties imitating now this now that Leaf, Odor, Blossom of the Garden still steadily retains it's own *staid* character, it's own sober and refreshing Hue and Fragrance. It deserves to be the Inmate of the House, and with due attention and tenderness will live thro' the winter, grave yet chearful, as an old family Friend, that makes up for the departure of gayer Visitors, in the leafless Season. But none of these are the MYRTLE! In none of these, nor in all collectively, will the MYRTLE find a Substitute.—All together, and joining with them all the aroma, the spices and the balsams of the Hot-house, yet would they be a sad exchange for the MYRTLE! O precious in it's sweetness is the *rich* innocence of it's snow-white Blossoms! And dear are they in the remembrance—but these may pass with the Season, and while the Myrtle Plant, our own myrtle-plant remains unchanged, it's Blossoms are remembered the more to endear the faithful Bearer; yea, they survive invisibly in every *more than* fragrant Leaf. As the flashing Strains of the Nightingale to the yearning Murmur of the Dove, so the Myrtle to the Rose—He who has once possessed and prized a genuine Myrtle, will rather *remember* it under the Cypress Tree, than seek to *forget* it among the Rose-bushes of a Paradise.

God bless you, my dearest Friend! and be assured that if Death do not suspend Memory and Consciousness, Death itself will not deprive you of a faithful Participator in all your hopes and fears, affections and solicitudes, in your unalterable

S. T. Coleridge

To J. H. Green

[?5 January 1828]

My dear Friend

Mrs Gillman bids me shift the blame of this Superfluity per [by] Post from my own to her shoulders—& say, that she bothered (anglice [in English], importuned) me not to wait for the chance of seeing you on Sunday but to ensure your coming against light obstacles.—Nay, quoth I, but a Surgeon hath no *light* obstacles. A pebble of an ounce weight might, it should seem, be easily kicked out of the way—but ask the Patient— and he will tell you (N.b.—I did not say this *out*) that one of a few grains is enough to gravel him—. But Women will have their way—& the purpose of this letter is to inform you, that my peccant Toe is not only very much sorer and more intolerant of the least pressure, but likewise not constantly but with intermissions, perhaps three or four times during the 24 hours painful—I can scarcely call it throbbing—it is a kind of heavy deep-seated pain—In the mean time, there has appeared an erysypelatous inflammation beginning at the top of the knee on the outside, extending permanently 3 or four inches, but at night the blush has shot downward in a narrow slip to within an inch or two of the instep—the worst part & that on which there are unfortunately two or three scratches or abrasions is just where the Calf thickens out on the anterior ridge of the Leg. I am lame—& have tried to keep down the inflammation, and to stop and as much as I can to prevent the Itching & Heat by the Liquor Carbonat: Ammoniae, & (which I find more efficacious) by sponging the Stocking with cold water. This Morning I found that the Stocking which I had kept on during the night, & wetted every time I awoke, had stuck to one of the Abrasions which had been oozing blood.

Tuesday Night I was feverish, with little sleep & that little disturbed by flying whirling confused Dreams with a number of crimson colored & luminous objects. My Spirits are depressed; but my mind calm and active—& all above knee not worse than usual—The pain across my body just below the Thorax, or between that and the navel, as soon as I awake

& as long as I remain in bed after waking, is not greater than it has been every morning for the last 6 or 7 years, is almost removed by rising and standing upright, and entirely removed the moment the faeces are eliminated. I have no pain & no soreness on either side; but make a great deal of light-colored clear Urine—and was thinking of boiling some over the candle in a Table-spoon to see whether it would co-agulate & thus (according to a Dropsy, Liver, and Kidney tall thin Quarto with a number of morbid-Anatomy Plates which I gave offence by calling *Cat's-meat*—not *quite* fresh) determine a schirrus, or abscess or tuburcle [tubercle?] in my Kidney—but I was afraid, it would co-agulate—& turned coward at the thought.—I know that nothing can be done, but by keeping myself still, & taking no stimulus that I can possibly do without—but yet it will be a great Comfort to me to see you next Sunday. And it is only on the possibility that something may have interfered or may interfere with *that*, that I could consent to avail myself of a leisure two hours on any other day, even tho' you should have them at your disposal.—If I know myself—& it is ten to one, I do not—but *if* I dare trust my own persuasions—I have no wish to have my life prolonged but what is involved in the wish to complete the views, I have taken, of Life as beginning in separation from Nature and ending in Union with God, and to reduce to an *intelligible* if not artistical form the results of my religious, biblical and ecclesiastical Lucubrations —& as I ground my hope of redemption from the afterdeath on the capability of a righteousness not my own, I have no other fear of Dying than that of being seized with the stolen goods on me—the talents which had been entrusted to me & which I had retained from the Persons, for whose benefit they should have been traded with—.

May God bless you | & your very affectionate, obliged & |

grateful Friend

S. T. Coleridge

P.S. There is something very aweful in that necessary inference from the Phaenomenon of the Races—assuming the rejection of the Ouran outang Hypothesis & that of Five Pairs of Adams & Eves°—that Individual Depravity in a nation of depraved individuals may sink so deep & diffuse itself thro' all the acts, affections, faculties, passions and habits of the Man as at length to master the formative principle itself & involve the generative power in it's sphere of influence—. What a dreadful inversion! a *guilty* Nature, and a necessitated Individual—an Individual sunk below guilt!—

To Joseph Henry Green

[Green was the first person to lecture on comparative anatomy in England, in a series of lectures given at the Royal College of Surgeons 1824–8. Coleridge took a serious interest in the lectures and referred to them in his *Aids to Reflection* (1825). Here he draws Green's attention to a scientific paper on the rhinoceros beetle in the *London Medical Gazette*.]

[2 May 1828]

My dear Friend

In the Medical Gazette, 26 April, No. 21, the 2nd. Column of the first page I thought, I found a striking illustration (of course, a 1000 such might be found) of the observation, 'how small a part of what we mean by the Body and the bodily functions are really the immediate object of the outward Sense, or can be termed *material*, as the contrary of immaterial or spiritual'.° In the Scarabaeus Nasicornis in it's first state 'we find the nerves arranged according to numerous small muscles attached to the *foot*—we see &c—muscles; but when this insect takes wing, there is a new developement of muscles for moving the wing; while those of the foot disappear, and (along) with them the Nerves'.—Now I humbly take for granted, that no one will pretend that the visible tangible molecules and fibres that compose the wing, were at the same time present and at work in manufacturing the new muscles and giving the nerves a new and correspondent arrangement; and likewise in the same moment in a third place removing and causing to disappear the muscles of the foot. But if not the component matter of the wing, then either the molecules of the wing muscles and those of the foot, the one moved *in* and the other moved by a fortuitous coincidence of opposite *freaks* without collusion which, I imagine, would protrude like the branching Antlers from the jaws of even a Boa Constrictor of Materialism who had contrived to swallow the whole Stag besides—*or* there must be a bodily Power or Power in the Body, working in evident reference to the wing.—And no less certain is it, that this is neither visible, audible, smellable, gustable, tangible, ponderable, nor any other ble but *intelligible*. Now I should like to hear first, what other definition of a spiritual Agent can be given but a presence that is intelligible but not sensible; and secondly, on what grounds the epithet, spiritual, can be denied to the bodily power aforesaid, seeing that the latter falls under the same definition. So true is the assertion of a Greek Neo-Platonist—τὸ καὶ Σῶμα πνευματικόν, ὁππο[σά]κις ζᾷ—i.e. Even the Body is spiritual as far as it *lives*.—Should you come up on Sunday (but do not put yourself to the slightest inconvenience—for I have no particular motive for wishing it) be so good as to bring with you the Letters on the true and false veneration of the Canonical Scriptures.°—

May God bless you &
S. T. Coleridge

To William Sotheby

9 Novr 1828
9, Waterloo Plains
Ramsgate—

My dear Sir

It is a not unfrequent tragico-whimsical fancy with me to imagine myself as the survivor of

> This breathing House not built with hands,
> This Body that does me grievous Wrong°—

and an Assessor at it's dissection—infusing, as spirits may be supposed to have the power of doing, this and that thought into the Mind of the Anatomist. Ex. gr. [e.g.]—Be so good as to give a cut just *there*, right across the umbilicar region—there lurks the fellow that for so many years tormented me on my first waking!—Or—a Stab *there*, I beseech you—it was the seat & source of that dreaded Subsultus, which so often threw my Book out of my hand, or drove my pen in a blur over the paper on which I was writing! But above all and over all has risen and hovered the strong half-wish, half belief, that then would be found if not the justifying reason yet the more than the palliation and excuse—if not the necessitating *cause*, yet the originating Occasion, of my heaviest—& in truth, they are so bad that without vanity or self-delusion I might be allowed to call them my *only* offences against others, viz. Sins of Omission. O if in addition to the disturbing accidents & Taxes on my Time resulting from my almost constitutional pain and difficulty in uttering & in persisting to utter, No!—if in addition to the distractions of narrow and embarrassed Circumstances, and of a poor man constrained to be under obligation to generous and affectionate Friends only one degree richer than himself, the calls of the day forcing me away in my most genial hours from a work in which my very heart & soul were busied, to a five guinea task, which fifty persons might have done better, at least, more effectually for the purpose;—if in addition to these, and half a score other intrusive Draw-backs, it were possible to convey without inflicting the sensations, which (suspended by the stimulus of earnest conversation or of rapid motion) annoy and at times overwhelm me as soon as I sit down alone, with my pen in my hand, and my head bending and body compressed, over my table (I cannot say, desk)—I dare believe that in the mind of a competent Judge what I have performed will excite more surprize than what I have omitted to do, or failed in doing—Enough of this—which I have written because I sincerely respect you as a good *man* to whose merits as an accomplished Scholar and Man of Letters his Rank and Fortune give a moral worth, as rendering this dedication of his time and talents an Act of free choice, and *exemplary*—and by the beneficial influence of such an example in that class of society, in which the cultivation of the Liberal Arts and Sciences affords the best, almost I had said the only, security against Languor, and a refined but enfeebling Sensuality—the more enfeebling, in proportion as it is diffused and inobtrusive. This is indeed the true meaning and etymon of the LIBERAL

Studies—digna Libero viro—those, which beseem a Gentleman, as containing in themselves and in their reflex effects on the Student's own mind and character a sufficing motive and reward—and are followed for Love not Hire.—Because you possess my inward respect, I would not stand in a worse light, than the knowlege of the whole truth would place me, or forfeit more of your esteem than my Conscience assents to.—I need not tell you, that pecuniary motives either do not act at all—or are of that class of Stimulates which act only as Narcotics; and as to what *people* in *general* think about me, my mind and spirit are too awefully occupied with the concerns of another Tribunal, before which I stand momently, to be much affected by it one way or other.

So much for the Past. Now for the answer to your Lett[er], which I have but just received in a pacquet by the Coach, & which must have been detained at the Coach office for a day & a half, according to the date of a Letter to Mrs Gillman inclosed in it, who is here with her Sister.—I mean by this Post to write to Mr Blanco White,° in answer to a Letter from him stating his scheme of a new Quarterly Review & soliciting my immediate assistance—& I will offer to him without any particular mention of your name, an article on Didactic Poetry, the age & state of manners to which it belongs; the merits and defects of the Georgics; the comparative fitness of the principal European Languages & the comparative Success of the several Translators, whose Versions are collected in the splendid Polyglot°—the former including the question of metres, and the two modes of translation, the identical, and the equivalent. I have not seen the Reviews, you mention; but do not entertain the least apprehension of having been anticipated. I shall have returned to Highgate (Deo volente [God willing]) within ten days, and as I shall bring with me the first half of the Article, having luckily the notes, I took, during a very minute and critical Perusal of the Georgics, first by itself, and a second time with Voss's & your Version, I hope & trust, that I shall be able to finish it before the close of as many days from the date of my return. —I know of no other respectable Channel—certainly none, to which I have any access—unless indeed Blackwood's Magazine might be considered such.—Indeed, on reflection—the wide sale of this work, and it's undoubted influence on the Literary Public, make it a *question*—and I will defer the statement of any particular article to Blanco White, till I hear from you—which likewise will give me the time, I unfortunately must devote to an article for a Newspaper, necessary for my immediate affairs—O how my soul shrinks from *Politics*—in the present state of things at least!—With respectful remembrance to Mrs and the Miss Sothebies, believe that in thought, will, and wish, I have been & remain your faithful & sincere Friend & Servt

S. T. Coleridge

P.S. My motive for wishing to know your feeling respecting the new Review & the Edingburgh Magazine is—that a certain tone & coloring of style is requisite for each.

To J. H. Green

Wednesday 12 Aug. 1829

My dear Friend

Suppose an absent man to have been moving the tips of his fingers round & round a small space of sunshine on a table or the like, & wholly unawares slides his hand under the focus of a Lens: the close neighbourhood, in which his hand had been playing about & about it, will but add to the vivacity of the sting—For the four last words substitute 'novelty of the Idea' and I shall perhaps have conveyed to you one small ingredient of the total impression left on my mind by your theory of the Beautiful & which has occupied my thoughts from the hour you left us on Sunday last.° It certainly did give a greater liveliness to the pleasure which every fresh inspection and turning round of the Idea afforded me, that tho' for years I had been experimenting on this or that fractional part of the Beautiful I could not recollect even an approximation to the Idea itself, to what the sense & state of Beauty *is*—and consequently with this the solution of the facts, that this or that quality is commonly found in objects which we call beautiful. The only thought indeed that I can recollect which possibly *might* have led me to the true Idea (for that it is such I have not the least doubt) but which most certainly failed of so doing, was an anticipation and half perception that in the distinctities of the Godhead the Beautiful or Essential Beauty belonged to the Spirit, or the Indifference (Mesothesis) of Will and Mind in the form of celestial *Life*, and in accordance with this and no less a consequence or corollary of your view, 1. the Good (= the Holy one, the abysmal Will) is the *Absolute Subject*—2. the Father, = I am, the Subjective: 3. the word or Reason (ὁ ἀληθὴς [the true]) the Objective: 4. the Spirit, or Life = Love, the Subjective Objective.° But tho' this did not lead me to the central Idea, (of which to the utmost of my Book-lore you are the Fons et origo [source and origin] your Idea necessarily leads to this, and both explains and confirms it. And this is not unimportant if (as I am disposed to think) in the enumeration of the Faculties or Attributes copresent in the *state* of the *sense* of Beauty, it shall be found requisite to place a higher Life (ζωὴ απαθὴς, cupido caelestis or Ἔρως ὁ οὐράνιος [the life free of passion; heavenly love; or spiritual love]) at the vertex of the line as the representative of the Will above Mind, as well as a lower life, at the Base, as the Exponent of Sensation, which must be assumed as present, tho' not in that degree in which it is an object of distinct consciousness, i.e. not *as a* Sensation but only as far as it is a necessary element in the attribution of independent Reality to objects of sense. But if the novelty & originality of your view have been one source of pleasure, still greater satisfaction have I received from the circumstance, that it is evidently a beautiful continuation & completion of the Idea so fully evolved in the introduction to the first of your two concluding lectures—on the distinctive character of the Human organisms —It is delightful to find that the same principle, which applied to the bodily organs and the functions, faculties and modes of Act and Being appertaining to or resulting from them distinguishes Man from the Beasts, constitutes in another form that capability, that exclusively human Sense, which more than any other distinguishes Man from Man, Nation from Nation°—

I feel perfectly assured that you have only to reproduce the idea and fix your mind on it for a while to be convinced that I do not over rate it's value and importance, and that whatever zest my personal affections may have given to the pleasure [of] the discovery, they have nothing to do with the substance of my satisfaction. As soon as I had full possession of your meaning, my mind seemed to have a promise of a new Resting-place—and the oftener I have reflected on it and the more relations and points of view I have examined it in, the clearer has the central & centrific° character of the Idea presented itself. The happy illustration of the centripetal and centrifugal, the Beautiful representing the former and the different modifications in the several Fine Arts corresponding to the latter, renders it even easy (i.e. for those to whom it is not impossible) to unfold the Idea into a complete Theory of the Fine Arts. At the same time it settles (and for the first time *satisfactorily*) the controversy respecting Taste—for it explains the difference of Tastes relatively to different objects even in men of equal cultivation, while yet it establishes the permanence of the ground of the sense of the Beautiful, and the independence of Beauty on accidental associations—i.e. distinguishes the Beautiful *in genere* [in kind] from the agreeable. It will therefore be a comparatively light task to shew in detail in what qualities positive and negative and what forms the fitness to excite the state and sense of the Beautiful consists, both as to the several material objects universally called beautiful, and as to those which all highly cultivated Minds have held such—But this is not all—I shall be wofully mistaken, if it will not be found to cast a new and important light on Psychology generally and to afford a clearer insight into the true essence of our great constituent powers—to the dispersion of the cloudy creations of Gall and Spurzheim.° For no living balance or union of communion can exist as the Mesothesis except by virtue of an *Identity* as the prothesis. Not only in the whole circle of the Fine Arts but in practical Morals, it will have a most salutary influence to have it an admitted principle—that the Beautiful is the centripetal Power, which dare never be *out of Act* even under the boldest and apparently wildest centrifugations. Another useful corollary is, that the Beautiful is an *Idea*—the *spirit* of this or that object—but not the object in toto [as a totality]—as Beauty adequately realized. As you truly observed, it is the subjective in the form of the objective—a fortiori [with all the more reason], not the objective in contradistinction from the Subjective. We behold our own light reflected from the object as light bestowed *by* it. The Beauty of the object consists in its fitness to reflect it—But I am called down—a party to day—the Chances, Col. Aspenwall &c &c—and another tomorrow—and Mice or the Devil's Imps are gnawing and nibbling within my right knee—Liver? Stomach? Kidneys?

To H. F. Cary

Monday Afternoon—[29 November 1830]

My dear & in the very center of my Being respected Friend! tho' I am so unwell as not without plausible grounds to suspect that your remarks may come too late for me to make any practical use of them; yet—should it please God to grant me a respite, such a sufficiency of bodily *negation* as (his grace assisting) would enable me to redeem the residue of my time—it would be so great a help to my chances of being useful to receive from a Man, like you, some *data* on which I might commence a sincere attempt to ascertain the causes of the Obscurity felt generally in my prose writings—whether in the way of expressing my thoughts, or in the injudicious selection of the Thoughts themselves—that I must press on you your kind promise to run your eye once more through my Work on the Constitution°—All I ask is, merely that you would mention the pages in the 2nd Edition, which you did not fully comprehend—for I am quite certain, that on such a subject what you found a difficulty in understand[ing], ought not, without an adequate preparation, to have been in the Book at all.—One cause of this defect I suppose to be the contrast between the continuous and systematic character of my Principles, and the occasional & fragmentary way, in which they have hitherto been brought before the Public.

Yet when I look at my *second* Lay-Sermon,° of which Mr Green was saying yesterday—that any reader who had not looked at the date in the title-page, would have taken for granted that it had been written within the last fortnight, and

in which I cannot believe it possible that any educated man
would complain of any want of common sense thoughts in
plain mother English—I cannot sincerely & conscientiously
attribute the *whole* of my failure to attract the attention of my
fellow-men to faults or defects of my own—You will believe
me when I say, that to win their attention for their own most
momentous interests is the Wish that so entirely predominates
over any literary Ambition, as to render the existence of the
latter *latent* in my own consciousness.—

My kindest Love & Regards to Mrs Carey—and with every
prayer of the Heart for you & your's I remain—

Your's truly
S. T. Coleridge

To J. H. Green

[29 March 1832]

My very dear Friend

On Monday I had a sad trial of intestinal pain and
restlessness; but thro' God's Mercy, without any craving for
the Poison [Opium], which for more than 30 years has been
the guilt, debasement, and misery of my Existence. I pray,
that God may have mercy on me—tho' thro' unmanly
impatiency of wretched sensations, that produced a disruption
of my mental continuity of productive action I have for the
better part of my life yearning [yearned?] towards God, yet
having recourse to the evil Being—i.e. a continued act of
thirty years' Self-poisoning thro' cowardice of pain, & without
other motive—say rather without *motive* but solely thro' the
goad *a tergo* [from behind] of unmanly and unchristian
fear—God knows! I in my inmost soul acknowlege all my
sufferings as the necessary effects of his Wisdom, and all the
alleviations as the unmerited graces of his Goodness. Since
Monday I have been tranquil; but still, placing the palm of
my hand with it's lower edge on the navel, I feel with no
intermission a death-grasp, sometimes relaxed, sometimes
tightened, but always present: and I am convinced, that if
Medical Ethics permitted the production of a Euthanasia, & a

Physician, convinced that at my time of Life there was no rational hope of revalescence to any useful purpose, should administer a score drops of the purest Hydro-cyanic Acid, & I were immediately after opened (as is my earnest wish) the state of the mesenteric region would solve the problem.

I trust, however, that I shall yet see you, as Job says, 'in this flesh'°—& I write now tho' under an earnest conviction of the decay of my intellectual powers proportionate to the decay of the Organs, thro' which they are made manifest, & which you must have perceived, of late, more forcibly than myself—I write, my dear friend! first to acknowlege God's Goodness in my connection with you—secondly, to express my utter indifference, under whose *name* any truths are propounded to Mankind—God knows! it would be no pain to me, to foresee that my name should utterly cease—I have no desire for reputation—nay, no wish for *fame*—but I am truly thankful to God, that thro' you my labors of thought may be rendered not wholly unseminative. But in what last Sunday you read to me, I had a sort of Jealousy, probably occasioned by the weakened state of my intellectual powers, that you had in some measure changed your pole. My principle has ever been, that Reason is *subjective* Revelation, Revelation *objective* Reason—and that *our* business is not to *derive* Authority from the *mythoi* [myths] of the Jews & the first Jew-Christians (i.e. the O. and N. Testament) but to *give* it to them—never to assume their stories as facts, any more than you would Quack Doctors' affidavits on oath before the Lord Mayor—and verily in point of old Bailey Evidence this is a flattering representation of the Paleyian Evidence°—but by *science* to confirm the *Facit*, kindly afforded to beginners in Arithmetic.° If I lose my faith in *Reason*, as the perpetual revelation, I lose my faith altogether. I must deduce the objective from the subjective Revelation, or it is no longer a revelation for me, but a beastly fear, and superstition.

I hope, I shall live to see you next Sunday. God bless you, my dear Friend! We have had a sad sick House—& in consequence, I have seen but little of Mr Gillman, who has been himself ill—and likewise Miss Lucy Harding. For me, it is a great blessing & mercy, Life or Death, that I have been & still remain quiet, without any craving, but the contrary.

Compared with this mercy, even the felt and doubtless by you perceived decay & languor of intellectual energy is a trifling counter-weight.—

Again, God bless you, my dear friend! | and
S. T. Coleridge—

To James Gillman, Jr.

Friday, 9 November 1832.

My dear James

I scarcely think that a Father can feel a livelier interest for a Son's Well-being and Well-doing (= εὐπραξία) than I feel in your's: and I do you but justice when I add, for your own sake, and from my faith in the foundation, the abiding Substratum of your character, tho' this is, doubtless, greatly enhanced by the accessory circumstance, that your Father is the Friend of a most important portion of my life, and your Mother a most dear and holy Name to me—a Blessing which plays, like an auspicious Flame, on my nightly Sacrifice of praise and thanksgiving.

My dear James! I am little *dis*contented with you—and not at all *mal*content. All I want and wish, but this I do want, I do most earnestly wish, is to see you rise one round higher on the Ladder of Thought and Feeling. Believe me, that He who takes his footing on the notion of the *Gentlemanlike*, will hardly attain, much less realize, the *idea* of a Gentleman: while the Christian—supposing the same social *Manège*, the same advantages of outward training—the Christian, respectful or forbearing to other men thro' the consciousness of his own actual defects and deficiencies, yet standing in awe of Himself from the knowlege of what he is *called* to be, is capable of becoming and aspires to become, who not overlooking the hues and qualities that difference man from man still looks thro' them; and in every exercise of prayer is compelled to lose them in the contemplation of the Reason, one and the same in all men, and the responsible Will and mysterious permanent Identity common to all men, and constituting while they

contra-distinguish our Humanity—the Christian, for whom in
this very habit of feeling respect for every man, even because
he is a Man, there arises that *manner* of shewing respect to
others which implies & with the ease and unconsciousness of
all *continual* feelings claims & anticipates respect for himself—
the Christian *comprehends, includes* the *Gentleman.* Or shall I not
rather say, he is the *Apotheosis* of a Gentleman? I was once
asked for a definition of Good Prose and replied—'Proper
words in their proper places.' And what then is good Verse,
rejoined the Querist: and my answer was—'The *most* proper
words in the *most* proper places.' So to the ? what should a
well-born Layman be? I would say—'A Gentleman'—and
what then a Clergy-man? 'A Gentleman in his Court-dress, as
always in attendance on the King from whom all Gentry is
derived.' For the Clergyman is a Christian, whose specific
business, whose recognized *profession* it is, at all times to
remember that he is a Christian, and were it but by his Dress,
and by a somewhat more heedful composure in his habitual
demeanour, to remind *others* that he is so.—

But both as Clergyman & Christian—or rather, as a
Christian, and therefore a fortiori [all the more so] as a
Clergyman, you have a threefold Ground of Respect, each
ground acquiring and indeed producing it's own appropriate
manner. First: *negative*—i.e. the respect you owe to a man, as a
man. Composure, mildness, and the absence of all passion,
overliness and contempt or contumely you would owe to your
self even tho' they were not owing to the individual in your
presence. But God, who permits him to retain *his* Image,
makes him your Creditor for this negative Respect, at least.
Secondly: *positive*—namely, the respect, you feel for intrinsic
worth, or in a less degree for the eminent gifts and talents with
which the Person has been endowed. Thirdly, and as the
intermediate of the first and second—Respect for the Relations,
both social & natural, as so many ordinances of the Divine
Providence. I respect a Senior, a Superior in rank or station, a
Matron, with the same feeling and on the same principle as I
take off my Hat when I enter the Aisle of a Church. The Apis
might be a clumsy Ox; but I would shew respect to him in
reverence of the higher power of which he was the appointed
Symbol:° and in my obeisance to William the fourth I should

feel myself discharging the debt of reverence, which as an Englishman I owe to the King that can do no wrong, that never dies.

Further, my dear James! as a Christian and a Moralist you will know and will hold it a duty of Self-reverence to avail yourself of the knowlege, that to be wronged confers on you in the same moment a superiority over the person who has wronged you, which you forfeit in proportion as you retaliate. In the very act of *retaliating* you change your position and lose your moral Vantage-ground. Worst of all, should the Impulse make you forget the permanent, the inalienable, indefeasible Relation, in which the Person has stood to you, and in which you stand to that Person. The more he forgets himself, the more do you remember *him*. I do not mean, I do not wish, that you should not shew that you felt the wrong, and with an emotion proportioned to your love and respect for the Author of it but let it be the impulse of the next moment to sacrifice the feeling on the altar of Memory and Gratitude: and let the scum, which has boiled up on the surface, remind you of the precious metal that glows beneath—the affections, the solicitudes, the love-travail of half a Life. I would have you connect a tender, a pleasurable feeling even with such a one's Foibles, whenever they were instrumental to or commingled with his well-purchased enjoyments, the alleviations of Cares and toils undertaken in no small part for your sake, and of which you have reapt and are reaping, the fruits. Life itself, this mortal Life, is but a trifle in a wise man's contemplation, and if you are a wise man, you will not let the trifles of Life upset you. Lastly, one of the securities for respecting and being respected is as seldom as possible to make your muscles the substitu[te] for your Tongue. What can be conveyed by *words*, express as seldom and as little as you can, in any other way.

God bless you &

S. T. Coleridge

To John Sterling

Tuesday Night [29 October 1833]
Grove, Highgate

My dear Sir

I very much regret, that I am not to see you again for so many months.° Many a fond dream have I amused myself with, of your residing near me or in the same house, and of preparing with your & Mr Green's assistance, my whole system for the Press, as far as it exists in writing, in any *systematic* form—that is beginning with the Propyleum, On the Power and Use of Words—comprizing Logic, as the Canons of *Conclusion*; as the criterion of Premises; and lastly, as the Discipline, and Evolution of Ideas—and then the Methodus et Epochae [Method and Epochs], or the Disqui[si]tion on God, Nature, and Man—the two first great Divisions of which, from the Ens super Ens [Being above Being] to the FALL, or from God to Hades; and then from Chaos to the commencement of living Organization—containing the whole scheme of the Dynamic Philosophy, and the Deduction of the Powers & Forces—are complete—as is likewise a third, *composed* for the greater part by Mr Green, on the application of the Ideas, as the *Transcendents* of the Truths, Duties, Affections &c in the Human Mind.—If I could once publish these (but alas! even these could not be compressed in less than three Octavo Volumes), I should then have no objection to print my MSS Papers on positive Theology—from Adam to Abraham—to Moses—the Prophets—Christ—and Christendom.—But this is a Dream! I am, however, very seriously disposed to employ the next two months in preparing for the Press a metrical translation (if I find it practicable) of the Apocalypse, with an introduction on the Use & interpretation of Scriptures—a Prophecy &c—and a *perpetual* illustration, as the Germans say—. I am encouraged to this by finding how much of *Original* remains in my Views, after I have subtracted all that I have in common with Eichhorn & Heinrichs°—I write now to remind you, or to beg you to recall to my Memory, the name of the more recent work (Lobeck?)° which you mentioned to me—& whether you can procure it for me or rather the Loan of it.—Likewise, whether you know of any German Translation & Commentary on Daniel, that is thought highly of?—I find Gesenius's Version° exceedingly interesting, & look forward to his Commentaries with delight.—You mentioned some works on the numerical Cabbala, the Gematria (I think) they call it—But I must not scribble away your patience—and after I have heard from you, from Cambridge, I will try to write to you more to the purpose—for I did not begin this Scrawl, till the hour had past, that ought to have found me in bed—With sincere regard

Your obliged Friend
S. T. Coleridge

To Adam Steinmetz Kennard

To Adam Steinmetz Kennard

13th July 1834. Grove, Highgate.

My dear Godchild

I offer up the same fervent prayer for you now as I did kneeling before the altar when you were baptized into Christ, & solemnly received as a living member of His spiritual body, the Church. Years must pass before you will be able to read with an understanding heart, what I now write. But I trust that the all-gracious God, the Father of our Lord Jesus Christ, the Father of Mercies, who by His only begotten Son (all mercies in one sovereign mercy!) has redeemed you from the evil ground, & willed you to be born out of darkness, but into light; out of death but into life; out of sin but into righteousness, even into 'the Lord our Righteousness'; I trust that He will graciously hear the prayers of your dear parents, & be with you as the spirit of health & growth in body, & in mind. My dear Godchild! you received from Christ's minister, at the baptismal font, as your Christian name, the name of a most dear friend of your father's, & who was to me even as a son, the late Adam Steinmetz; whose fervent aspirations and ever paramount aim, even from early youth, was to be a

Christian in thought, word, & deed, in will, mind & affections.

I too your Godfather, have known what the enjoyments & advantages of this life are, & what the more refined pleasures which learning and intellectual power can bestow, & with all the experience that more than threescore years can give, I now on the eve of my departure declare to you (and earnestly pray that you may hereafter live & act on the conviction) that health is a great blessing; competency obtained by honourable industry, a great blessing; & a great blessing it is to have kind, faithful & loving friends & relatives, but that the greatest of all blessings, as it is the most ennobling of all privileges, is to be indeed a Christian. But I have been likewise, thro' a large portion of my later life, a sufferer, sorely afflicted with bodily pains, languor, & manifold infirmities; & for the last 3 or 4 years have with few & brief intervals, been confined to a sick room, & at this moment, in great weakness & heaviness, write from a sick bed, hopeless of recovery, yet without prospect of a speedy removal. And I thus, on the brink of the grave, solemnly bear witness to you, that the Almighty Redeemer, most gracious in his promises to them that truly seek Him, is faithful to perform what He has promised, & has preserved under all my pains & infirmities, the inward peace that passeth all understanding, with the supporting assurance of a reconciled God, who will not withdraw his spirit from me in the conflict, & in his own time will *deliver* me from the Evil One. O my dear Godchild! eminently blessed are they who begin *early* to seek, fear, & love their God, trusting wholly in the righteousness & mediation of their Lord, Redeemer, Saviour, & everlasting High Priest, Jesus Christ. O! preserve this as a legacy & bequest from your unseen Godfather & friend,

S. T. Coleridge

NOTES

2 *& the 20th.* William Paley (1743–1805), Archdeacon of Carlisle, published *Reasons for Contentment* in 1792 to discourage revolutionary activity. The pages specified by Coleridge are concerned with some of the advantages of poverty. Paley later became one of Coleridge's bugbears, as a prominent champion of the Church using the wrong (materialist) arguments on its behalf.

Allen. Robert Allen (1772–1805), schoolfellow and college-mate of Coleridge's; one of the first both to join and to withdraw from the Pantisocracy scheme.

4 *religious feelings.* Resolved, that is, to take his life.

5 *Claud.* Claudian, *In Eutropium*, ii. 13, with minor variants.

Tiverton. From another brother, Captain James Coleridge, whose regiment was stationed in Devon.

6 *canine.* Canine appetite, i.e. voracious appetite; common name for the disease bulimia.

Pantocracy. Also 'Pantisocracy': Southey's and Coleridge's scheme for a classless community (the name means 'a form of government in which all are equal in power') that was to have been established on the banks of the Susquehanna River in America.

proprius. Spheterizomai is a Greek verb meaning 'to claim as one's own'. Coleridge's coinage, with the addition of the negative prefix, means 'to render communal'. Southey in turn used 'aspheterization', which he defined as 'the generalization of individual property'.

7 *odours awhile.* An adaptation of a line from Coleridge's own poem 'The Faded Flower'.

brassy hue. Not published in this form.

Allegory. A transparent disguise. In the days of the Roman empire, the island of Cos was famous for producing 'Coan vestments' so light that one could see through them.

Compliments. Joseph Hucks was Coleridge's companion on the walking tour; Robert Lovell married Mary Fricker; both were founding members of Pantisocracy.

8 *MY BROTHER.* Shadrach Weeks, servant to Southey's rich aunt, Miss Tyler, in Bristol; he had been brought up as almost a 'brother' to Southey.

9 *to the Heart.* The last six lines of this sonnet, published as 'Pantisocracy', may not be Coleridge's: for the complicated publishing history, see *Poetical Works*, ed. E. H. Coleridge (Oxford, 1912), i. 68 n.

10 *To love her*. Mary Evans.

for Good. Rom. 8: 28. The verse continues, 'to them that love God'.

11 *Optimist*. Coleridge was at the time a follower of the philosopher David Hartley and of the Unitarian scientist Joseph Priestley, and was consequently a 'necessitarian' in denying the freedom of the will, but an optimist in believing that since God is good, present evil must be ultimately good.

12 *on the Nativity*. 'Religious Musings', modelled on Milton's poem 'On the Morning of Christ's Nativity'.

13 *Wynne*. C. W. W. Wynn (1775–1850), a former schoolmate of Southey's, and his benefactor (p. 13).

14 *disciple*. Luke 14: 26.

17 *the boldest Order*. *Joan of Arc*, an epic poem published in 1796, celebrates a defeat of England by France and would therefore be rightly understood to challenge current government policy.

19 *Dr Pangloss*. A tutor in Voltaire's *Candide* (1759), whose lesson under the most discouraging circumstances is that 'all is for the best in the best of all possible worlds'.

Sorrow. Untraced.

22 *Temptation*. Coleridge adapts lines from Milton's *Paradise Lost*, iv. 83–6, 'whom I seduc'd / With other promises and other vaunts / Than to submit, boasting I could subdue / Th'Omnipotent.' The speaker is Satan.

23 *Sense*. The ability to recognize worthlessness. The word is derived from a mnemonic in Latin grammar.

24 *sloth-jaundiced*. Coleridge's word in 'Lines on a Friend' (1796), l. 43.

25 *changed my route*. Coleridge was on a tour seeking subscribers for his periodical, *The Watchman*.

26 *Arkwright*. Jedediah Strutt (1726–97), himself a cotton manufacturer and inventor, partner of Arkwright (1732–92), the inventor of the spinning frame, since 1771.

the Christian. Joseph Wright (1734–97), still known as 'Wright of Derby', whose paintings of industrial subjects, usually with dramatic chiaroscuro, have now historical as well as aesthetic interest; and Erasmus Darwin (1731–1802), physician, inventor, and author of such successful didactic poems as *The Botanic Garden* (1791). The author of *The Origin of Species* (1859) was his grandson and his biographer.

theory of the earth. James Hutton (1726–97), whose *Theory of the Earth* (1785) challenged traditional geological thinking by suggesting that the formation of the earth was a continuous process without beginning or end.

27 *unbelief*. Heb. 3: 12.

28 *your God*. John 20: 17.

29 *will be done*. Combines Matt. 6: 10 and 26: 39.

Freedom. Or 'Friends of Liberty', i.e. political radicals organized into groups so named.

30 *Magazine*. Founded in 1792 with the motto 'Unite, persevere, and be free', the London Corresponding Society was the first in a linked network of associations of working men established in urban centres in England and Scotland to press for political reform. Its *Moral and Political Magazine*, to which Thelwall was a major contributor, appears to have lasted only six months, June–Dec. 1796.

lost them. Poems on Various Subjects, 2 vols., 1787.

31 *English Pagan*. Thoth was an Egyptian god depicted as having the head of an ibis on a human body; Coleridge is probably alluding to alchemical or 'hermetic' writings, however, for Thoth was identified with Hermes Trismegistus. The 'English Pagan' is Thomas Taylor (1758–1835), translator of Plato and Platonists.

32 *octavos*. C. F. Dupuis, *Origine de tous les cultes, ou religion universelle*, 1795.

unsexing. Jonathan Swift used the name for Esther Johnson, addressed in his *Journal to Stella* (composed 1710–13).

34 *£2 10 0*. Coleridge's want list would tend to confirm the account of his reading given earlier in the letter, for it concentrates on Neoplatonists and pagans; the fifth-century Christian poet Sidonius Apollinaris is the odd man out.

35 *Sister*. Mary Lamb.

36 *Why will ye die?* Alluding to 1 Kings 19: 11–13.

Godwin. Coleridge's plan to write a refutation of *Political Justice* was never realized. (For Godwin, see the Biographical Register and the Index.)

Idolatry. The *Monthly Magazine*, to which Coleridge was an occasional contributor, first appeared Feb. 1796. Coleridge alludes to an article in the issue of Nov. 1796, 'Concerning some Apologists of Hero-Worship', which asserts that such great English philosophers as Bacon, Hobbes, and Hume were in favour of idolatry, and recommends the establishment of a 'national pantheon'.

37 *Thunder-storm*. 'Sonnet to the Wind', *Cambridge Intelligencer*, 22 Oct. 1796.

Gurney. Untraced.

38 *great things*. In 1796, Thelwall had published a successful pamphlet, *The Rights of Nature*, in response to Edmund Burke's *Letters on the Prospect of a Regicide Peace*; in November of that year, he announced the imminent publication of a second 'letter' and proposed, but never published, at least two more in the series. The notice about these works outlines topics to be covered, and they are as ambitiously wide-ranging as Coleridge's joke about the schoolmen suggests: Letter 3, on property, for example, has 28 subheadings.

39 *obscure*. Coleridge is responding to Thelwall's objection to his 'Sonnet,

composed on a journey homeward; the author having received intelligence of the birth of a son, Sept. 20, 1796' (above, p. 32).

40 *Berkleian.* Coleridge announces his conversion from the system of materialism associated with David Hartley and Joseph Priestley to the idealist philosophy of George Berkeley (1685–1753)—but both systems reject the dualism of 'body' and 'soul'.

Gray. 'Ode on the Pleasure Arising from Vicissitude', ll. 47–8.

Della Cruscan. That is, a member of the school of poetry associated with Robert Merry (1755–98), who had lived in Florence, belonged to its Della Cruscan Academy, and signed his contributions to periodicals 'Della Crusca'.

41 *Uniformity.* The Act of 1662, requiring that all clergymen accept the Book of Common Prayer as the only guide for public worship.

43 *was no more.* An abridged version of Rev. 10: 1–6.

made perfect. An abridged version of Heb. 12: 18–23.

oracle of God. Milton, *Paradise Lost*, i. 19–12, substituting 'me' for 'thee'.

44 *Immortality.* 1 Cor. 15: 53, wording slightly altered.

Botany Bay. Thelwall's objection was perhaps that Coleridge's poems seemed to be addressed to the wicked: the Magdalen Hospital was an asylum for the reform of prostitutes, and Botany Bay, in New South Wales, a colony founded by transported felons.

Physician. A paraphrase of Matt. 9: 12.

Poor Man? Adapted from Isa. 61: 1.

good works. Adapted from 2 Cor. 7: 10.

high places. Eph. 6: 12.

these bonds. Acts 26: 29.

45 *perfect.* Matt. 5: 48.

first Address. 'A Moral and Political Lecture', delivered in Bristol in January or early February 1795, and printed shortly afterwards.

Robespierre. Maximilien François Marie Isidore de Robespierre (1758–94), one of the great leaders of the French Revolution, and chief organizer of the Terror (1793–4), during which nearly 20,000 executions took place across France.

Hexameter Poem. Luise (1795), by J. H. Voss.

Universal Love. 2 Pet. 1: 5–7.

46 *divine nature.* 2 Pet. 1: 4.

49 *Godwin.* See note to p. 36.

50 *buds anew.* Untraced.

Materialists. Thomas Beddoes (1760–1808), whom Coleridge knew in Bristol, and Erasmus Darwin (note to p. 26 above), whom he met in Derby, were both eminent physicians. Coleridge goes on to name others whom he knew only through their publications: Alexander Monro (1733–1817), John Hunter (1728–93), and John Ferriar (1761–1815).

51 *Plastic & vast, &c.* Coleridge's own 'Eolian Harp' (1795), ll. 44–7.

52 *my own Wit.* These verses were first published from this text, as 'Lines to Thomas Poole', in 1893.

Woolman. An American Quaker (1720–72), influential by his essays and example in the anti-slavery movement. His remarkable *Journal*, a spiritual autobiography, was first published in 1775.

53 *Sans culotte.* Plebeian, from the French term for working-class revolutionaries.

54 *Parson Adams.* The unworldly clergyman of Fielding's novel, *Joseph Andrews* (1742).

55 *Angel still.* Untraced.

56 *Shenstone's.* Coleridge alludes to the affectionate comic portrait in William Shenstone's poem *The Schoolmistress* (1742).

Renyolds. Joshua Reynolds (1723–92), the most eminent portrait painter of his time, first president of the Royal Academy, friend of Samuel Johnson, and author of *Discourses* (1769–91).

57 *weary of herself.* Milton, *Samson Agonistes*, ll. 594–6.

Review. The issue of March 1797 contained reviews of Coleridge's 'Ode to the Departing Year' (1796) and Southey's *Poems* (1797).

incumbent Deity. Untraced.

59 *Quarle.* Defoe's *Robinson Crusoe* (1719) and the Crusoesque *Adventures of Philip Quarll* (1727), by Peter Longueville, were popular children's reading; Belisarius (*c.*505–65), the great Roman general, was the subject of an historical romance—published in French in 1766, but translated almost immediately and reprinted many times—by Marmontel, who perpetuated the legend that Belisarius had been blinded and reduced to beggary.

64 *Presentation.* The right, that is, to send a student to Christ's Hospital, the famous 'bluecoat' school founded under Edward VI.

65 *Euphrasia.* Legendary daughter of Evander, King of Syracuse, who upon the fall of her father, instead of escaping with her husband and child, sought him out in prison and kept him alive by suckling him; heroine of Arthur Murphy's successful tragedy *The Grecian Daughter* (1772).

67 *Freedom.* See note to p. 29.

68 *still small Voice.* 1 Kings 19: 11–13.

Alchemists. Although the Greek word, which means 'all-golden', does not appear among the common terms of alchemical literature, Coleridge might have encountered it in his wide reading. He seems to be referring to the Philosopher's Stone, the substance that would turn base metals into gold, which was one of the dreams of alchemy, along with the panacea or universal medicine.

69 *at Jerusalem.* John 4: 21.

Cowper. The Task, v. 496–508.

71 *Wordsworth.* An early draft version of the ending to 'The Ruined Cottage', which was later recast, omitting these lines, as part of *The Excursion*: see Wordsworth, *Poetical Works* (Oxford: Clarendon Press, 1949, repr. 1966), v. 400–1.

72 *dance of thought.* Coleridge quotes his own 'Fears in Solitude', l. 220.

Pyrrhonisme. Pascal, *Pensées*, Nos. 246, 287, translated by John Warrington (1960).

73 *Inanimate.* Coleridge's *Osorio*, v. i. 11–14.

74 *my Lessing.* Coleridge hoped to earn back the money spent on his trip to Germany with books that would be published after his return—specifically, a volume of 'travels' and a biography of the great German dramatist and critic G. E. Lessing (1729–81). See note to p. 76.

75 *Miss Speddings.* Mary (b. 1768) and Margaret (b. 1774?), sisters of Wordsworth's schoolmate John Spedding (1770–1851). They lived at this time with their widowed mother at Armathwaite Hall, Bassenthwaite.

76 *Germany.* The letters were never published as a separate work, but were put to occasional use, notably as 'Satyrane's Letters' in *The Friend* and *Biographia Literaria*. For the biography of Lessing, Coleridge did extensive research, but eventually abandoned the project.

him about it. As manager of Drury Lane Theatre, R. B. Sheridan (1751–1816) had encouraged Coleridge and Wordsworth in their attempts to write tragedy (*Osorio* and *The Borderers*, respectively), but rejected the results. Coleridge's *Osorio* was revised and produced in 1813; *The Borderers* was published in 1842. See Coleridge's comment p. 77.

Farmer's Boy. A popular new poem by Robert Bloomfield (1766–1823).

Trade. Source untraced.

Curran. At the urging of his friend John Philip Curran (1750–1817), the Irish politician and judge, Godwin spent six weeks in Ireland in the summer of 1800.

77 *Grasmere.* See note to p. 76. 'Stewart' is Daniel Stuart.

78 *Horn Tooke's System.* The study of language through speculative etymology in Επεα Πτεροεντα *[winged words]* or, *The Diversions of Purley* (2 vols., 1786, 1805) by the political radical John Horne Tooke (1736–1812), who had been tried and acquitted of treason along with Coleridge's friend Thelwall.

79 *vibrations.* Coleridge was probably thinking of associative 'processes' in referring to the union of words and feelings, and directing Godwin to avoid the theory of actual physical vibrations in the nervous system adopted by the principal philosopher of association, David Hartley (1705–57).

published. Coleridge's blank verse translation of Schiller's historical plays *The Piccolomini* and *The Death of Wallenstein* (1799) was published in 1800.

Calvert. William Calvert (1771–1829).

81 *Impressions.* Hume's *Treatise of Human Nature* (1739) begins with a distinction between 'impressions' and 'ideas', respectively the vivid experience of sensations and emotions, and the 'faint images of these in thinking and reasoning'. Coleridge objected to the debasing of the term 'idea'.

Descartes. 'Third Meditation', translated by John Cottingham.

suâ stat. Virgil, *Aeneid*, x. 770–1.

82 *Bark.* Peruvian Bark, i.e. quinine.

but a Bruise. Cf. *Tempest*, v. i. 286, 'not Stephano, but a cramp'.

Sara. Sara Hutchinson, arriving to spend several months with the Wordsworths.

83 *Mr Jackson.* The Coleridges' landlord and neighbour at Keswick.

Wissenschaftslehre. On the Concept of the Theory of Knowledge, 1794.

Gilbert's. Coleridge's Bristol friend William Gilbert (*c.*1760–*c.*1825), author of *The Hurricane* (1796), 'poor' Gilbert because he was insane.

84 *equalled this.* That is, in the apparently nonsensical speeches of Shakespeare's clown, Touchstone, in *As You Like It.*

Lucretius. In Thomas Creech's well-known verse translation (1682) of Lucretius, *Of the Nature of Things*, a note on 'empty space' in i. 381–3 occupies four columns of notes, labouring and obscuring the obvious.

Clarkson. The Wordsworths' friends Thomas and Catherine Clarkson, active members of the movement for the abolition of the slave trade.

87 *Necessity.* See note to p. 11. Coleridge's major attempt to refute the associationism of Hartley's influential *Observations on Man* (1749) appears in ch. 7 of *Biographia Literaria.*

89 *Little-ists.* Poole had used this term in warning Coleridge of the dangers of discrediting Locke and leaving nothing in the place of the former giant.

91 *in America.* Joseph Priestley (1733–1804), Unitarian and eminent scientist, had been driven out of England in 1794. He originally planned to join a community to be formed by his son, on the Susquehanna River (the intended site also of the Pantisocracy scheme), but when no community materialized, he settled in Northumberland, Pennsylvania.

92 *Tragedy. Abbas, King of Persia*: never performed, though the MS, with Coleridge's comments, survives.

93 *wishes to see.* Godwin's *Antonio, a Tragedy* (1800), and Thomas Campbell's didactic poem, *The Pleasures of Hope* (1799).

from Heaven. A favourite phrase from Juvenal, *Satires*, xi. 27.

mornings.—. . . Two lines heavily inked out.

94 *wiser man.* Coleridge's own phrase from the second-last line of the 'Rime of the Ancient Mariner'.

Dinners. See note to p. 78.

Paley's. See note to p. 2, and Index.

95 *the World.* Untraced.

    now over. There had been food riots in the west of England, and Poole was active in relief work.

96 *quarrel.* A variant of 'When thieves [or knaves] quarrel, honest men come to their good'—'get their goods' in Benjamin Franklin's version.

    go down. Adapts a biblical formula, e.g. in the apocryphal Baruch 3: 11, 'them that go down into the grave'.

97 *wonderful vale.* Southey had made a brief visit in September, and was about to leave for Lisbon.

98 *Wallenstein.* In Schiller's play, which Coleridge had translated, Max Piccolomini, in love with his commander Wallenstein's daughter, remains loyal to Wallenstein although his own father is not.

    Rickman. Southey's friend John Rickman (1771–1840), economist and statistician.

    Ribbon. The 'ribbon' of the Order of the Garter, emblem therefore of Nelson's ambition.

99 *Wheat & Barberry.* The wholesome and its destroyer: barberry is a host to black rust, which attacks wheat.

    Mole & Mulla. A mountain and a river referred to in Spenser's *Colin Clout's Come Home Again*, ll. 56–9; Southey had presumably been trying to identify them with particular geographical features.

    Stolberg. F. L. Stolberg, 'Der Irrwisch' (1772).

100 *Vapidarians.* Tepidarians, i.e. tea-drinkers.

    Sleep. An adaptation of 'Christabel', ll. 375–6.

102 *Friends.* Alluding to an ironic line in Sheridan's play *The Critic*: 'If it is abuse—why one is always sure to hear of it from one damned good-natured friend or other!'

103 *manner.* In *Lyrical Ballads* (1800), ii. 169–70: 'I marvel how Nature could ever find space / For the weight and the levity found in his face . . .'.

    Gesner. The First Navigator, an idyll by Salomon Gessner (1730–80), which Coleridge was at the time planning to translate.

104 *strong Wine.* Untraced.

    welcome. Sotheby had proposed a visit to Coleridge. The angel Uriel, 'Regent of the Sun', appears in *Paradise Lost*, iii. 621–735.

    diligence. Both parts of Coleridge's Latin remarks come from Cicero's letters, the first being a slightly modified version of Ep. xvi. 7, and the second (from 'De ceteris') a paraphrase of a passage in i. 2.

105 *loved me too.* Coleridge conflates lines from Giordano Bruno's *De innumerabilis immenso et infigurabili* (1591) and Virgil's *Eclogues*, v. 52, incidentally changing a negative ('non') to a positive ('quam') in the part from Bruno.

    Æolus. Gessner's story concerns the love of a young man for a girl on an island; in contriving to meet her, he becomes the first mariner.

Coleridge objects to Gessner's mythological machinery, especially to the presence of the minor gods Cupid (Love) and Aeolus (Wind).

Love. An echo of a phrase in Lucretius *De rerum natura*, iv. 1071. The Latin that follows is Coleridge's own, probably an attempt to conceal the thought from the women in Sotheby's household.

106 *task*. Misquoting Virgil, *Aeneid*, vi. 129.

Messias. F. G. Klopstock (1724–1803) published the first canto of his epic poem *Messiah* in 1748, and the last in 1773. Coleridge and Wordsworth sought him out in Germany, and Coleridge's record of their discussion is given in 'Satyrane's Letters' in *Biographia Literaria*. The motto comes from Virgil's *Eclogues*, v. 45–6.

107 *Mortimer's*. John Hamilton Mortimer (1741–79), historical painter.

Preface. The controversial 'Preface' to the 1800 edition of *Lyrical Ballads*.

Intricate &c &c. *Polyolbion* (1622), xxvi. 17–22.

vol. II. p. 27.—. In *Poems*, Vol. ii (1801—Vol. i being the 1800 *Sonnets*), Bowles printed a Latin poem by the Dean of Winchester with his own verse translation.

108 *Augustine. Confessions*, iv. 8.

Autumn. Sotheby had published his translation of Virgil's *Georgics* in 1800. He later presented Coleridge with a handsome copy of the *Georgics* in six languages (his own the English version), published in 1827.

Dark Ladié. 'The Ballad of the Dark Ladie', composed in 1798 and published as a fragment in 1834.

Dash. Two Lake District waterfalls.

109 *blood-red Wine*. A phrase from the folk ballad 'Sir Patrick Spens', from which Coleridge also took the epigraph for 'Dejection: An Ode'.

110 *Letters*. William and Dorothy Wordsworth were in France, making arrangements for the maintenance of William's illegitimate daughter Caroline and her mother, Annette Vallon. On their return, William married Mary Hutchinson.

old Molly. Mary Fisher (1741–1808), a neighbouring cottager who did part-time domestic work for the Wordsworths.

St Bees. Coleridge had just returned from a nine-day walking tour in which he passed through St Bees, to which he had probably been attracted by reports of a library there. He appears to mean that he had made the tour *instead* of spending several days at St Bees, as he had once intended. Thomas Ashburner (b. 1754) was a crofter and neighbour of the Wordsworths.

111 *Lloyd's children*. Charles Lloyd (1775–1839), contemporary of Coleridge's and Charles Lamb's, published verse with both of them and lived for a year in Coleridge's house. He married in 1799 and had eventually nine children.

112 *Lady Rush.* Wife of Sir William Rush, a wealthy Suffolk landowner; Wordsworth had accompanied the whole Rush family on a trip into Scotland in 1801.

Orestes. Sotheby's tragedy, recently published in one volume with his masque *Oberon.*

113 *First Navigator.* Coleridge's projected translation of the poem by Gessner mentioned previously, pp. 103–5 and notes.

Tomkyns. The engraver P. W. Tomkins (1759–1840), who was to illustrate the text.

Volume. See the note to p. 107; *Poems*, pp. 113–23 contain the first canto of an unfinished poem entitled 'The Spirit of Navigation and Discovery'.

114 *Sermon.* A facetious translation of the phrase 'nearer to prose' from Horace, *Satires*, i. 4.

Aristotle. Coleridge has amplified a passing remark made by Edward Young in 'An Essay on Lyric Poetry' (1728).

Aspen Grove. Coleridge, 'To Matilda Betham from a Stranger' (1802), ll. 34–41.

115 *external objects.* Coleridge refers to his 'Hymm Before Sunrise, in the Vale of Chamouni', based on a poem by Frederika Brun.

Naiads, &c &c. The divine powers of a particular place; of a particular person; of trees; and of streams, rivers, or lakes.

116 *meets the ear.* Milton, *Il Penseroso*, l. 120.

the Cross. The significance of Milton's 'Haemony' is still disputed, but Coleridge's allegorical linking of *Comus*, ll. 629–38, with the Last Supper and the communion service represents a significant tradition in Milton criticism.

of this world. In an Appendix to his essay 'On the Demoniacs mentioned in the New Testament' (*Works*, 1788, i. 485–9), Nathaniel Lardner quotes and gives the reference for a passage in which Josephus describes a plant with the property of driving out demons that is, however, difficult to get at—it can, for example, be pulled up by a string fastened to a dog, but then the dog will die. In quoting Lardner's reaction, Coleridge has made his words more emphatic than they are in the original.

117 *Es tee see.* Coleridge also puns thus on his initials in his satirical poem 'A Character', ll. 72–3; in fact, the rather free Greek became a favourite motto.

118 *of the Alps.* Coleridge's poem, published in 1798.

what she does. Coleridge adapts the words of Christ on the cross, Luke 23: 34.

120 *Old Allen.* The Allens were related to the Wedgwoods by marriage, John and Josiah Wedgwood having each married an Allen daughter.

121 *Sharp*. Richard—known as 'Conversation'—Sharp (1759–1835), a well-to-do businessman, member of the Wedgwood circle.

122 *love indeed*. A slightly varied version of his own lines, from the end of 'The Pains of Sleep'.

123 *the world*. Coleridge has playfully constructed the word 'anti-podagra' (anti-gout) on the model of anti-Christ, and quotes an appropriate verse from 1 John 4: 3.

Gunville. Josiah Wedgwood's country house in Dorset, where Coleridge had recently spent time with Tom Wedgwood.

124 *my Soul*. Adapts Ps. 59: 3.

125 *Sister*. Not Sara Hutchinson but another sister, Joanna.

126 *the Ghost*. 'I find it written of Simonides', published in the *Morning Post*, 10 Oct. 1803, and never reprinted by Wordsworth. It tells the story of a Greek poet who piously arranged for the burial of an unknown corpse, and who was later saved from a fatal voyage by its ghost.

127 *Optics*. His letter of 23 Mar. 1801, pp. 89–91.

exquisitely wild. Coleridge is quoting Wordsworth's description of the boy, from 'To H. C. Six Years Old', l. 12.

129 *Gravel*. Gout that exhibits symptoms in different parts of the body at different times; and urinary disorder.

Mackintosh's. James Mackintosh (1765–1832), philosopher, was a brother-in-law of both Daniel Stuart and the Wedgwoods, and Coleridge may have seen him as a rival; in any case, he strongly disliked him. The anonymous editorials to which Coleridge refers recommended severe treatment of French prisoners of war in case of an invasion, saying, 'the principle of no quarter is not a principle too harsh for us to inculcate . . . no mercy should be shewn till we are secure.'

130 *dreaming Clarence*. To the bottom of the sea, as evoked by the Duke of Clarence in his dream of drowning, in *Richard III*, I. iv. 9–63.

'foe intestine'. Coleridge's landlord, William Jackson, had proposed to sell Greta Hall. The quotation marks simply draw attention to a pun: the cliché 'intestine foe' refers to enemies within a state; Coleridge means that his digestive system gave him trouble.

Williamtayloricè. William-Taylor-ly, a reference to Southey's friend William Taylor of Norwich (1765–1836), well known for his linguistic innovations.

Anubioeides. 'Time in the form of Anubis': Anubis was the Egyptian god of the dead, often depicted with the head of a dog or jackal. Lethe is the river of forgetfulness in the Underworld.

Ottery. The second volume of the *Annual Review* (1804), almost 1,000 pages long and printed in double columns, reviewed books published in 1803, including a volume of Coleridge's poems. William Taylor was responsible for approximately 55 reviews, Southey for 35—among them the review of James Stanier Clarke's *Progress of Maritime Discovery* to which Coleridge refers, and a review of the second edition of Malthus's *Essay on the Principles of Population* for which Coleridge had provided 'Hints'. Southey pleased Coleridge also by using a little Latin joke of his in a one-sentence dismissal of a volume of verse, Luke Booker's *Calista*, and by quoting—perhaps at Coleridge's suggestion— 'our old and delightful poet, W. Browne of Ottery' (author of *Britannia's Pastorals*), in a review of John Davis's *Travels in the United States of America*.

131 *Crit. Rev.* It is unfortunately impossible to know to which of Taylor's articles in the *Critical Review* Coleridge refers, for Taylor contributed over 60 reviews between Dec. 1803 and Nov. 1804, and although his contributions to the *Annual Review* have been identified, the remarks about Milton and Tasso there have eluded discovery. As to Egypt, Coleridge is objecting to Taylor's remark in the *Annual Review*, ii. 307 that the French might as well be allowed to take over Egypt, for all the use it was to the British.

Madoc. In the press at the time; published 1805.

Marsyas and Apollo. Poets are unlikely to make money. Coleridge's immediate allusion is to the golden touch of Midas, and to Apollo as the patron of poets; but Midas was also said to have made an enemy of Apollo by declaring Pan to be a better flute-player. The satyr Marsyas had once similarly challenged Apollo as a musician; when Marsyas lost the contest, Apollo flayed him alive.

132 *Bellygerent.* Southey reported in October that their house had been sold, but in December sent word that the sale had been broken off. 'Bellygerent', 'belly-carrying', was Southey's term for the purchaser, 'one White, a fellow all paunch'.

137 *Anguish to me.* Stuart was then contemplating marriage, but did not in fact marry until 1813.

138 *head and heart.* The letter is unfortunately lost; the subject must have been the value of incentives to religion.

139 *first Essay.* In the projected *Friend*.

blind Eye. The surgeon who operates on a cataract.

140 *Obligation.* Book ii of *The Principles of Moral and Political Philosophy* (1785).

141 *this garden.* An allusion to a familiar passage in Boswell's *Life of Johnson*, in which Boswell complained of a book insidiously subversive of religion, saying that the author should have posted warnings outside his booby-trapped 'garden of flowery eloquence'.

142 *Friends.* Quakers, members of the Society of Friends; the coincidental title of Coleridge's periodical *The Friend* (1809–10) led to some misunderstandings.

Spectator. The most successful of Coleridge's predecessors in the mode of the periodical essay, the *Spectator*, conducted by Joseph Addison and Richard Steele, appeared six days a week from Mar. 1711 to Dec. 1712.

143 *Debate on the Address.* A new session in Parliament had begun 23 Jan. 1810 after a seven-month break. Since the King was ill, his customary address had been replaced by a commissioned speech, outlining the official position on current affairs, notably the state of the war with France. The speech was then 'debated' in both Houses, and the debate reported in the newspapers.

Satyrane's Letters. A selection of Coleridge's letters from Germany, published in the *Friend* in 1809.

responsibility. Sailors are invoked in illustration of Beattie's arguments in *An Essay on the Nature and Immutability of Truth* (1770; 2nd edn. 1771), but not in the passage on fate and free will (pp. 354–5) to which Coleridge appears to be referring. Beattie quotes a *History of St. Kilda* as proof of the belief of uneducated people that 'fate and providence are much the same thing', and comments 'that the sentiment of moral liberty is one of the strongest in human nature. For how many of their vices might they not excuse, if they could persuade themselves, or others, that these proceed from causes as independent on their will, as those from which storms, earthquakes, and eclipses, arise . . .'.

144 *Fourdrinier.* The stationer who supplied paper for the *Friend*.

Greek Articles. This paragraph takes up a current scholarly controversy bearing upon the doctrine of the Trinity. In 1798, Granville Sharp published *Remarks on the Use of the Definitive Article in the Greek Text of the New Testament*, proposing a rule or 'canon' for the interpretation of compound subjects in Greek, so that in the phrase 'Our God and Lord Jesus Christ', 'God' and 'Jesus' are understood as one and the same. Sharp's rule was defended by Christopher Wordsworth in *Six Letters to Granville Sharp* (1802) and by T. F. Middleton in *The Doctrine of the Greek Article* (1808).

147 *Ruth, p. 110.* Coleridge's point is that both Scottish poets, Scott and Thomas Campbell, author of *Gertrude of Wyoming* (1809), offend against the Commandment, 'Thou shalt not steal.' The couplet that he quotes from *The Lady of the Lake* has an analogue in ll. 124–5 of Wordsworth's 'Ruth', published in 1800: 'For him, a Youth to whom was given / So much of earth—so much of heaven.'

a canto. 'P——' stands for 'piss': someone suffering from a strangury has difficulty urinating.

148n. *Priscian.* A grammarian who flourished *c.*500, author of a Latin grammar in 18 books, mentioned here as a representative of staid scholarship.

et passim!— Further instances of Scott's lack of originality: Bracy is the Bard in Coleridge's 'Christabel'; the story of the travelling gentleman appears in Matthew Bramble's letter of 15 Sept., from Scotland, in Smollett's *Humphry Clinker* (1771).

149 *Hart Leap Well.* Wordsworth's poem, published in 1800.

King Lear. Untraced; perhaps anecdotal.

150 *Mrs Radcliff's style*. Ann Radcliffe (1764–1823) was one of the most popular writers of Gothic romances, e.g. *The Mysteries of Udolpho* (1794), *The Italian* (1797).

as well as new. 'Makes look almost as good as new': an allusion to Burns's poem, 'The Cotter's Saturday Night', l. 44.

Aberfoil. These lines are Coleridge's parody of Scott's octosyllabic verse in *The Lady of the Lake*.

caput mortuum. 'Dead head', or dregs, a term used in alchemy and in chemistry in Coleridge's time for the residue left after distillation.

151 *Dr Robertson's*. William Robertson, DD (1721–93), learned author of a well-known *History of Scotland*.

expected. Southey, a prolific author, published both the first volume of his *History of Brazil* and an epic poem, *The Curse of Kehama*, in 1810.

delightful Tale. Crabb Robinson had made Coleridge a present of his new translation (1811) of *Amatonda*, written by C . L. Heyne under the pseudonym of Anton-Wall.

152 *Apelles himself*. The greatest painter of antiquity is named simply as a representative of the artist of genius confronting a philistine public.

Murad. *Amatonda* tells of four Persian brothers—Solimar, Murad, Selim, and Hassan—who are encouraged to seek careers as soldier, courtier, poet, and dervish respectively, in the hope that they may be rewarded by Amatonda, Queen of the fairies, who embraces only those who live at peace with themselves. Hassan refuses to become a dervish, but stays at home in Beitulsalam, marries a young neighbour, and is embraced by the fairy. Solimar and Selim return home to live in humble contentment; only Murad is corrupted by power.

153 *Cantharadine*. Cantharides, dried Spanish flies, were used as an aphrodisiac. Coleridge is objecting to erotic elements in such French oriental tales as Voltaire's *Zadig* (1747) and the popular fairy-tales—originally written to *satirize* the vogue for fairy-tales—of Anthony, Count Hamilton (1646?–1720), who is mentioned in Crabb Robinson's preface to *Amatonda*.

155 *Jean Paul*. Pseudonym of J. P. F. Richter (1763–1825), popular author of whimsical novels and aphorisms, and of an influential treatise on poetry, *Vorschule der Ästhetik* (1804).

156 *Clarkson*. See note to p. 84.

157 *Devil, was sick*. 'The Devil was sick, the devil a monk would be; / The Devil was well, the devil a monk was he' (proverbial).

158 *Mr Street*. T. G. Street (fl. 1796–1827), at this time editor and joint proprietor of the *Courier*.

164 *Chivalry*. Apparently Coleridge's own verses. A second line, 'And all the thrilling Tales of Chivalry', is crossed out in the manuscript.

Tam o'Shanter. That is, from old to new and from sophisticated to rustic:

the references are to the author of the second-century Latin romance, *The Golden Ass*, and to Robert Burns's comic poem 'Tam O'Shanter' (1791).

166 *I need not say.* Coleridge implies that he would challenge Montagu to a duel.

171 *such an act.* Coleridge's poem 'To William Wordsworth, composed on the night after his recitation of a poem on the growth of an individual mind' (1805)—his tribute to *The Prelude*.

Longman's Table. Crabb Robinson had been present at a March dinner-party given by Longman, the publisher, at which the quarrel had been part of the literary gossip of the historian Sharon Turner.

172 *seeming otherwise. Othello*, II. i. 122.

173 *Oil of Vitriol.* Concentrated sulphuric acid, therefore not soothing but exacerbating.

done with them. Not a quotation, but an allusion to the parable of the talents in Matt. 25: 14–30.

174 *Socinian.* A Socinian denies the divinity of Christ. As leader of the Unitarian congregation in Bristol, Coleridge's former friend, the Revd John Prior Estlin, resented the association of Satan with Socinian principles.

175 *gradually.* Coleridge echoes the Apostles' Creed: '[He] was crucified, dead and buried; He descended into Hell; the third day he rose again from the dead . . .'.

176 *offendeth in all.* Jas. 2: 10.

heart. A slip for 'head'?

177 *Kennel.* We would say 'gutter': the kennel was the channel running down the middle of a street, to carry away rain-water and rubbish.

my unbelief. Mark 9: 24.

178 *Socinian.* See note to p. 174.

Charlotte. Morgan's wife and her sister, Charlotte Brent.

179 *that dieth not.* Based on Mark 9: 48.

180 *years and ten.* Coleridge's 'Monody on the Death of Chatterton' (1794 version), ll. 1–4.

the Rocks. A variant version of 'The Picture, or, the Lover's Resolution' (1802), ll. 17–27.

refocillation. 'Revival', a coinage from the Latin *refocillo*, 'to revive'.

181 *Mrs H. More.* Hannah More (1745–1833), celebrated bluestocking author who had turned in the 1790s to writing tracts that advocated social reform. She was associated with the evangelical Clapham sect.

very harsh. See note to p. 176.

182 *'Messiah'.* Cottle sent for Coleridge's critical attention a draft of the poem he published later in the year.

of Eternity. A free version of the apocryphal Wisdom of Solomon 2: 23, 'But God created man for immortality, and made him the image of his own eternal self . . .'.

184 *Poverty.* An attempt had been made to raise money for Coleridge by the common charitable method of subscription, but it had led to unpleasant talk about him.

185 *Ladyship.* The Beaumonts had been lent a copy made by Sara Hutchinson of Coleridge's tribute to *The Prelude*, 'To William Wordsworth'; the long quotation below is from that poem.

186 *Monody.* 'Monody' here means a poem in which a mourner bewails someone's death, as in Coleridge's own 'Monody on the Death of Chatterton'. Coleridge may be referring to a public lecture—of which there is now no record—in which he compared Milton's monody 'Lycidas' with Cowley's 'On the Death of Mr. William Harvey'.

former Poem. The Prelude.

188 *upon me.* Aristophanes, *The Frogs*, l. 314.

Senses. By a radical simplification, John Locke's *Essay Concerning Human Understanding* (1690) was generally considered to be the foundation of an empirical psychology that represented the mind as empty until furnished by sense-impressions.

Ouran Outang state. Coleridge cites two popular didactic poems, the first book of Pope's *Essay on Man* (1733–4) and Erasmus Darwin's *Temple of Nature* (1803) to illustrate the pervasiveness of the view that man differs only in degree, not in kind, from other animals; neither work explicitly supports the theory (though it was current in the eighteenth century) that mankind evolved from the higher primates.

189 *Point of View.* These were the words Wordsworth had used in his letter to Coleridge, 22 May 1815.

190 *Single Patron.* For Allston, see the Biographical Register. George Dawe, RA (1781–1829), a successful Academy painter, exhibited a painting and a bust of Coleridge in 1812.

included. In *Biographia Literaria*, Coleridge clarified his divergence from Wordsworth's views about the nature of poetic diction and the relationship between poetry and prose.

191 *merely mechanic.* Coleridge's system of 'Dynamic Philosophy' was itself subject to constant revision, but its fundamental tenet—the progressive manifestation of divine spirit in the world—may be seen e.g. in the preceding letter to Wordsworth, pp. 188–9.

intermixed. An order for snuff.

192 *Self-miscomplacence.* Lack of self-satisfaction.

195 *Mad. de Stahl.* In the account of German life, literature and philosophy in her popular work *De l'Allemagne* (*Germany*), published in 1810.

197 *from Jove.* The opening lines of Dryden's translation and Johnson's

imitation (*The Vanity of Human Wishes*) of Juvenal's Tenth Satire; and Milton's *Paradise Lost*, ix. 396.

caput mortuum. See note to p. 150.

his libels. In 1816, Hazlitt wrote several damaging reviews of Coleridge's *Statesman's Manual* and *Christabel, Kubla Khan, The Pains of Sleep*; the following allusions show that Coleridge was thinking particularly of the *Christabel* review in *The Examiner*.

198 *now printing.* Coleridge was planning the revision of his periodical *The Friend* for publication in 3 vols. (1818), and contemplated including successful newspaper essays concerned with the two great statesmen. (He did not in the end include either piece.) In Appendix C of his first 'lay sermon', *The Statesman's Manual* (1816), he hinted at Charles James Fox in his reference to 'a French nature of rapacity, ferocity, and presumption'.

Logos. Chiefly because of John 1: 1, 'In the beginning was the Word,' the Greek term 'Logos' or 'Word' has traditionally been identified with Christ; it is also the root of 'logic' and hence of the following titles.

Spinoza. Coleridge groups together three thinkers whom he believed to be misunderstood and underrated by his contemporaries: Giordano Bruno (1548–1600), who was executed as a heretic; the mystic Jacob Boehme (1575–1624); and the great Jewish philosopher Benedict Spinoza (1632–77).

Unitarianism. Coleridge perhaps means to imply that there is nothing new about Unitarianism but its name, and that that is misleading. The Unitarians deny the divinity of Christ and reject the doctrine of the Trinity. Like earlier churches, then, they teach the *unicity* and not the *unitariness* of the godhead: such may be Coleridge's line of thought.

thy shore. Coleridge quotes his own poem of 1801, 'On Revisiting the Sea-Shore'.

200 *with thanks.* Interested presumably by the Swedenborgian element in Blake's work, Tulk had lent Coleridge a copy of *Songs of Innocence and of Experience* (1794); in a letter to another correspondent, Coleridge remarked, 'You perhaps smile at *my* calling another Poet, a *Mystic*; but verily I am in the very mire of common-place common-sense compared with Mr Blake, apo- or rather ana-calyptic Poet, and Painter!'

goldbeater's skin. Coleridge means, perhaps, skin as thin as gold leaf—an apt image for the clinging garment of flesh characteristic of Blake's figures.

of this poem. Although he fears that Swedenborgianism may underestimate the gulf between divine and human, Coleridge finds the opposite extreme in the 'modern Saints' (meaning probably the Calvinists) much worse. Both parties printed tracts for free distribution.

203 *Pediluvia.* Purgative medicines for stomach and bowels.

Antar. Antar. A Bedoueen Romance. Translated from the Arabic (1819), by

Teerick Hamilton. Coleridge alludes below to remarks made in the introduction, p. iv.

Lady Errol. Mrs J. H. Frere (for whom see the Biographical Register).

Brahmanism. The Hindu reformer has not been identified.

205 *Hercules.* The 'matrimonial goddess' Hera (in Latin, Juno) was responsible for childbirth; Boreas, the North Wind, was supposed to bring ill health: Coleridge means that Gillman has been as busy tending pregnant women and invalids, as Hercules in his legendary 'labors'.

Attic Evening. An evening of good fellowship and conversation; see note to p. 235.

206 *Academus or . . . the Lyceum.* The two places associated with the teaching of Plato and Aristotle respectively.

Prolegomena &c. Prolegomena zu einer jeden künftigen Metaphysik, i.e. Prolegomena to any future metaphysic (1783).

Literary Life. This maxim, attributed to Socrates by Diogenes Laertius (and encountered by Coleridge in Bacon's *Apophthegms*), is the theme of the opening of Chapter 12 of *Biographia Literaria*, and the touchstone of much of Coleridge's literary criticism.

208 *better melody.* Edmund Spenser, 'October', *The Shepheardes Calendar*, ll. 109–14, 61–2, 73–8 (with minor variants).

209 *Ravensmuir. The Bride of Lammermoor* (1819). 'Ravenswood' is a family name in the novel. Coleridge explains his opinion of Scott's work more fully in a later letter, pp. 216–18.

211 *paragraph. Lycidas*, ll. 64–84, in which the poet's complaint about the futility of his work is answered by reference to God's final judgment: 'As he pronounces lastly on each deed, / Of so much fame in heav'n expect thy meed.'

they came. The poem—a sonnet?—is untraced.

215 IN HAND. Spenser, 'October', *The Shepheardes Calendar*, ll. 97–102 (with 'Want' for the original 'Love' in the second line).

216 *Scott.* In the letter preceding, p. 209.

217 *my position.* Coleridge names three popular actors of his own time: 'Master Betty', a child prodigy who had had a vogue in 1804–5; Edmund Kean (1787–1833), the great Shakespearian actor; and Charles Matthews (1776–1835), the famous comic actor who happened also to be a Highgate neighbour.

218 *Beggar-girl.* Coleridge compares Scott's fiction with its eighteenth-century precursors. Parson Adams and Blifil appear in Fielding's novels; Strap, Lieutenant Bowling, and Tabitha Bramble in Smollett's; Lovelace, Miss Byron, Emily, and Clementina in Richardson's; and the Widow Wadman, Mr Shandy, Uncle Toby, and Trim in Sterne's. Anna Maria Bennet's *Beggar-Girl*, published in 1797, is a late entry.

219 *Ashantees.* West African tribes, the Fanti and Ashanti.

220 *D'Urfé, Scudéri, &c.* Coleridge is disparaging both Scott's originality and the effort involved in his kind of fiction by suggesting that it is the sort of rubbish found in the circulating libraries, and that it is derivative. The authors to whom he refers wrote some of the celebrated French romances of the seventeenth century—Madeleine de Scudéry (1607–1701) and Honoré d'Urfé (1567–1625).

Phantasus. A collection of short pieces by Coleridge's German friend Ludwig Tieck, published in parts in 1812–16.

Alnaschar-like. In the *Arabian Nights* and *Spectator* 535, a day-dreamer.

221 *Gospel.* Untraced.

39 Articles. Socinians deny the divinity of Christ, considering him simply as a great man. Coleridge believed there was a connection between the chief Socinian dissenters of his own day, the Unitarians, and the dominant party within the Church of England, the liberal tradition which he traced to Jacobus Arminius (1560–1609) and Hugo Grotius (1583–1645), in that both emphasized mortal and material aspects of Christianity in contrast to Coleridge's own emphasis on spiritual religion.

222 *Comforter.* Mrs Gillman.

226 *proserpence.* 'Creeping along', Coleridge's coinage from the Latin verb *proserpo.*

227 *continuity.* 'From Dan to Barsheba' is a proverbial expression, based on Judges 20: 1, for great extent (Dan being the most northerly, Beersheba the most southerly of the cities of the Holy Land). William Harris (1720–70), author of biographies of James I, Charles I, Cromwell, and Charles II, was celebrated for his annotation, many pages of his work containing nothing but footnotes.

228 *Sales.* St Francis of Sales (1567–1622). Where he uses the phrase is not known.

229 *on Ants.* P. Huber, *The Natural History of Ants* (1820), a translation from the French.

for Morality. For Coleridge's opinion of the inadequacies of Locke and Paley, see pp. 89, 140, 270, and notes to pp. 2, 188.

230 *Clerisy.* Coleridge introduced this term into English in his work *On the Constitution of the Church and State* (1829), where it denotes not only the clergy but the educational and cultural establishment of a country, its intelligentsia.

234 *Daeianira's gift.* Deianeira, the wife of Hercules, was tricked by the centaur Nessus into giving her husband a poisoned garment that clung to him and caused his death.

235 *Noctes atticae.* 'Attic nights', the title of a collection of essays by Aulus Gellius, but used here (as p. 205) simply to mean evenings of good fellowship.

Sonnet to me. No published source has been traced for this sonnet, although Coleridge's college friend T. F. Middleton (later Bishop of Calcutta), who introduced Coleridge to the sonnets of W. L. Bowles, published at least one other sonnet on Cambridge and Coleridge, in his *Country Spectator* on 22 Jan. 1793.

Mrs Chisholm. A Highgate neighbour with whose daughter Derwent may have been romantically involved about this time. Derwent had evidently represented himself in a letter to her as 'a mere poor child of charity' (below).

236 *respecting you.* Coleridge is complaining that since he gets no news from Derwent directly, he has to rely on reports from others at Cambridge—Calvert, Worship, and Henry Nelson Coleridge—and that what he hears has not been encouraging.

237 *aspen Leaf.* Coleridge himself had used this phrase to describe Hartley, in a letter of 1801.

years old. William Wordsworth, 'To H. C. Six Years Old' (1802), from which poem the quoted phrases below are taken.

Melancholy. From the poem cited above, ll. 19–20.

241 *fresh currency.* Francis Jeffrey, editor of the *Edinburgh Review*, had shown himself consistently hostile to Coleridge and his associates; Thomas Medwin's recent *Conversations of Lord Byron* (1824) recorded Byron's regret that Coleridge had given up poetry for 'German metaphysics'.

242 *Leibnitz.* That is, pre-Kantean philosophy: Leibniz died in 1716, Wolff in 1754.

the name is. As a friend of Allston's, C. R. Leslie (1794–1859) had known and admired Coleridge for a decade. The resemblance to Coleridge in his portrait of Dousterswivel in the frontispiece to *The Antiquary* in the 1823 collection of Scott's *Novels and Tales* is debatable; the point is that if it *were* associated with Coleridge, it would reinforce his image as a pedantic obscurantist.

to Man. Lorenz Oken, *Lehrbuch der Naturgeschichte* (1813–26).

243 *on the subject.* Coleridge is uneasy at the prospect of his nephew's connection with John Murray and William Gifford, respectively the publisher and the previous editor of the *Quarterly*—Coleridge himself having had unhappy relations with them.

Millman. Henry Hart Milman, author of historical poems (e.g. *The Fall of Jerusalem*, 1820).

244 *Society.* 'On the *Prometheus* of Aeschylus', a paper delivered 18 May 1825.

Amanuensis. Probably John Watson (d. 1827), an apprentice to Gillman and friend to all the family, who had been studying in Germany for over a year.

246 *a Saddle.* Steamboats were a fairly recent innovation, and Coleridge

could appreciate the difference between the new way of making the Ramsgate journey and the old ways by sail or by road.

Susan. Apparently a maidservant brought from Highgate, not to be confused with Susan Steele, the Highgate neighbour mentioned below and p. 257.

251 *Pattison.* There was no master of this name at Eton. Coleridge may have hoped to persuade John Patteson—whose name he always spelled with an 'i'—to interest himself in Henry Gillman's cause. Patteson was married to Coleridge's niece Fanny, Edward Coleridge's sister.

252 *Routinier.* 'Routineer', a person who acts by routine, i.e. someone who does a job mechanically.

253 *downright Last.* Lotteries were abolished in England in 1826, the last being held on 18 Oct. that year.

255 *Essay the First.* The contrast between a passive memory or association and active methodizing is further developed, as Coleridge says, in a series of essays on method in *The Friend*: see the edition by Barbara Rooke in the Bollingen *Collected Works* (Princeton and London, 1969), ii. 448–57.

256 *Irish Bull.* 'A self-contradictory proposition' (*OED*), popular as a type of joke. Boswell gives an instance in Johnson's remark about a bad horse, 'When he *goes* up hill, he *stands still.*'

257 *Letter to me.* A Highgate neighbour, Mr Stanley, had sent Mrs Gillman word of a driving accident involving her husband. He had been thrown from his carriage but was not seriously hurt.

Hygeia. Goddess of health. Miss Steele (later for a time engaged to James Gillman, Jr.) was the daughter of Highgate friends and accompanied Coleridge and Mrs Gillman on this holiday.

260 *Adams and Eves.* Contemporary anthropology offered several incompatible theories about how there came to be different races among mankind: the 'Ouran Outang' hypothesis (p. 188) argued that man had evolved from the higher primates, but that some races were further removed from them than others; the theory of polygeny entailed five couples of different races from the start, from whom all members of the human race were descended. Coleridge, interpreting the account of Creation in the Bible in the light of current scientific knowledge, believed that all mankind descended from one family, but that some races were more degenerate than others.

261 *spiritual.* This sentence expresses a theme that is prominent in Coleridge's philosophical writings, notably the *Aids to Reflection* (1825), but it has not been traced in exactly this form. Coleridge may be paraphrasing himself.

262 *Scriptures.* That is, a draft version of the work published posthumously as *Confessions of an Inquiring Spirit* (1840).

grievous Wrong. Coleridge quotes his own poem 'Youth and Age' (1823), ll. 8–9.

264 *Blanco White.* Joseph Blanco White (1775–1841), an Irish–Spanish Catholic priest who escaped from Spain in 1810, became a convert to Protestantism and eventually (1835) a Unitarian. His publications include *Letters from Spain* (1822) and *Evidences against Catholicism* (1825). The *London Review* folded after two numbers.

Polyglot. See note to p. 108.

265 *Sunday last.* Green and Coleridge had a common interest in aesthetic theory. Green lectured on anatomy and the fine arts at the Royal Academy from 1825 to 1852.

266 *Subjective Objective.* The logical structure implicit here is common in Coleridge's work: the first factor or Prothesis generates Thesis and Antithesis, which may be held in balance in a Mesothesis or unite to produce a new Synthesis.

Nation. That is, taste.

267 *centrific.* 'Centre-making'.

Gall and Spurzheim. Founders of a system of phrenology, that is, of a 'science' of psychology based on the interpretation of the shape of the skull. Coleridge had to his amusement been analysed by Spurzheim as having very little 'Ideality' but a great deal of 'Locality' or sense of place.

268 *Constitution. On the Constitution of the Church and State* (1829).

Lay-Sermon. 'Blessed are ye that sow beside all Waters!' A Lay Sermon (1817).

270 *in this flesh.* Job 19: 26.

Evidence. That is, even by the dubious standards of evidence acceptable in a court of law, such arguments as those found in William Paley's *Evidences of Christianity* would scarcely be accepted.

Arithmetic. To help students concentrate on mathematical method, it appears to have been customary to give the solution or 'facit' (Latin for 'it makes') along with the problem.

272 *Symbol.* The ancient Egyptians worshipped the god Apis in the form of an ox.

274 *many months.* Coleridge evidently believed that Sterling was about to leave the country; in fact, he had recently *returned* from Germany.

Heinrichs. Taking into account, that is, the latest biblical scholarship on the subject of the apocalyptic writings in works by J. G. Eichhorn (*Commentarius in Apocalypsin Joannis*, 1791) and J. H. Heinrichs (*Apocalypsis Graece*, 1818), Coleridge finds that he still has something original to say.

Lobeck. Probably C. A. Lobeck's recent *Aglaophamus* (1829), which treats of the Eleusinian, Orphic, and Samothracian mysteries; Coleridge is interested in early analogues to the visionary and prophetic books of the Bible.

275 *Gesenius's Version.* Possibly W. Gesenius's Hebrew–German dictionary (1810–12), which had a special section on the vocabulary of the Books of Daniel and Ezra.

INDEX

In the following list, titles of works appear under their authors' names, 'n.' refers to a footnote by Coleridge, and 'qu.' means 'quoted'.

Index 303